GUIDE TO THE

COLORADO
MOUNTAINS

TENTH EDITION

GUIDE TO THE

COLORADO
MOUNTAINS

TENTH EDITION

edited by Randy Jacobs
with Robert M. Ormes

The Colorado Mountain Club Press
Golden, Colorado

WARNING: Mountain climbing and hiking are high-risk activities. This guidebook is not a substitute for your experience and common sense. The users of this guidebook assume full responsibility for their own safety. Weather, terrain conditions, and individual technical abilities must be considered before undertaking any of the climbs and hikes in this guide. The Colorado Mountain Club does not assume any liability for injury, damage to property, or violation of the law that may result from the use of this book.

Published in the United States by The Colorado Mountain Club Press
710 10th St. #200, Golden, CO 80401
(303) 279-3080 1 (800) 633-4417
e-mail: cmcoffice@cmc.org
website: http://www.cmc.org/cmc

Manufactured in the United States

Front cover photo: Vallecito Peak, San Juan Mountains by David Anschicks
Back cover photos: Wilson-El Diente ridge (top) by Terry Root and Mt. Moss (bottom) by Chester Stone
Typography and interior design by Lyn Berry

Guide to the Colorado Mountains / edited by Randy Jacobs with Robert M.
    Ormes -- 10th ed
    ISBN 0-9671466-0-7
    Library of Congress Card Number: 99-069864

Table of Contents

List of Maps

Bob Ormes and the
Guide to the Colorado Mountains

by John Devitt

"You simply had to be there!"

Those of us who knew Bob Ormes realized that they were dealing with a quirky, very intelligent, humorous character combining the best aspects of a mountaineer, explorer, writer, teacher, master of practical jokes and best buddy. Fairly described as a sporadically-gregarious introvert, an acquaintance of his selection could quickly be made to feel like an old friend. Although a skilled writer himself, no written account of his personal history has really captured his in-person reality. You simply had to be there.

From modest beginnings as the son of the Colorado College librarian, he took his degrees from that school and first became a high-school English teacher, and briefly, a marginal girls' basketball coach. He began to find his real calling at Fountain Valley School, where he was in charge of rock-climbing instruction and general hilarity in addition to his position as an English master. An English instructorship at Colorado College followed, and his association there continued until his retirement.

A long-time Colorado Mountain Club and American Alpine Club member, Bob's impact on mountaineering began early as he visited many summits with the legendary Albert Ellingwood in the 1920's. He became an expert rock climber and made many early ascents of difficult peaks and rocks.

A little-known but permanent aspect of Bob's influence on Colorado was his role in naming previously neglected peaks in the state. This interest began with his irritation that so many mountains were named Baldy, Old Baldy, Bald Mountain, and so on. He gave a number of mountains names noted for their color and appropriateness.

Around 1950, the original CMC Publications Committee — Betsy Cowles Partridge, Carl Blaurock and Henry Buchtel — persuaded Bob to be editor of the new Colorado guidebook they were beginning to hatch. Among other things, they were looking for a writer sprightly enough to, for example, direct prospective climbers of that rotten rockpile Lizard Head to "Take photograph and go away." (Bob had made the third ascent.) This was easily the most noted quotation from the first edition, which was published in 1952. This book was based largely on many contributions from club members, and the extensive CMC trip report files. Later, principally in the 1970's and 80's, Bob took over the publishing of the book, and by the 8th edition the text had largely become his. By then, the *Guide to the Colorado Mountains* had established a unique niche in mountaineering circles, and still remained the only comprehensive climbing guide to the entire state. What has made the book legendary over the past 48 years is its nonchalant conversational style, which reflects the author's wry humor and love of life.

As the guide approached its fifth decade in print, its existence was in jeopardy. Much needed updates were long overdue, rendering large sections almost useless. In addition, over the years the guide had been supplanted by more detailed interpretive guides to most mountainous regions in the state. For members of the Colorado Mountain Club the guide seemed an obvious project, especially so for Gary Grange during his tenure as CMC president in 1988. Grange fostered the drawn out negotiations for transfer of the copyright from Ormes to the club. Both sides sensed the urgency of the project and CMC members were anxious and willing to format a revised edition competitive with present guidebooks. This effort became the 9th edition, released in 1992.

The *Guide to the Colorado Mountains*, now in its 10th edition, is still Bob Ormes' book. It continues to exist with interjections of his jovial personality, style and belief that "climbing should be more than just following Baedeker routes." Our goal was to review the many descriptions, correct inaccuracies, and clean up the book's most notorious uncertainties and weaknesses. However, we have been careful not to unduly tamper with the greatest gift of Colorado's Grand Old Man of the Mountains. To do so would extinguish a birthright for future mountaineers that the rest of us have delighted in. Bob Ormes has passed away and we who are still climbing his mountains miss him.

Acknowledgements

The *Guide to the Colorado Mountains* represents the work of an organization that is dedicated to the appreciation of Colorado's mountains. The Colorado Mountain Club can trace its involvement with the guide all the way back to the first edition, published in 1952. The original CMC Publications Committee of Betsy Cowles Partridge, Carl Blaurock and Henry Buchtel conceived the idea of a new Colorado guidebook and persuaded Robert Ormes to be the first editor. Ormes continued in that capacity for nearly four decades, eventually taking over all responsibilities for publishing the book.

Gary Grange, during his tenure as club president in 1988, negotiated an agreement with Ormes for transferring the rights to publish back to the CMC. The club's Publications Chairman Gary Hall, than formed a steering committee for the purpose of preparing a new 9th edition to be released in 1992. The committee that produced the successful 9th edition of the book consisted of Gary Hall (Guide Steering Committee Chairman), Randy Jacobs (project editor), Walter Borneman, Steve Coley, John Devitt, Roger Fuehrer, Mike Foster, Gary Grange, Jim Gresham, Jean McGuey, Al Ossinger, Don Peel, Terry Root and David Zimmerman. Walter Borneman, president of Cordillera Press, provided practical experience and knowledge about the book trade and marketed the guide to retailers. Pre-publication sales were coordinated by Roger Fuehrer. The Betsy Cowles Partridge Foundation provided critical funding for producing the 9th edition.

A new revision committee that formed in 1997, headed by CMC Publications Chairman Terry Root, has continued to revise the guide resulting in the current 10th edition. For production funding of the 10th edition, we express our gratitude to the Scientific & Cultural Facilities District (SCFD), the Denver Group and the High Altitude Mountaineering Section (HAMS) of the CMC, and to numerous donations from individuals in the CMC. The rights for the book currently reside with the Colorado Mountain Club Press.

Randy Jacobs has served as editor for the last two editions of the book and the resulting manuscript reflects his attention to accuracy and detail along with retaining Ormes' original language and style. CMC computer liaison and technician Lyn Berry did the layouts and desktop publishing for both the 9th and 10th editions. CMC Publications Manager Tom Beckwith helped with technical questions on the 10th edition. Cartography, except as noted, was by Randy Jacobs. Steve Coley helped in coordinating photo selection for the 9th and Terry Root did the same for the 10th. Mountaineering historian Bill Bueler and geologist Jack Reed provided introductory material that has contributed to both editions.

These past two editions, as previous ones, have relied heavily on routine CMC trip reports from countless trip leaders, as well as articles from *Trail and Timberline* (a CMC bi-monthly magazine in continuous publication since 1918). We are indebted for proofing the entire document to Walter Borneman, Alex Carson, Mike Foster, Linda Grey, Gary Hall, Jean McGuey, and Chester Stone, and for reviewing selected sections by Nadia Brelje, Dave Butler, George Cowles, Fred Facer, Gary Grange, Jackie Johnson, Bob Martin, Jo Ann Moon, Dave Myers, Glen Phillips, Rich Riefenberg, Mike Tabb, and Barbara and Joe Wasung.

Several area coordinators took responsibility in the 9th edition for review and corrections in the various ranges around the state and this material, for the most part, has continued into the 10th edition. Area coordinators were Russ Allen (Park Range North), Lyn Berry (Indian Peaks), Steve Coley (Mosquito/Tenmile Range and Flattops), John Devitt (Elk Range), Madeline Framson (Rocky Mountain National Park), Jim Gresham (Front Range), Gary Hall (Tarryall/Kenosha Mountains, Rawah Range, Sangre de Cristo Range and West Elks), Randy Jacobs (San Juan Mountains West), Jean McGuey (Gore Range), Al Ossinger (Sawatch Range), and Terry Root (San Juan Mountains East). In addition, we are grateful to those who contributed field reports for both editions, including Arden Anderson, Gary Anderson, Dave Anschicks, Allen Best, Rob Blair, Steve Bonowski, Nadia Brelje, Dennis Brown, Patricia Butler, George Chenoweth, Polly Craig, Hille Dais, Jack Dais, Jeffrey Davies, Gary Davis, Jack DePagter, Ken Drybread, Virginia Ellis, Dick Fenton, Roger Fuehrer, George W. Fuller Jr., Gary Grange, Linda Grey, Thomas Healy, Ward Hobert, Bryce Johnston, Dave King, Bob Kinter, Joseph Kramarsic, John Layman, Betty McCord, Van McDaniel, Steve Mitchell, Ken Nolan, Randen Olson, Paul Pixler, Janet and Steve Ray, Bill Ramaley, Rich Riefenberg, Dave and Jan Robertson, Barbara Schmerler, Jennifer Sears, Chester Stone, Jim Towns, David Wasson, Russ Weber, and Vic Wuensch.

Colorado Mountains

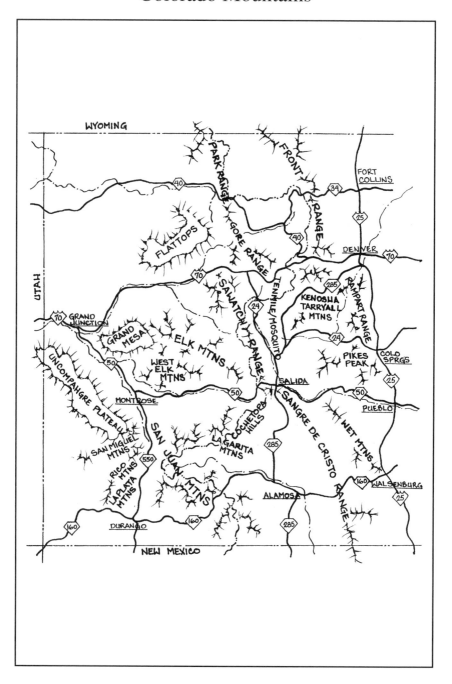

The Mountains - By and Large

Colorado's mountains are generally not hard to climb. The mining boom, which began in 1859 and lasted into the first decade of this century, has left a heritage of roads and trails through the timber. These, along with newer trails built specifically for recreation by the Forest Service and other organizations, link auto roads to the timberless upland; they make the mountain tops accessible.

Most of Colorado's summits can be reached by at least one route that is no more than steep mountain-side hiking. Some routes to the peak-tops have slow stretches involving hand-over-hand rock scrambling and, at times, exposed sections demanding steady nerves. Nearly all can be reached without technical equipment, provided the climbers are knowledgeable and experienced in basic mountaineering skills. There are, however, plenty of summit approaches for those who want to try out their ropes and other technical hardware.

The sheer nature of some mountain ranges, the Needles and Grenadiers for instance, harbor standard routes described as anything but walk-ups. Occasionally, for these exceptions, we refer to the Yosemite rating system which classifies climbs class 1 through 5. One being easy hiking; 2, scrambling and hand holds; 3, some exposure; 4, rope may be necessary for belaying; and 5, technical climbing.

Using This Guide

Many mountaineers have their goals; the fourteeners, the highest 100, the highest 200, etc; and a wealth of interpretive guides have grown around the need to satisfy these specific objectives, activities or localities. But one of the beauties of the Ormes Guide has been a statewide focus on diverse destinations not always addressed in more recent guidebooks. A bibliography in the back of this book lists these more detailed guides, for those who desire a further supplement to the information described within these pages.

The Rocky Mountains in Colorado are comprised of many, mostly north to south, ranges. Therefore, it is logical that this guide be laid out in sections depicted by those ranges. The mountainous regions described here are grouped within 7 geographic sections that do not necessarily conform to strict topology; rather they are convenient to the format — Front Range, Sangre de Cristo Range, Park Range, Sawatch Range, Elk Range, the San Juan Mountains and finally, the Northwestern Plateau. Each of these 7 general sections is further reduced into manageable range units (42 in all), which are ultimately defined by auto access.

Certain abbreviations are used to conserve space, most are self-explanatory. "FSR" refers to Forest Service Road, "FSR-100" for example means Forest Service Road 100. Be aware that in some counties, forest road numbers and county road numbers coincide. "CMC" is used commonly for the Colorado Mountain Club, and "*T&T*" for its monthly publication *Trail & Timberline*. "CT" and "CDT" are used for Colorado Trail and Continental Divide Trail, respectively. "4WD" is short for four wheel drive, as in vehicles. It would be prudent to note here that many mountain roads accessible to conventional automobiles under normal conditions may be impassable during inclement weather, even to 4WD vehicles.

Finally, although considerable effort has been dedicated to confirming and correcting descriptions, it is not possible to catch all inaccuracies. Also, access across private lands and land-use regulations on public lands change. Please send notifications of any discrepancies in this edition or changes required in future editions to: The Colorado Mountain Club Press, 710 10th St. #200, Golden, CO 80401.

Maps

Detailed maps for orienteering purposes are a necessary part of every mountaineer's equipment. This guide lists the appropriate Geological Survey (USGS) 7.5 minute topographic maps (1:24,000) for each of the 42 range units. These maps are the most suitable and detailed for field use. In addition, each range unit lists the appropriate National Forest (NF) maps for general direction and facility information. Beyond these specific government printed documents, there is a wide range of map options available to mountain travelers.

The USGS also has several other topographic map sources for the state; the county map series (1:50,000), and the 30x60 series (1:100,000). In addition, government printers have the more prominent National Parks and Monuments mapped in topographic format, some in shaded relief which imparts a 3-dimensional quality to the sheet. All USGS maps can be purchased commercially as available or directly from the USGS, Box 25286, Federal Center, Denver, CO 80225.

The schematic access maps which accompany each of the 7 general sections in this guide, and the more detailed schematic vicinity maps should be considered for general planning purposes only and not for orienteering. There are 8 local areas maps provided that serve to highlight particularly popular climbing basins, often where groups of fourteeners are clustered. These are for general interest and should not replace a USGS topographic map for climbing purposes.

Names Of Peaks

Generally in the Ormes Guide, we adhere to the names of peaks (and other features) as assigned by the United States Board of Geographic Names (USBGN). However there are hundreds of unnamed summits in Colorado and some controversy as to how to deal with them, especially in this era of increasing interest in these "forgotten" summits by peak baggers. There are many summits that have unofficial names that have sprung up because of local usage or traditional agreement in the climbing community. Examples of these are some of the "T" designation summits in the San Juans and the many peaks with letter names in the Gore Range. Even though these names do not typically appear on the USGS topographic maps or in other official sources, we choose to use them in the guide because of widespread usage.

If a peak has no generally recognized name, we refer to it simply by the word "Peak" followed by its elevation. Some guidebooks use the term "Unnamed" followed by the elevation. To us this implies that the summit should be, and will be, named someday. But in truth, the USBGN has very restrictive guidelines that result in few, if any, new peak names annually in Colorado. The majority of hundreds of unnamed summits in Colorado are likely to remain unnamed long into the future. Likewise we have resisted the temptation that some guidebook authors have taken upon themselves recently; to apply names of their own choosing.

Weather and Seasonal Conditions

Though mountain weather tends to be unpredictable, Colorado's relatively dry climate makes for pleasant camping and climbing conditions. The open season for high peaks is more or less from late June through early October, with wide variations in different years and with different climbs. Lower altitude mountain trails and trips are possible off and on through the winter as snow tends to melt off on sunny slopes up to 8000 feet.

Mountain storms are more frequent in the afternoon than in the morning, and climbers should be prepared to turn back short of their goal to avoid a building thunderstorm. Lightning, an obvious hazard to mountain travelers, is a common occurrence during midsummer afternoon thunderstorms. Start early so that you reach your goal and are descending before storms build. If caught in an electrical storm, descend a few hundred feet, at least, below the ridge tops or summits. Lightning travels down wet gullies and towards water in streams and lakes. Stay away from them and isolated or tall trees. Put metal objects (ice axes, frame packs) away from you and position yourself so that you touch the earth only with the soles of your boots.

Autumn can be a delightful time to be in the mountains. But keep a close look on the skies for fierce early winter storms, and wrap yourself with plenty of orange so as not to be mistaken for suitable game.

This guide describes the summer-time routes to the mountains and generally does not address winter climbing which is now attracting a great deal of activity from late autumn through early spring. These adventures are for experienced mountaineers with specialized, cold weather equipment and emergency essentials, and a complete knowledge of the route to be followed.

Mountaineering Clothing and Equipment

Effective, good quality clothing and other gear will often determine the difference between a safe, enjoyable day in the mountains and an unpleasant or even potentially disastrous experience. For clothing, modern synthetics, like polypropylene and "pile" are light, insulate well and dry quickly. But traditional wool clothing is still effective and often available cheaply through surplus stores. Avoid cotton entirely, as it loses all insulating ability when wet. The following suggested list is for a typical, non-technical, day climb during the summer in the Colorado mountains.

    1. Day-pack - 1500 to 3000 cubic inches
    2. Leather boots - mid weight
    3. Socks - wool, with silk or poly liners
    4. Long underwear - light weight, poly tops and bottoms
    5. Shirt or sweater - poly or wool
    6. Pants - poly or wool
    7. Parka shell - waterproof, windproof
    8. Pants shell - waterproof, windproof
    9. Hat and gloves - stocking cap or balaclava and poly/wool gloves
"The Ten Essentials" (emergency shelter, extra clothing, extra food, extra water, first aid kit, flashlight, map and compass, matches/fire starter, pocket knife, sunglasses/sunscreen)
    If traveling on snowfields, include gaiters and ice axe.

Safety

Remember that good mountaineering is safe mountaineering. When on an outing, assistance can be hours, even days, away. Keep these basics in mind:

    1. High altitudes require adequate clothing and rain gear. Adequate sun glasses and skin protection are necessary in the blinding glare of lingering summer snowfields and the rarified atmosphere. Rough mountain slopes demand sturdy boots. Be aware of the symptoms of hypothermia, a rapid loss in body temperature from exposure to cold, wind and wetness. Wear proper clothing to insulate and keep you dry.

Coming off a fourteener   *David Hite*

2. Know your physical limits and avoid fatigue. Weariness compounds the difficulty of mountain terrain. Many mountaineering accidents happen on the descent when climbers are tired.

3. Avoid the rotten rock hazard in every way possible. A party should bunch together in a loose-rock couloir, and on wider slopes they should angle away from the direct line of fall.

4. Snow slopes should be tested carefully. In the early morning, snowfields can be as hard and slick as ice. However, in the afternoon, they may be soft and mushy. Neither condition is particularly conducive to comfortable, or safe, foot travel. The steeper the snow, the more concern for caution and knowledge in traversing such conditions. If you encounter snowfields, carry an ice axe and know how to use it. Take an avalanche awareness course.

5. Climbing alone is not recommended. If you do, leave word where you are going and stay with your plans. Keep a wide margin of safety in your movements. Mountaineering convention says that a group of four is the minimum number for safety. That way, if an accident occurs, two can go for help while one remains with the injured. When traveling together as a party, avoid becoming separated.

6. Some routes up the mountains are technical or approaching technical. Do not challenge yourself beyond your genuine abilities. Be aware that ascending steep, exposed pitches is sometimes easier than descending them. Look back often during your climb to mark difficult or confusing return routes in your memory.

7. Climbing and hiking at altitude poses dangers. The lower barometric pressure results in lower oxygen intake and reduced levels of oxygen in the blood stream. Effects from altitude sickness can be severe and result in death. Acclimate slowly on extended trips in the mountains, know what the symptoms are of altitude sickness, and descend immediately in the event of illness.

This guide assumes that climbers are acquainted with the techniques needed to forestall most backcountry disasters; i.e., orienteering and map reading, wilderness survival, mountaineering expertise, etc. If not, the Colorado Mountain Club regularly holds schools, seminars and training sessions to instruct in these backcountry skills.

Backcountry Regulations and Ethics

All outdoor enthusiasts have a responsibility to maintain the pristine conditions of the backcountry. Most of the mountain terrain in Colorado lies within the jurisdiction of the United States Forest Service, and the USFS has adopted guidelines and regulations to help preserve our backcountry. Lawful compliance includes the following. Check with the local ranger district while planning your trip to confirm restrictions on campfires. These and other regulations are common in the summer. It is good practice to use a fuelstove for cooking, and reserve your small campfires for social focal points. Remember that Indian sites, old cabins and other structures, if on federal ground, are protected by law. They have a historic value and are not at the disposal of souvenir hunters. Fishing and hunting permits are required for those activities.

More strict occupancy codes have been legislated to protect fragile wilderness areas, although some heavily used non-wilderness areas also have restrictions. Within wilderness areas, groups must be restricted in size, camps and tethered animals are not permitted within a hundred feet of lakes and streams, and pets must be keep on a leash. For further information on public lands, the appendix section lists the full addresses and phone numbers of the appropriate land management agencies as designated in each range unit of this guide.

Beyond these general regulations, all users of Colorado's high country have an obligation to conduct themselves in a responsible manner, thus reducing their impact. Even the popular phrase "Take only pictures, leave only footprints" could be revised, for delicate alpine flowers succumb to the fate of a hiker's heavy boot print. Refrain from cutting switchbacks and other mindless activities that lead to trail erosion. Use existing campsites, and resist the temptation to develop new ones by digging drainage channels, building fire-rings, etc. Restore your campsite to its pristine conditions when you depart.

Much concern has been voiced at the increasing erosive influence our species has had on the more popular fourteeners, as well as other common high-country destinations in the state. Consequently, as we head for the hills to meet the challenge our mountains provide, we are taking an increasing toll on the vulnerable summits we love to climb. In recent years, the CMC Conservation Committee, in conjunction with the club's trail committee, has begun to stabilize existing routes, or build adequate new ones up these mountains. Peak baggers can help by avoiding obviously destructive practices, such as the popular rock (or boot) glissade on vulnerable scree slopes.

Some mountain areas are privately owned; large tracts, for instance, in the San Luis Valley, or the more common patchwork of patented mining claims throughout the state. This guide may not refer to all private property signs, given the changing nature of those postings. However, it should be obvious that all private property should be respected, whether mentioned or not.

Spring climbing   *Mike Endres*

We encourage the use of established trailheads and parking areas, whenever possible, to leave cars. When not feasible, remember that even out-of-the-way forest roads are likely to be used by others, including the USFS and the logging industry, so pull well off to leave the way clear.

Mountain bikes are becoming more popular on trails, and will be seen increasingly to the consternation of many hikers, backpackers and animal packers. However, mountain bikers do have a responsibility to other trail user's pre-existing rights: courteously dismount when faced with pedestrians or equestrians, stay in control at all times for your own safety as well as others, be aware that if ridden improperly your bike can destroy a well designed trail, and remember that mountain bikes are not allowed in wilderness areas.

Walking gently and talking softly is in tune with the backcountry code, and increases your overall wilderness awareness. In this age of increased recreational use of our backcountry, the Colorado Mountain Club supports the efforts of two leading organizations that are making a difference. The **Colorado Fourteeners Initiative** (CFI) is a non-profit organization with a goal of protecting and preserving the fourteeners by minimizing the impact of climbers on these popular peaks. Their address is CFI, 710 10th St. Suite 220, Golden, CO 80401. Contact CFI at their website (www.ColoradoFourteeners.org) for a list of minimum impact routes for climbing all of the fourteeners. **Leave No Trace** (LNT) is a national non-profit organization dedicated to educating people about responsible use of the outdoors, with special emphasis on minimum-impact travel. They publish a series of booklets focusing on LNT techniques for specific areas including the Rocky Mountains. For more information, contact LNT at their Colorado office: PO Box 997, Boulder, CO 80306 or go to their website at http://www.lnt.org.

The Mountaineering Heritage

by William M. Bueler
Author: *Roof of the Rockies: A History of Colorado Mountaineering*

The history of mountaineering not only in Colorado, but in the American West, began with Lt. Zebulon Pike's 1806 attempt to climb the great peak which bears his name. This is not to say that no peak had been climbed before then, because plainly the Indians had the ability to reach most summits in the American Rockies. Since the Indians left no written accounts of climbs, however, any before 1806 must be considered "pre-historic."

We know that at least a few Indians had not only the ability, but also the motivation, to reach the high points. For one peak, Longs, we have a firsthand account of a pre-white ascent. This was given in 1914 by an old Arapahoe who told of a climb made by himself and other young braves in 1859, at a time when Longs had not yet been ascended and was still considered unclimbable by white settlers. The Arapahoe, Gun Griswold, also told of earlier ascents, apparently frequent, by his father—Old Man Gun—who had excavated a small pit on the summit. He would place a coyote as bait beside it, then climb in to wait the arrival of eagles, which he would grab for their feathers. On another peak—Blanca, the state's fourth highest—a shelter wall of presumably Indian origin was found by the first white climbers—a Wheeler Survey party in 1874. Its purpose is unknown, but it might also have been an eagle trap, or perhaps a lookout or a shelter for a vision-seeker.

The first white people to travel through the mountains were the Spanish, who probed north from New Mexico from the late 17th Century on. They knew the San Luis Valley well, and traveled north along the western edge of the Great Plains as far as Wyoming. Zebulon Pike reported after he arrived in Santa Fe that the Spanish were well acquainted with Pike's Peak—thus one should not say, as has sometimes been said, that Pike "discovered" it. The only specific reports of Spaniards leaving the valleys and passes to head into the higher country relate to mining in the San Juans and Sangre de Cristos. The Spanish names for many southern Colorado ranges and individual peaks indicate their general familiarity with the geography of that part of the state.

Pike's attempt to climb his peak—which ended on an uncertain minor summit—was a relatively small incident in a very harrowing mid-winter expedition. By the time his men were captured by Spaniards in the San Luis Valley and taken to Santa Fe they had suffered weeks of bitter cold, deep snow and near starvation, but in the end had made a significant contribution to understanding the complex ranges and river drainages of the Colorado Rockies, and left a timeless tale of adventure and courage.

The next government expedition to Colorado, that of Major Stephen Long in 1820, had the good fortune to reach the Rockies in summer. Approaching up the South Platte River, the first high peak spotted was Longs—named for the Major. The expedition's doctor, botanist and chief chronicler was 23-year-old Edwin James who, with two soldiers, climbed Pikes Peak. James gave an excellent description of the ascent and the summit view. He also related their concern about Indian war parties in the area, and their chagrin when, as the state's first careless campers, they started a small forest fire which destroyed most of their supplies.

The expedition's trapper guide told James that although Indians and hunters had tried many times to climb the peak, none had succeeded. It is hard to imagine that the Indians, if they really tried, could not have attained the summit. But given the lack of any specific evidence that they did, credit for the first ascent—the first recorded for any major mountain in the West—goes to James.

Hunters and trappers, first French then American, had begun to enter the Colorado mountains late in the 18th Century. Since it was always in the beaver trapper's interest to find new streams which had not yet been trapped out, they had a positive incentive to explore new territory—at least that portion of it below timberline. One can only assume that curiosity must have taken some of them up nearby easy peaks, but like the Indians, they didn't write about their adventures. In fact, the explorations of these generally illiterate men would have disappeared from history had not some of them become guides for official explorers and wealthy travelers after changing fashions and a declining number of beavers brought the trapping era to a close in the 1830's. Kit Carson was the most famous of these ex-trapper guides, and he achieved lasting fame when he signed on as chief guide for the explorer John C. Fremont, whose voluminous writings made both Carson and the Colorado Rockies famous throughout the nation. Carson had come to know the Rockies as well as any trapper, and it is appropriate that one of Colorado's greatest peaks is named for him.

On four expeditions Fremont traveled through most of Colorado's parks and crossed numerous passes. But his best known adventure was his 1848 mid-winter attempt to cross the San Juans. He was seeking a railroad route to the west coast and, according to his backer, Senator Benton, decided to go in winter so he could learn firsthand "all the disadvantages of the route." He certainly did that. By the time the remnants of the 33-man expedition straggled into Taos, New Mexico, 11 men had died, and some of the survivors were troubled by charges of cannibalism for the rest of their lives.

Another ex-trapper, named Kelly, guided the traveler Thomas J. Farnham through central Colorado in 1839. Farnham recorded Kelly's lament: "The game is all driven out . . . Ah! those were good times; but a white man has no more business here." Kelly had a very limited trapper's-eye view of the world. As of 1839, Colorado's good times were not yet over!

The Narrows, Longs Peak, 1913   *CMC Archives*

The impact of the next group of people to reach the Colorado mountains was totally different from that of the trappers. Whereas in 30-some years of activity the trappers left almost no visible mark on the mountain country, the influx of miners which began with the 1859 Pikes Peak Gold Rush had, within a decade and a half, spread trails, roads, mines, heavy equipment, towns and cities all over the region. Their impact changed the access to the mountains forever, and even today is the most visible man-made presence throughout much of the near-timberline and above-timberline country. We still hike on miners' trails, poke curiously into their diggings, and occasionally even find shelter in what remains of their cabins.

Although the miners' main purpose in the mountains was not, of course, to climb them, there are many reports that they sometimes did. Many a walkup peak in the Front, Sawatch, Mosquito and San Juan Mountains was first ascended by a miner on his day off. It is possible that some of the rougher peaks also succumbed, but the evidence is generally lacking. Later mountaineers of the modern era often found cairns, bottles, tools, cans and other signs of miners' presence on the easier summits near mines and mining towns, but most of the rougher peaks were devoid of such signs.

One non-walkup peak that did attract some early miners as well as other adventurous settlers was Longs. There were several attempts in the 1860's, and it is possible that two men who probably arrived as part of the mining boom succeeded in 1865. But proof is lacking, so credit for the first non-Indian ascent goes to the 1868 party led by Major John Wesley Powell—the one-armed Civil War veteran better known for the first boat trip down the Grand Canyon. After Longs, Powell continued west and made another climb at least as difficult, if not quite as historic: the highest peak in the rugged Gore Range—appropriately named Mount Powell.

The following year, 1869, became a milestone in man's growing knowledge of the Colorado mountains when Harvard Professor Josiah D. Whitney led a surveying team to the Mosquito and Sawatch ranges. Miners who had scoured these ranges were floating rumors of peaks over 17,000 feet high, and one thing certainly on Whitney's mind was to see if, in fact, there were any peaks higher than the highest in California—which, not incidentally, had been named for him. His Colorado survey results were sufficiently precise (Mount Lincoln was given as 14,300, only 14 feet above the presently given height) that he could go back east secure in the knowledge that Mount Whitney was not surpassed. The survey named Mounts Harvard and Yale (where second-in-command William Brewer taught), thus initiating the "Collegiate Peaks" tradition.

By 1870, the Elk and San Juan ranges remained the major terrae incognitae in the state. These are among Colorado's most scenic mountains, as well as the most interesting geologically and most challenging alpinistically. Their exploration by the Hayden and Wheeler surveys from 1873 to 1876 was Colorado's closest approximation to the Golden Age of mountaineering in the Alps. When the surveys entered these ranges, their geography was virtually unknown. Three years later most of the prominent peaks had been climbed and the ranges were covered by some of the best topographic maps of that era.

Both the Hayden and Wheeler surveys explored the Elks in 1873. A member of the Wheeler team, apparently climbing alone, recorded the first mountaineering venture in the range when he got within 200 feet of the top of a "pyramidal" peak. Some have assumed this was the peak later named Pyramid, but the description could also fit North Maroon. The Hayden men attacked less ambitious peaks, but with greater success. They climbed Snowmass and Castle, the easiest of the range's six fourteeners.

As significant as were the survey explorations of the Elks, they were surpassed in historic interest by the exploration of the San Juans. This is largely due to the literary efforts of Franklin Rhoda, the 20-year old chronicler of the 1874 Hayden party. His 40-page account in the survey report is one of the best of the last century in American mountaineering; it stacks up well against the far better known writings of Clarence King and John Muir, for instance. Rhoda goes into enthusiastic detail on the summer's work, giving an excellent description of camp life in addition to some very memorable climbs: Uncompahgre—near the summit of which they had one of the summer's numerous encounters with bears; Sunshine—where they were caught on the summit by an electrical storm (there is no better description than Rhoda's of what that experience is like); Sneffels—where the deep Blue Lakes Basin reminded them of the great hole in the Earth in Jules Verne's *Journey to the Center of the Earth*, with Verne's fictional Mount Sneffels rising above; Mount Wilson—whose narrow south ridge gave them their most difficult and dangerous climb, and which was one of the hardest climbs done in the West in the 19th Century. In all, they climbed 35 summits over 12,000 feet in order to triangulate for mapping the great San Juan uplift.

The Wheeler Survey men were more interested in military mapping than in geology or topography, and they covered more territory with fewer men. Not surprisingly, their maps were not as detailed nor their written reports as readable. Nevertheless, Lt. William Marshall's report was also an important contribution to Colorado's mountain literature. The Wheeler men also climbed many San Juan peaks, including Uncompahgre, Handles, Redcloud and Rio Grande Pyramid among the higher ones. The Wheeler topographer, J.C. Spiller, made a serious attempt on Mount Wilson and almost made it. He left a can with his name in it at his high point: a gap in the south ridge at over 14,000 feet. The can was found by William S. Cooper during the second successful ascent of Wilson in 1908.

Aztec Mountain, 1920 CMC summer outing   *CMC Archives*

The surveys also climbed many peaks outside of the Elks and San Juans. In the Sawatch, for instance, the Hayden men climbed Elbert, Massive, Harvard and La Plata, the first, second, third and fifth highest in the state. All of these, however, had been climbed before by miners or others. The Mount of the Holy Cross at the then virtually unexplored northern end of the range provided by far the most interesting adventure. The official photographer of the survey was William H. Jackson, who had heard about the mountain with a great cross of snow on its east face and was determined to photograph it. An element of mystery surrounded the mountain because, although the cross was visible from many distant peaks, the closer one got to it the more it was hidden by Notch Mountain—a long, high ridge immediately to the east. Thus, near views were impossible until you stood upon the Notch ridge itself. Jackson had deduced this fact, so he and his assistants hauled his heavy cameras up Notch. The photograph which resulted became the most famous ever taken of an American mountain.

After the survey's explosion of mountain adventure in the 1870s, there followed three decades in which relatively little of historic significance occurred. Nevertheless, miners, hikers and mere tourists continued to wander up many of the state's hundreds of walkup summits located near towns and roads, while a number of climbs were made on the rougher peaks. Longs Peak became a popular excursion, and Blanca Peak, erroneously reported by the surveys to be the highest in the state, was assaulted by several parties from the east between 1877 and 1889. Most of these managed to get lost without reaching the top, but one of them stumbled by mistake onto the summit of Little Bear, thus claiming a peak as interesting as Blanca from a mountaineering point of view.

There were also a handful of quite challenging first ascents of interest. These included Holy Cross via the east (cross) face; a possible climb of South Maroon by a local boy; and several climbs in what is now Rocky Mountain National Park by Frederick Chapin, whose 1890 book *Mountaineering in Colorado: The Peaks About Estes Park* was the first devoted exclusively to climbing in Colorado. Another high and difficult peak, El Diente, in the San Miguels, was climbed by visiting British mountaineer Percy Thomas in 1890; but this fact did not become known until 1931, when a young Coloradoan, Dwight Lavender, made the discovery. Lavender had been rummaging through old copies of the *British Alpine Journal* when he came across an 1891 article by Thomas, who wrote that he had climbed Mount Wilson. Lavender argued convincingly that he had actually climbed El Diente and been prevented by clouds from seeing the slightly higher Wilson, a mile to the east.

The next era of major importance after the surveys was from 1907 to 1910. During those four successive summers, Percy Hagerman and Harold Clark thoroughly explored the Elks and climbed all the range's fourteeners. Capitol, Pyramid and North Maroon, some of the toughest in the state, were first ascents. They also climbed many lower peaks, including Hagerman, Daly, Clark and Cathedral (later, in 1919).

The year 1908 brought the most significant expedition to the San Juans since 1874. William S. Cooper and John Hubbard made first ascents of Pigeon, Vestal and Arrow, three of Colorado's finest mountains. They also repeated the survey climbs of Vermillion, Uncompahgre and Mount Wilson. The only place they used their rope during this summer of ambitious climbs was at the gap on Mount Wilson's south ridge which stopped Spiller of the Wheeler Survey and which the Hayden men crossed only with great difficulty; the toughness of this climb speaks well for the mountaineering skills of the 1870's survey climbers.

The founding of the Colorado Mountain Club (CMC) in 1912, and the appearance of its journal *Trail and Timberline* in 1918, helped greatly to jell climbing interest and facilitate communication among mountain devotees.

Albert R. Ellingwood is perhaps the outstanding figure in the history of Colorado mountaineering. While a Rhodes scholar at Oxford he acquired European-level rock climbing skills, and he introduced them to the Rockies after returning in 1914. In 1916, Ellingwood led climbs of the last remaining unclimbed fourteeners, Kit Carson, Crestone Peak and Crestone Needle. The only person to accompany him on all of them was Eleanor Davis Ehrman, certainly the outstanding woman mountaineer of that era; she was still able to tell people about these historic climbs in 1990, at the age of 104.

Ellingwood, with Barton Hoag, climbed Lizard Head, Colorado's hardest peak, in 1920. In 1925, he returned to Crestone Needle, and with Davis and two others, climbed the Ellingwood Arete, a major 2,000-foot technical climb on the northeast face. The Ellingwood Ridge on La Plata, which he climbed alone in 1922, remains the best known rock scramble in the Sawatch Range. Ellingwood also introduced serious rock climbing to the Garden of the Gods in Colorado Springs; made many pioneering climbs in Wyoming; and passed on his skills to younger climbers, including Robert Ormes of guidebook fame, and Denver's Carl Blaurock, whose 60-plus-year climbing career beginning in 1909 was surely the longest and most active in Colorado history.

An important phase in the exploration of the San Juans began in 1929 with the founding of the San Juan Mountaineers (SJM), eight or ten local climbers who were also CMC members but specialized in climbing the San Juans. This small but very active group probably did more climbing in the San Juans in seven years than all other climbers put together before the 1940's. The SJM members were the first to seek out difficult rock and snow routes in the San Juans and make winter high-peak ascents. They climbed virtually every significant peak and pinnacle in the region, dozens being first ascents. Their most active organizer and climber, Dwight Lavender, was also the moving force behind the compilation of the pioneering work, *The San Juan Mountaineer's Climber's Guide to Southwestern Colorado* (1932), a typewritten book of history and route information which set the pattern for later guidebook writers. Lavender accomplished much at an early age; he died of polio in 1934, at 23.

By the 1930's only one major range remained mostly untouched by climbers: the Gores. This rugged uplift only 60 miles from Denver had seen a few climbs of its high point, Mount Powell, but most of the other main peaks were virgin when a handful of climbers "discovered" them in the early 1930's. A CMC summer outing in 1935 racked up probably as many first ascents as any other group ever did in Colorado in a couple of weeks of climbing. The Gores had been saved from earlier invasion by several factors: their summits fell well below the magic 14,000-foot contour; there was no legacy of mining roads and trails; and early designation as a primitive area prevented development.

The fourteeners have always served as natural magnets for Colorado mountaineers. They are generally (but not always, particularly in the Needles-Grenadiers region) the most prominent as well as the highest peaks. And their number (now 53 or 54, depending on how you count) constitutes a substantial yet manageable wish list for anyone with a car, strong legs and free weekends. The idea of completing the list appears first to have occurred to Carl Blaurock and William Ervin in 1920 when, sitting on top of Mount Eolus, they counted up the fourteeners each had climbed and resolved on the spot to climb the remainder. By 1923, they had become the first to do so. Albert Ellingwood soon followed and by 1940, there were seven more finishers. By 1950 there were 33, and then the onslaught began. By 1990, over 500 people had climbed them all. Climbing them on a weekend today may not be the wilderness experience it once was, but you still get a lot of good exercise and see a large portion of Colorado's best mountain scenery.

As the number of virgin peaks dropped toward zero, climbers began searching for new and more challenging routes up the steep faces and sharp ridges that had previously been shunned. Professor James Alexander's 1922 climb of his chimney on the east face of Longs was a notable opening move in this new era of alpinism. Ellingwood's 1925 route on Crestone Needle followed. Other milestones were: Stettners Ledges on Longs (1927); the north face of Sneffels (peripheral route 1931; direct route 1933); the northwest face of Capitol (1937); the Wham (north) ridge of Vestal (1941); the east face of Monitor (1947); the northeast face of Blanca (1948); and the Diamond on Longs (1960).

By 1970, only a few peaks, mostly minor, had been overlooked by climbers. And most of the obvious route variations had been pioneered. The chance to make history on the high peaks had thus become very slight. Consequently, most of the recent history of mountaineering in Colorado has been made on the rock outcrops and canyon walls of which the state also has an abundance. To follow this phase of history, with its emphasis on technical routes and the competitive raising of technical standards, one may turn to the climbing journals.

Although the arena for getting one's name in the history books by making new and significant ascents is now small, the scope for building a personal history of memories of great days in the mountains is as wide open as ever.

Geology of The Mountains

by John C. Reed, Jr., *U.S. Geological Survey*
edited by Michael Waters

Like nearly all landscapes, the mountain landscape of Colorado is the product of two sets of interacting processes—those that elevate parts of the Earth's crust and those that work to reduce the Earth's surface to a near-level plain. These two sets of processes have interacted for more than 4 billion years.

The part of the story for which we have a record in Colorado begins about 1.8 billion years ago. Thick sediments and volcanic debris were carried to great depths below the surface by tectonic forces, where heat, pressure and igneous intrusion converted the original material into schists and gneisses—the dark metamorphic rocks now exposed in the eroded cores of many of the major mountain ranges and in most of the deeper canyons. Twice more these ancient metamorphic rocks were injected by molten magma. The second episode, about 1.0 billion year ago, produced the great mass of granite and associated gem-bearing pegmatite that now makes up Pikes Peak.

In the time between the intrusion of the Pikes Peak Granite and the beginning of the Paleozoic Era about 570 million years ago, basement rocks that had lain many miles below the Earth's surface were exposed by erosion. Eventually, shallow seas inundated much of the interior of the continent. For the next 200 million years, sand and mud built up layers of sandstone and shale; calcium carbonate from shells and skeletons of marine organisms formed extensive deposits of limestone. These sedimentary deposits reached combined thicknesses of a few hundred to a thousand feet. We see them grandly exposed today in Glenwood Canyon, at the Garden of the Gods, and capping some of the highest peaks of the Sawatch, Tenmile, and Mosquito Ranges.

This period of quiescence ended about 320 million years ago when plate-tectonic movements raised and faulted great mountain blocks in what is now much of the southwest United States. In Colorado the ancestral Rocky Mountains comprised two major ranges: one in the approximate position of the present Front Range, the other in the general area of the Uncompahgre Plateau and the present San Juans. The record of their former grandeur lies in great thicknesses of red sandstone and conglomerate formed from the rocks stripped off their heights as they were uplifted and eroded. These strata are now exposed along the Front Range in the Flatirons and Red Rocks, in the Maroon Bells of the Elk Mountains, in Crestone Peak in the northern Sangre de Cristos, and on the flanks of the San Juans. As the ancient ranges rose, the earlier sedimentary formations were eroded from the uplifts, exposing the underlying basement rocks. The positions of the former mountains are now marked by areas where the older sedimentary rocks are absent and the younger strata rest directly on the basement rocks. The uplift continued for perhaps 70 million years. When it ceased, erosion gradually reduced the peaks to a near-level plain, across which meandered sluggish muddy rivers, flanked by swamps in which dinosaurs flourished. Their bones are displayed in the fossil quarry at Dinosaur National Monument.

About 85 million years ago, the sea once more spread across Colorado. Beaches and sand bars formed a widespread deposit of white sand that we now know as the Dakota Sandstone. Farther offshore, other deposits accumulated. When the sea withdrew, about 75 million years ago, sediments as much as two miles thick blanketed the eroded stumps of the ancestral Rocky Mountains. The stage was set for the Laramide orogeny, the mountain-building episode that helped outline the present ranges of the Rockies.

About 70 million years ago, plate convergence occuring in western North America increased and began to affect the area of the present Rockies. The continental crust began to buckle and shorten like an accordion, resulting in uplifts and downwarps in which the long-buried basement rocks were elevated or depressed thousands of feet. This combination of folds and inclined faults shortened the continental crust between Grand Junction and Denver by some 25 to 50 miles, and the resulting uplifts became the sites of most of the major modern ranges.

As the Laramide uplifts rose, molten magma began to rise through the crust and intrude in a narrow belt that trends northeastward from the southwestern San Juans to the Front Range northwest of Boulder. These masses solidified at depth to form bodies of granite and related rocks; others vented to the surface and fed volcanoes. This narrow belt of igneous rocks, known as the Colorado mineral belt, contains almost all the enormous deposits of gold, silver, lead, and zinc that supported the great Colorado mining districts.

The Laramide orogeny lasted perhaps 30 million years. Erosion continued and by about 35 million years ago, the Laramide mountains were a series of hills and low, isolated mountains that rose above a rolling plain. Remnants of this erosion surface are the oldest records of the history of the present mountains that are preserved in the modern landscape. During the formation of this surface, igneous activity resumed and intensified. The most complete record is in the San Juans, where between 35 and 26 million years ago, huge depressions ringed with volcanoes erupted hundreds of cubic miles of volcanic ash in clouds that surged outward for fifty miles or more. As the glowing ash settled, it welded together to form the thick, light-colored layers of tuff so conspicuous in many of the peaks and canyons of the San Juans. Volcanoes also erupted in other areas, including the West Elks, and the Never Summer Range. Volcanic debris in South Park dammed streams, pending a lake in which the beautifully preserved fossil leaves and insects were entombed at Florissant Fossil Beds National Monument. The Spanish Peaks, southwest of Walsenburg, are the eroded cores of volcanoes that erupted at about the same time. In addition, great masses of igneous rocks were intruded in many ranges, now exposed in the southern Sawatch Range, the San Miguels, the Elk Mountains, and parts of the Front Range. Intrusions of this age were responsible for the formation of the great molybdenum deposits at Henderson, Climax, and Mount Emmons.

About 26 million years ago, plate-tectonic interactions along the western edge of the continent changed, so that much of western North America began to pull apart instead of shorten. This extension had two effects in the area of the Colorado mountains. First, the nearly flat land surface was broken and displaced by faults. Most noteworthy of these fault breaks is the down-dropped block known as the Rio Grande rift, marked by the San Luis valley between the Sangre de Cristos and San Juans and by the upper Arkansas valley between the Sawatch and Mosquito Ranges. The second effect was that the entire region, which had lain only a few thousand feet above sea level after the Laramide orogeny, was elevated six thousand feet or more. As faulting and uplift proceeded, erosion by wind, water, and, later, by glaciers carved the landscape, shaping the present peaks and ranges and incising the major canyons. The crystalline basement rocks, the thick layers of hard sandstone and conglomerate on their flanks, and the intrusive bodies of young granite were more resistant to erosion and, thus, tended to form high peaks. Less resistant rocks, such as the younger sedimentary rocks, were carved out as valleys and basins. Faulting and probably uplift continue today, but at slower average rates.

The action of glaciers in shaping the modern landscape is obvious. The ice-polished and striated rock surfaces, the U-shaped cross sections of the mountain valleys, the scattered erratic boulders, and the moraines all speak of the effects of glacier erosion. In comparison with glaciers in higher, wetter, or more northerly ranges, the effects of former glaciers in the Colorado mountains were relatively minor: they merely applied the final touches to a nearly finished work of sculpture, most of which had already been shaped by other processes. No great continental ice sheets edged into Colorado during the Ice Ages, but during at least two glacial intervals, one ending about 130,000 years ago and one ending about 14,000 years ago, wetter and colder climates triggered the advance of glaciers down the major mountain valleys, carving the cirques, polishing the valley walls, and scouring the basins for the mountain lakes. The Colorado mountain landscape was essentially complete by the end of the last of these glacial advances—this was the time when the first humans appeared on the scene.

THE FRONT RANGE

The Spearhead   *Terry Root*

Front Range (Northern)

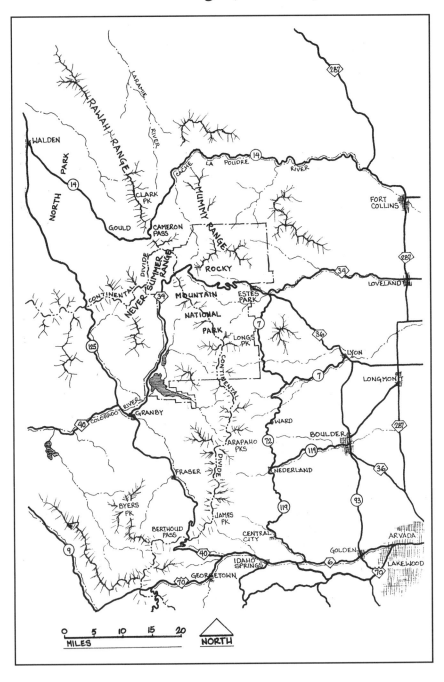

The Front Range

The Front Range of Colorado is a term applied somewhat arbitrarily to the wide band of mountains visible from the eastern plains, extending south from Wyoming to Colorado Springs. Geographically, the range is much smaller than implied in either casual contemporary conversation or as indicated by this section. However, for convenience and current popularity, we adhere to the "expanded" boundaries. In this context, the range is actually a compilation of many mountain chains. The most notable is the northern section comprising Rocky Mountain National Park and the Indian Peaks, which slowly change to the south into a muted collection of rounded ridges in the Rampart Range, setting the stage for an exuberant encore at the Pikes Peak massif.

Many localities along the Front Range reflect the once powerful and fierce interaction of the more prominent Indian nations of mountain and plain, particularly in Rocky Mountain National Park and south to Indian Peaks, where geographic landforms have been christened with Indian names.

Because of their prominent location near the first camps and settlements, the mountains of the Front Range received an expected abundance of attention from early pioneers and explorers. Many pages of flowing prose describe the infatuation of the civilized newcomers with the wild west; from the first War Department surveys of Zebulon Pike and Stephen Long, to the unlikely rambling itinerary of a world traveling Englishwoman, Isabella Bird. But the pioneers sensed a spirit in these mountains, for they proposed descriptive titles like Snowy Range and Shining Mountains to distinguish their beloved region.

Until dependable transportation links were extended deep into Colorado's Rockies, the Front Range was the primary focus of mountain recreation. It is not surprising, therefore, that the mountains of the Front Range were among the first to be named, explored and prized for purely recreational qualities. The creation of Rocky Mountain National Park in 1915, reflected the concern of these early day nature seekers to protect large tracts of land for outdoor enjoyment. This evolution of thought would radically alter the unbridled economic focus of the Colorado mountains established in the last half of the nineteenth century, and lay the groundwork for a nature conservation movement that would gain momentum and slowly move westward through all of the state's ranges.

FRONT RG

Rawah Range

Jurisdiction:
Roosevelt NF, Canyon Lakes Ranger District
Colorado State Forest

Map area reference:
Page 34

Maps:
USGS: *Boston Peak, Chambers Lake, Clark Peak, Gould, Johnnie Moore Mountain, Rawah Lakes*
Forest Service: *Roosevelt NF, Routt NF*

This linear range, 15 miles long, running from north-northwest to south-south-east on the southeast border of North Park, tops at around 12,000' in pinkish Front Range granites that are deeply cut on the east side by glacial erosion. It is bounded on the north by the timbered saddle south of Johnnie Moore Mountain, and on the south by Cameron Pass, which separates it from the Never Summer Mountains and the northwest corner of Rocky Mountain National Park. The range is crossed by Hwy-14, connecting Fort Collins and Walden, and serving as the most obvious access. We use the name Rawah, Indian for wilderness, for this southern part of the Medicine Bow Mountains.

The Rawah Range has cirques and lakes typical of glaciated mountains. The west side, much of it in forest below the 11,000' timberline, is in the Colorado State Forest. The central lake district on the east side is in the Rawah Wilderness.

Colorado State Forest/North Michigan Reservoir Campground Access:

On the west side of the range there are trails to Kelly, Clear and Jewel Lakes. For access to all three, turn off Hwy-14 about 2 miles north of Gould onto Jackson Co Rd-41. This is the entry point into the Colorado State Forest via North Michigan Reservoir. Pick up a pass (fee required) and a map at the guard station, and continue around the reservoir. Rd-41 continues about 6 miles north to a barricade. About 1.5 miles north of the reservoir is the turnoff to **Jewel Lake**. Where the county road ends at the barricade, continue on foot following the abandoned road to a fork near Dry Creek. Here, go east to **Kelly Lake** or continue parallel to the range for the trail up Clear Creek to **Clear Lake**. Many old roads in the State Forest have recently been abandoned and barricaded to prevent resource damage. This may require you to hike a little longer to your destination than in previous seasons, but please respect all closures.

An alternate approach due east of Warden on Jackson Co Rd-12 G, ends at the State Forest boundary, and gives access to Muddy and Willow Creeks. Both Clear and Kelly Lakes can be reached from this approach, albeit with a long walk.

Clark Peak (12,951') is a short climb of 1,700' directly northeast from Jewel Lake. It combines well with **Sickle Mountain** (12,654') 0.5 mile west-north-west, and a Sickle Ridge descent. From 0.5 mile downstream from Jewel Lake, a branch trail takes you east about halfway up 12,433' **Pipit Peak**.

From Clear Lake there are steep climbs of **North Rawah Peak** (12,473') 1.5 miles north, **South Rawah Peak** (12,644') 0.75 mile east-northeast, and **Snowbank Peak** (12,522') 0.75 mile southeast.

Kelly Lake, at 10,805', is beneath some of the roughest part of the range. **Mount Ashley** (12,376') is a mile east at the head of the Kelly Lake Gulch, and not difficult to reach. **Island Lake Peak** (12,175') is closer, east-northeast, and sufficiently cliffy to require some exploring and perhaps experimenting with routes. For Whitecrown, Snowbank and South Rawah, you should retreat 0.5 mile on the trail and then angle up the steep slope to the right to gain the ridge. For South Rawah alone, go north and a little left to the saddle west of Snowbank, and then north-northeast to the ridge. South Rawah is 0.75 mile north of Snowbank along the ridge, and 550' above the low point of the ridge.

Hwy-14/Blue Lakes Trailhead/Chambers Lake Access:

Medicine Bow Trail starts about 10 miles south of Mountain Home, Wyoming, and runs down the range crest to Rawah Lakes, where it ties into the **Rawah Lakes Trail**, one of the better-built scenic trails. This latter trail passes the Rawah Peaks on the east, and with the West Branch and Fall Creek Trails, continues to the Chambers Lake area, west of Fort Collins on Hwy-14. This 40-mile trail system is mainly above timberline, except where it dips into the spruce timber of high valleys. Snow normally closes this trail by the end of September and keeps it closed until mid-July.

Since the peak climbs are beautiful and fairly short, and the trail approaches long, the Rawah climbs are particularly inviting as a backpack expedition along the above trail sequence, beginning at Blue Lake Trailhead, 1.25 miles above Chambers Lake on Hwy-14. To get there from Fort Collins, go north on US-287 8 miles to Hwy-14, and then west 53 miles, paralleling the Cache la Poudre River, to the trailhead.

Clark Peak (12,951') is the high point of the range. Take the **Blue Lake Trail** 5 miles west and northwest to the pass north of **Blue Lake**, and climb 2 more miles southwest on the ridge to the summit.

Cameron Peak (12,127') is an easy mile east from the saddle above Blue Lake. It is well worth the climb for the view into the cirques farther north.

From the foot of the Blue Lake Trail a mile northwest of the pass at 10,100', you can turn up **West Branch Trail** and climb 1,000' (1.5 miles) to **Carey Lake** and **Island Lake**. **Island Lake Peak** goes best from Island Lake and a climb around south to the south saddle.

Whitecrown (12,440') is a mile farther north on the ridge, a pretty straight mile-long climb of 1,400' north-northwest from Carey Lake.

It is 3.5 miles down from Carey Lake, or 2 from the Blue Lake Trail terminus, to the Rawah Trail, which the West Branch Trail joins at the junction of North Fork and West Branch Creeks, at 9,600'. This point can also be reached from the West Branch Trailhead, at 8,600', (0.5 mile north of Tunnel Campground) 7 miles north of Chambers Lake and Hwy-14 on Larimer Co Rd-103 (FSR-190), also known as the Laramie River Road. The West Branch Trail starts here and climbs 4 miles and 1,000' to the junction. About 1.5 miles west of this junction, at 10,450', the **North Fork Trail** branches to the southwest off the Rawah Trail and climbs 1 mile to **Twin Crater Lakes** at 11,050'. **South Rawah Peak** (12,644') is a climb of 1.25 miles across the basin to the northwest.

North Rawah Peak (12,473') is nearly 1.5 miles of ridge walk north-northwest from South Rawah, but there is only a moderate loss of altitude and a good cirque to look at on the way; and from North Rawah there is a short descent east to another side trail that assures good footing homeward from the north side of Lake Four. This trail drops to the Rawah Trail, which returns to the junction with North Fork Trail, about 3.5 miles in all from North Rawah Peak.

Hwy-14 Access:

Big South Trail starts at Big South Trailhead, west of Fort Collins 48 miles on Hwy-14, and runs south along the Cache la Poudre River. It connects with the **Flowers Trail** 7 miles from the highway, and enters Rocky Mountain National Park at mile 10. Just inside the park boundary, the **Mummy Pass Trail** heads east along Hague Creek, a sizable stream with interesting rock formations along the way, making this a pleasant trip.

Greyrock Mountain Trail climbs north 2 miles to **Greyrock Mountain**. The trailhead is about 8 miles west of US-287 on Hwy-14.

The Diamond, Longs Peak   *Roger Fuehrer*

FRONT RG

Rocky Mountain National Park

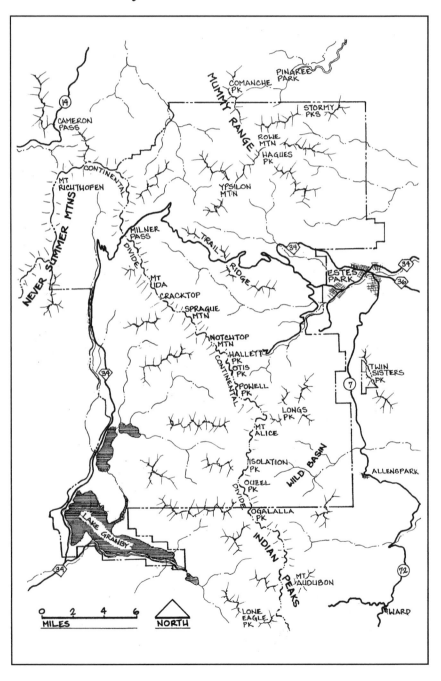

Rocky Mountain National Park

Jurisdiction:
Rocky Mountain National Park

Map area reference:
Page 34 and 40

Maps:
USGS: *Allens Park, Comanche Peak, Estes Park, Fall River Pass, Grand Lake, Isolation Peak, Longs Peak, McHenrys Peak, Mount Richthofen, Shadow Mountain, Trail Ridge; Rocky Mountain National Park (1:62,500)*
Forest Service: *Roosevelt NF*

Within Rocky Mountain National Park, the Front Range angles south-south-east and south 20 miles from La Poudre Pass through the Wild Basin back ridge. The mountains are of typical Front Range granite and generally speaking rather flat-crested but with very deep cut glaciation on the east slopes. The glaciation has produced many alpine lakes, often with cliffs at the back. Longs and Hallett Peaks, Lumpy Ridge and some of the lower points have been areas of intensive rock climbing for many years. As is always true in the Rockies there is loose rock, ready to fall at a touch, even on the cleanest cliffs.

Because the park is full of hazards, including cliffs and ice, it is highly recom-mended that all climbers consult park rangers for trail and route conditions. Technical climbs are those for which ropes or other aids are used. For overnight camping anywhere away from car campgrounds, permits are required. Check with the backcountry office at park headquarters. Making reservations well in advance is recommended.

The Never Summer and Mummy Ranges are small subgroups to the Front Range that lie mostly within the park, to the west and north, and are included as part of this section.

US-34/Milner Pass Access:

Mount Ida (12,880') is reached from 10,750' **Milner Pass**, the Continental Divide crossing on US-34 Trail Ridge Road, 30 miles west of Estes Park or 21 miles from Grand Lake. Follow the trail south 0.5 mile, then northeast a mile or so. Then you cut off to the right side, climbing to the ridge and divide, which you follow south-southeast 3.5 miles. Mount Ida looks down on the Gorge Lakes. If you wish to extend your outing to include **Chief Cheley Peak** (12,804'), **Cracktop** (12,760') and **Mount Julian** (12,928'), proceed from Mount Ida southeast down the saddle, ascend the west side of the ridge to reach Chief Cheley. For Cracktop, descend from Chief Cheley northeast to the next saddle and ascend to Cracktop, then descend to the next saddle northeast to reach Mount Julian.

Gorge Lakes, the remote gems of alpine scenery which lie between Mount Ida and Mount Julian, are one of the best trailless trips in the park. You can go toward Mount Ida as above but turn off east from the divide, 0.5 mile and 400' short of the summit. Near the end of the ridge you turn west to Arrowhead Lake. This is an altitude loss of 1,200', which you regain in segments as you go up past the lakes.

Bear Lake Access:

Little Matterhorn (11,586') is a favorite of experienced climbers, being very handsome to look at and from, and offering the suggestion of a rock climb by the easiest route. A rope should be available whether it is used or not. From **Bear Lake**, 9,400', walk the trail 4.5 miles west and north to the **Odessa Lake** outlet. Cross the creek and climb west and across the creek from Tourmaline Gorge. When you have bushwhacked to timberline continue west-southwest to south to reach the ridge west of the end point which constitutes Little Matterhorn.

Another route approaches the summit ridge from the opposite side. From 3 miles up the Odessa Lake Trail you turn off left for **Lake Helene** and switchback downhill northwest from it until you can cross the west fork of Fern Creek and head up an obvious gully to the ridge.

Flattop Mountain (12,324') is a 4 mile trail climb from Bear Lake parking area, 9,400'. It is about 1.5 miles west and north around **Ptarmigan Point** (12,363') to **Notchtop** (12,129'), another 0.5 mile northwest to **Knobtop** (12,731'), and 0.75 mile more north to **Gabletop** (11,939'), all with very little loss of altitude. Notchtop, like Little Matterhorn, is down east of the gentle divide ridge. It presents good technical climbing on its south face to those who approach from the valley below.

Sprague Mountain (12,713') is also at the end of a pleasant 4 mile walk northwest along the divide from Flattop, and **Stones Peak** (12,922') is another 1.5 miles northeast of Sprague, but you have to get to Flattop first. **Hallett Peak** (12,713') is 0.5 mile south and east around the **Tyndall Glacier** head from Flattop. **Otis Peak** (12,486') is another 1.5 miles south around Chaos Canyon, and **Taylor Peak** (13,153') is 2 miles more south past **Andrews Glacier** and the rough cliffs above Loch Vale. From Flattop to Taylor without the other peaks en route is a trip of 2.5 miles with only 200' altitude loss. Hallett and Otis are side trips of about 250' elevation gain each. Another option is to glissade down Andrews Glacier to Loch Vale and out at Glacier Gorge. If you choose this exit, check with the backcountry office on the safety conditions of the glacier.

On trail to Mount Ida   *Frank Cechner*

Glacier Gorge Access:

McHenrys Peak (13,327') is climbed from **Black Lake**, 5 miles from Glacier Gorge Junction by marked trail. One skirts the lake to the left, climbs 0.5 mile farther south up the brook to near **Frozen Lake** and then climbs 0.5 mile west to **Stone Man Pass**, and turning right, takes the ridge to the top. On your way by Frozen Lake, you'll pass the striking **Spearhead** (12,575'). Although it is popular with technical climbers, there is a much used pedestrian route. Climb to the saddle southwest of the peak and finish with a short scramble up the ridge. **Chiefs Head** (13,579') is a ridge climb of 1 mile southeast from Stone Man Pass.

Mount Powell (13,208') can be climbed from Sky Pond, to which a 4.5 mile trail, only cairn-marked the last part of the way, leads from Glacier Gorge Junction. It is a climb of 0.75 mile from the pond up the north side of Powell, some of it probably on steep snow.

Thatchtop (12,668') juts northeast a mile from Powell. Take the Loch Vale Trail from Glacier Gorge Junction 2.25 miles to the first sharp bend past the trail junction with Glacier Gorge. Just south across the creek you will get into the start of a reverse S-shaped couloir. It leads up to the easier tundra slope above. The climb is 2,800' from trail to summit in not much over a mile. You are in very handsome country here, with everything showing its teeth at you.

Thatchtop is as often climbed from **Solitude Lake**. Take the **Black Lake Trail** 4.5 miles to a timberless patch just north of Shelf Creek, which comes in from the west side of the canyon. Bushwhack up the right side of the creek to Shelf Lake, 1,000' higher. From Solitude Lake, a little farther up the shelf, cut north up a steep half-mile slope to the summit.

Solitude Lake also offers an interesting alternate approach to McHenrys Peak. Climb west into the cirque, then scramble up exposed slabs to the McHenrys-Arrowhead saddle. A short scramble to the left leads up to **Arrowhead** (12,640') or follow the ridge to the right, passing any obstacles on the right, to McHenrys.

Pagoda Mountain (13,497') is best reached from the 13,100' Longs-Pagoda saddle and the north-northeast ridge. You take the 5 mile Black Lake Trail from Glacier Gorge Junction and keep southeast from Black Lake to Green Lake. Ascend the couloir southeast to the saddle between the last gendarme of Keyboard of the Winds and the Pagoda ridge. Ascend the southeast side of the ridge to the summit. It is a 7 mile trip one way, with a 4,300' climb.

Longs Peak Trailhead Access:

Longs Peak (14,255') is one of Colorado's great mountains, accessible to tourists under favorable conditions, yet well armored with steep to perpendicular faces. You need four USGS maps to see it topographically. It was named for Major Stephen H. Long, who explored the plains in 1820. The first recorded climb was made by Major Powell and *Rocky Mountain News* founder William Byers in 1868, but Indians are said to have had an eagle trap on top earlier. Enos Mills gave it fame in his yarns. Since then, its national park status, ranger patrolled trails and good rock have helped to keep its climbing tradition active.

From Estes Park drive 10 miles south on Hwy-7 and 1 mile west to the Longs Peak Ranger Station at 9,400'. Climb 7 miles west by trail to the **Boulderfield** at 12,600'. The Boulderfield is also reached by a 9 mile trail from Glacier Gorge Junction on the Bear Lake Road. From the Boulderfield a marked route, rated technical, climbs directly south ascending the north face toward the summit. It goes over boulders and then up a rather steep cliff band to a sketchy trail higher up. The longer traditional route goes west through the **Keyhole** and turns south along marked rock ledges. At the end of the ledges section you will go up to the top of the Trough and out on to the beautiful south exposure called the Narrows. Last is a fairly short climb north up the Homestretch. This standard "tourist" route is only dangerous if wet or icy, particularly in the Trough or on the Homestretch. Camping by permit is possible at the Boulderfield or at the Battle Mountain backpack site, a halfway point near timberline on the north side of the trail and north of Alpine Brook. For the many rock routes, which run all the way from easy to very difficult, consult *High Peaks Guide* by Richard Dumais or *Rocky Mountain Climbs* by John Harlin.

The Sharkstooth   *Kent Keller*

Storm Peak (13,326') and **Mount Lady Washington** (13,281') flank the Boulderfield. Rock hop up Lady Washington's north ridge for an unparalleled view of the east face of Long's. Storm goes by way of a short, steep climb up its east face.

The most accessible route on **Mount Meeker** (13,911') is 11 miles with 4,500' gain. Take the **Longs Peak Trail** to the **Chasm Lake Trail**. From the **Chasm Lake** shelter cabin climb on or skirt the snowfield southwest to the left of the Ships Prow. At the upper part, follow cairns appearing on ledges to the south, reaching the Loft. From there it's an easy tundra walk southeast to the official west summit. Some negotiate the knife edge to the eastern summit. Another approach from Chasm meadow is to ascend the Meeker northeast ridge to both summits. Yet another route is one that takes you through the Wild Basin scenery on the way (see Wild Basin Access).

Wild Basin Access:

The southern peaks, Pagoda and Chiefs Head, are often climbed from upper Wild Basin, off of Hwy-7, 12 miles south of Estes Park or 2 miles north of Allens Park. Take the **Sandbeach Lake Trail** 3.5 miles from its start at Copeland Lake.

Chiefs Head (13,579') goes by the 3 mile North Ridge, including **Mount Orton** (11,724'). For **Pagoda Mountain** (13,497'), climb Hunters Creek to the first lake at 11,200', then angle northeast over a low ridge toward Mount Meeker and climb the loose rock gully to the saddle west of Longs. Longs can be climbed from here via the Keplinger Couloir, the original Powell Expedition route, or with **Mount Meeker** by heading for the saddle between the two. For those who want to make Mount Meeker in one day, bushwhack from the Horsetooth Peak-Lookout Mountain saddle, 10,200', to and up the southeast ridge.

The peaks west of Wild Basin are best enjoyed from the lakes designated by the park service as camping areas: Sandbeach, Thunder, Ouzel and Bluebird. A back-country permit is required.

Mount Alice (13,110') and **Tanima Peak** (12,420') present formidable east fronts, but both can be climbed together from Thunder Lake. The pack in is on a 7.5 mile trail west from 8,400' at Wild Basin Trailhead to 10,600'. Start for the peaks along the north side of **Thunder Lake**, climbing west 1.5 miles to **Boulder-Grand Pass** at the head of the drainage, 12,061'. Tanima is a climb of 0.5 mile east-southeast; Alice is nearly a mile north. It is possible to make a steep return from Alice by going southwest at the top, then south and east, following the gulch 1.5 miles southeast along the headwater creek of the North St Vrain. You can take a gentler route from Alice down the north-northeast ridge 0.5 mile, then down a long ridge that cuts off at right angles to it, to the **Lion Lakes**.

Longs Peak   *Neil Purrett*

Separately, Alice can be climbed from the **Lion Lakes Trail**, ascending a south-east ridge forming a T with the divide, as per the descent described above. Turn south on the divide to the summit. Likewise, Tanima goes by itself on a popular route starting south of Thunder Lake, on a log-jam crossing near its outlet. Ascend the east ridge and traverse to the south side. Follow the ridge to the top, expecting many false summits along the way.

Isolation Peak (13,118') is accessible from Thunder Lake Trail. A dimly marked trail goes south around the bench and up west to **Box Lake**, **Eagle Lake** and **Frigid Lake**, about 2.5 miles in all. From Frigid there is a good route south around the ridge end and slantwise southwest up the slopes of Isolation. There is permit camping also on the **Bluebird Lake Trail** at **Ouzel Lake**, 10,000', or near **Bluebird Lake**, 1,000' higher. They are 5.5 and 7 miles respectively from the trailhead. Isolation Peak can be climbed quite directly from Bluebird. You continue west from the north side of the lake all the way to the 12,200' pass south of the summit, then work your way up the short steep ridge. Or, from **Isolation Pass**, Isolation Peak is west and **Mahana Peak** (12,632') is an easy climb east.

Copeland Mountain (13,176') juts far into the southwest corner of Wild Basin with a rough north face. The easiest route goes from the outlet of Ouzel Lake, 9,800', where you bushwhack south 0.5 mile up a timbered ridge and then south-west to timberline another good 0.5 mile. From there it is a mile of rather steep trudging.

For **Ouzel Peak** (12,716') and **Ogalalla Peak** (13,138'), start at the outlet of **Pipit Lake** and ascend southwest to the ridge. Then travel east to Ouzel's summit. Continue on the west side of the divide south 1.5 miles to Ogalalla. These peaks can be reached from **Cony Pass** if free of snow later in the season. To reach the pass, cut off the Bluebird Lake Trail and follow the drainage south and west to **Junco Lake**.

Elk Tooth (12,848') starts at the **Finch Lake Trail** to **Pear Lake**, then goes cross-country to **Hutcheson Lakes**. From the lower lake ascend west avoiding the steep cliffs to the ridge southeast of the summit. Follow the ridge to the summit and descend the same, a total of 9 miles and 4,210' elevation gain.

A popular one day over-the-divide hike is to start early at the Wild Basin Trailhead, hiking to Thunder Lake, Lake of Many Winds and ascending the Boulder-Grand Pass. Descend into East Inlet and pick up all the gorgeous multitude of lakes ending at Grand Lake. You can also do this in reverse, albeit with more elevation gain.

Twin Sisters Trailhead Access:

Eastward across the Tahosa Valley from Longs is the good trail up to **Twin Sisters Peak** (11,413'). Look for the start 1 mile south of Wind River Pass on Hwy-7, 9 miles south of Estes Park.

Grand Lake Access:

From **Grand Lake**, on the west side of the park, there are well maintained trails. **North Inlet Trail**, which takes off from Grand Lake's water treatment plant, connects via Flattop Mountain with Bear Lake, 16.5 miles. It also has a 3.5 mile side trail south to **Lake Nokoni** and **Lake Nanita**, 11 miles from Grand Lake and 2,240' higher, or 10,800'.

Ptarmigan Mountain (12,324') is a short steep climb up ridge from the pass between the two lakes.

East Inlet Trail starts at West Portal, at the east end of Grand Lake, and climbs to camping at **Lake Verna**, 7 miles, and on up the valley in sloppier style to Fourth and Fifth Lakes, the latter above timberline and a cliff-blocked mile north of Isolation Peak.

Shadow Mountain (10,155'), south of Grand Lake, is a good conditioner. Drive south across the Grand Lake-Shadow Mountain channel and turn right. From the road end walk south along the east side of Shadow Mountain Lake. The trail starts a gentle climb after 1 mile. You ascend through 4 miles of timber to a fire lookout 1,500' above the lake.

Mount Craig (12,007') is an imposing western extension from the divide. To climb it, take the East Inlet Trail from 8,367' Grand Lake 5 miles east to **Lone Pine Lake** at 9,900'. Head south from the southeast corner of the lake, following a minor ridge and bench for 0.25 mile to the mouth of a steeply climbing U-shaped valley. After about 600' of climbing in the valley it is feasible to work out of it to the right, where you continue on slopes of lessening steepness to the summit. It is wise to keep details of your route well in mind as any deviation on the descent may lead you into serious trouble.

Ptarmigan Mountain (12,324') and **Andrews Peak** (12,565') can make a combined ridge climb from a camp at Lake Verna, 7 miles east of Grand Lake on the East Inlet Trail. To climb Andrews, which is 1.5 miles north from the lake, you go diagonally upslope, angling well left of the fall line. A 12,000' bench makes it easy to avoid the high spots of the ridge on the 2 mile traverse to Andrews Peak. These peaks are on the spur of the divide north of Mount Craig.

A backpack up Tonahutu Creek offers the approach to a couple of the most secluded summits in the Park. From 4 miles north of Grand Lake on US-34, take the Green Mountain Trail 2 miles, then follow the Tonahutu Creek Trail another 5 miles. Turn left on a faint trail leading past **Haynach Lakes** 2 miles to the northeast ridge of **Nakai Peak** (12,216') and follow it to the top. For **Snowdrift Peak** (12,274') follow the Tonahutu Creek Trail 7 miles until just below Bighorn Flats, then finish up Snowdrift's northeast ridge.

FRONT RG

Never Summer Range

Jurisdiction:
Arapaho NF, Sulphur Ranger District
Routt NF, Parks Ranger District
Rocky Mountain National Park

Maps:
USGS: *Bowen Mountain, Fall River Pass, Mount Richthofen*
Forest Service: *Arapaho NF, Routt NF*

This 10 mile range from Cameron Pass to Bowen Mountain is a southward continuation of the pink granite line of Rawah peaks. Its beautiful name is a translation of the Arapaho one. The cloud names were the idea of James Grafton Rogers, a founder of the Colorado Mountain Club. Although Nokhu Crags give the range a rough north end, its other summits are generally of even slopes and are less deeply cirqued than either the Rawahs or the Front Range mountains to the south. Accesses start on either Hwy-14 west of **Cameron Pass** or on US-34, Trail Ridge Road just north of Grand Lake.

As the Never Summer Range has its most popular side in RMNP, park regulations for camping and registering for overnight trips are in force and information should be sought from park officials.

Hwy-14/Cameron Pass Access:

Mount Richthofen (12,940') is the high point of the range. One of the survey parties of the 1870's, probably Clarence King's, named this mountain after a scientific friend, Baron Ferdinand von Richthofen, who had worked with them on the California survey, and later first mapped the mountains of inner China. Mount Richthofen is reached from Hwy-14. From 2 miles south and west of Cameron Pass a lumber road leads south and east a mile or so to the start of the trail to **Lake Agnes**. Walk 3.5 miles south, passing the lake on either side, climb to the saddle and then east. Upper rock slopes are very unstable. From the lumber camp the climb is 3,300', 4 miles.

Teepee Mountain (12,360') is an exciting side trip from Richthofen. Scramble south 0.25 mile, passing obstacles on the right. A short, steep crack provides a way up the west face of the summit block.

To climb **Static Peak** (12,560') continue north from Richthofen's summit, descend 540' to the saddle and ascend 160' to the summit. Return via Richthofen.

FRONT RG

Nokhu Crags (12,485') east of Lake Agnes, is climbed by its north-northeast ridge. Go south-southeast 1.5 miles on the ditch road from Cameron Pass and then follow the ditch around to the ridge. Near the summit, work the gullies to the west of the ridge, scrambling on rotten rock. Bring a rope to rappel the obvious notch, if you wish to visit Nokhu's nearly identical south summit.

US-34/Trail Ridge Road Access:

The **Grand Ditch,** which picks up water all along the east side of the range and takes it across the divide at 10,175' **Poudre Pass,** has a road which is closed to vehicular traffic but available for horse and foot travel. A road climbs to near the south end of it from the Never Summer Ranch, 9 miles north of Grand Lake on US-34, Trail Ridge Road. From the Colorado River Trailhead, 3 miles farther north, the **Red Mountain Trail** climbs up to the ditch road also. There are several crossings of the ditch. Farthest north is the **Colorado River-Poudre Pass Trail**, which keeps to the

Nokhu Crags, east face   *Chester Stone*

White crowned sparrow   *Neil Purrett*

Colorado River all the way from the trailhead, where Trail Ridge Road starts its climb out of the valley, to Poudre Pass, 7 miles north and northeast.

Thunder Pass Trail, the only one giving horse access to the range, leaves the Colorado River-Poudre Pass Trail at mile 2 and climbs about 7 miles over the pass and on to 11,500' **Snow Lake**, cupped under Nokhu Crags and Static Peak. The next crossing of the ditch is at Big Dutch Creek, where a trail goes west to timberline under the **Lake of the Clouds**. Mosquito Creek, Opposition Creek and Red Gulch also have crossings.

Mount Richthofen is twice as long a climb from the west end of Trail Ridge Road when compared with the Hwy-14 approach. From the Colorado River Trailhead, take Colorado River-Thunder Pass Trail north 4 miles to 0.5 mile past the ditch crossing, and climb the 2-mile ridge to the west.

Lead Mountain (12,537') can be combined with Richthofen, or climbed separately from the same trail. You cross the ditch and cut left (southwest) for a half mile, then go up Skeleton Gulch to the northwest ridge or the east saddle for the finish on the sharp ridge. By itself, starting on the Red Mountain Trail, head up Big Dutch Creek where you can cross and go west on Lake of the Clouds Trail as far as timberline. From there the climb is to the saddle east of the peak and up the knife-edge ridge to the west.

Howard Mountain (12,810') and **Mount Cirrus** (12,797') are approached from Lake of the Clouds at the head of Big Dutch Creek (see above for Lead Mountain). You can climb up the Cirrus ridge 0.5 mile west-northwest from the lake, then dip to its 12,400' south saddle and then climb up to Howard. For a shorter descent route, start east on the Howard ridge and cut east-southeast via Pinnacle Pool to Mosquito Creek. Follow the creek down to the ditch.

Mount Nimbus (12,706') is climbed from the Opposition Creek Valley. Use the Red Mountain Trail from the Colorado River Trailhead but cut up along Opposition Creek, where a ditch crossing lets you follow that drainage west to the north ridge of the peak, 2.5 miles from the ditch. It is 0.4 mile and 200' altitude loss to continue south to 12,520' **Mount Stratus**.

For **Green Knoll** (12,280') take the Never Summer Ranch Trail to Ditch Road. Wade at low water level point across Grand Ditch and follow the switchback trail ascending northwest, then go cross country above timberline to the summit. Stratus may be reached on a narrow ridge to the northwest.

Baker Mountain (12,397') which is cliffed on the east, is best approached from the Never Summer Ranch. It is about 4 miles up the hillside and then west along the Grand Ditch to the Baker Gulch crossing, a good place to start the steep climb from 10,300' to the top, a mile north-northeast. Total altitude gain is about 3,400'.

Parika Peak (12,394') is about 2.5 miles west via **Parika Lake Trail** from the same crossing of Baker Gulch, or in all 6.5 miles. From the lake, head west to the Continental Divide, 0.5 mile. Parika is 0.25 mile north from this saddle and **Fairview Mountain** (12,246') is 0.25 mile south.

Bowen Mountain (12,524') is also climbed from the ditch road south of where it crosses Baker Creek. Head west-southwest then west 1.5 miles to the valley head, about 12,200', and then south-southeast along the ridge 0.5 mile to the top.

Cascade Mountain (12,303') is best climbed from the south. Take County Rd-4 west, 9 miles north of the US-34/US-40 intersection or 7 miles south of Grand Lake Road on US-34. Follow the dirt road north to the trailhead that leads to the **Wolverine Trail**, then stay on the Wolverine Trail ascending Blue Ridge overlooking **Bowen Lake**. Ascend the ridge to the Cascade summit.

Mummy Range

Jurisdiction:
Roosevelt NF, Canyon Lakes Ranger District
Rocky Mountain National Park

Maps:
USGS: Comanche, Estes Park, Pingree Park, Trail Ridge
Forest Service: Roosevelt NF

Most of the Mummy Range lies within Rocky Mountain National Park, whose north boundary now passes through Fall Mountain. Thus all accesses from the south and southeast of Fall Mountain are through the park.

The Mummy Range gets its name from the resemblance it has to a reclining mummy. It is a 20 mile front range, 10 miles east of the Continental Divide between the Poudre and Fall Rivers. The west slopes tend to be smooth, the east cirqued.

Pingree Park Access:

Comanche Peak (12,702') and **Fall Mountain** (12,258') are end points of a 2 mile northwest-southeast ridge, west-southwest of Pingree Park. They are best climbed from the Colorado State University Camp there. From US-287 northwest of Fort Collins, drive 25.5 miles west on Hwy-14 and turn left on Larimer Co Rd-63E, and travel 14.0 miles to Tom Bennett Campground. Continue about 1.5 miles to Beaver Creek Trailhead, east of Sky Ranch, and follow the trail to Comanche Reservoir. A pack trail crosses south over the dam and continues to the summit, 6 miles and 3500' in all. Follow the smooth ridge south-southeast to Fall Mountain.

About a mile before Beaver Creek Trailhead, you will pass the Cirque Meadow Trailhead, from where trails lead to **Emmaline Lake** and **Mummy Pass**. The **Mummy Pass Trail** continues west 4.5 miles from Mummy Pass to a trail on the upper Cache la Poudre River, and these in turn connect with long trails to Big South Trailhead on Hwy-14 to the northwest, and Fall River and Trail Ridge Road to the southwest. There is a trail across the range west of the Comanche Peak-Fall Mountain ridge but none south of Mummy Pass.

Stormy Peaks (12,418') and **Sugarloaf** (12,120') are reached from the Stormy Peaks Trailhead 0.4 mile beyond Tom Bennett Campground and 0.1 mile up the left fork of the road. About 5 miles up the trail is Stormy Peaks Pass. Stormy Peaks are 0.5 mile to the north and northwest, and Sugarloaf is 1.5 miles to the west.

US-34/Trail Ridge Road Access:

Hagues Peak (13,560') is usually climbed by a long but beautiful route from Horseshoe Park, on US-34. Starting at the Lawn Lake Trailhead at 8,600' the 6 mile **Lawn Lake Trail** climbs to the **Black Canyon Trail** at 10,800'. Follow the Black Canyon Trail southeast about 0.3 mile at the trail junction, then head north and northwest to the summit of **Mummy Mountain** (13,425'). Continuing to Hagues, descend north to the saddle and contour northwest below the ridge crest about 0.5 mile to another small saddle. Follow the saddle on the north side near **Rowe Glacier**, and approach the summit from the upper basin. **Rowe Peak** (13,400') and **Rowe Mountain** (13,184') can be approached by climbing or skirting the small glacier in a northerly direction. Return via the Hagues-Mummy saddle and Lawn Lake.

The **Ypsilon Lake Trail** leaves the Lawn Lake Trail 1.5 miles above the start in Horseshoe Park. It is 3.5 miles to the lake, at 10,600'. This route is used by rock climbers and those who want to give their ice axes a workout on the "Y", high on Mount Ypsilon.

Mt. Ypsilon, east face　　　*Mike Endres*

Fairchild Mountain (13,502') is a non-difficult climb from Ypsilon Lake. Heading north from the outlet, you climb 600' in altitude, the last of it on a timbered ridge that runs northwest. As the ridge steepens, turn right, north again, and contour north-northwest 0.5 mile to the upper Fay Lake. From here you can see your route. Fairchild is a long mile directly north and 2,300' higher. There are non-technical routes to Ypsilon Mountain from **Ypsilon Lake**, by detouring either north toward Fairchild or south over Chiquita.

The easiest approach to the southern summits is by way of the Fall River Road. It is one-way west from US-34 at Horseshoe Park. **Mount Chapin** (12,454'), **Mount Chiquita** (13,069') and **Mount Ypsilon** (13,514') are climbed in the order named from Chapin Pass. The trail starts north from 0.25 mile above the second left road hairpin in the series of zigzags climbing out of Fall River, about 6.5 miles west of Horseshoe Park, or if you walk down Fall River Road, 1.5 miles from the Trail Ridge Road. The trail, starting at 11,000' takes you 0.1 mile to the pass, where you leave it to go northeast along the ridge. Mount Chapin is 200' higher than the saddle to the north of it, and easily bypassed; Chiquita loses you only 100', but is also easily bypassed. The trip to Ypsilon is about 5 miles.

Indian Peaks

Jurisdiction:
Arapaho NF, Sulphur Ranger District
Roosevelt NF, Boulder Ranger District

Map area reference:
Page 34 and 40

Maps:
USGS: *Allens Park, East Portal, Empire, Grand Lake, Isolation Peak, Monarch Lake, Nederland, Ward*
Forest Service: *Arapaho NF, Roosevelt NF*

This section extends from Ogalalla Peak at the southern boundary of Rocky Mountain National Park to Rollins Pass, and consists of the **Indian Peaks Wilderness**. This wilderness was established in 1978, giving this unique and fragile environment a strong measure of protection from commercial use, as well as over-use by hikers and campers. The Indian Peaks, especially the east side, is one of the most heavily used areas in the country. The fragile environment, sitting on the edge of existence, requires both protection and intelligent use by visitors to ensure its continuation as an exciting place to visit. Check with the ranger districts for regulations about use and travel, and to obtain the necessary camping permits.

The Indian Peaks are situated along the Continental Divide, with ten of the biggest named after prominent Indian tribes of the Great Plains. From north to south Ogalalla Peak, Paiute Peak, Pawnee Peak, Shoshoni Peak, Apache Peak, Navajo Peak, Arikaree Peak, plus North and South Arapaho Peaks, are situated directly on the divide, while Kiowa Peak sits east of Arikaree. There are more than 15 other major peaks in this section, as well as several glaciers.

The rugged beauty of the Indian Peaks was carved during the ice age. The glaciers left unique summit domes, jagged ridges, cirques, and pristine valleys. The present glaciers, however, are examples of how wind and abundant snowfall combine to form small glaciers and numerous snowfields on the east side of the highest ridges. The prevalent rock of the summits is the Idaho Springs schist and gneiss.

The main approaches are on either side of the divide. On the east is Hwy-72, the Peak-to-Peak Highway, and its continuation, Hwy-119. On the west is US-40 from Winter Park to Granby. Many of the trails over the divide link these various access points and trailheads with numerous combinations of long walks or loops.

Indian Peaks Wilderness   *Neil Purrett*

The Rollins Pass Road, route of David Moffat's Denver, Northwest & Pacific Railroad over the divide, is now a scenic drive although some sections are rough. It connects Rollinsville on Hwy-119 to Winter Park on US-40 via 11,670' Rollins Pass. At the present time, the old railroad tunnel near the pass is closed making it impossible to completely cross the divide on this exciting drive.

Peaceful Valley Trailhead/Middle St Vrain Creek Access:

From 9 miles north of Ward, 10 miles south of Allens Park, on Hwy-72, go west on County Rd-114 1.5 miles to Camp Dick Campground and parking. The Buchanan Pass Trail starts at Camp Dick, crosses the creek to the north side and goes 3 miles to the Indian Peaks Wilderness boundary. Four wheel drive vehicles may also drive the road on the south side of the creek from Camp Dick to the same wilderness boundary.

The **St Vrain Glacier Trail** goes up the Middle St Vrain Creek from the wilderness boundary to timberline, within a half mile of **Gibraltar Lake**. The trail, which is now a closed roadway, parallels the creek on the east side. Within about 3 miles of the start at the wilderness boundary, the old roadway crosses the creek and becomes a real trail.

To reach **Ogalalla Peak** (13,138') hike to the end of the St Vrain Glacier Trail and continue along the creek drainage past Pika Lake, a small tarn nestled beneath **Elk Tooth** (12,848'). Continue on into the head of the Middle St Vrain Valley and climb steeply into the cirque containing the northernmost of the **St Vrain Glaciers**. There is a very steep slope with loose talus between the glacier and the summit of Ogalalla. Climb the talus to the low spot of the ridge on the Continental Divide. Once there, it is a short but rewarding hike to the summit. Ogalalla Peak can also be climbed from Wild Basin in Rocky Mountain National Park (see that section).

The **Buchanan Pass Trail** connects Middle St Vrain valley with Monarch Lake, west of the divide (see Lake Granby Access). It is a 14 mile traverse over **Buchanan Pass**. From the Indian Peaks Wilderness boundary along the Middle St Vrain Creek, turn left at 2 miles following the sign for Buchanan Pass Trail. The trail crosses the creek on a bridge, traverses through forests uphill, passes the trail turning right to Red Deer Lake and continues into a large valley heading towards 11,837' Buchanan Pass. Near timberline, the Beaver Creek Trail turns left downhill, and continues to Coney Flats and Brainard Lake.

Sawtooth Mountain (12,304') is the easternmost point of the Continental Divide in all of North America. It is an easy climb of 0.4 mile south-southeast from Buchanan Pass. Its narrowness and 600' south side cliff make it one of the striking sights from the Peak to Peak Highway, to say nothing of the exposure and excitement of being on the top.

The **St Vrain Mountain Trail** loops over **St Vrain Mountain** (12,162') connecting Allens Park with Peaceful Valley. From the St Vrain Glacier Trail, the mountain trail turns right 0.3 mile from the Indian Peaks Wilderness boundary. The Allens Park end is at the end of the road leading south from the center of town. St Vrain Mountain is an excellent viewing point well east of the divide revealing a wide span of the Indian Peaks range.

Brainard Lake Trailhead Access:

From just north of Ward on Hwy-72, turn west on County Rd-102. Follow the road 5 miles to **Brainard Lake** where there is parking at both the Mitchell Lake and Long Lake Trailheads. These parking areas are crowded in busy seasons, and the trails from them are not the places to go for peace and solitude. Various circular hikes may be made from this access point using the Mount Audubon Trail, the Blue Lake Trail and the Pawnee Pass Trail.

Pawnee Pass Trail runs over an 11 mile route from Brainard Lake to Monarch Lake west of the divide (see Lake Granby Access). It can be used with the **Buchanan Pass Trail** to make an excellent high country loop. Spur trails run to Crater Lake, under the spire of **Lone Eagle Peak** from the Cascade Creek side, and to 13,000' Isabelle Glacier on the Brainard Lake side. The route, being an old pack trail formerly known as the Breadline Trail, has high quality construction, especially through the rocky crags on the west side of Pawnee Pass.

Mount Audubon (13,223') and **Paiute Peak** (13,088') are easily climbed via the **Mount Audubon Trail** from the Mitchell Lake Trailhead. From Audubon, and with extra energy, one can drop 600' on the ridge to the west and climb up to Paiute Peak a mile away.

Mount Toll (12,979') can be climbed from Paiute Peak by going south, dropping almost 700', then climbing steeply in a rotten, 5th class rock couloir to the sharp summit. This peak may be easily climbed from the west side of **Blue Lake**, accessible via the Blue Lake Trail from the Mitchell Lake Trailhead, by gaining the 12,550' saddle between Toll and Pawnee Peaks. The climb to the top of Toll is less treacherous on this south side.

Pawnee Peak (12,943') and **Shoshoni Peak** (12,967') are both within climbing distance from the Long Lake Trailhead. Take the Pawnee Pass Trail 4 miles to 12,541' Pawnee Pass, then head north along the rocky top of the divide 0.5 mile to Pawnee, or south a mile to Shoshoni. The route to Shoshoni traverses Point 12,878' which has a steep drop off on the west side. Pawnee Peak may also be climbed from the saddle to the south of Mount Toll.

For **Apache Peak** (13,441') and **Navajo Peak** (13,409'), take the Pawnee Pass Trail 3 miles to where it climbs away from Lake Isabelle. Continue along the South St Vrain Creek another mile to a little lake south of Shoshoni Peak. For Apache, the route goes another mile southwest and west to its south saddle, with 1,000' of climbing at the end. The peak is 250' higher, a short distance up-ridge north-northwest. For the fine steep cone of Navajo, showpiece of the group, go up Airplane Gulch, the left hand choice of two ravines that are south-southwest

On route to Shoshoni Peak   *Neil Purrett*

of the lakelet. From Niwot Ridge, the summit can be taken either directly or on a clockwise spiral. Rope may be needed.

Arikaree Peak (13,150') can be climbed by the route used for Navajo Peak as far as the climb up Airplane Gulch to Niwot Ridge. Then cross the basin to the south, a drop of 400', to Arikaree's east saddle and climb the peak by its east ridge. **Kiowa Peak** (13,276') also goes by this saddle by boulder hopping up its short west ridge.

Please note that the 3.5 mile stretch of watershed between **Niwot Ridge** and the east ridge of South Arapaho Peak, including Kiowa Peak, has been closed by the City of Boulder.

Eldora Access:

From Nederland on Hwy-72, go west to Eldora and a mile beyond on County Rd-130 to **Hessie Trailhead**. Continue 5 miles to Buckingham Campground and **Fourth of July Trailhead**.

Arapaho Pass Trail climbs from the trailhead to the divide west of Arapaho Peaks at 11,906' then drops down Arapaho Creek to Monarch Lake (see Lake Granby Access), 12 miles in all. The west side may be shortened by using the Caribou Trail. From **Arapaho Pass**, go west past **Lake Dorothy**, then northwest to **Caribou Pass** which sits high between Caribou Lake and Columbine Lake. From the pass, the trail heads westward to meet the trail connecting the Junco Lake Trailhead with Columbine Lake (see Meadow Creek Reservoir Access). Follow this trail northwest 1.5 miles to the end. **Santanta Peak** (11,979') is a short grass stroll north from Caribou Pass, west of Arapaho Pass, and is approachable from either side of the divide.

North Arapaho Peak (13,502') and **South Arapaho Peak** (13,397') are rendered conspicuous by the lower smoother ridge to the south of them as well as by their own roughness. Start the ascent from Fourth of July Trailhead, hike 2 miles west toward Arapaho Pass to the location of the Fourth of July Mine at 11,252'. Then climb northeast 1 mile to the saddle between Old Baldy and South Arapaho Peak at 12,800'. From this place, climb 0.5 mile west up-ridge to the South summit and then 0.75 mile to the North summit via a paint-marked route. Arapaho Glacier lies east of both summits.

An alternate climb of **Arapaho Peaks** may be started at the Rainbow Lakes Campground. Drive north from Nederland 8 miles on Hwy-72 to the turn-off for the University of Colorado Camp (Boulder Co Rd-116, FSR-298). Follow the dirt road 4.5 miles to the trailhead. The hike from Rainbow Lakes is on a marked trail and traverses **Caribou Mountain** (12,310') and Caribou ridge before reaching the saddle between Old Baldy and South Arapaho Peak, and the trail from Fourth of July Mine.

Mount Neva (12,814') and **Mount Jasper** (12,923') can be climbed together from Fourth of July Trailhead. Take the **Diamond Lake Trail** from the campground using a left fork off the Arapaho Pass Trail about 0.5 mile from start and hike 3 miles to Jasper Lake. From the lake go northwest and climb 800' to the top of the east ridge, then follow the ridge 1.5 miles west to the summit of Jasper. From Jasper follow the divide west and then north 2 miles to Neva. Drop off the north side (good glissade) and past the east side of Lake Dorothy to Arapaho Pass. Return to the campground on the Arapaho Pass Trail, a total of about 10 miles. Mount Neva may also be easily climbed from the west using the Junco Lake Trailhead near Meadow Creek Reservoir (see Meadow Creek Reservoir Access).

The **Devils Thumb Pass Trail** starts from Hessie Trailhead at 9,000', about a mile west of Eldora on County Rd-130. It follows Jasper Creek for about 3 miles, then climbs to **Jasper Lake** and continues west to Devils Thumb Lake and climbs the steep face near **Devils Thumb Pass** at 11,747'. About 1 mile from the Hessie Trailhead, the Devils Thumb Pass Trail turns right while the trail to Lost Lake, Woodland Lake and King Lake crosses the creek on a bridge. Ascend a short steep pitch to a broad meadow where the Indian Peaks Wilderness boundary is signed. After traversing the meadow, the trail connects with the older trail following Jasper Creek and continues up to Jasper Lake. From **Devils Thumb Lake** the trail climbs south-westward up the steep slope and attains the Continental Divide near point 12,123', about 0.5 mile south of Devils Thumb Pass. West of the pass, the trail descends to Devils Thumb Park as the King Lake Trail, also called Corona Trail on the USGS map.

For a round trip hike using Devils Thumb Pass and **King Lake Trail**, follow the trail to Devils Thumb Pass then turn south on the King Lake or **Corona Trail** which runs along the Continental Divide. Go 3 miles to the saddle south of **King Lake** and descend on the King Lake Trail to the lake. Return to Hessie on the King Lake Trail which follows the South Fork of Middle Boulder Creek all the way to the bridge that is 1 mile from the trailhead.

The **Devils Thumb** (12,150') is the rocky spire rising in magnificent fashion near the northwest side of Devils Thumb Lake. The high point on the divide (12,440') just to the northeast of the spire can safely be climbed across the alpine tundra from Devils Thumb Pass.

Lake Granby/Monarch Lake Access:

Take US-34 5.4 miles north of Granby or 8.9 miles south of Grand Lake to County Rd- 6. Turn east, and follow the gravel road 9.4 miles to the east end of Lake Granby. The Roaring Fork Trailhead is across the bridge, then left and about 1 mile west along the north shore of Lake Granby. **Monarch Lake**

Lone Eagle Peak   *Terry Root*
Inset: *Climbing the north ridge*

Trailhead is across the same bridge then straight 0.5 mile to Monarch Lake and parking. Routes that begin at Monarch Lake include the High Lonesome Trail, **Cascade Creek Trail** (which becomes the Pawnee Pass Trail from Brainard Lake), and **Buchanan Pass Trail**.

The **High Lonesome Trail** connects Monarch Lake with **Devils Thumb Park**, keeping below timberline most of the way. It passes by the Meadow Creek Reservoir near the Junco Lake Trailhead.

Lone Eagle Peak (11,920'), named for Charles Lindbergh, the first solo flier of the Atlantic, is a spire-shaped ridge-end a mile west of the divide. From the trailhead at Monarch Lake, take the Cascade Creek Trail for 9 miles east to **Crater Lake**, and camp under the peak at 10,500'. This lake itself is worth the hike, being one of the most isolated and nestled alpine lakes in the entire wilderness. The conventional route circles east under the peak and goes south about 0.6 mile before turning to climb the east flank. The route starts up considerably south of the big chimney to the east, and follows the knife edge north (and down!) to the top. The peak has claimed fatalities; care should be taken to note landmarks for the return trip. Though topographically only a spur of Mount George, it is spectacular and frequently visited. The rock, generally sound, provides some fine technical climbs.

Thunderbolt Peak (11,938') a rugged western offshoot of the Continental Divide, can be climbed by leaving the Cascade Creek Trail a mile before its intersection with the Pawnee Pass Trail. Head northeast up any of the steep gulleys to the gentler slopes on the crest and pick your destination; the named point on the west end of the ridge or actual high point 0.5 mile southeast of it.

It is also possible to reach some of the Continental Divide Indian Peak summits from the west by starting at or near Crater Lake. Climb in the valley and up Fair Glacier 2 miles to the 12,750' saddle south of it. **Mount George** (12,876') is a ten minute stroll west from the saddle. **Apache Peak** (13,441') is 0.3 mile east up-ridge, and **Navajo Peak** (13,409') is another 0.5 mile southeast along the divide. **Arikaree Peak** (13,150') is another 0.75 mile further on an obstacled ridge that drops 150' before climbing the last 300' to the summit.

Mount Irving Hale (11,754') and **Hiamovi Mountain** (12,395') can best be reached from Roaring Fork Ranger Station near the east end of Lake Granby. The trail, starting at 8,300', climbs 3 miles up the Roaring Fork to 9,800', then takes a side creek east 2 miles to Hiamovi-lrving Hale saddle. The trail continues another 2 miles east to **Stone Lake** and **Upper Lake** at 10,730', the head of Hell Canyon. Irving Hale is an easy mile south from the saddle. Hiamovi is 2 miles east-northeast via the ridge.

Ogalalla Peak (13,138'), can be climbed from the west by first camping at Upper Lake. Go northwest to the saddle between *Hell* and *Paradise* (Paradise Park in Rocky Mountain Park), then climb east up-ridge and across gentle alpine slopes 2 miles to the summit.

Watanga Mountain (12,375') and **Mount Adams** (12,121') can be climbed using the trail from the Roaring Fork Station. From the trail junction along the creek at 9,800', turn north and hike 1.5 miles to Watanga Lake at 10,800'. Adams is another 1.5 miles north. Veer right to the saddle, and then left to the summit. For Watanga, angle south-east past the small lakelets to a ridge at timberline. It is then about 2 miles northeast to the top.

Cooper Peak (12,296') and **Marten Peak** (12,041') are connected by a saddle 0.75 mile south of Upper Lake. You can make a slantwise climb to the saddle at 11,600', and get up the left ridge to Cooper Peak, and you can at least explore the summit of Marten Peak. Both summits look down on Gourd, Island and other lakes.

Meadow Creek Reservoir/Junco Lake Access:

Turn northeast on FSR-129 just east of Tabernash on US-40. Drive about 10 miles on this road to Meadow Creek Reservoir, and follow the road to the east side. Junco Trailhead and parking are about 0.5 mile beyond the reservoir. The trail goes south-east following Meadow Creek to Columbine Lake, or via Caribou Pass to the divide at Arapaho Pass and down the North Fork to the Eldora Access.

Mount Neva (12,814') is easily climbed from the Junco Trailhead. Take the trail all the way to Columbine Lake at timberline. Stay on the right side of the lake and climb 0.25 mile south-southwest to the saddle. Angle south up Neva's west face to the top.

Devils Thumb Park Access:

Devils Thumb Park may be reached via jeep roads and water board roads from Fraser on US-40. Inquire locally as to conditions and accesses.

Corona Trail (also called Kings Lake Trail) covers 6 miles from Devils Thumb Park to Rollins Pass. Many climbing and hiking enthusiasts use this as a good access to fine adventure along the southern section of the Indian Peaks Wilderness.

FRONT RG

Front Range (Southern)

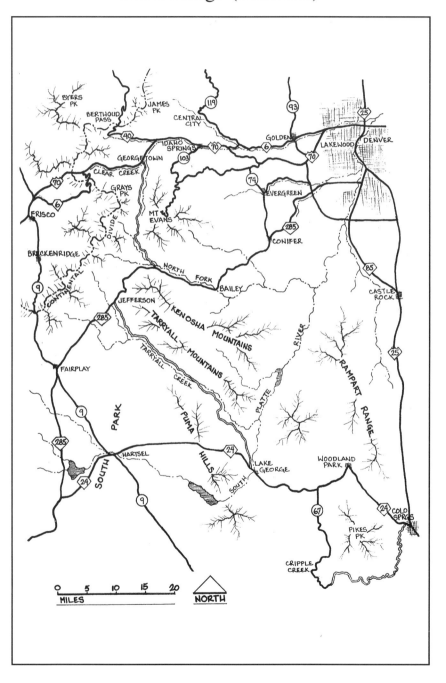

Clear Creek Section

Jurisdiction:

Arapaho NF, Clear Creek Ranger District
Pike NF, South Platte Ranger District

Map area reference:

Page 34 and 66

Maps:

USGS: *Berthoud Pass, Bottle Pass, Byers Peak, Empire, Fraser, Grays Peak, Harris, Idaho Springs, Loveland Pass, Montezuma, Mount Evans*
Forest Service: *Arapaho NF, Pike NF*

From James Peak to Guanella Pass, 18 miles south, the Continental Divide makes a great westward bend around the heads of Clear Creek and West Fork Clear Creek. On the divide north of Loveland Pass are Vasquez Peak, Jones Pass, Pettingell Peak, Citadel Peak and Hagar Mountain. East of the Pettingell Group, the two Clear Creeks are separated by a spur with Bard, Engelmann and others. North of Jones Pass, a Middle Park spur, called the Vasquez Mountains, goes off west and north to Byers Peak. When the divide turns east, near Loveland Pass, it leads to Grays and Torreys. The Evans massif is on a big eastern spur.

The Williams Fork Mountains go northwest from the divide at the Eisenhower Tunnel on I-70. They are treated in this section as a subset of the Front Range.

In the foothills closer to the metro area is a system of county and state parks that are the envy of many urban districts. They are touched on in this section.

US-40/Berthoud Pass Access:

From the Continental Divide crossing on US-40 at 11,300' **Berthoud Pass**, one can look northeast along the divide or south across the west fork valley at Engelmann Peak. You can climb along the divide in either direction. Hikers sometimes skirt north of Colorado Mines Peak and follow the divide to Mount Flora, Mount Eva, and sometimes Witter Peak. When there is no snow cover, loose talus may encourage you over Colorado Mines Peak.

Stanley Mountain (12,521') is a trip of about 3 miles. From the pass, climb west up through the ski area to the ridge, where you turn southwest along the Mount Nystrom Trail.

Breckinridge Peak (12,889') and **Mount Flora** (13,132') can be climbed from Empire, at the foot of Berthoud Pass on US-40. Take the main road north up North Empire Creek from the middle of town, 2 miles to Conqueror Mine, which

FRONT RG

is posted as "No Trespassing". Continue along a sharp right switchback as far as you can go with conventional vehicles. Follow the road about 1.75 miles to a large clear area about 1.5 miles east of Breckinridge. Flora is a mile further west.

Alternatively, you can reach Breckinridge Peak from the Mad Creek Road. Take the North Empire Creek Road 1 mile north and turn left. Follow the road through timber cuts to its end, 1 mile south of the peak.

US40/Jones Pass Access:

The road to 12,541' **Jones Pass** is a good road, but too steep for many cars. It leaves US-40 7 miles west of Empire at the hairpin turn which starts the climb to Berthoud Pass, and turns onto a gravel road just before the gate at the Henderson Mine. It is 5.5 miles from US-40 to the top of Jones Pass. From the pass you can see the Arapaho Peaks to the north-northeast, and the Gore Range and Holy Cross country to the west. At the top of the pass, the road deteriorates to a jeep trail, and drops on switchbacks into the Williams Fork drainage.

Vasquez Peak (12,947') is approached from the Jones Pass Road. Drive to where the road emerges from the trees, crosses the creek and makes a sharp left bend to leave the creek, about 3.5 miles from US-40. The peak is across the valley, 2,000' above and 1.5 miles north-northeast.

Mount Nystrom (12,652') is also available from here. Go up the road as far as you like. From Jones Pass, or a shortcut below it, you go about 1.5 miles north to where the ridge splits, and then walk a mile northwest from the divide along the Mount Nystrom Trail.

The peaks between Clear Creek and West Fork—Englemann, which one can see south across the West Fork valley from Berthoud Pass, Robeson and Bard, which are south of Englemann, and Parnassus and Woods, which are to the west—can all be reached from the Urad Mine Road. Turn left off the Jones Pass Road 0.2 mile west of US-40, and go south and west about 1 mile and across the old tailings pond. The route then takes an abandoned jeep trail (closed to vehicles) south from the mine area, 1 mile to near timberline on Ruby Creek. From here, **Mount Parnassus** (13,574') is 1.5 miles due south, and **Woods Mountain** (12,940') is 1.2 miles southwest. **Bard Peak** (13,641'), the highest, is 2 miles south-south-east. **Robeson Peak** (13,140') is about a mile north of Bard, and **Englemann Peak** (13,362') is about a mile north of Robeson. If Bard is the objective, climb to the Bard-Parnassus saddle. If you go north to Englemann, descend its north-northwest ridge to the old mine area.

Fraser (US-40)/Vasquez Mountains Access:

The group consists of the horseshoe ridge around St Louis Creek, and is accessible from the north off US-40 in the vicinity of Fraser. A system of fine trails connects these Middle Park ridges.

The Mount Nystrom Trail starts at the top of the Winter Park ski area, and follows the ridge south to **Stanley Mountain** (12,521'), then turns west, crossing over Vasquez Pass and **Vasquez Peak** (12,947'), and then climbs to **Mount Nystrom** (12,652'); a total of 15 miles.

The St Louis Trail comes directly to Mount Nystrom from its beginning on a ridge knoll. Start in Fraser, and travel up the St Louis Creek Road to the Fraser Experimental Forest road junction; then go east to another Water Board road junction. Here, take the road that goes south up Fools Creek, 2,400' and 9.5 miles to the 11,956' knoll (the last 2 miles are rough and steep). The trail follows the ridge 4 miles south to Mount Nystrom, and continues 2.5 miles to St Louis Pass and **St Louis Peak** (12,247').

Mt. Bancroft, east ridge   David Anschicks

It is 7 more miles from St Louis Peak west then north along a ridge on the Byers Peak Trail to **Bills Peak** (12,703'). There are lines of descent down both sides of this Byers Massif, which follow creeks, suggesting backpack trips.

St Louis Peak and Lake can also reached by first driving to the end of the St Louis Creek road from the Fraser Experimental Forest road junction (see above). The trail from here leads to St Louis Lake, at 11,531', and also to the Byers Peak Trail at the top of the ridge.

Byers Peak (12,804) is the prominent mountain with the large snow field visible to the west from Fraser. It is easily climbed by using the water board road going right and west from the Fraser Experimental Forest road junction. This road passes near an old log cabin and continues up West St Louis Creek. Drive to the end of the road at about 10,700', then hike a trail west through the forest, then south up the exposed ridge of the peak. Also from this ridge, turn north, hike along the Byers Peak Trail through trees, then follow above timberline travel to Bottle Pass, with **Ptarmigan Peak** (11,773') to the left, and **Bottle Peak** (11,584') to the right.

James Peak Group Accesses:

James Peak (13,294') is accessible from several different approaches. One of the most popular is from the Fall River Road which leaves I-70 (exit 238) 2 miles west of Idaho Springs. Drive 8 miles to the abandoned St Marys Ski Area at 10,300'. Park here and hike left on a dirt road going another mile to **St. Marys Lake**. Hike right of the lake and continue up the glacier. Continue west across the alpine meadow and ascend the east ridge 2.5 miles to the peak.

An even closer start for James Peak can be made from **Loch Lomond** (11,200'). Turn left at Alice, go through town and turn left and then quickly right. Continue along a chiprock road for 3.5 miles to the loch. A short climb northeast from the lake end puts you on the gentle ridge slopes. A rougher route leads west past the lakes into the cirque head right beneath the Continental Divide. The hike from James to **Mount Bancroft** (13,250') is a long mile south-southwest. **Parry Peak** (13,391'), highest of the group, is 1 mile west of Bancroft. The best descent is from the saddle east of Parry. Contour a little south of Bancroft, then follow the east to east-southeast ridge, then back to the loch. For Bancroft and Parry only, the shortest approach is also from Loch Lomond.

For **Mount Eva** (13,130') and **Witter Peak** (12,884') turn west at the switchback 6.5 miles up the Fall River Road. Follow this road to **Chinns Lake** in another 3.5 miles. Hike west 2 miles to the Continental Divide where Eva is 0.5 mile north and Witter a mile south, then east.

James Peak may be climbed from the north by starting at **East Portal** and using the South Boulder Creek Trail. Cross the railroad tracks and climb over the fence, then follow the trail across the private property and up the creek to **Heart Lake** at 11,300'. Hike south above timberline, skirt around 11,700' **Haystack Mountain**, then go up the flat north face of James Peak to the top. Other trails and routes radiate from East Portal and lead to numerous high lakes that are nestled beneath the east side of the Continental Divide.

To reach James Peak from the west, a route starts where the water siphon crosses US-40 at Jim Creek Valley, south of Winter Park. Hike Jim Creek to the road end in the midst of heavy timber, and head directly up the slope to the east and climb to the divide at 11,860' **Rogers Pass**. It is 2 miles south along the ridge to the peak. Alternatively, drive to Riflesight Notch at 11,080' on the Rollins Pass (Moffat) Road. An old road climbs from the Notch south along the hillside for 2 miles to Rogers Pass, and from there the **Ute Trail** takes you another mile along the divide to the 0.5 mile climb to the top on the flat-faced north ridge.

James Peak was named for Dr. Edwin James, the first man on record to climb a 14,000' peak in the continental United States. He and two other men climbed Pikes Peak in July, 1820. Major Stephen H. Long, the expedition leader, tried to change the name to James Peak, but Pike's name was too well established. In the 1860's, James' name was given to the mountain west of Central City. It was long referred to as Jim Peak.

US-6/Loveland Pass Access:

US-6 tops out on the Continental Divide at 11,990' Loveland Pass. **Grizzly Peak** (13,427') is visible as one drives toward Loveland Pass from the west. It is a good high-country ridge tour of 2.5 miles from the pass. Climb east along the divide most of a mile, then angle to the right to skirt the 12,915' ridge point and continue along the ridge southeast. Grizzly is sometimes climbed from the northeast via Grizzly Gulch, reached from Stevens Gulch Road (see I-70 Access). **Mount Sniktau** (13,234') can be reached by climbing east along the divide, then north another mile.

I-70 Access:

Pettingell Peak (13,553') is reached from the Herman Gulch Trailhead at 10,300'. Take exit 218 on I-70, 3 miles west of Bakerville, to the trailhead on the north side of the highway. The route is 4 miles long. Take the west fork a short way from the trailhead into **Herman Gulch** and finally to Herman Lake. Climb west for a more direct route, aiming just left of the summit, or roughly north to the ridge, then along the divide to the summit.

Bard Peak (13,641') and **Mount Parnassus** (13,574') are also climbed from the Herman Gulch Trailhead 3 miles west of Bakerville. Start on the trail and very shortly take the right fork into Watrous Gulch. The trail contours around the gulch to the south ridge of Parnassus, which is climbed to the top. Bard is a mile to the east along the crest. **Woods Mountain** can also easily be climbed from Watrous Gulch or Mount Parnassus and **Peak 12,805'** is another mile southwest from Woods.

Hagar Mountain (13,195') is climbed from Dry Gulch, 4 miles west of Bakerville on I- 70. After 0.2 mile, keep to the north side of the creek, eventually reaching the summit on its south ridge. **Citadel Peak** (13,294'), between Hagar and Pettingell, can be climbed from either. There is some tricky rock scrambling near the top.

The entrance to Dry Gulch is flanked by **Mount Trelease** (12,477') and **Mount Bethel** (12,705'), the latter named for a prominent CMC'er who was responsible for bestowing names on several Front Range Peaks early in the century. Both are steep but easy ascents from a mile up the gulch.

Grays Peak (14,270') and **Torreys Peak** (14,267') are named for the famous 19th century botanists Asa Gray of Harvard, and John Torrey of Princeton. They are often climbed together. From Bakerville (exit 221) on I-70, 6 miles west of Georgetown, drive south 4 miles or less in Stevens Gulch to a road closure at the Stevens Mine. The Grays Trail is 4 miles long with 3,000' gain, starting from the northwest side of the creek. Torreys is north from Grays along a 0.75-mile ridge, with a 550' drop. To do Torreys' northeast ridge, follow the above route until you can make for a mine shack in the saddle on the Torreys-Kelso ridge. The ridge provides some scrambling with moderate exposure.

For a northeast route up Grizzly, or a west side approach to Torreys, turn right on the Grizzly Gulch Road about 1.5 miles up the Stevens Gulch Road south of Bakerville. **Grizzly Peak** is 4.5 miles and 3,100' from the road. A mile above the Grizzly Gulch jeep road, angle left (south) from the creek and find a route to the east ridge to finish.

Kelso Mountain (13,164'), a mile west of the camping area in Stevens Gulch, is best reached from the south, from the above mentioned Torreys-Kelso saddle.

Guanella Pass Access:

Guanella Pass between Georgetown on I-70 and Grant on US-285 (where it is known as Grant's Pass), is on the Clear Creek-South Platte Divide 10 miles south of Georgetown. En route you pass the hydro-electric power plant that levels off-peak power demands by pumping water from the lower pond to the upper during off-peak hours. A branch road turns right 3 miles south of Georgetown at a switchback, and climbs west to the old railroad grade of the Argentine Central, then follows it for 7 miles to Waldorf. This is where one of the many tunnels planned for the divide was to go through to Peru Creek and the Snake River. From 11,600' Waldorf, you can jeep southwest to **Argentine Pass** or west up the railroad switchbacks to 13,000' on McClellan Mountain. The slopes on this side of the valley, including that of Mount Edwards, are grassy, steep walking country. There is good above-timberline camping above Waldorf.

Mount Edwards (13,850') can be reached by climbing west from Waldorf, about 2 miles, or along its southeast ridge from Argentine Pass. Both ways are gentle climbing. **McClellan Mountain** (13,587') is an easy 0.75 mile hike northeast from Edwards. **Argentine Peak** (13,738') is an easy 1 mile ridge walk south from the pass.

Squaretop Mountain (13,794') is 3 miles west of 11,670' Guanella Pass. Except for an abrupt section near the west end, it is a gentle high country ridge climb. **Gray Wolf Mountain** (13,602') is 3 miles northeast of the pass; look for breaks in the willows. Or do it in winter and walk on top of them. **Mount Bierstadt** (14,060'), is 3 miles east-southeast of the pass. From the parking area, walk far enough south to get past the marshes, and then go east up to the ridge.

Mount Bierstadt   *H. L. Standley*

A longer and wilder approach to both Bierstadt and Evans leaves the pass road about 5.5 miles north of Grant, at Burning Bear Campground. The trail follows Scott Comer Creek and its Lake Fork to **Abyss Lake**. The section of trail along the Lake Fork traverses high and north of the creek. From the junction of Lake Fork and Scott Gomer Creek, one can cut southwest on a cairn line, then up the south ridge of Bierstadt. For **Mount Evans**, hike on the Rosalie Trail from its intersection with the Scott Gomer Creek trail near the creek junction, and climb south to the saddle at 11,660'. Turn east and hike to Epaulet, then walk north-northwest to Evans.

A fun climb of Mount Evans is the one across the Sawtooth Ridge from Bierstadt. When in doubt, cut down to the north side of the ridge. This is good route finding practice!

Hwy-103/Mount Evans Road Access:

Mount Evans (14,260') has a road to the top. From I-70 at either exit 252 for Evergreen or exit 240 at Idaho Springs, follow Hwy-103 to Echo Lake, 21 or 14 miles respectively. From Echo Lake, it is 14 miles to the top. At 12,834' **Summit Lake**, 10 miles from Echo Lake, it is a steep half mile south to the summit. Climb anywhere east of the cliffs.

Mount Bierstadt is often packaged with Evans. Descend the west ridge of Evans 1.5 miles and turn south along **Sawtooth Ridge** 0.75 mile to Bierstadt. The Sawtooth can be skirted on a high north side traverse, about 13,200' at the low point. From Bierstadt, return on the traverse and climb 0.75 mile northeast to the 13,650' saddle west of Summit Lake, and descend east down a steep couloir, or go over **Mount Spaulding** (13,842') and down its east ridge.

Rosalie Peak (13,575') is a down-ridge walk of 2 miles from the Mount Evans Road. Leave the road where it crosses the flats 2 miles south-southeast of Summit Lake, and travel southeast. You will drop to about 12,900'.

Mount Evans was named for the second governor of Colorado Territory. Mount Bierstadt was named for the 19th century artist, whose romantic paintings of mountains are well represented by the oil depicting Longs Peak. The painting is currently hanging in the Western History room of the Denver Public Library. Rosalie Peak was named for his wife.

Williams Fork Mountains

FRONT RG

Maps:

USGS: *Dillon, Loveland Pass, Mount Powell, Sheephorn Mountain, Sylvan Reservoir, Ute Peak*
Forest Service: *Arapaho NF*

This minor range runs west 6 miles from a mile south of Hagar Mountain on the Continental Divide to Ptarmigan Peak, and then 25 miles north-northwest parallel with the Blue River. For climbers, its main interest is the view it gives of the Gore Range across the valley.

A road climbs east to the crest in 6 rather steep miles from the Grand-Summit County line, 12.5 miles south of Kremmling, 29 miles north of Dillon Reservoir dam.

The road over Ute Pass starts 12 miles north of Silverthorne on Hwy-9. It climbs 1400' to the pass crest in 5.5 miles and runs down to the Williams Fork road in 3 more.

I-70 Access:

Coon Hill (12,757'), the high point, can be reached from the west portal of the Eisenhower Tunnel on I-70. Walk up Straight Creek 0.5 mile and pick a route to the left.

You can walk 12 miles of the crest on the **Ptarmigan-Ute Peak Trail**. The Ptarmigan Trail itself starts up from the bottom of Straight Creek, but an easier approach starts in Silverthorne. Take Hwy-9 north from I-70 exit 205 to Tanglewood Drive. Pass the Ramada Inn to Road 2021. Turn right and drive 1.0 mile to a pull off. Watch for trailhead signs and be careful of private property in the trailhead area. The trail leads to **Ptarmigan Peak** (12,498'). The ridge to the north connects to **Ute Peak** (12,303') and on out to Ute Pass via the Ute Peak and Ute Pass Trails.

Going east along the ridge from Ptarmigan Peak brings you to 11,777' **Ptarmigan Pass** and a trail coming up Laskey Gulch from I-70. Parking for Laskey Gulch is a small pull off just below the second truck runaway ramp. It is an 8.4 mile loop from Laskey Gulch to the Ptarmigan Trailhead. The loop from Ptarmigan Trailhead to Ute Pass is 17 miles. Both loops require car shuttles.

About 1.5 miles northwest of Ptarmigan Peak, a trail descends north to camping on the Williams Fork and its auto road. Nearby Sugarloaf Campground is 25 miles from Parshall on US-40.

FRONT RG

County and State Parks

Jurisdiction:

Jefferson County Open Space
Colorado State Parks and Recreation

Maps:

USGS: *Evergreen, Indian Hills, Kassler, Morrison, Squaw Pass*

The Front Range foothills west of Denver offer nearly year round hiking opportunities. Much of this area has been developed by Jefferson County, and by the city and county of Denver, as mountain parks for nature-seeking urbanites. The Colorado Division of Parks and Outdoor Recreation has developed parks state-wide, but here we focus on those local to this section.

Jefferson County Open Space:

In 1972, Jefferson county residents approved a sales tax to fund the preserving of open space within this largely mountainous county, a suburban refuge to sprawling Denver. Many miles of maintained, non-motorized trails now exist in 21 park areas. Some have nature centers and facilities for camping. A few highlights are included here: check for regulations at the Open Space main office in Golden.

Bergen Peak (9,708') can be climbed by trail starting at Elk Meadows Park. From I-70 exit 252 for Evergreen, take Hwy-74 about 3.5 miles to the Meadow View Trail parking area on the west side of the road. Or continue on Hwy-74 another 2 miles to Stagecoach Blvd, and go west to a parking area for the south end of the Meadow View Trail.

Mount Falcon (7,851'), with views of peaks and prairies and located within Mount Falcon Park, is unique for what it might have been. In the early 1900's, John Brisben Walker owned over 4,000 acres surrounding the mountain, and built a spacious stone castle just north of the peak. He dreamed of making a theater in Red Rocks, which his property overlooked, and of building a Summer White House for presidents, on a ridge just east of his castle. The trauma of World War I, and hard times for Walker, ended his plans for the Summer White House, although a cornerstone was laid. The park, the mountain and its system of trails, are accessible from two trailheads. The lower trailhead starts south of Morrison on Hwy-8. The upper trailhead is by Parmalee Gulch Road, off US-285, 4 miles west of Hwy-470; follow the signs to the parking area, about 3.5 miles. An observation tower atop Mount Falcon elevates you above the trees so you can observe Walker's territory. You can also visit the proposed president's summer home site, and the ruins of Walker's castle, which burned in 1918.

Colorado State Parks:

The Colorado Division of Parks and Outdoor Recreation was established in 1959 to further the recreational experience beyond forest service properties. Many of the 40 state-wide areas are focused around reservoirs, where water sports are the primary attention-getters. There are, however, many mountainous locations within the system of interest to the hiker/climber, including but not limited to: Golden Gate Canyon State Park northwest of Golden, Mueller State Park west of Colorado Springs and Colorado State Forest (described here in detail under the Rawah section) east of Walden. Most of the parks have campgrounds, and some have visitor centers and interpretive programs. Please note that a park pass must be purchased. For further information, contact Colorado State Parks in Denver.

The unusual rock formations at **Roxborough State Park** remind us of Red Rocks Park to the north and Garden of the Gods to the south. This area has recently been incorporated into the Colorado State Park system. The trails here are restricted to daytime pedestrian use only. You get there from Denver by driving south on Wadsworth Blvd (Hwy-121) to Chatfield Recreation Area, and beyond to the road end at the Martin-Marietta plant. Go left as for Waterton Canyon and Roxborough State Park, and follow the signs. Or follow Santa Fe Blvd (US-85) 4 miles south from Hwy-470 to Titan Road. Turn right and travel west, then south, about 3.5 miles to the park entrance. **Carpenter Peak** (7,160'), at the west boundary of the park, rises above the sedimentary formations. Start at the attractive visitors center where you can learn something about the area's past. A trail continues to the summit.

Southwest Section

Jurisdiction:
White River NF, Dillon Ranger District
Pike NF, South Platte Ranger District

Map area reference:
Page 66

Maps:
USGS: *Alma, Breckenridge, Boreas Pass, Como, Grays Peak, Jefferson, Keystone, Montezuma*
Forest Service: *Pike NF, White River NF*

For this section, Argentine Peak to Hoosier Pass, there are several high paved and 4WD roads from which the many summits, on and off of the Continental Divide, are accessible.

Snake River/Peru Creek/US-6 Access:

One of the larger areas for exploration is the Snake River, a valley with good camping, mine roads and peaks in all of its several branches. The Montezuma Road turns south from US-6 7.5 miles east of Dillon, just beyond the Keystone Ski Area, and runs east 4.5 miles to a split in the valley. Peru Creek comes in from the east; the Snake River takes you on a turn to the south. For Peru Creek, continue east. You can follow it 4.5 miles to where it curves north and steepens at about 11,000'.

Argentine Peak (13,738') is 1.25 miles east. Climb the slope or use the old Argentine Pass Road, which climbs to the saddle north of the peak in a steep zigzag. See also the route from Waldorf under the Clear Creek Section.

From lower in Peru Creek valley, old mine roads lead south from both Cinnamon Gulch and Warden Gulch, 9 and 7 miles from US-6, to the ridge connecting **Decatur Mountain** (12,890'), **Revenue Mountain** (13,134'), and **Silver Mountain** (12,849'). On the north side of Peru Creek, a little west of Warden Gulch, a walking road climbs steeply into the ponds and meadows of Chihuahua Gulch. About 2 miles up the gulch, the road cuts back southeast to climb into Ruby Gulch, to old diggings at 12,150'. This is on a south face route to **Grays Peak** (14,270'), about a mile from the top. The ridge on the right connects **Ruby Mountain** (13,277') and **Cooper Mountain** (12,792'), both climbable. If you do not turn with the road into Ruby Gulch, but continue north 1.5 miles to the headwall of Chihuahua Gulch, you will be on the 12,600' saddle connecting **Torreys Peak** (14,267') on the east and **Grizzly Peak** (13,427') on the west. Each is about a mile. **Lenawee Mountain** (13,204') is the west wall of the gulch, connected to Grizzly by a rugged ridge. You can descend south off Lenawee down the Argentine-North Fork Trail to circle back to Peru Creek.

An article in the June 1978 issue of *T&T* by Mike Foster presents three approaches by way of Chihuahua to the south-southeast ridge of Grays, which he says provide a variety of passages from moderate scrambling to moderate class 5.

If you keep on the main road south up the Snake River to Montezuma, you can probably get your car up most of the steep but good road to the Quail Mine, 3 miles east of the little town and 1,200' higher. A walk-road continues to **Santa Fe Peak** (13,180), a mile southeast; continuing south along the ridge brings you to **Sullivan Mountain** (13,134'), **Geneva Peak** (13,266') and **Landslide Peak** (13,238'). These peaks can also be reached from the east side of the divide (see US-285 access).

By going from Montezuma to a junction 1.5 miles south and keeping left up the Snake River, you can drive a jeep, or car with high clearance, a good part or all the way to 12,096' **Webster Pass**, 6 miles south-southeast from Montezuma. Here you are between the easily accessible **Handcart Peak** (12,518') on the west, and **Red Cone** (12,802') on the east. From the base of the pass at 11,400', an old walk-road climbs west a mile to a mine high on **Teller Mountain** (12,615').

Going southwest out of Montezuma on a 4WD road, you reach the ghost town of Saints John, the remains of the Wild Irishman Mine and **Glacier Mountain** (12,443').

West of Keystone Resort, a road runs south 8 miles up Keystone Gulch. Turn south at the stoplight on US-6 just west of the village center, cross the bridge, turn right on Soda Ridge Road then left in 0.4 mile at the Keystone Gulch Road. The 11,940' Erickson Mine at the end of the road gives a good look at the Gore and Tenmile Ranges. You can climb to **Keystone Point** (12,408') and walk a gentle ridge east 2.0 miles to Glacier Mountain, or go north 1.0 mile to **Bear Mountain** (12,585') and **Independence Mountain** (12,614'). The gulch road itself is a popular cross country ski tour in winter.

Hwy-9 Access:

Hwy-9 intersects I-70 at Frisco and provides several approaches from Breckenridge to Fairplay.

Tiger Road turns east 2.6 miles south of Farmer's Korner at the south end of Dillon Reservoir. Near the end of the improved road, turn south on FSR-355, a 4WD road that becomes increasingly difficult as it approaches Georgia Pass.

From the 11,585' pass, walk the ridge west to **Mount Guyot** (13,370'). Georgia Pass is more easily reached from the south via Michigan Creek, using the US-285 access below. Tiger Road continues as FSR-6 (4WD) up the Swan River Middle Fork, putting you close to **Sheep Mountain** (12,495') and the Continental Divide summits of Glacier Peak and Whale Peak, likewise more commonly approached from the US-285 access.

From the northeast part of Breckenridge, a road goes east up French Creek, driveable 5 miles or so. It is a pleasant 4 mile walk south up the valley to **French Pass** at 12,046' on the divide. From the pass, a fairly sharp steep ridge leads a mile west to **Bald Mountain** (13,684'). By climbing instead to the ridge 0.5 mile east, you can walk 1.5 miles north along it to **Mount Guyot** (13,370').

The shortest route to Bald Mountain is from **Boreas Pass** (11,481'), reached by road from the south end of Breckenridge. The Boreas Pass Road connects over the Continental Divide to Como on US-285. Most of the road follows the old Denver South Park and Pacific Railroad grade, a very pleasant drive that gives good views of the Tenmile Range on the west. From the pass, start east of the ditch and head north for 2 miles to Bald Mountain.

Boreas Mountain (13,082'), like Bald Mountain above, is easily reached from Boreas Pass. Head up the slope east-southeast and climb 1,500' in little over a mile.

Boreas Pass also gives access to **Red Peak** (13,215') to the southwest. Go west, keeping to the north side of the humps on a gently climbing contour into a saddle 2 miles west-southwest from the pass. Climb the steep ridge south-southwest another 1.5 miles to the high point. The same summit can be reached from **Hoosier Pass**, the 11,541' Continental Divide crossing at Hwy-9 south of Breckenridge. It is about 5 miles of ups and downs starting east up a slope with deadfall, and turning north along the divide ridge.

Mount Silverheels (13,822') was named for a dance hall girl in Buckskin Joe, a town above Fairplay. She nursed the miners through a smallpox epidemic after all the "proper" women had left camp. Leave the car at the second major drainage, about 1.7 miles south of the Hoosier Pass summit on Hwy-9. Climb east over Beaver Ridge, then a little north and down to Beaver Creek. From there the wide, west ridge of Silverheels is an obvious way east to the top. Alternatively, from 4th Street in Fairplay, drive 6 miles north-northwest on Beaver Creek. Take the trail 2 miles north up Beaver Creek and climb 1.5 miles east to the top. The number of back country roads makes this trailhead hard to find.

Mr. Marmot   *Ellen Kress*

US-285 Access:

Between Guanella Pass and Boreas Pass, the South Park approaches from US-285 to the divide are generally longer than those from the Snake River and Hwy-9 accesses.

At Duck Creek Campground, 7.5 miles north of Grant on US-285, a road goes northwest for about 8 miles following Geneva Creek. The road has recently been gated about 5 miles in, closing off access to a half dozen peaks. An alternate route makes a nice circle tour. Take the Smelter Gulch Trail, from 3 miles in on the road, north 3 miles to Shelf Lake. A short climb west puts you on **Decatur Mountain**. Follow the divide around west, then south, knocking off in rapid succession **Revenue Mountain**, **Silver Mountain**, **Santa Fe Peak**, **Sullivan Mountain**, **Geneva Peak**, and **Landslide Peak**. This is long but easy walking. Descend east off Landslide, picking up the Kirby Gulch Trail and following it as it circles north back to the Geneva Creek road.

Hall Valley has a road system that leads to good camping and excursions. From the old townsite of Webster on US-285, 3 miles west of Grant and 4 miles north of **Kenosha Pass**, a road runs northwest 5 miles to the Hall Valley Campground at 9,750'. Continue about 1.5 miles before the road gets rough, or 4 miles in a jeep. At 11,600', you are a mile south of **Teller Mountain** and 0.5 mile southwest of **Handcart Peak**, both steep climbs.

From Hall Valley Campground, a less conspicuous 4WD road climbs right and north-northwest 3 miles up Handcart Gulch and continues a last mile up to **Webster Pass** on a more-or-less washed out trail. **Red Cone** is on your right. Handcart Peak is on your left. The descent takes you northwest into the Snake River drainage and in 6 miles to Montezuma.

Whale Peak (13,078') makes a good climb from Hall Valley. Turn off 1.5 miles beyond Hall Valley Campground at a trail marked Gibson Lake (10,316'). From there it is 2.5 miles to the small lake at 11,850', another bent mile to the top on either flanking ridge.

Glacier Peak (12,853') and Whale Peak can be climbed from Jefferson Lake, for which you turn north from US-285 at Jefferson and follow the signs to Jefferson Lake. From the parking area at the lake, walk 1 mile west across the dam, then follow a trail halfway along the west shore, then slant north and northwest through the timber 0.5 mile to the top of the ridge at 12,245'. Glacier Peak is another mile at the northwest end. The 3 mile climb gains about 2,100'. To visit Whale Peak, go north and east from Glacier a mile along the divide, with a loss of 200'. Return on the southeast ridge of Whale to a desirable descent route.

Georgia Pass, the historic 11,585' divide crossing christened by southern miners in 1860, is also approached from Jefferson on US-285. Start as for Jefferson Lake above, then follow signs towards Michigan Creek Campground and Georgia Pass, 10 miles in all. It is 3 miles northeast to Glacier Peak from the pass crest. **Mount Guyot** (13,370') is a mile west of the pass, a steep but simple ridge climb. From Georgia Pass, the road descends north into the Swan River drainage. It is unmaintained, steep, and only recommended for 4WD vehicles.

Kenosha and Tarryall Mountains

Jurisdiction:
Pike NF, South Park and South Platte Ranger Districts

Map area reference:
Page 66

Maps:
USGS: *Cheesman Lake, Eagle Peak, Farnum Peak, Glentivar, Green Mountain, Jefferson, McCurdy Mountain, Mount Logan, Shawnee, Spinney Mountain, Tarryall, Topaz Mountain, Windy Peak*
Forest Service: *Pike NF*

The Kenosha and Tarryall Mountains are two separate, back to back ranges sharing a wilderness area, several access points and trail connectors. As a set, they extend from Kenosha Pass on US-285 to Wilkerson Pass on US-24. They are bounded by the North Fork South Platte River on the north, and the South Platte River on the east and south. This section treats these two ranges as one large contiguous mountain region.

The Kenoshas are oddly warted smoothtops that run southeast along a 14 mile split ridge just east of Kenosha Pass on US-285. The Tarryall Mountains stretch 25 miles northwest-southeast from Jefferson to just north of Lake George, with Tarryall Creek running parallel to it on the northeast side. The Tarryalls were named by miners in 1859 who panned gold "as big as watermelon seeds" out of the creek. Late comers, angry that they could find no good placers for themselves, said the creek should have been called Grab-All; they headed across South Park and founded Fairplay. The north and south ends are a timbered ridge; the middle is higher, wider, and rougher, and characterized by a wealth of warts, spikes, knobs, etc., of very red granite. It once had a large concentration of bighorn sheep, but they are scarce now.

The Tarryalls are traversed by Park Co Rd-77, about 43 miles long from Jefferson to Lake George, and parallel to the Tarryall Creek. Much of the land about the creek is private, but there are convenient campgrounds and trails into the range. Another road (FSR-211) goes north from Rd-77, about 6 miles from Lake George, and passes west of Cheesman Reservoir and connects to the roads near the South Platte River at Deckers. The Lost Park Road (FSR-127) starts from US-285 1 mile north of Jefferson, and heads east and southeast into the heart of the two ranges.

The **Lost Creek Wilderness** comprises large sections of the Tarryalls and the Kenoshas. This secluded area gets its name from the Lost Creek drainage that begins deep within the massif, but becomes "lost," and disappears in a dramatic labyrinth of granite pinnacles, rocks, and needles, only to re-emerge near the southern wilderness boundary as Goose Creek. Consequently, the scenic luster and numerous remote locations make the Lost Creek Wilderness one of the more popular destinations for nearby urbanites.

Kenosha Pass (FSR-126) Access:

One can drive on FSR-126 east from US-285 at **Kenosha Pass** about 1.25 miles to Kenosha Creek, 10,050', then continue on a jeep road about 4 miles to the **Twin Cones**. Don't be alarmed if you can count three; Mount Blaine is between and east of the twins. For a long high walk go down one ridge 6 or 8 miles, cross Craig Park's marshes, and come up the other ridge.

Lost Park Road (FSR-127) Access:

The interior and western sections of these mountains are best approached on the Lost Park Road. Turn east about 3 miles west of Kenosha Pass (1 mile north of Jefferson) and travel 23 miles to the Lost Park Campground near the wilderness boundary. From here, trails lead north to North Fork Lost Creek and the Colorado Trail, east through East Lost Park and Wigwam Park, and south to Indian Creek, and the Ute Creek Trailhead.

Bison Peak (12,431') and **McCurdy Mountain** (12,164') are climbed by use of the Indian Creek Trail to Bison Pass, then the McCurdy Trail eastward. The peaks are side trips to the north of the trail of less than a mile and a little over 500' elevation gain. Since there are many rock obstructions and some down timber from an old burn, this top country is confusing, so be careful not to get lost.

North Tarryall Peak (11,902') is a bushwhack climb of 1.5 miles from the 10,670' pass that is 13.5 miles from the start of FSR-127. You can also start 2.5 miles further southeast; head west and cross a marshy area and then climb 3 miles up the east ridge to the top.

Knobby Crest (12,429') is the high point of the Kenoshas. To climb it, drive FSR-127 11 miles to FSR-817, and turn left, which takes you in 0.2 mile to a dead end. This is a trailhead for the Colorado Trail. Follow the CT east and uphill for 1.5 miles to the upper end of the North Fork Lost Creek park. From this meadow at 10,900' bushwhack north and attain the crest of the Kenosha Mountains. Continue northwest to the summit. Views include a sweep from Evans through the Sawatch and Sangre de Cristo Ranges to the Great Plains. The crest can also be climbed directly from the trailhead. Take the connector to the Colorado Trail at 10,120', cross the trail and continue a short distance to some beaver ponds. From the ponds, bushwhack north toward a large rock outcrop high on the ridge. Pass it on the east and continue north to the summit.

North (12,319') and **South** (12,323') **Twin Cones**, along with **Mount Blaine** (12,303') are best climbed from the Rock Creek Trailhead (formerly the Ben Tyler Trailhead). Turn left on FSR-133 about 7 miles from the start of FSR-127, and drive 1.5 miles to where the Colorado Trail crosses. The trail begins another 0.75 mile north, follows the creek for a while, and reaches the summit ridge within 3.5 miles. Turn off-trail to the left (west) and hike above timberline to the summits. The Ben Tyler Trail continues down the other side of the Platte River Mountains to US-285, and another trail leads southeast through Craig Park.

Park Co Rd-77/Ute Creek Trailhead Access:

The **Ute Creek-Indian Creek Trail** starts near a footbridge 4 miles southeast of Tarryall Reservoir, 8.5 miles northwest of the village of Tarryall on Park Co Rd-77. It crosses the creek and climbs northnortheast 3.5 miles along Ute Creek from 8,700' to 11,300', where it meets the **McCurdy Trail**. You can go north down Indian Creek to the Lost Park Road, or turn east on the McCurdy. The latter climbs 1.5 miles to the flank of Bison Peak, turns to flank McCurdy Mountain, 1.5 miles southeast, and then continues by a swing southeast over (informally named) Jumble Mountain (11,758'). It then turns south and west to return to Tarryall Creek at Twin Eagles Trailhead, at the mouth of Hay Creek, 6 miles on Park Co Rd-77 downstream from the Ute Creek Trailhead.

Bison Peak (12,431') and **McCurdy Mountain** (12,164') are side trips from this trail of less than a mile each, and a little over 500' altitude gain. There are rock obstructions and some down timber from an old burn, so be careful to not get lost in this confusing top country.

Bailey (FSR-543) Access:

Windy Peak (11,970') names its quad. From the foot of the hill at Bailey on US-285, drive southeast 5 miles on Park Co Rd-68 which becomes FSR-543 once you leave the paving. Keep right at the fork, and continue about 2.5 miles to the Colorado Trail crossing and park. Go west on the Colorado Trail to the fork for Craig Meadows, then bushwhack south about 2 miles to the summit. This peak can also be climbed from the trail up Rolling Creek. Begin on the CT as described above and shortly turn left (south) on the trail leading to Wigwam Park. This trail first crosses Freeman Creek, then follows Rolling Creek, eventually topping out on a 10,600' saddle. From the saddle cut to the right and follow Windy Peak's southeast ridge staying on the crest, or to the right of it, 2.5 miles to the summit.

The Castle (9,691') which rises from the west side of **Wellington Lake**, is a semi-technical climb, and not for the inexperienced. To avoid the access through the private campground at Wellington Lake, use the CT trailhead described above, and hike 1.5 miles on the Wigwam Park trail to where it reaches the south fork of Rolling Creek. Then bushwhack east to The Castle. Pass the lesser summit on the north. The jumble of rock points can then be explored or climbed, according to the party's makeup.

Freeman Peak, or **Buffalo Peak**, (11,589') at the south end of the Kenoshas, is well fortified by bushwhacking terrain on steep slopes. From Wellington Lake on FSR-543, fork right and continue over Stoney Pass on FSR-560 approximately 6.5 miles to the Wigwam Trailhead. Follow the trail from 8,200' along Wigwam Creek for 2 miles, then cut off right and work your way north up the slope, then northeast. It is about 2 miles of hard work.

FSR-211/Goose Creek Access:

Park Co Rd-77 connects with Jefferson Co Rd-126 by FSR-211, an isolated, southwest-northeast road through the range, also called the Matukat Road. To reach a popular point of departure on Goose Creek into Lost Creek Wilderness, travel about 8 miles northnorthwest along Park Co Rd-77 from US-24 near Lake George, then go east and north on FSR-211 some 10 twisting miles, to the turnoff onto FSR-558 leading another mile to the Goose Creek Trailhead. A popular loop backpack via Refrigerator Gulch, McCurdy Park and Hankins Pass in the heart of the Tarryall Range starts here.

For travelers approaching from the north on US-285, the northern end of FSR-211 is found by heading south on Jefferson Co Rd-126 approximately 20 miles through the towns of Pine and Buffalo Creek.

Wilkerson Pass (US-24) Access:

The name **Puma Hills** applies to a clump of timbered knobs running to 11,000' summits on both sides of **Wilkerson Pass** on US-24. The **Badger Mountain Lookout** (11,294') is just northeast of Wilkerson Pass on US-24. The scramble up is about 1,800' in about a mile.

Packer Gulch Road (FSR-144) Access:

The high point of the Puma Hills, an 11,570' unnamed point, is 1.5 miles southwest of **Farnum Peak** (11,377') and a 0.5 mile southwest of the end of the Packer Gulch Road (FSR- 144). You can get there by driving about 1.5 miles west on FSR-234 from Tarryall Reservoir, then turning left on Packer Gulch Road (FSR-144). Keep left at the fork at mile 2.5. The road climbs to 11,000'. The higher summit is the second one, 0.5 mile southwest of the road end. Farnum Peak may also be climbed from the road end by bushwhacking northeast.

Rampart Range

Jurisdiction:
Pike NF, Pikes Peak Ranger District

Map area reference:
Page 66

Maps:
USGS: *Cascade, Dakan Mountain, Devils Head, Mount Deception, Palmer Lake, Woodland Park*
Forest Service: *Pike NF*

The Rampart Range runs south from Devils Head to Garden of the Gods at elevations around 9,000'. It is a good place for early and late season climbing, when the high mountains are snowed-in. There are many roads, campgrounds, ranches and resorts through this range of almost indistinguishable ridges and valleys. It is well sprinkled with spectacular hunks of granite, and here and there a prominent summit to climb. The area is heavily used, considering its location between Colorado Springs and Denver.

Rampart Range Road (FSR-300) Access:

The Rampart Range Road (FSR-300) runs from the Garden of the Gods at Colorado Springs to Hwy-67 near Sedalia, a mountain route of over 50 miles. The road is winding and goes slow for its entire length. An alternate approach begins at Woodland Park, 20 miles northwest of Colorado Springs on US-24. For this access, head north on Baldwin Street as you enter Woodland Park from the east, and intersect the Rampart Range Road 4 miles up.

The turnoff for Rampart Reservoir is about 5 miles south on FSR-300 from the Woodland Park approach; a 13 mile trail circles the shoreline.

Ormes Peak (9,727') was named by the Saturday Knights, the state's oldest hiking group, for Robert Ormes' father, Manley D. Ormes. To go there, drive 2 miles farther than the reservoir exit on the main road, and take the road east. Keep right at mile 1 and continue 1.5 miles east and southeast to a saddle where the road turns north. Walk 0.6 mile, keeping to the ridge line.

Blodgett Peak (9,423'), overlooking the plains, is a 2 mile walk from Ormes east and northeast on the indefinite ridge; take your map and compass.

Devils Head (9,748') is the summit of greatest interest on the Rampart because of the rough points of rock that rise from it like the horns of a mythical monster. A short trail climbs to the fire lookout on top from 8,800' Devils Head

Campground. To reach the campground, drive approximately 35 miles north on FSR-300 from Woodland Park or 10 miles south from the road end on Hwy-67 near Sedalia.

East Side (I-25) Access:

The east side approach to the Rampart Range is tricky only because of private property which exists as a continuous 50 mile barrier between the highway and the national forest. The most accessible entry occurs at Monument, 20 miles north of Colorado Springs on I-25 (exit 161). Here, Mount Herman Road (FSR-320) begins southwest of town and continues 10 miles to connect with the Rampart Range Road north of Woodland Park. A second possibility is to use the United States Air Force Academy parkways which take you within 1 mile of the NF boundary. Keep in mind that the USAFA is a military installation, and as on all military reservations, visitors must obey rules.

As one drives I-25 south from Denver to Colorado Springs in the piedmont country between mountain and plain, the unpretentious ridges of the Rampart Range rise as an appropriately modest transition to the high mountains further west. Some of these high peaks can be identified from obscure points on the Rampart.

Mount Herman (9,063') is one such point, easily accessible almost all year long. From 3rd Street in Monument, cross the railroad tracks west of town and follow the signs to Mount Herman Road. The obscure trail up the west side of the mountain to the top begins at a widened curve 4.2 miles up the road from the Pike NF boundary sign.

A group of accessible summits, often called the Academy Peaks because of their location, are due west of the USAFA. Enter the academy at the north entrance on 1-25 (exit 156B), 5 miles south of Monument. Ask for directions from the guard as to the quickest route to the hospital (no medical emergency!); the most direct route goes west of the guardhouse and left on Stadium Blvd, then right on Academy Drive to the hospital on Pine Drive. Take an unmarked dirt side road opposite the hospital on Pine Drive to the trailhead, and follow the trail up rugged Stanley Canyon. During the winter months, a giant ice flow blocks the canyon about half way up. Just before the reservoir, head 0.5 mile north and east to **South Peak** (9,385'), and 0.25 mile north to **North Peak** (9,368'). In past years, North Peak has been confirmed as a Peregrine Falcon nest site, and access has been restricted at certain times of the summer as posted at the trailhead.

Pikes Peak Region

Jurisdiction:
Pike NF, Pikes Peak Ranger District

Map area reference:
Page 66

Maps:
USGS: *Cripple Creek North, Manitou Springs, Mount Big Chief, Pikes Peak*
Forest Service: *Pike NF*

Pikes Peak is farthest east of the big peaks, hence its early fame to explorers and pioneer immigrants. Today, it is accessible by road, trail and rail. Hikers and climbers should be aware that following and/or hitchhiking either the Pikes Peak Toll Road or the Pikes Peak and Manitou cog railway is illegal. Nevertheless, the mountain has a well established system of trails and a ring of lesser summits, some of which constitute significant climbs of their own.

Colorado's mountain historian Louisa Ward Arps supplied many items of interest for this book, including the following information on Pikes Peak.

The peak was the first 14,000-foot mountain in the United States to be climbed. This was on July 13, 14 and 15, 1820, with such brilliant mid-summer weather that Dr. Edwin James, botanist of the Long Expedition, wondered if the blue of the tundra flowers was not partially acquired from the sky. Dr. James' climbing companions were a soldier and a civilian employee of the expedition. The climb was successful in spite of the fact that the climbers broke most modern mountaineering rules; the soldier, instead of "going light," carried a gun (in case of hostile Indians); they carried no emergency rations; they left their warm clothes in camp; the party did not stay together—the civilian got tired and took a nap below timberline, causing Dr. James to lose time and patience hollering for him. But the worst mistake was failing to put out their fire the morning after they bivouacked on the ascent. When they came off the mountain they found their cached supplies burned and a good part of the forest with them. Colorado's first careless campers!

Fourteen years before, in 1806, the man for whom Pikes Peak is named, Zebulon Montgomery Pike, left his main party in a breastwork built of 14 logs on the present site of Pueblo, and, with three companions, set out, "to ascend the north fork (Fountain Creek) to the high point of the blue mountain, which we conceived would be one day's march, in order to lay down the various branches and positions of the country." One of the legends that have grown up about this attempt is that Pike actually climbed Cheyenne Mountain; another is that he said Pikes Peak would never be climbed. Mountaineering scholars now think he came up South Turkey Creek and climbed Blue Mountain or another of the summits southwest of Cheyenne Mountain.

Pikes Peak and Garden of the Gods   *Donna Kelley*

Barr Trailhead Access:

The most popular and well-known trail up **Pikes Peak** (14,109') starts on the west end of Manitou Springs, for which you drive west on Manitou Avenue (US-24 business route) and fork left on Ruxton Avenue to the cog railway depot. Just beyond you will find the small trailhead perpetually crammed with cars, unless it's the dead of winter.

The 12 mile climb starts at 6,600' and involves more base to summit altitude than any other in the state. It is very punishing unless you are in condition, and even if you are, it will be more comfortable to camp en route. The usual place is at Barr's Camp, 9,800', named for Fred Barr who built all but the first three miles of the trail, maintained the camp and built other trails up North Cheyenne Canyon and Bottomless Pit as well. Since its official opening on July 4, 1920, **Barr Trail** has remained a local landmark and is used by casual dayhikers as well as determined peakbaggers.

Hwy-67 Access:

Hwy-67 goes south from Divide and US-24, continuing south to Cripple Creek and Victor. On the way it passes several inviting approaches for the west side of the massif.

A much less demanding climb up Pikes Peak, from the west, begins at Crags Campground. Start on Hwy-67 4 miles south of Divide and travel east 3 miles to the campground on FSR-383. Keep to the right side of the stream as you walk east up the creek. An old lumber road will take you most of the way to timberline. Then climb to a shallow saddle between points 12,792' and 12,888' and follow a spur to the highway. Shortcut the road on the ridge crest southeast to the summit, 7 miles in all.

Sentinel Point (12,527') is an obvious cone 3 miles west of Pikes Peak. The base of the cone is easily approached on the trail to Horsethief Park, but climbing it is another matter. The trail begins on the south side of the highway tunnel approximately 8 miles south of Divide on Hwy-67. It is a 0.5 mile walk to the lower end of the park where there is a split into a right and left fork. Hike up the left fork then bushwhack and scramble for a finish on the summit from the northwest, or continue up the right fork and ascend south on the trail towards Pancake Rocks. Follow a rough ridge northeast and north 2 miles to the summit. The unusual **Pancake Rocks** are a good destination for those who run out of steam en route.

Gold Camp Road/Old Stage Road Access:

The south side of the massif is best reached by the Gold Camp Road (FSR-370) and the Old Stage Road (FSR-368). The Gold Camp Road was initially graded for the Colorado Springs and Cripple Creek District Railway, called the Short Line, which ran between 1901 and 1922 as one of three railroads serving the famous gold camp. The upper end of the road, from North Cheyenne Canyon to St Peters Dome, is closed until further notice. The Old Stage Road, which predated the railroad grade to Cripple Creek, serves as a detour to the upper end of the Gold Camp Road.

The easiest approach to the lower Gold Camp Road is to follow US-24 west to 26th Street in Colorado Springs, and continue southwest into Bear Creek Canyon to the Gold Camp Road. The road is usually barricaded several miles up near the parking area for the trail up North Cheyenne Canyon and Bear Creek. To detour the closure for the upper end, follow the signs towards the Cheyenne Mountain Zoo via Penrose Blvd from the Broadmoor Hotel in the southwest section of the city. Keep an eye peeled for a residential street marked as Old Stage Road at right. It is 7 steep miles to reconnect to the upper Gold Camp Road near the viewpoint and trail to **St Peters Dome** (9,680').

From the parking area on the lower Gold Camp Road, continue beyond the barricade to the trail in popular North Cheyenne Canyon, or up the seasonally barricaded High Drive to the Bear Creek Trail.

Mount Garfield (10,920'), **Mount Arthur** (10,807') and **Tenney Crags** (10,094') are climbed to the north 3 miles up Bear Creek Trail or from the same location starting at the Jones Park trail connector in North Cheyenne Canyon. **Cameron Cone** (10,707') is an uninteresting 2 miles north-northeast of Arthur.

Almagre Mountain (12,367') is the bald ridge which rises 6 miles south-southeast of Pikes. It is reached from 3 miles beyond Jones Park on the Bear Creek Trail, with a long pull up loose talus on its north slope to the summit.

Mount Rosa (11,499') is a low, but distinctive and noticeable cone at the head of North Cheyenne Canyon. Hike 1 mile beyond Camp Nelson to the North Cheyenne-East Beaver Creek divide and bushwhack east to the summit from the meadow.

There is a less aerobic approach to both Almagre and Rosa from the upper Gold Camp Road opposite Rosemont Reservoir on FSR-379. Follow FSR-379 north 1 mile for the route to Rosa from the above meadow, or continue on FSR-379 two additional miles for Almagre from the south.

THE SANGRE DE CRISTO RANGE

Crestone Needle   *Robert Norris*

Sangre de Cristo Range

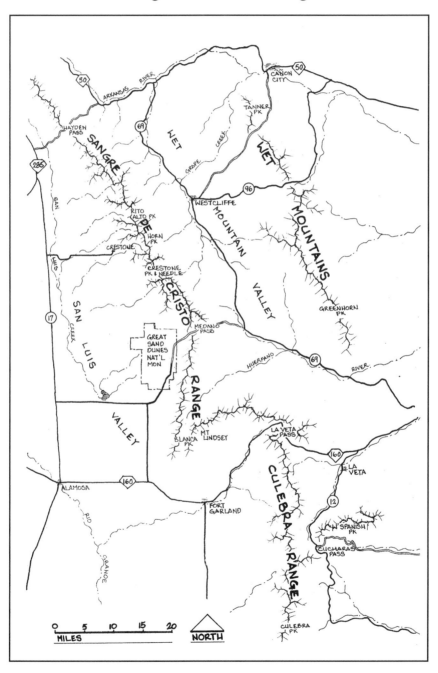

The Sangre de Cristo Range

The Sangre de Cristo Range has "the glamour of lost history—dim memories of Indian bands, of French explorers and Spanish troops; they have the spell of the remote, the mystery of recesses that are little known; they are the kind of mountains one's imagination builds." So wrote pioneer climber Albert Ellingwood after his party's first ascent of the Crestones in 1916.

"Sangre de Cristo" is the Spanish name for the mountain crescent between Salida, Colorado and Santa Fe, New Mexico. Translated "Blood of Christ", it refers to the alpine glow of sunrise and sunset. To the west of the range lies the flat-floored San Luis Valley with its artesian water and its national monument of thousand-foot sand dunes. The lower central portion, most interesting to mountaineers, is accessible from the Wet Mountain Valley, which parallels the range on the east. Except for Blanca, which is of igneous rock, the higher Sangre de Cristo summits are composed of folded and layered metamorphosed sedimentary rocks of Pennsylvanian to Permian age, notably the greenish, durable agglomerate of the Crestones.

Much of the Blanca massif and the area south of the dunes are on the Sangre de Cristo Grant and the Luis Maria Baca Land Grant #4. The history of the Baca Grant starts in 1821 when the Spanish rulers granted the Vegas Grandes land grant to Don Luis Maria Cabeza de Baca, descendant of the Cabeza de Vaca who walked across the southwest in the 1530's. By the 1860's, when the US Government set out to settle claims for Spanish and Mexican land grants, many families had settled on the Vegas Grandes (Big Meadows) without permission of Don Luis and his heirs. Instead of putting these settlers off the land, the government offered the Baca heirs their choice of equal acreage elsewhere. They chose two parcels in New Mexico, two in Arizona, and one in Colorado in the San Luis Valley—the fourth of the five grants. The Baca heirs ceded the San Luis Grant, 99,128.39 acres, to their lawyer, who sold it to land speculators. The speculators were as unsuccessful as the gold mines that were found near the town of Crestone. In the 1930's, a middle-aged Philadelphia tenderfoot with money, Alfred Collins, turned the Baca Grant #4 into a spectacularly successful cattle ranch. He sold it 20 years later.

Time and again surveyors of this Baca Grant tried to get to the top of the Sangre de Cristo Range to establish the boundary line, but they always failed. They wrote words like "inaccessible" and "unsurveyable" on their maps across the faces of Kit Carson, Humboldt, and the Crestone Peaks.

The range divides naturally into three groups: North, Main, and Sierra Blanca. For convenience, included in this part of the book are the Wet Mountains, Spanish Peaks and Culebra Range which share the Sangre's mystic lure.

SANGRES

Scrambling on Bushnell Peak   *Denise Snow*

North Section

Jurisdiction:
San Isabel NF, Salida Ranger District
Rio Grande NF, Saguache Ranger District

Map area reference:
Page 94

Maps:
USGS: *Bushnell Peak, Coaldale, Poncha Pass, Wellsville*
Forest Service: *San Isabel NF, Rio Grande NF*

The 17 mile string of crests from Poncha Pass to Hayden Pass is seen clearly from Poncha Pass. The summits are not far under 13,000'. This section is easily accessible from US-50 on the Arkansas River side and US-285 on the San Luis Valley side.

ARKANSAS RIVER SIDE - US-50 Access:

US-50 parallels the Arkansas River from Canon City to Salida, mostly in a tight canyon. About 4 miles west of Salida, US-50 intersects US-285 in Poncha Springs.

Poncha Mountain (10,134') is the northwest point of the range. To reach it, drive south on US-285 from Poncha Springs. From the intersection with Chaffee Rd-206, near the south edge of town, continue south, up Poncha Creek, about 2 miles. Park at a large turnout on the east side of US-285 near the mouth of the first prominent tributary that heads southeast. Bushwhack east across Poncha Creek to the west ridge of Poncha Mountain, and continue on this ridge about 1.25 miles to the summit.

For **Methodist Mountain** (11,707'), drive through Salida on US-50. In the middle of town, turn south on Chaffee Co Rd-107. Go for about 0.5 mile, then take the left fork, Rd-108, and after about 0.3 mile, take the right fork. Continue about 1.4 miles south, and park at the beginning of Methodist Mountain jeep road. Hike about 4 miles to the summit. Chaffee, Saguache, and Fremont Counties meet on the peak about 0.6 mile south of Methodist Mountain.

Methodist Mountain can also be reached via the **Rainbow Trail** from Bear Creek. Drive about 2 miles southeast from Salida on US-50, and turn south on Chaffee Rd-101. Go about 5.5 miles to the trailhead. For about 2.5 miles the road is adequate for passenger cars, then it becomes a jeep road. Take the west leg of the Rainbow Trail 6 miles to Methodist Mountain. To reach **Simmons Peak** (12,050'), bushwhack about 2 miles southwest.

SANGRES

Hunts Peak (13,071'), the most conspicuous point of the range as seen from US-285 north of Salida, is a steep mile-long climb by the east ridge. From the trailhead on Bear Creek Road mentioned above, take the Rainbow Trail southeast about 5 miles to the **Hunts Lake Trail** just east of Spring Creek. The Hunts Lake Trail can also be reached via the Rainbow Trail from Kerr Gulch Road, about 4 miles southeast of Howard. Take Hunts Lake Trail about 2.5 miles southwest to **Hunts Lake**. From the lake, climb northwest to the east ridge, and continue southwest along the ridge about 0.5 mile to the summit.

Red Mountain (12,994') is about 2 miles southeast along the ridge from Hunts Peak with a lot of side-hilling or 600' of lost altitude on the way.

Twin Sisters Peak (13,012') can be reached via the Kerr Gulch Road or the Hayden Creek Campground, about 5.5 miles southwest of Coaldale. Take the **Stout Creek Trail** to the Stout Creek Lakes. The peak is about 0.5 mile due west of the lakes. You can climb straight to the summit; this is toward and up the right side or head of the cirque. The Twin Sisters were named from the Arkansas valley, with reference to the two very symmetrical ridge faces they have on that side. The left one as seen from the Arkansas valley is a mile northeast and down-ridge from the above summit. The peak seen to the right is on a parallel ridge northwest of Cherry Creek. Its ridge end, the symmetrical part as seen from the valley, is 1.5 miles northeast of the range crest.

Bushnell Peak (13,105') is a mile southeast along the ridge from the Twin Sisters and can be done with them. Bushnell can also be climbed from the **Bushnell Lakes**. From the Hayden Creek Campground, take the Rainbow Trail 2.5 miles northwest to the **Bushnell Lakes Trail**, and follow this trail 2.5 miles to the Bushnell Lakes. The peak is less than 0.5 mile south of the uppermost lake. The best route is to use the easiest gradient; work northwest to the Stout Creek ridge, then to the range crest, and southeast along that to the summit.

Hayden Creek Road leaves US-50 at Coaldale, about 5 miles northwest of Cotopaxi, 21 miles southeast of Salida, and climbs 5.5 miles to Hayden Creek Campground, at about 7,700'. The road continues from the campground southwest up the ridge 5 miles, to cross the range at 10,709' **Hayden Pass**, then drops by a very steep route to the San Luis Valley and Villa Grove, 6.5 miles. Take only high clearance, 4WD vehicles over this pass. From the pass, ridge walk about a mile northwest to **Galena Peak** (12,481').

To reach **Nipple Mountain** (12,199') follow the Black Mountain Trail a little over 4 miles southeast. At the intersection with the Steel Canyon Trail, climb easterly to the summit. **Mount Otto** (12,865') is 1.5 miles northwest beyond Nipple along the crest, contouring around a couple small bumps.

SAN LUIS VALLEY SIDE - US-285 Access:

Several trails go in to the northern Sangres from US-285 on its 16 mile stretch between **Poncha Pass** and Villa Grove. The first, from 2 miles south of Poncha Pass, goes as a jeep road up Dorsey Creek (keeping right) to the northeast, then continues as a trail through the timber to 10,700', where it is a mile south and 1,000' below Methodist Mountain. Pagosa Mountain is the north end point. Under the name of **Simmons Peak Trail** it turns southeast and contours under the range crest to a point about 0.5 mile past **Salamander Lake**, 10,800', where it is 0.5 mile southwest of Simmons Peak, named for an Arkansas valley pioneer.

Simmons Peak (12,050') is best climbed from 0.25 mile east of Salamander Lake via the timber-free slope left of the trail, then east along the ridge.

Saguache Co Rd-57 runs north from about a mile north-northwest of Villa Grove on US-285, taking you to a "T", where you can drive east on a jeep road to the forest boundary at about 9,300'. From here, a steep but generally open ridge climb of about 3,700' in 2 miles will take you to the summit of Twin Sisters. If you want more, go southeast a mile, passing right of the midway ridge point, and climb Bushnell Peak. The west-southwest Bushnell ridge takes you back to the starting place.

The Hayden Pass jeep road runs east from Villa Grove, climbing about 2,000' in the last 2 miles. From the crest, the **Black Mountain Trail** runs southeast parallel to the range crest on the west side about 6 miles to a 12,503' summit point on the long northwest ridge of **Cottonwood Peak**, then turns off down Black Canyon to the Orient Mine. See Valley View Hot Springs Quad.

SANGRES

Rito Alto Peak, with Crestones behind   *David Anschicks*

Main Section

Jurisdiction:
San Isabel NF, San Carlos Ranger District
Rio Grande NF, Saguache Ranger District

Map area reference:
Page 94, 104 and 107

Maps:
USGS: *Coaldale, Crestone Peak, Electric Peak, Horn Peak, Medano Pass, Rito Alto Peak, Valley View Hot Springs*
Forest Service: *San Isabel NF, Rio Grande NF*

This large section runs from Hayden Pass to Mosca Pass. It is easily reached from both the east (Wet Mountain Valley) on Hwy-69, and from the west (San Luis Valley) on US-285 and Hwy-17. The crest peaks run generally from well over 13,000' through 14,000', with no saddles under 12,000', except at Hayden Pass and from Medano Pass south. Except for a section in the Crestone area, the summit climbs do not present problems so long as visibility is good and the cliffs can be seen and avoided.

The Rainbow Trail, 55 miles long, skirts the east flank of the Sangre de Cristo Range from Bear Creek to Music Pass, 22 miles south of Westcliffe. The average elevation of this trunk trail is 9,000'. It crosses 40 streams, many of them with side trails running up them to the lakes and range crest of the Sangre de Cristos. Named for its arc shape, the trail was constructed over the period 1912-1930 at a cost under $15,000. Like the flanking trails, it was built largely for fire protection but serves also for horseback and pack trips, and is useful as a cross line for backpackers. This part of the range has the most interesting side trips: those to Lakes of the Clouds, to Hermit Pass, to Macey Lakes, to South Colony Lakes, and to the Venable-Comanche loop.

The Wet Mountain Valley was settled by several colony groups, including one peopled by Germans, from which Colony Creek and Colony Lakes take their names. The valley is one of the lesser of Colorado's large mountain parks, wide enough so that the spectacular line of summits can be seen from most points.

Some very rich silver mines were developed in the neighborhood of Westcliffe, and two railroads came in. The first was a narrow gauge which washed out, the second was a standard gauge which went up Texas Creek. Silver Cliff, a mile east of Westcliffe, came into being when the citizens felt they were being cheated by a water company, and moved their dwellings up the road.

SANGRES

WET MOUNTAIN VALLEY SIDE - Hillside (FSR-300) Access:

The flanking road for the east side of the range is Hwy-69. It runs from Texas Creek on US-50 through Westcliffe and the Wet Mountain Valley, southeast to Walsenburg and 1-25.

There is a northern line of access from Hillside on Hwy-69, 11 miles south of Texas Creek, 14 miles north of Westcliffe. Take the right fork (FSR-300) just south of Hillside and go west about 3 miles to the Lutheran Rainbow Trail Camp, at 8,400', where there is parking for 7 to 10 cars. Lake Creek Campground is on the opposite (north) side of the road. A jeep road continues west, following North Lake Creek past Balman Reservoir, and on to the Cloverdale Mine. A trail continues up the main drainage to a 12,700' pass and continues as **Garner Trail** into the San Luis Valley. It is about 5 miles down Garner Creek to the road on that side.

Cottonwood Peak (13,588') is a little over a mile northwest of the **Garner Creek Pass**. To reach it from this side, turn off the pass trail about a mile up Cloverdale Basin from the mine, and climb 400' on the right side (northwest) to Silver Lake. Strike directly up to the saddle north of the lake, then climb south to the summit along the ridge. The ridge climb is 800' in a mile. **Thirsty Peak** (13,213') is a short climb southeast from the pass.

Wulsten Baldy (12,823') is a north-northeast offshoot of Cottonwood, 2.5 miles removed. To climb it, turn off as for Silver Lake, but angle back as you climb, so as to come to the ridge north of the big hump between Wulsten and Cottonwood. **Eagle Peak** (13,205') rises directly behind the Cloverdale Mine. The best approach however is to stay on the trail until past the last timber, and then angle southeast for the ridge leading back north to the top. From the low spot left of the ridge bump you have an easy mile north along the crest.

To reach the **Brush Creek Lakes**, drive west from Hillside toward the Lutheran Rainbow Trail Camp about 2 miles. Turn south on a jeep road and go 3 miles to the North Brush Creek Trail. Take this trail about 3 miles west to the Brush Creek Lakes. Here, the North Brush Creek Trail turns south and continues on as the Crossover Trail, a sort of elevated Rainbow Trail.

To reach **Lakes Peak** (13,375'), follow the trail south from Upper Brush Lake to the ridge crossing at 12,300', then climb due west. From this ridge crossing, the Crossover Trail drops south to a cirque heading the South Branch of North Brush Creek, at 11,600', then ascends around the next ridge, crossing it at 12,500', and then zigzags down to timber at 11,500' in Middle Brush Creek. It climbs Middle Brush Creek to 12,400' **Banjo Lake** and up to the next ridge south, 500' higher. It then descends to and along the South Brush Creek.

Electric Peak (13,598') is directly above Banjo Lake. It is best climbed however by going up the ridge north of Middle Brush Creek from where the trail crosses it, an easy 1.5 miles west-southwest. **Mount Niedhardt** (12,844') is a ridge walk of less than one mile southwest from Electric Peak, and **De Anza Peak** (13,362') is a little less than 2 miles southeast along the range crest. The stretch from Brush Creek Lakes across the ridges to timberline in South Brush is about 9 miles in beautiful high country, which makes it very inviting as a backpack loop.

Gibbs Peak (13,553') is the most prominent summit from a considerable stretch of the valley. It is climbed from South Brush Creek. Bushwhack south along the east side of Horseshoe Bend Creek until you are pretty high in the basin, then cut off left (east-southeast) to the saddle of the ridge connecting Gibbs to the range crest, for an easy finish.

WET MOUNTAIN VALLEY SIDE - Hermit Lake Road Access:

Hermit Lake Road travels west from Westcliffe. You can easily catch it on the south side of town from Hwy-69. Lakes of the Clouds Trail is reached by driving on the Hermit Lake Road to its intersection with the Rainbow Trail, then taking the Rainbow Trail north about 3 miles. The **Lakes of the Clouds** are about 4 more miles southwest.

Mount Marcy (13,490'), 1.5 miles northwest of the Lakes of the Clouds, is climbed most easily from them by a route north to its gentle east-northeast ridge, and up that.

Spread Eagle Peak (13,524' and 13,423') has its saddle 1 mile south (half left as you face up canyon) from the lakes. The climb to either or both summits (the western summit is the higher) goes by way of the saddle and along the connecting ridge. Spread Eagle is descriptive of the formation, the summits being the wings which sweep away from the lower hump or head between. From its intersection with the Rainbow Trail, Hermit Lake Road continues as a jeep road up Middle Taylor Creek to **Hermit Pass** at 13,000'.

Rito Alto Peak (13,794') is a climb of only 0.75 mile and 800' northwest from the pass, or from the ridge by **Horseshoe Lake**, 1,800'.

Hermit Peak (13,350') is an even shorter climb if you go south from the pass. **Eureka Mountain** (13,507') is 1.5 miles southeast along the ridge from Hermit Peak. An attractive trip is to climb from Hermit Lake to the pass, walk down range over Eureka and drop southeast on a good slope back of the cliffs to **Goodwin Lake**, then climb north over the saddle east of Eureka to Eureka Lake, and either contour northwest to Horseshoe Lake or cut down the hill east before that.

Sangre de Cristo Range
(Hermit Pass to Music Pass)

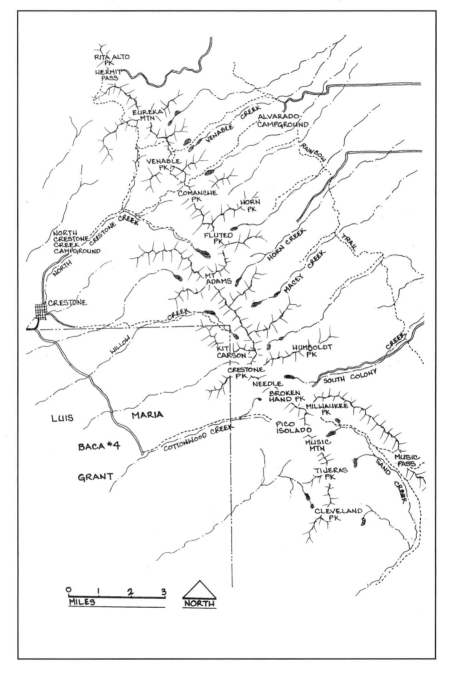

North Taylor Creek has a trail too. From the intersection of Hermit Lake Road and Rainbow Trail, take the Rainbow Trail north a mile at 8,600'. It is about 4 miles up North Taylor to a little lake under Rito Alto Peak. The north ridge of this valley, Spread Eagle Peak, is not difficult from here.

WET MOUNTAIN VALLEY SIDE - Schoolfield Road (Rd-140) Access:

Schoolfield Road (Rd-140), which leaves Hwy-69 3.5 miles south of Westcliffe, takes you west 6 miles to Abbots Lodge and Alvarado Campground, at 9,100'. This approach is used for each of four valleys.

Goodwin Lakes Trail is about a mile northwest along the Rainbow Trail from Abbots Lodge. From the Rainbow, it climbs 4 miles to the lower lake at 11,400', where you are under the upper Goodwin Lake and an easy route to Eureka Mountain by its south-southeast face.

The **Venable** and the **Comanche Trails** go up to complete a loop at 12,800' behind the range crest. On the Venable Trail, one sidetracks to Venable Falls, looks across south from Venable Lakes at the Phantom Terrace, and cuts left from a little east of **Venable Pass** across the east face of **Venable Peak** (13,334'), on a high shelf route to the range crest saddle, where one meets the other trail from the south. It is about 6 miles to the range crest either way, and 0.5 mile on the western slope.

Venable Peak, **Spring Mountain** (13,244') and **Comanche Peak** (13,277') are all within half a mile of the trail, and present no difficulties beyond a little steepness. The round trip is a big day without these additions, and since there is camping (preferably on the Comanche side) we recommend it as a deluxe overnight tour.

The fourth valley is **Cottonwood Creek**, for which you walk southeast about a mile on the Rainbow Trail from Alvarado Campground. The Cottonwood Creek Trail climbs 4 miles to 11,600'. **Horn Peak** (13,450') can be climbed by the long northeast ridge from near the start of the trail, or by a route which uses the trail for altitude gain then climbs the west ridge.

WET MOUNTAIN VALLEY SIDE - Horn Road (Rd-130) Access:

To catch Horn Road (Rd-130), travel on Hwy-69 4.4 miles south of Westcliffe to Rd- 119 (Colfax Lane), then another mile south on Rd-119 to Horn Rd (Rd-130). Travel west to the parking lot for trails up Dry Creek, Horn Creek, and Macey Creek.

SANGRES

SANGRES

Dry Creek Trail is reached from a 0.5 mile stretch of Rainbow Trail running northwest from Horn Creek. It climbs in 5 miles from 9,200' to 11,800'. Camping is good between the falls and the lakes.

Horn Peak, like Gibbs Peak farther north, is far enough east of the crest to dominate its section of the valley. The route climbs northwest from the lower **Dry Lake** to the peak's west ridge saddle. From the saddle, it is a good 0.5 mile, and steep, to the top.

Another route to Horn Peak is by Hennequin Creek. From Horn Creek, go about a mile northwest along the Rainbow Trail to Hennequin Creek. Climb southwest along the creek about 0.5 mile, then up either ridge to the summit.

Horn Creek Trail climbs 4.5 miles from the Rainbow Trail to the upper Horn Lake. Little Horn Peak you pass on the right; Little Baldy is the long ridge running to the valley head on the left.

Mount Adams (13,931') is at the upper lake valley head on the right. The ridges cut it off from all but a point or two on Hwy-69. When you do see it, it is a wedge shape and looks high, hard, and handsome. Climb north-northwest from the upper lake to the ridge, a mile or less, and then left up that to the finish. A rope is recommended.

Little Horn Peak (13,143') and **Fluted Peak** (13,554') are connected by a mile of narrow but quite passable ridge. From the bowl between the two peaks, climb north to the saddle, then east to the summit of Little Horn. Reverse on the ridge and go up to the range crest and northwest along the cirque crest to Fluted.

The **Macey Creek Trail** likewise starts in effect from the Horn Road parking place. It is 2 miles south on the Rainbow Trail, then about 4 miles southwest to the upper Macey Lake, 11,865'.

Colony Baldy (13,705'), 0.75 mile east of Lake 11,643', is climbable on its west- southwest face. Climb south from the lake, then east up the face.

North Colony Creek has a trail which runs about 5 miles in from the Rainbow. It can be approached on rather long stretches of the Rainbow Trail from either Horn Creek or South Colony Creek.

WET MOUNTAIN VALLEY SIDE - South Colony Creek Access:

South Colony Creek is a favorite haunt of mountain climbers who go there to enjoy the Crestones, the roughest and some of the most pleasant parts of the Sangre de Cristo. From Westcliffe, drive 4.4 miles south on Hwy-69, then south about 5.5 miles on Colfax Lane (Rd-119), where you turn west and go about a mile. From here, a rough jeep road climbs an increasingly rocky and steep route to the road end, where it is a short pack in to the **South Colony Lakes**. There are good, but heavily used, camping knolls near the lakes.

Humboldt Peak (14,064') is an anthill type mountain (small rocks for sand grains) a mile northeast of the first lake, which is 11,667'. The short but tedious hike, best from farther up the valley, offers as reward a fine view of Crestone Needle and Peak across the valley. Most years it sends a snowslide down its south face to South Colony Creek.

Except for parties thoroughly familiar with the routes, rope should be taken for the other climbs from this camping area.

Kit Carson Peak (14,165') is about 2.5 miles northwest from upper South Colony Lake. Rock-whack to the 13,150' plateau at the west end of the Humboldt ridge via the ridge or the head of the cirque west of upper Colony Lake. Pass to the left of the unspectacular rock-pile hump (**Peak 13,799'**) to the saddle beyond it, 13,450'. You should go across the top of the ridge (**Peak 13,980'**) immediately west and climb down to the notch beyond, losing about 350'. The 600' climb up a wide ledge-and-rock gully leading to the summit is steep but not difficult.

Crestone Needle (14,197') and **Crestone Peak** (14,294') are often climbed together. From the northwest end of lower South Colony Lake, climb generally

Crestone Group

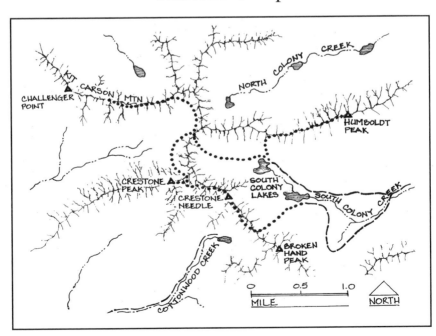

Traversing the Crestones   *Denise Snow*

toward the low point of the Needle's left (east-southeast) ridge, and after 0.2 mile, find a zigzag cairn-marked route more directly up until you cross the ridge at the third pinnacle northwest of the low point. Contour left around the first rib to get into an easy, steepish hard-rock gully for the summit climb. The first gully is airier and parties may require rope for one short steep section, though the rock is not difficult. On the descent, be looking for the way back left to the ridge, or you will get too low. The gully from the lowest point of the ridge is very rotten and a helmet may fend off rocks from above. At least one fatality has occured in this gully from rockfall.

The Needle-to-Peak traverse looks precipitous, but though slow, it is not difficult. Drop from the Needle to the saddle west-northwest (fixed hand rope will move your party faster) and keep contouring left. You can begin climbing after you pass the red saddle. A technically easier route contours 200' below the red saddle to a huge red gully not previously visible, and up the gully to the high saddle. From the high saddle between the summits, climb left. Return to same and go down the northwest couloir. Sand on smoothed rock or ice problems may make this very slow. Traverse right as soon as you can, and go down to the plateau and a steep couloir for descent. Below the upper lake, keep well to the left to find the trail to the lower lake and so avoid deep willows. Strong parties make three and sometimes all four fourteeners in a day. Crestone Peak can of course be climbed by this descent route, but the best traverse from it to the Needle is harder to find going east-southeast.

The stretch of the Sangre de Cristo Range immediately south of the Crestone group is similar to the Crestones in rock type and thus interestingly rugged and steep.

Broken Hand Peak (13,573') is directly south of the lower South Colony Lake. There are interesting routes on this side, and an easier approach from beyond the notch separating this peak from Crestone Needle. The notch itself is rather too steep and dirty for comfort, but you can get behind it from higher on the right as for Crestone Needle, and then drop to it on the easy side.

Milwaukee Peak (13,522') can also be reached from the back, or southwest side of Broken Hand. It goes best if you drop to about 12,500' to traverse across the slope of Broken Hand to get into the west basin of Milwaukee for the ascent. Climbers have also gone south, directly up-cirque, to the saddle between Broken Hand and Milwaukee, then up the sharp west ridge of Milwaukee's false north summit, and south to top.

The **Marble Mountain Trail** is reached by the Rainbow Trail from South Colony Creek Road. It is used as the approach for the Marble cave and other caves, as well as the mountains.

Marble Mountain (13,266') is a smooth frontal ridge running parallel to the valley and range. It is climbed on this steep side, more or less directly from the trail end at 11,500'. It is also possible to climb Marble Mountain sans trail, by climbing straight up the first ridge crest south of South Colony Creek. This way you use the Rainbow Trail for only 0.25 mile.

WET MOUNTAIN VALLEY SIDE - Music Pass Access:

The trail to **Music Pass** is open to 4WD vehicles. For this you take the same road as for South Colony Creek, but at the end of Colfax Lane (Rd-119), go 0.25 mile east and then turn south. Keep right at the first "Y" then left at the second and third. A little over 4 miles south, you enter the forest at about 9,300' on Grape Creek. The road continues on as the Music Pass jeep trail. Travel several miles to a barricade, where you must continue the remaining distance to the pass on foot. Sand Creek, on the other side of the pass, gives access to several fine rough peaks. It is said that Music Pass was named either for the melodic sound created by the wind as it crosses this notch, or for the moans of the shifting sand dunes at the western end of Sand Creek.

Music Mountain (13,355') is a little over 2 miles west and a little north from Music Pass. Walk on a trail from the pass 1 mile to Sand Creek and up to about 50 yards past the first timber. Here you should pick up a trail cutting left for lower **Sand Creek Lake**, 11,471', about a mile southwest. Go counterclockwise

SANGRES

around the lake to the north side, where there is a clearing with a game trail that leads to timberline and good slopes.

Tijeras Peak (13,604') is a mile south-southeast along the ridge from Music Mountain, and presents a formidable ridge-crowned wall to lower Sand Creek Lake. From the north side of the lake, go part way into the Music Mountain basin, then turn south. Look for a break through the steep mid-section of the canyon side. The upper slopes lead southwest less steeply to a short stretch on the northwest ridge for a finish.

Milwaukee Peak (13,522') heads the Sand Creek valley. It should be approached from upper Sand Creek Lake, 11,745'. Follow the trail northwest to the saddle north of the peak, then south along the ridge. Marble Mountain can be combined with Milwaukee. It is north and east along the ridge, with some 600' drop to regain.

Pico Asilado (13,611') is a higher summit of the Milwaukee Massif, 0.5 mile-west- southwest of Milwaukee. It is hard to see from below and named for its remoteness.

Cleveland Peak (13,414') 2 miles south-southwest from lower Sand Creek Lake, is a long airy approach from a camp there. Go south about 0.5 mile and then climb west up into the basin. At the back end of the basin, hike south up grassy slopes to a saddle. Contour southwest around Tijeras' south ridge point into another saddle and scramble the broken ridge south over **Peak 13,401'** and on to Cleveland.

WET MOUNTAIN VALLEY SIDE - Medano Pass Access:

The Medano Pass road leaves Hwy-69 about 8 miles west-northwest of Gardner, or about 21 miles southeast of Westcliffe, and continues on west-northwest to just beyond the forest boundary. From here, it continues as a jeep road about 2 miles to the pass at 9,950'. The road continues west of the pass and ends up in Great Sand Dunes National Monument. Be aware that the last several miles of the road is in the sand dunes, which could lead to some frustrating moments for unwary drivers.

Mount Seven's top summit (13,297') is about 3 miles straight west of Medano Pass. From the pass, take the jeep road 0.5 mile southwest to a trail junction at 9,600' on Medano Creek. The right fork goes northwest to Medano Lake. From the lake, you can climb west to the north ridge then 0.5 mile south to the summit.

SAN LUIS VALLEY SIDE - Valley View Hot Springs Access:

From near the junction of US-285 with Hwy-17 in the San Luis Valley, 4 miles south of Villa Grove, a road runs east to Valley View Hot Springs. About 5.3 miles east on this road, a jeep road cuts off to the northeast and goes about 2 miles to the Orient Mine. This mine was once an iron source for Pueblo's Colorado Fuel and Iron Company.

From mile 3 on the Valley View Hot Springs Road, a road runs north, and about 1.3 miles along the north road, a jeep road turns off northeast about 2 miles to become the **Quarry Trail** at 8,475'. It climbs about 4 miles to the Black Mountain Trail at 11,600' on Nipple Mountain (see above with North Sangre de Cristo Section).

About 0.5 mile north of the Orient Mine, you can pick up the Black Canyon Trail at 8,900' and climb northeast about 3 miles to a trail junction at 11,000'. The left fork zigzags north to the 12,503' end of Cottonwood Peak's northwest ridge. The right fork continues 0.5 mile toward the canyon headwall under the northwest face of Cottonwood Peak. One can continue to the basin head and then climb out southwest to the ridge to make a round trip with the better route below.

Cottonwood Peak (13,588') has a trail to within easy distance of the summit. From the Valley View Hot Springs turnoff, you can drive about 0.5 mile south to the Hot Springs Canyon jeep road. Take the road to about 10,200', then continue by trail to about 13,000' on the peak's west ridge.

The **Garner Trail** starts a little less than a mile south of the Valley View Hot Springs turnoff, and 0.5 mile up Garner Creek. The trail climbs over the range crest to Cloverdale Basin and Rainbow Lake.

Thirsty Peak (13,217') is a short climb east-southeast from the Garner Trail pass. It takes its name from the Michel-Arnold traverse of the Sangre de Cristo. In the summer of 1961, Bill Amold, Lester Michel and Jim Michel, age 14, trekked the range from Poncha Pass to Music Pass in a period of 9 days, with the help of food caches. The trio arrived at this peak in a dried up condition and had to satisfy their thirst by gazing down at the Brush Creek Lakes. They survived, and two days later began to get daily drenchings.

The Major Creek jeep road is about a mile south of Garner Creek. It runs about 4 miles east-northeast up Major Creek to a fork at 10,000'. The left fork climbs about 2 miles to the range crest at 12,450', and continues 0.5 mile on the other side to a junction with the Crossover Trail in the head of the south branch of North Brush Creek.

Electric Peak (13,598'), the highest point north of Rito Alto Peak, is most easily approached from this range crossing. It is about 1 mile southeast along the ridge crest; a pull of 800', a level off, and a pull of 400' more.

Mount Niedhardt (12,844'), whose name honors an early settler, is a mile-long ridgewalk due south off the range crest. You can descend the drainage due west to the south fork of Major Creek.

SAN LUIS VALLEY SIDE - Saguache Rd-AA Access:

Cotton Creek Trail is best approached from Saguache Rd-AA, about 6 miles south of the US-285/Hwy-17 junction. From the Hwy-17/Saguache Rd-AA junction, you drive east 5 miles, north 2, and east 2 to the trailhead. The trail goes up canyon to a junction. The right fork goes about 3 miles south-southeast to **Cotton Lake** at the 11,500' timberline. It continues south a long mile to the 12,500' pass separating the long Mount Owen massif from the main range, and then heads around west down Rito Alto Creek.

Mount Marcy (13,490') is about 2 miles northeast of the lake on good slopes. From the pass you can skirt east and south around the bowl to climb **Spread Eagle Peak** (13,524'), or head northeast to **Peak 13,513'**, 1 mile west-northwest of Spread Eagle. Conversely, heading west from the pass takes you up the short but narrow east ridge of **Peak 13,490'**, highpoint of this westward extension.

The left fork of the Cotton Creek Trail climbs 1 mile of steep slope to cross the range crest at 12,800', and drops a little way on the other side to the Crossover Trail, meeting it at its south end at the head of South Brush Creek. This suggests a loop trip with the Major Creek Trail via the more rugged side of the range.

From the Hwy-17/Rd-AA junction, go straight east on Rd-AA 8 miles to the Wild Cherry Creek Trailhead. This trail climbs about 5 miles from 8,600' to **Cherry Lake**, 11,800'. **Mount Owen** (13,340') is a steep but climbable mile due north from the lake.

To reach the Rito Alto Creek Trailhead, go east about 5 miles on Saguache Rd-AA from the Hwy-17/Rd-AA junction, then south about 3 miles on Saguache Rd-64, then east 3.5 miles. The trail climbs about 4.5 miles east-northeast up Rito Alto Creek to 10,900', junction point for the pass trail north to Cotton Lake, then continues 1 mile south to **Rito Alto Lake**, 11,327'. About 0.5 mile southeast of Rito Alto Lake, a fork of the trail goes northeast 1.5 miles to meet the Hermit Pass Road at 13,000'. **Rito Alto Peak** (13,794') is an 800', 1 mile climb north-northwest up-ridge from the pass.

The south fork is the continuation of the Rito Alto Pack Trail, which goes over the ridge at 12,200', around the head of San Isabel Creek, then over a 12,400' pass, and down the north fork of North Crestone Creek. This latter pass offers a short brisk climb of 1,000' northeast up the ridge to **Eureka Mountain**.

A mile south of the pass on the Eureka Mountain ridge, at 11,600', the trail from Alvarado Campground comes in from the east over 12,800' **Venable Pass**. Venable Pass is a mile east and a climb of 1,200' from the Rito Alto-Venable trail junction.

SAN LUIS VALLEY SIDE - Crestone Access:

More trails are reached from Hwy-17 on the latitude of Moffat, which sends a 12 mile road east along the north side of Baca Grant #4 to the village of Crestone.

For Dimick Driveway, take a jeep trail north-northwest about 1.5 miles from the townsite of Crestone. The driveway goes up Dimick Gulch, north over the divide into San Isabel Creek, and northeast up San Isabel Creek. A trail continues on to **San Isabel Lake** at 11,625', then north to join the Rito Alto Trail under Hermit Peak. This suggests loop trips of various kinds.

For the **North Crestone Trail**, go straight north from Crestone about 1 mile, then a little over 0.5 mile northeast to North Crestone Creek Campground. Cars can go about 1 mile up-creek from the campground to a small parking area at about 9,000'. About 1.5 miles up the creek from the parking area, the **North Fork Trail** turns off left, and climbs 1.75 miles in the North Fork to a junction. On the left is the Rito Alto Trail to the northwest, well under the range crest and parallel to it. On the right is the trail to **Venable Pass**, 12,800'. From Venable Pass, you can follow the Venable Trail south on the east side of the range crest to Phantom Terrace and then along the west side to Comanche Pass, and then descend the Crestone Creek Middle Fork to the junction with the North Fork. From the road end this makes about a 13 mile loop, more or less comparable with the Venable-Comanche loop from Alvarado Campground in the Wet Mountain Valley.

By keeping right about 1.5 miles above the road end in North Crestone Creek, you pass the North Fork and Middle Fork Trails and take the Lake Fork, which takes you about 3 miles east-southeast to **North Crestone Lake** at 11,800', under Mount Adams.

Fluted Peak (13,554') is a short stiff climb of 1,800' from the lake. Go north then northeast to the ridge saddle, then south to the top. **Mount Adams** (13,931') goes by its steep and airy northwest ridge. First climb southwest from the upper lake end to the saddle, about 1,000', then up the ridge, for which you should have a rope along.

There is a jeep road that goes about 2 miles east from Crestone to two trailheads. The left one follows South Crestone Creek about 3.5 miles to **South Crestone Lake**, still in timber at 11,800'. Mount Adams is a climb of about 1.5 miles and 2,100', going up the basin on either side ridge.

The excellent **Willow Creek Trail** takes off east from just east of the South Crestone Creek Trail, and climbs from 8,600' to scenic 11,564' **Willow Lake** on a 4 mile route. A camp on the north side of the lake gives short routes to Mount Adams, Challenger Point, and Kit Carson. For the latter two, it is the easiest approach. For Mount Adams, climb north from the lake to the west ridge of Adams at about 12,900'. Follow the ridge about 0.5 mile east to the summit. The same ridge and a likewise distance but west, leads up **Peak 13,546'**. Southeast along the crest from Adams is **Peak 13,580'**. It goes by an easy west slope.

For **Challenger Point** (14,081'), named for the fateful shuttle flight, climb above the cliffs on the north side of Willow Lake, go above the waterfall, and work your way to the south side of the valley. Climb the steep slope just left of a narrow couloir which descends from the top of the valley wall and follow the ridge top south-southeast to the inconspicuous summit. For **Kit Carson Peak** (14,165'), continue east, dropping 400' into a notch at the summit buttress. Climb a broad ramp that takes you up, then down the southeast side of the summit pyramid, then go up a wide, cairned couloir.

SAN LUIS VALLEY SIDE - Baca Grant #4 Access:

The trailheads for Cottonwood Creek, Deadman Creek, Pole Creek, and Sand Creek are on the Luis Maria Baca #4 Grant. The approach is the same as the Crestone access above. Do not enter the grant without permission. Inquire about

Crestone Peak from Bears Playground   *H. L. Standley*

road conditions. You should make sure where you are going and not squirrel around; this is sand country and even your jeep can go down wallowing.

To reach the **Cottonwood Creek Trail**, drive about 4 miles southeast from Crestone to the trailhead at 8,400'. The trail is rough and steep, and climbs about 3.5 miles to a junction. The left fork goes to **Cottonwood Lake** at 12,310'. The right fork goes into the bowl just west of Milwaukee Peak, and continues over Milwaukee's north ridge into the Sand Creek valley. Milwaukee is a short steep pitch from the pass.

Pico Asilado (13,611') is just right of Milwaukee Peak, and best climbed from the saddle between the two, whether alone or with the latter. The saddle is at 13,200', the last 400' very steep. From it you turn back to the right along the ridge. This peak, though it is the highest point between the Crestones and the Sierra Blanca massif, is all but invisible from both valleys flanking the range.

The Crestones are also within reach of a camp on Cottonwood Creek. For **Crestone Peak** (14,294'), take the left branch of the trail and climb northeast toward Cottonwood Lake. Just below the lake, turn left along a stream that comes in from the north, and climb north into a bowl and then up the red couloir to the summit. **Crestone Needle** (14,197') and **Broken Hand Peak** (13,573') can be climbed from the saddle east of Cottonwood Lake.

Another Baca jeep road of interest, if passable, goes to and up Pole Creek a short distance, from where a trail continues on to **Pole Creek Lake** at 12,000'. For **Cleveland Peak** (13,414'), climb to the saddle southeast of the lake, then northeast along the very flat west ridge to the summit. **Peak 13,384'** is a short pull southwest from the same saddle and **Peak 13,050'** is likewise a short excursion northeast from the west end of Cleveland's flat ridge.

Two Baca roads converge at Liberty, name of the quad and start of the Sand Creek Trail. The trail climbs up Sand Creek about 12.5 miles to **Music Pass**. The trail can also be reached from Medano Creek by a long hike across the northern part of the Great Sand Dunes National Monument. Park near the mouth of Little Medano Creek. Since Sand Creek is more easily approached from the east side, the climbs in it are treated with those on that side of the range.

SAN LUIS VALLEY SIDE - Great Sand Dunes National Monument Access:

The Great Sands Dunes are an extraordinary playground and camping spot reached by driving 22 miles east from 0.5 mile north of Mosca on Hwy-17, or by going 7 miles west from Blanca on US-160, then north on Hwy-150. The shifting beige sand rises 1,000', and its smooth undulating shapes are often photographed with the Sangre de Cristo Range as a dramatic rocky backdrop.

The dunes formed as the prevailing southwesterly winds carried the sandy soil towards the low notch in the range, where Medano, Mosca and Music Passes are located. The heavier sand, naturally sifted from the finer dust, was deposited here. There are no trails on the dunes, and remember that the surface temperature of the sand can be uncomfortably warm at mid-day. Medano Creek, which forms the east boundary of the dunes, completely disappears into the sand near the monument headquarters.

The Medano Pass Road is a jeep road that goes about 6 miles north from the Dunes headquarters then turns up Medano Creek going about 8 miles more to 9,950' Medano Pass. From 3 miles off the top it connects with a better road up from Bradford on Hwy-69 in the Wet Mountain Valley. Mosca Pass goes directly east from Dunes headquarters.

Huerfano Valley, Blanca group behind   *Mike Endres*

Sierra Blanca

Jurisdiction:
San Isabel NF, San Carlos Ranger District
Rio Grande NF, Divide Ranger District- Del Norte

Map area reference:
Page 94 and 118

Maps:
USGS: *Blanca Peak, Mosca Pass, Twin Peaks, Zapata Ranch*
Forest Service: *Rio Grande NF, San Isabel NF*

The name sierra is often used for a whole range. We apply it here to the massif of which Blanca Peak is the highest individual mountain or peak. It includes, besides Blanca, the cluster around it: Little Bear, California, Lindsey, and their ridges.

Huerfano River Access:

The Huerfano River provides access to a spectacular valley on the north side of Blanca Peak and Ellingwood Point. For the more experienced mountaineer, a climb of these fourteeners from this side avoids the traffic congestion common on the Lake Como side.

Leaving Hwy-69 at Gardner, southeast of Westcliffe, proceed southwest past Red Wing on gravel to Sharpsdale junction at mile 12.5. A road goes west-northwest to Mosca Pass at 9,750'. It continues a little higher to a relay installation with no special advantages for viewing. A trail goes down the west side 3 miles to the Great Sand Dunes National Monument.

Continuing southwest 4 miles from Sharpsdale, you will reach the Singing River Ranch. From here you will need a high clearance vehicle to negotiate a stoney stretch of road through the ranch (do not trespass!) and parts of the remaining 5 miles leading to the Forest Service closure at 10,700'. There is good camping just before the road closure, high above the Huerfano, or lower down along the river. The **Huerfano Trail**, a route across the valley connecting on the west side with the Zapata Drive Trail, crosses the Huerfano River 4 miles from the ranch.

California Peak (13,849') may be climbed from this trail, which zigzags up 2 miles to the ridge at 11,845'. The summit is south another 2.5 miles on good enough footing. A shorter, alternate route departs the **Lily Lake Trail** 0.25 mile south of the Forest Service closure. Bushwhack straight up a ridge west-northwest to the summit ridge.

SANGRES

Mount Lindsey (14,042') was known as Old Baldy until renamed in 1954 for Malcolm Lindsey, a devoted leader of the Denver Juniors Group in the Colorado Mountain Club. To climb it, follow the trail up the Huerfano River about 4.5 miles south of the forest boundary and 0.5 mile past the Lily Lake turnoff. A trail of sorts can be found in the first draw coming into Huerfano River from the left. You follow this and climb 2 miles to the ridge saddle, at 12,500'. From here you climb 0.25 mile northeast to the higher ridge, at 13,150', and then southeast to the top.

Iron Nipple (13,480') and the centennial, **Peak 13,828'** northeast of it, can be visited from the same 13,150' ridge saddle. Stay right of any obstacles. Jim Schofield describes a climb of these two summits along with others from Huerfano Valley in the February 1972 *T&T,* and pronounces them his favorites. Little **Peak 13,081'** sits astride the ridge between giants Blanca and Lindsey. To reach it from Lindsey's 12,500' saddle, contour south and east until well past the towers and then straight north up the slope. **Peak 12,915'**, on a narrow northwest spur from Iron Nipple, is a showcase from down valley and is sometimes mistaken for the latter. Well guarded by cliffs, it goes by a gulley on the northwest side, by leaving the trail to Lindsey just before treeline. Once on the ridge, simpler slopes lead southeast 0.25 to the rocky summit.

Blanca Group

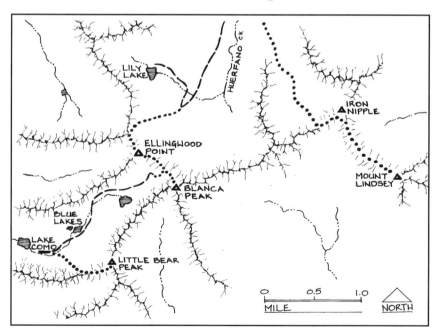

Blanca Peak and Ellingwood Point   *H. L. Standley*

Blanca Peak (14,345') shows a fine steep north face to this valley. Blanca and **Ellingwood Point** (14,042') may be climbed together in a long and difficult day. For a party of any size, the best route proceeds up the **Lily Lake Trail**. Proceed 1.6 miles up the trail to the southern most bend in the trail at 11,600', an area with good campsites and cabin ruins. Leave the trail and head west-southwest toward a low point on the north-south ridge running north off Ellingwood. Go up loose talus and grassy ledges reaching steeper slabs near the saddle. Work your way along the west side of the ridge on grassy ledges until you can gain the summit ridge up a steep rock pitch north-northwest of the summit. Note this point for your descent. From the top of Ellingwood, it is a short 0.5 mile to Blanca's summit. Smaller groups with technical abilities can have good and not too slow rope play at the right edge of Blanca's north face, where there is a couloir and rib combination. Experienced mountaineers armed with a rope can enjoy the northeast ridge to Blanca (Gash Ridge) returning over Ellingwood as noted above. To reach the ridge, leave the Huerfano at or north of where it bends west to Lily Lake, and head directly up the ridge to the south on good rock to a sub-peak at 13,400'. The exposed but firm ridge west soon reaches the Gash where you may drop 50' into the notch on rope and climb up two roped pitches over smooth sandy rock. Traverse south 150' below the summit to finish up a couloir.

Mount Lindsey   *H. L. Standley*

Blanca/US-160 Access:

At this writing, the traditional southern route to Blanca is closed. Permission is not being given because of problem campers and climbers. Contact the San Luis Valley Ranches Headquarters in Alamosa or the caretakers in Blanca if you want to see if this policy has changed. The traditional approach goes north-northeast from the west edge of Blanca on Smith Road-Cedar Road. About 0.5 mile short of Arrowhead Lodge, about 5.5 miles from US-160, there is a road off left (north) which soon deteriorates to 4WD. The route keeps right as the road winds up the valley, and in about 3 miles comes to a cabin and mine. The trail, starting left of the cabin, climbs along the left side of a dry wash to a ridge, crosses that, and continues to climb along the right side of Blanca Creek. In a mile or more, it crosses and doubles back to a ruined cabin west of the creek. There is good camping here and also at timberline. There is a choice of routes from near the head of the valley. The usual one goes east to a saddle on the Hamilton-Blanca ridge, and up that. **Hamilton Peak** (13,658') is about 0.4 mile south of the saddle.

Little Bear Peak (14,037') is also climbed from this camp. Go only a short way toward the basin from the cabins, and then left up south slopes and along a rotten ridge to the summit. You can also get up Little Bear from a camp about 2 miles farther up, near timberline in Blanca Creek drainage. By crossing a rock field west-southwest you come into a long couloir. Go up the couloir to South Little Bear, then along the ridge, just west of the crest, to the summit.

SANGRES

Hwy-150 Access:

Lake Como, on the west side of the massif, gives a jeep road access to both Blanca and Little Bear which involves less altitude and mileage for climbs. From US-160, 7 miles west of Blanca (15 east of Alamosa) drive north on Hwy-150 3.2 miles toward the Great Sand Dunes National Monument. Turn northeast and follow the road 2 to 3 miles. From this point an exceedingly rough and hazardous 4WD road climbs about 5 miles more up Holbrook Canyon to Lake Como at 11,750'. A trail climbs another 2,000' to the valley head. **Blanca Peak** is on the right, and **Ellingwood Point** (14,042') on the left of the 13,750' saddle to the north. To climb **Little Bear**, which is only 1 mile east of Lake Como, keep up valley about 0.5 mile from the lake and then head south to a notch on the ridge. Angle down on the south side of the ridge and into a wet bowling alley couloir, then up that to the summit, staying left in the couloir. Ellingwood Point honors Albert Ellingwood, the first Colorado climber to try peaks the hard way. A Rhodes scholar, he had learned balance climbing in England's Lake District.

Able climbers have sometimes done the full ridge between Blanca and Little Bear. It is rickety and gives us the impression that it must be held together.

The Zapata Ranch entrance is about 12 miles north from US-160 on Hwy-150, and 1 mile south of Sixmile Lane, the road to the Dunes from Mosca on Hwy-17.

Rappel off Little Bear Peak   *Robert E. Thompson*

SANGRES

Two trails go east from this vicinity: one up Raspberry Canyon, connecting with the Huerfano Trail and giving access to California Peak, and one up South Zapata Creek to **South Zapata Lake**.

Twin Peaks (13,580' and 13,534') are about a mile up the South Zapata Lake basin on the right (west) side on quite climbable grades. To climb **Peak 13,660'**, go past the lake to where you can climb northeast up steep talus to the narrow southeast ridge. Blanca Peak, which is 2 crow miles southeast from the lake, has a feasible route from here that includes Ellingwood Point. Go southeast and east-northeast a mile to the ridge crest at 13,200' and then climb as from the preferred large party route from the east (see Huerfano River Access above).

La Veta Pass/US-160 Access:

Mount Mestas (11,569') and **Rough Mountain** (11,138') flank US-160 on the route from I-25 to **La Veta Pass**. Mount Mestas, named for a La Veta (town) soldier lost in combat, is so near and so conspicuous that it must have been climbed or a least tried a number of times on impulse from the road. The best route takes off from a mile short (southeast) of the pass at 9,200', and bushwhacks 1.5 miles east-southeast to the 10,600' saddle between Mestas and Rough. Rough is close at your left; Mestas, steep at first, becomes a 1.5 mile ridge walk.

Wet Mountains

Jurisdiction:
San Isabel NF, San Carlos Ranger District
Map area reference:
Page 94
Maps:
USGS: *Badito Cone, Bear Creek, Beulah, Curley Peak, Hardscrabble Mountain, Mount Tyndall, Royal Gorge, Rye, San Isabel, St Charles Peak, Westcliffe, Wetmore*
Forest Service: *San Isabel NF*

These mountains are a short north-northwest trending range; they represent a southward structural continuation of the Front Range. The range is bordered on the east by a thrust fault along which the core rocks, largely Precambrian granites and metamorphics, were shoved up and eastward over the younger flanking sedimentary rocks. The western edge of the Wet Mountains consists in part of a series of steeply upturned sedimentary rocks which have been faulted. Tertiary volcanic rocks and Quaternary alluvial deposits obscure the western border structure of the northern half of the range. Greenhorn Mountain, at the south end, is a large anticlinal structure.

The range is the broad 45 mile wide frontal ridge seen from I-25 between Pueblo and Walsenburg. Except for a short crest at the south end, it is all below timberline; an area of woods, meadows, campgrounds, brooks, and a few lakes. There are two state highways which cross the range: Hwy-165 northwest from Rye, and Hwy-96 from Wetmore to Westcliife. The latter gives a fine look across at the Sangre de Cristo Range.

There are several trails in the range whose moderate ups and downs are well-suited to horsebacking. In general these are open to 2-wheel and snow vehicles.

Greenhorn Mountain, or Cuerno Verde, highest in the range, recalls a confrontation in 1779 between the Governor of New Mexico, Juan Bautista de Anza, and the Comanche Greenhorn. On his journey to dispose of Greenhorn, de Anza became the first white man to enter the south-central ranges of Colorado.

South Range Access:

There are two main dirt roads in the southern section of the range. Begin on the Ophir Creek Road (FSR-400), which leaves Hwy-165 at Ophir Creek Picnicground, 6.7 miles northwest of **Lake San Isabel**, and travel 8 miles to the top of Promontory Divide. The Gardner and Greenhorn Roads begin here. The Gardner Road runs down off the southwest side to Hwy-69 near Gardner. The

Greenhorn Road (FSR-403) runs south-southeast parallel to the range crest all the way to the west side of North Peak, 0.3 mile south of **Blue Lakes**, where it is closed off.

From mile 2.1 on the Greenhorn Road, there is a close approach to the well-timbered **St Charles Peak** (11,784'). You go by way of the St Charles Trail and have a 2 mile walk and short climb. The other terminus of the trail is on Hwy-165, 2.7 miles south-southeast of Ophir Creek, and 0.75 mile north of Greenhill Divide. St Charles Peak is 5 miles from that (east) side access.

Greenhorn Mountain (12,349') is a 2.5 mile climb from the south end of Greenhorn Road, at the upper end of Greenhorn Trail. To treat it as a mountain, climb up to it from the west end of Rye on the Greenhorn Trail, which starts at 7,475', and takes you 7 miles up Greenhorn Creek to the road. You are at the north end of the 4-bump summit ridge, and can either flank it on an abandoned road for a couple miles and then climb up, or follow the ridge to Greenhorn, 1.5 miles south-southeast.

The South Creek Trail starts at the south boundary of Pueblo Mountain Park, 2 miles south-southwest of Beulah on Hwy-76, and bears west on an old road back of Walters Ranch. It runs for 10 miles to Lion Park, 0.7 mile north-northwest of Greenhill Divide. A branch of this good trail runs into Squirrel Creek.

North Range Access:

The northern summits of the range are easily accessible from FSR-143, which can be reached from the north at Canon City on US-50, or from the south at Silver Cliff on Hwy-96. The most straight forward approach begins at the Fourth Street viaduct in Canon City. Go south on Fourth Street approximately 1 mile to a sharp left bend in the road; then make an immediate right onto Fremont Co Rd-143 (Oak Creek Rd). Continue south and enter the national forest after 7 miles, where the road changes its designation to FSR-143.

One mile beyond, at a blind curve in the road, is the trailhead to Stultz Trail, a popular point to begin the climb west to **Tanner Peak** (9,351') and **Curley Peak** (9,622'). The Stultz Trail intersects Tanner Trail several miles up. Tanner Trail, which takes off from FSR-143 3 miles beyond the Stultz Trailhead, is an alternate approach to the same peaks.

FSR-143 continues to the forest boundary on the west side of the range, where it changes back again to Fremont Co Rd-143. Rd-143 nears its jurisdictional limit at the Custer County line where it is nearly 20 miles to Silver Cliff. The road network changes its nomenclature several times, and ends as Rd-255 at Silver Cliff on Hwy-96.

Spanish Peaks

Jurisdiction:
San Isabel NF, San Carlos Ranger District

Map area reference:
Page 94

Maps:
USGS: *Cuchara, Fishers Peak, Spanish Peaks, Cucharas Pass, Herlick Canyon, Starkville*
Forest Service: *San Isabel NF*

These visually paired mountains are a little farther east than Pikes Peak, so share with it the honor of being the first seen by people who come to southern Colorado from the east. Indians called the pair the Wahatoya, breasts of the world. As you approach them, you see the radiating dikes which run along for miles, and usually more or less line up with the summits. The dikes came when the area was cracked in many places by an intrusive mass that forced its way toward the surface from beneath. The summit rocks are Tertiary intrusives. The dikes at Stonewall are a part of this system.

Once there was a trail that circled all that mass, an almost closed figure 8, pinched close together under the saddle between the peaks. The trail was reportedly 29 miles long. Some segments were roads; there were several roads and trails that came to it from down below. Only pieces of it are now accessible; there is little continuity.

La Veta/Hwy-12 Access:

The Spanish Peaks are best reached off Hwy-12, which connects south and east from US-160 through La Veta to I-25 at Trinidad. The high point of Hwy-12 is at 9,941' **Cucharas Pass**. From here FSR-415 bears generally east over 11,248' **Cordova Pass** (formerly Apishapa Pass), giving a close approach to the West Spanish Peak. FSR-415 then descends to a junction with I-25 at Aguilar.

The **Wahatoya Trail** starts from mile 7 on the Wahatoya Creek Road, which dead ends about 8 miles south from the town of La Veta on Hwy-12. The trail climbs 2,000' to the 10,300' saddle between the two peaks, then descends to the road in South Fork Trujillo Creek (the road access is closed below), where it meets the old Spanish Peaks Trail. The Peaks Trail at one time led around the south and east flank of the East Spanish Peak to a long exit road down Bear Creek to Walsenburg. In the opposite direction, it went west-southwest to the Apishapa Creek Picnic ground on Apishapa Pass Road (FSR-415). Much of this trail is on private property, with no public access, and is not maintained.

The well-maintained **Apishapa Trail** runs northwest from Apishapa Creek Picnic Ground, on the downhill side of the Apishapa Pass Road, to the West Peak Trail.

East Spanish Peak (12,683') is easily climbed from the saddle between the peaks. **West Spanish Peak** (13,626') can be climbed from the same saddle, but is usually approached by Hwy-12 and the Cordova Pass or Apishapa Pass Road (FSR-415). The West Peak Trail takes you northeast 2 miles to the start of the climbing ridge, where you are on rocks most of the way.

Trinidad/I-25 Access:

Fishers Peak (9,586') is the highest of the late Tertiary or Quaternary lava flow mesas east of I-25. Its block top is detached from Fishers Peak Mesa (Raton Mesa) to form an abrupt though flat summit. It is visible from far north, and conspicuous south of Walsenburg. The approach is from I-25 about 2 miles south of Starkville, 4.5 miles north of Morley, where a jeep road goes southeast up Clear Creek. Go up Clear Creek about 0.5 mile, and take the left fork to Bell Tank. Climb north to the ridge and east to the summit. At the top, where you are confronted by vertical rock, you can find a chimney to break through. It's a good fall climb, with Persian carpet colors to compensate you for having to push the oak brush around. See Starkville and Fishers Peak USGS Quads.

Jump!   *David Anschicks*

Culebra Range

Jurisdiction:
San Isabel NF, San Carlos Ranger District

Map area reference:
Page 94

Maps:
USGS: *Cuchara, Cucharas Pass, Culebra Peak, El Valle Creek, McCarty Park, Ojito Peak, Stonewall, Taylor Ranch, Torres, Trinchera Peak*
Forest Service: *San Isabel NF*

Culebra is Spanish for snake, a name first given to a creek in the area. The range runs south 30 miles from La Veta Pass to the New Mexico line, with the high section centering south of the middle.

The west slope of the Culebras is on the Sangre de Cristo Grant, the vast tract which includes the lower Trinchera Ranch. It was deeded in the 1840's by Governor Armijo of Santa Fe to Narcisco Beaubien and Stephen Lee of Taos. Narcisco was a 12 year-old boy, Lee a sheriff and distiller of Taos Lightning; they received the grant for no other reason than that they asked for it. When both were killed by Indians, Beaubien's father inherited his son's share, and bought out Lee's heirs for $100. In 1867 ex-Governor William Gilpin of Colorado and associates bought his grant, and divided it into the Costilla and Trinchera Estates, the better to peddle it to colonists in Europe. Their London-published promotion books are lavishly illustrated and one contains the statement that the San Luis Valley never gets cold!

The Culebra peaks are not difficult climbs, but access routes are limited due to private property. Do not use any routes without checking access rights. On the west side there is a jeep road in to McCarty Park, but this is north of the high section. There are some long trail approaches, but all through private land, and closed.

San Luis Valley Side/Hwy-152 Access:

Culebra Peak (14,047') has been traditionally climbed from the west side. This is possible only from the Taylor Ranch, which with the Forbes Trinchera property adjoining it to the north, controls the full length of the high part of the Culebra Range on this side. Sale of the ranch in 1999 has closed access. Contact the CMC office for updated information. In the hope that this traditional access will reopen for climbers, the following route description applies.

From San Luis, Colorado's oldest town, drive southeast on Hwy-152 to Chama. Go east from Chama, and immediately after crossing Culebra Creek, turn off

SANGRES

right. At the "T" in the road, 0.6 mile south, turn east again, and keeping right, you will reach the Taylor Ranch in 2.7 miles. At the foreman's house, you pay a head fee and get instructions for reaching timberline camp. The road is more steep than rough, and some conventional cars can make it.

About 4 miles from the ranch house, the road forks, with the left branch dropping to Culebra Creek and Whiskey Pass Road. Continue on the center fork east to water at 11,700'.

For the climb, angle southeast 1.25 miles to the 13,200' saddle and follow the main ridge line to summit. **Red Mountain** (13,908') is an easy conquest a mile south along the ridge. On the return, you skirt left of the Culebra summit. **Peak 13,565'** is a mile north of Culebra's east summit.

Routes to several other peaks north of Culebra are also within the Taylor Ranch domain, and require permission and use of the Whiskey Pass Road. Here we give the string of peaks which can be reached this way, all on the El Valle Creek Quad.

Mariquita (13,405') the northernmost, is approachable on the Whiskey Pass Road up El Valle Creek. From the end of the road, go about 2 miles northeast along the left (north fork) trail to the divide west of De Anza Peak. Mariquita is another 2 miles in the same (northeast) direction, the last 0.75 mile of the way on the range crest. **De Anza Peak** (13,333') is about 1 mile due east of the end of the left (north fork) trail.

To get to **Whiskey Pass** from where the road ends in El Valle Creek, take the left (north fork) trail, and after about a mile there is another fork in the trail. Take the right fork, which runs south around the hill into the south fork El Valle Creek. This trail continues up into the basin under the 12,550' Whiskey Pass, giving access to De Anza Peak and **Beaubien Peak** (13,184'), 0.5 mile south of the pass.

Culebra Creek, route of the Whiskey Pass Road, splits about 8 miles east of Chama. The north fork, with the road's extension, is El Valle Creek. The south fork is Carneros Creek, formerly used to approach Culebra Peak. Carneros has a left fork, Bernardino Creek, with a trail in it climbing about halfway from Culebra Creek to the range crest.

From the trail's end to **Francisco Peak** (13,135'), is a climb up the valley 0.5 mile then 2 miles northeast. **Lomo Liso Peak** (13,128') is 0.75 mile south-south-west back along the crest ridge from Francisco. **Miranda Peak** (13,468') is about 2 miles east 30 degrees south, on the east side of the end of the Bernardino Creek Basin. There are few places on the west side of the range where the cliffs forbid access.

Purgatoire Peak (13,676') and its 13,466' north twin are a handsome ending to the main range string. They lie only a mile apart at the head of San Francisco Creek, but are separated by a 12,827' saddle. The approach, subject to Taylor Ranch permission, is from the townsite of San Francisco, where you drive a jeep road 2 miles southeast then 4 more miles east up Alamosito Creek. Then bushwhack to the end of the valley to the saddle. See La Valle and Culebra Peak Quads. **Vermejo Peak** (13,723') is about 1.5 miles northeast of Purgatoire's north twin.

East Side/Hwy-12 Access:

At the north end of the range the approaches are from Hwy-12, which connects La Veta and Trinidad.

Road-410 (FSR-410) leaves Hwy-12 a mile south of La Veta and goes about 9 miles by way of Indian Creek into the wooded country near La Veta Railroad Pass. The **Indian Trail** takes off about 2.25 miles west of the forest boundary and runs down about 3.5 miles to where it is blocked at the Forbes Trinchera boundary along the range crest. After about a mile break due to private property, the trail continues down along the east side of the range to Blue Lake Campground.

The trail continues south from Blue Lake Campground about a mile to where the North Fork Trail comes in from the southeast. It is about 5 miles down this trail to the upper end of the North Fork (Purgatoire) Road. This road climbs 6 miles west and northwest from North Lake, which is 15 miles south of Cuchara and 7.5 miles north of Stonewall Gap on Hwy-12.

The road in to **Blue Lake** lets you approach the higher north-end peaks. It turns off Hwy-12 about 4 miles south of Cuchara and climbs 4 miles to 10,400'.

Teddys Peak (12,575') is a climb of 2,100', either by ridge or by valley, from 0.5 mile north of the Bear Lake Campground. Teddy Roosevelt hunted in the Trinchera country.

Trinchera Peak (13,517') is the northern one, prominent as a symmetrically rounded summit seen from as far off as I-25. There is an old mine jeep road almost to its summit, winding about 4 miles south and southwest from Blue Lake Campground. Trinchera combines well with 12,955' English Saddle, a mile north along the ridge.

Leaning North Peak (13,100') and **Leaning South Peak** (13,203') so called from their appearance from the east, are reached from the saddle south of Blue Lake on North Fork Trail. **Mount Maxwell** (13,335') is directly up the ridge from Potato Patch Campground at the end of the North Lake Road. A trail zig-zags up the ridge to the top. **Quatro** (13,487') named for the "IV" shaped snow-banks on its east side, is a mile north of Maxwell along the ridge.

The boundary between national forest land on the north and the CF&I holdings on the south, runs from Mount Maxwell on a line about east 23 degrees south. Thus the Whiskey Pass Road and all others to the south are within private prop-erty and closed to the public.

The east road toward **Whiskey Pass** goes west 6 miles from 0.5 mile south of **Monument Lake,** and dead ends on the side of Whiskey Creek at 10,218', where it joins with 2 trails. The right-hand one goes north and west 4 miles to the head of Whiskey Creek's north branch, and continues way up the cirque to 12,300' on the south face of Mariquita. This peak is a pull of 0.5 mile north and De Anza is about the same distance southwest. See El Valle and Stonewall USGS Quads. The left-hand trail from the road end doubles back south, and splits after about 0.5 mile. Its right branch goes up to 10,900' in a middle branch of Whiskey, but too far below the range crest to help much. The left trail goes 3.5 miles up the south fork close under Whiskey Pass. Beaubien Peak is 0.75 mile south-south-west up a steep slope.

At a point 1.5 miles down the Whiskey Road from its upper end there is anoth-er trailhead. This trail winds off south and west. A side trail climbs west to **Lost Lake** at 11,525'. When it turns east, this trail connects with the jeep trail system west from Duling Lodge. Duling Lodge is a mile south of Stonewall Gap, and behind the wall. A jeep road runs west from the lodge up Duling Creek 3.5 miles to a junction. The right fork turns north 2 miles to **Duling Lakes**, near the link-age point with the trail from Whiskey Pass Road. The left fork goes west and winds up a ridge and into Abbot Creek.

A jeep road runs from Duling Lodge up Abbot Creek, and after about 4.5 miles branches. The north branch connects with the Duling Creek trails. The south branch connects with a trail that climbs the ridge to Culebra, and with others that follow Las Vigas Creek, Vallejos Creek, and the South Fork of the Purgatoire.

THE PARK RANGE

Looking for spring snow, Tenmile Range   *Mike Endres*

Park Range (Northern)

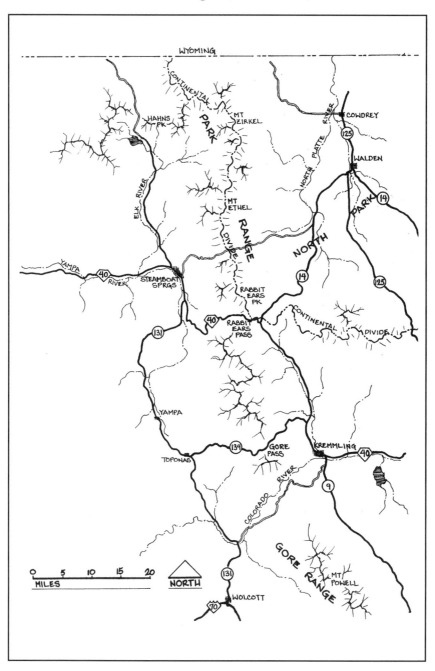

The Park Range

The Park Range has the distinction of being one of the major mountain systems in the state, although the tribute is rarely recognized. Starting out as the Sierra Madres in Wyoming, the Park Range continues in Colorado for 180 miles bearing south-southeast to its end at the Arkansas River just below Salida. Unfortunately, the range is deprived of the appearance and continuity of a mighty mountain chain because of several geologic interruptions. The first breach is at dramatic Gore Canyon where the Colorado River has channeled through on the western edge of Middle Park. The next is at Tenmile Canyon and another functional separation of the range. Finally, at Hoosier Pass the range is visually disconnected where the Continental Divide crosses it on the perpendicular. These obstacles effectively cut the range into four smaller ones; the so-called North Park, Gore, Tenmile, and Mosquito Ranges.

Large sections of the range are exposed to the state's great parks - North Park, Middle Park and South Park - providing expansive views of its craggy summits from afar and giving the range its name. Early explorers and nature seekers were intrigued and mystified by these geologic depressions in the midst of the towering mountains, and they wrote romantically about the mountains and the recessed plateaus as integral but contradictory forms. One of South Park's early English explorers, George Ruxton, knew the place as the home of abundant wildlife and nomadic bands of Utes in the summer. At that time the trappers had already given it the name of Bayou Salado, for the salt springs at its southern border. And nearly thirty years later as Helen Hunt Jackson gazed out over the still deserted plain, she described how the immensity of the place compounded the views so that "the effect to the eye is as if there lay only mountains to the very outermost edge of the world."

The heavily mineralized Tenmile and Mosquito Ranges on the southern end of the chain were some of the earliest mountains in the state to be prospected and developed. Today, the transformed mining and ranching communities that flank the Park Range quarry a different sort of commodity, no less enthusiastically than a century before. However, in contrast to those early-day vagabonds, the year-round recreation areas and glitzy resorts that have grown up along the Park Range do offer a unique and comfortable base for today's mountaineer to rise above.

For most of its length, this north-south chain of mountains is largely overlooked by serious mountaineers and peakbaggers, with the exception of several modest fourteeners in the Tenmile and Mosquito Ranges. And despite its proximity to the metro area, the Gore Range is strangely untrampled even though it has some of the best climbing in the state outside of the San Juan and Elk Mountains.

North Section

Jurisdiction:
Routt NF, Hahns Peak/Bears Ears and Parks Ranger Districts

Map area reference:
Page 132

Maps:
USGS: *Boettcher Lake, Buffalo Pass, Davis Peak, Farewell Mountain, Floyd Peak, Hahns Peak, Mount Ethel, Mount Zirkel, Pearl, Pitchpine Mountain, Rabbit Ears, Rocky Peak, Teal Lake, West Fork Lake*
Forest Service: *Routt NF*

The north section of the Park Range is the higher southern extension of the Sierra Madres of Wyoming. As it reaches into Colorado, it forms the western boundary of North Park, extending some 50 miles south to Rabbit Ears Pass. The Continental Divide follows the range crest, separating the Yampa from the North Platte drainages. The summits, some of which are remnants of a Tertiary age erosion surface, are lower in height than the Rawahs that border North Park on the east. Three of the highest named peaks exceed 12,000'. The geologic structure of the range is that of an asymmetrical, faulted anticline, similar to other north-south oriented ranges in Colorado. The high peaks are composed of Precambrian age metamorphic and igneous rocks.

Most Colorado climbers overlook the north section of the Park Range in search of higher, more accessible peaks further south. Despite the fact that a number of excellent technical climbing routes have been documented in the Mount Zirkel-Sawtooth Range area, the area remains little known and does not attract many climbers. Ascents of the higher peaks, with the exception of Mount Zirkel, have not attained popularity.

The naming of lakes, streams and parks appears to have taken precedence over that of mountain peaks. Most of the geographic features were named by the Forest Service. Routt NF Rangers Ray Peck and Percy J. Paxton are known to have named many of the alpine lakes (using mostly women's names) and other features in the range. Many features were also named by early homesteaders, miners and ranchers. The Fortieth Parallel Survey, under the guidance of Clarence King, conducted the first mapping expedition in the region, and named both Mount Zirkel and Mount Ethel.

The main stretch of high country (Mount Zirkel to Mount Ethel) is in the Mount Zirkel Wilderness, 30 miles long and 6 to 11 miles wide. The only road across the range is over 10,325' Buffalo Pass near the south end. It connects Hebron, 11 miles southwest of Walden on Hwy-14, with FSR-60 running northeast out of the center of Steamboat Springs. Road conditions vary from year to year: high clearance or 4WD vehicles are recommended.

The Forest Service maintains an extensive trail system in the range. One can hike parallel to the crest on the Wyoming and Grizzly-Helena Trails, or cross the range at various places on trails that are oriented perpendicular to the range. The Forest Service has implemented overnight camping restrictions at Gilpin, Gold and Three Island Lakes due to adverse environmental impacts from overuse. All campsites must be at least 0.25 mile from these lakes.

The **Wyoming Trail** (#1101) extends from the Wyoming state line (9,260') south to Round Lake (10,050'), some 50 miles in length. Segments of the trail that are above timberline, and follow the divide through the Mount Zirkel Wilderness, offer the venturesome spectacular scenery in all directions. Hikers should be prepared for highly variable trail conditions. North of Lost Ranger Peak, in the large boggy area, no trail is discernible. By contrast, motorized vehicles are permitted on the segment from the Wyoming line south to the **Manzanares Lake Trail** crossing. The Wyoming Trail was initially used from 1910 to 1916 by sheep ranchers near Rawlins, Wyoming, as a driveway to market at Steamboat Springs and later as a driveway to reach grazing allotments located in the Routt NF. With the decline of these allotments over the years, today the trail is used primarily for recreation by backpackers hiking the Continental Divide.

The **Grizzly-Helena Trail** (#1126) runs north-south parallel to the range along the east flank. Much of this trail is being designated part of the Continental Divide Scenic Trail along the northern section of the Park Range. To lessen visitor impact in the Mount Zirkel Wilderness, the Forest Service decided to divert CD trekkers from the crest of the range through the heart of the wilderness, to the east flank via the Grizzly-Helena Trail. The trail traverses approximately 17.5 miles from the North Fork of the North Platte River (8,600'), south to the end of Teal Lake, FSR-615 (8,800'). Many trails extend westward from the Grizzly-Helena to the crest of the range. To access the trailhead at the north end, take County Rd-6 18 miles west and north from Cowdrey to Pearl, turn left on County Rd-6A, and continue to Big Creek Lakes, and on southward on a jeep road around the east side of the lakes.

The **Big Creek Trail** (#1125) begins at the Big Creek Lakes Campground at 9,000', and continues westward into the Mount Zirkel Wilderness to the Main Fork Trail along the Main Fork of the Encampment River, approximately 9 miles. At mile 6.5 from Big Creek Lakes Trailhead, Seven Lakes may be accessed 0.1 mile south. Directions to the trailhead are the same as for the north end of the Grizzly-Helena Trail, except when you reach Big Creek Lakes, turn right and proceed to the trailhead on the west side of the lakes.

PARK RG

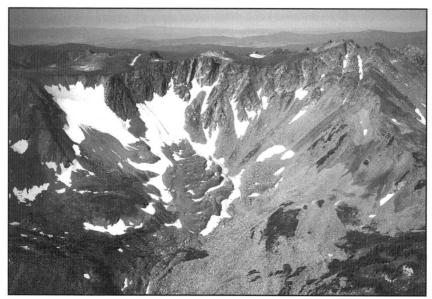

Mount Zirkel   *Russ Allen*

Fish Creek Trail (#1102) extends approximately 10.5 miles between the Fish Creek Falls Trailhead, 3 miles east of Steamboat Springs (7,400'), and the Dumont Lake Campground (10,000') on the old Rabbit Ears Pass Road. Numerous lakes near the Continental Divide, including Long, Round, Fishhook and Dumont are accessed from this trail. To reach Dumont Lake Trailhead, turn off the old Rabbit Ears Pass Road to the stone monument near Dumont Lake Campground. From the stone monument you can hike or continue north on 4WD FSR-311 to the old Base Campground. The trail continues north and then west to Fish Creek Falls.

North Park Access:

Expansive **North Park** is centered around the Jackson County seat of Walden, from which Hwy-14 radiates east over Cameron Pass and southwest over Rabbit Ears Pass on US-40. Hwy-125 crosses from southeast at Willow Creek Pass to the northwest at the Wyoming border. North Park's unpaved county roads can pose a mud problem when sufficiently wet.

Mount Ethel (11,924') ". . .is visited best on horseback, and with a camp outfit and packhorse. . ." according to a Routt NF brochure published in 1917. Today, the best approach for reaching this seldom climbed peak is from the **Rainbow Lake Trail** (#1130), which begins at the Livingston Park Trailhead. To reach the trailhead from Walden, go west 5 miles on Jackson Co Rd-12, then straight ahead 4.5 miles on Rd-18, then left 1.7 miles on Rd-5, then straight ahead 3 miles on Rd-22. Then take the left fork for 1.1 miles, then the right fork for 2.9 miles to the trailhead. For the last couple of miles, high clearance vehicles are advised. From the trailhead at 8,750' Livingston Park, follow the Rainbow Lake Trail to the intersection with the Grizzly-Helena Trail. Continue approximately 6.6 miles on the Rainbow Lake Trail past the Rainbow Lakes to **Upper Slide Lake** (10,740'), a good area for camping. To summit, continue north on Rainbow Lake Trail beyond Upper Slide Lake. Upon reaching the tundra above the trail switchbacks, go west, then south up Ethel's gentle north slope.

Lost Ranger Peak (11,974') can be best approached from North Park on the Rainbow Lake Trail (#1130), 10.5 miles from the Livingston Park Trailhead, or on the **Lost Ranger Peak Trail** (#1131), 8.5 miles from the trailhead at Red Canyon Reservoir. The Wyoming Trail (#1101) passes just east of the summit, affording easy access to CD trekkers. The story of the peak's name, as related by FS personnel, states that ". . .a ranger who was lost in an early fall snowstorm was located on Lost Ranger Peak by one of the rangers from an adjoining district. The Hahns Peak district rangers have for years joked that it was the North Park district ranger who was lost and found by the Hahns Peak ranger. Needless to say, the North Park rangers have told the same story, only the Hahns Peak ranger was the man who was lost."

Flattop Mountain (12,118'), second highest peak in the range, lies directly on the Continental Divide. It is best approached from the North Park side. Follow County Rd-12 approximately 11.5 miles west of Walden, then go left at a "T" for 2 miles and through the Lone Pine Ranch to the National Forest boundary. Continue west on FSR-640 to the Grizzly-Helena Trailhead on the north side of the road. From the trailhead, follow the Grizzly-Helena Trail (#1126) 1.3 miles north to the **Bear Creek Trail** (#1180). Go northwest 4 miles on the Bear Creek Trail to **Ute Pass** (11,000') and follow the Continental Divide ridge north 1 mile to the long flat summit. CD trekkers may traverse this peak by staying on the divide between Red Dirt and Ute Passes.

Rabbit Ears Peak (10,654') is a northern Colorado landmark located 2 miles north of **Rabbit Ears Pass** on US-40. The conspicuous rabbit ears, which can be seen from near Kremmling to the northern edges of North Park, are a vestige of late Tertiary basalt flows that once covered the area. From the Rabbit Ears Pass marker, near Dumont Lake Campground, proceed north 0.3 mile, turn right on a jeep road for 2.6 miles as it meanders to the south base of the peak. At road's end, continue on the trail 100 yards to the most westerly basalt tower and on east to the adjacent pinnacles. Ascent of the tower and pinnacles requires technical climbing. However, one need not ascend these to enjoy excellent views in all directions.

PARK RG

Routt Co Rd-129 Access:

Routt Co Rd-129 begins just north of Steamboat Springs on US-40, and continues north and northwest to the Wyoming border. This route provides a main access to the west side of the range at the popular Slavonia Trailhead on FSR-400. To reach Slavonia, proceed 19 miles north from Steamboat Springs on Rd-129 to FSR-400. Turn right and continue northeast approximately 11.5 miles to the road's end.

Mount Zirkel (12,180'), highest peak in the range, is best approached from the west via the **Gilpin Lake Trail** (#1161). From the trailhead at Slavonia (8,480'), continue 4.5 miles to Gilpin Lake (10,338'). Good campsites exist around the lake; however, the Forest Service is now prohibiting overnight camping due to overuse. Bushwhack northeast up to the ridge, and north to the unnamed 12,006' point. Continue northeast on a ridge to a flattish area, then northwest to the summit. A good, slightly longer route begins just west of Slavonia on the **Gold Creek Trail** (#1150). Follow this trail past Gold Creek Lake 8 miles to **Red Dirt Pass** (11,570'), then west up slope to flattish area, and on 1.2 miles northwest to the summit. CD trekkers staying on the divide can best climb Zirkel from Red Dirt Pass after crossing, or before descending into, Fryingpan Basin. Although the rock is generally good, the north ridge route is not recommended for backpackers. Contrary to map information, public access is not available from the east at the Shaffer Ranch Trailhead. Steamboat Springs climbers Michael Covington and Kevin Rusk established a number of technical climbing routes on Zirkel's west side during the 1960's and 1970's. The most well-known include the Hummingbird, Flower Wall, and Window routes (all about 5.8). Zirkel's west side technical routes are best accessed from the Slavonia Trailhead via the Gilpin Lake Trail.

Big Agnes Mountain (12,059'), third highest in the range, is approached from the Slavonia Trailhead. Take the Gilpin Lake Trail (#1161) 1.2 miles to the trail junction at 9,040' where the **Mica Basin Trail** (#1162) bears left. Continue 2.5 miles on Mica Basin Trail until it turns west to climb out of the basin. Bushwhack 0.25 mile north to Mica Lake. Grassy areas around Mica Lake provide good camping. To summit, proceed east from Mica Lake into the cirque and north up Agnes' south slope. Scrambling and various technical climbing routes are also available on Big Agnes. Summit ridge traversing along the Sawtooth Range, of which Big Agnes is a part, and Titan Tower routes, are well-known.

Hahns Peak (10,839') is a laccolith located 7 miles southwest of the range crest. Intrusive igneous rock created a domed geologic structure that was subsequently eroded to the symmetrical landform we see today. Joseph Hahn, for whom the peak is named, discovered gold in the area in 1862. In the spring of 1866, after spending a long winter in his cabin near the base of the peak, he set out on an ill-fated attempt to reach civilization. Weak and exhausted from a lack of food, Hahn died of exposure on the bank of Muddy Creek near Kremmling. To reach the peak, travel north on Rd-129 from Steamboat Springs 32.5 miles to the hamlet of Columbine. At Columbine, turn right onto the rough, unmarked road and proceed southeast 1.6 miles to 9,400'. Leave your car here and proceed on foot up the jeep trail that zigzags up the west and north sides to within 0.25 mile of the fire lookout on the summit.

Hahns Peak   *Donna Kelley*

Park Range (Southern)

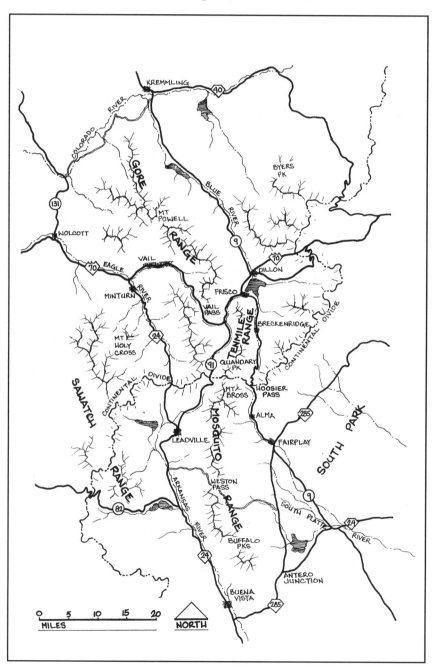

Gore Range

Jurisdiction:

White River NF, Holy Cross and Dillon Ranger Districts

Map area reference:

Page 140 and 152

Maps:

USGS: *Dillon, Frisco, Mount Powell, Piney Peak, Squaw Creek, Vail East, Vail Pass, Vail West, Willow Lakes*
Forest Service: *White River NF*

The Gore Range shortcuts 70 miles south across the big east bend of the Continental Divide, connecting Rabbits Ears Pass and Fremont Pass. Thus it is a slightly S-curved southern extension of the north section of the Park Range. It is cut through about 1/3 of the way down by the Gore Canyon of the Colorado River, and near the south end, by Vail Pass. Most of the high peaks are contained within the Eagles Nest Wilderness, and the range crest is the border between White River and Arapaho National Forests. The range is named after an Irish baronet, Sir St George Gore, who hunted in the West from 1854 to 1857. He outfitted himself in luxury, hired Jim Bridger as a guide, and with a party of 40, devastated the wildlife through much of the central Rocky Mountains. Although the range carries his name, the closest he came to the area was a pass from Middle Park to the Yampa Valley, which Jim Bridger later named "Gore's Pass". Sir St George's game was buffalo — he was not interested in the high peaks off to the south.

Geologically, the Gore mountains are a fault block range. The northern Gore peaks are metamorphic schist and gneiss produced from sedimentary rock. The central section is divided between schist and gneiss, prevalent on the east ridges, and granite up to the crest on the west side. The Willow Lakes section is granitic. Topographically, the Gore and Tenmile Ranges are linked with the westward edge of the Front Range to the east.

The range is more one of ridges than of separated peaks, but the ridges are generally strings of pinnacles and small peaks. There is a world of rock climbing, mostly a mixture of easy scrambling and route finding problems. Pitkin Lake, Willow Lake (Zodiac Spires) and Tenmile Canyon have seen most of the rock climbing activity. Major faces and ridges provide technical climbing opportunities. Almost all of the high peaks can be climbed without a rope by normal routes under good conditions. An ice axe should be carried on all early season climbs. Great care in descending the sometimes rotten rock, and good judgment in selecting routes, are of paramount importance for climbing in the Gore Range.

PARK RG

One of the Gore climbing patterns is to get up into one of the high cirques and then move along a length of the range near the crest, climbing from valley head to valley head, such as Joseph Kramarsic did throughout the 1980's. For ridge hopping, the Gore probably has no equal; you could spend any amount of time trying to keep along the top of any of several ridges, spinal or lateral.

There was almost none of the mining which provided roads up through the steep timbered valleys in other mountain areas. Though the range offers many trail hikes, and many destinations are heavily used, much of it still remains, as designated, wilderness. An aura of exploration and discovery still exists in these mountains, perhaps because many of the peaks in the interior of the range have been climbed only a handful of times. The CMC was instrumental in the early exploration of this range, with many first ascents from holding the annual summer outings of 1935 and 1948 in the range. The unusually system of assigning letter designations to the peaks was a result of a 1932 trip into the range by Carl Erickson and Edmund Cooper. They used it for indicating the peaks surrounding Black Creek basin and the CMC subsequently nurtured and expanded that system.

On the east side, the Gore Range is paralleled by the Blue River and Hwy-9. It is bordered on the south and west sides by I-70. The section of main interest, about 15 miles long, lies between Green Mountain and Dillon Reservoirs, with the range crest about 6-9 miles west of Hwy-9. Gravel and dirt roads from these highways provide access to the trailheads. Views of almost the entire range can be had from the top of Vail and Beaver Creek Ski Areas, and from the Ute Pass Road opposite Slate Creek.

EAST SIDE RANGE - Spring Creek Road Access:

The **Gore Range Trail** is 54.5 miles long, including the section identified as the Wheeler-Dillon Trail on many maps. The northern terminus is 0.5 mile north of Mahan Lake on the jeep road, and the southern is at Wheeler Flats across from Copper Mountain Resort. The trail runs along the east flank of the range largely below timberline around 10,000', and gives access behind the private properties on Hwy-9 to the canyons, the ridges between them and the lakes.

The Spring Creek Road (Grand Co Rd-10) runs west from Hwy-9 about 11 miles south of Kremmling or 28.9 miles north of Silverthorne on I-70 (exit 205). Note that logging roads can cause confusion and signs do change along this road. Shortly past the National Forest boundary (7 miles) turn right at the Mahan Lake turnoff onto Sheep Mountain Road. A left turn at the first Y and a right at the next, brings you to the Mahan Lake-Elliott Ridge junction, about 4.5 miles total. The left fork of this jeep road (FSR-1831) runs another 4 miles southeast to Mahan Lake. The right branch (Elliott Ridge Trail) is blocked to vehicles at Blue Lake but continues as a 5.5 mile walk route along Elliott Ridge almost to the top of **Meridian Peak** (12,426').

About a mile north of Meridian Peak, weak trails meet the **Elliott Ridge Trail** from both sides of the range. The one on the east side drops into upper Cataract Creek and connects by way of Mirror Lake and Upper Cataract Lake with the Gore Range Trail. The one on the west side (Soda Lakes Trail) crosses upper Meadow Creek and the ridge into Piney Creek above Piney Lake, with forks running off west and northwest into lower country.

The easiest, though long, east-side approach for climbs of **Eagles Nest** (13,400') and **Mount Powell** (13,560') begins at Blue Lake, goes along Elliott Ridge, then descends into the upper Cataract Creek valley, either by Mirror Trail or the southwest side of the valley. To climb Eagles Nest, descend and hike about 0.25 mile beyond a small lake, cross the creek, and pick a route east-northeast up steep slopes of broken rock to the low point of the Eagles Nest-Mount Powell ridge. Follow the ridge north to the summit.

For Mount Powell from the upper Cataract Creek valley, go upstream from the same small lake, and climb on grass and sheep trails toward the 12,040' pass (see Vail Village Access) at the head of the valley. A little below the pass, veer left towards a large gully that angles upward in a southeasterly direction. A cliff band one-third of the way up is easily climbed. Follow the upper gully to the summit plateau, then east to the summit. It is important for the descent to note the point where the gully and summit plateau meet.

EAST SIDE RANGE - Cataract Creek Access:

The most popular access route to the Gore Range Trail is from 8,630' **Cataract Lake**. Follow Hwy-9 16 miles north of Silverthorne (I-70 exit 205) and turn left onto Heeney Road (Rd-30). Continue 5.3 miles around the end of Green Mountain Reservoir, turn west onto County Rd-1725 and go 2.3 miles to the Cataract Creek Campground.

The **Surprise Trail** runs south 2.6 miles to the Gore Range Trail, meeting it a little below water lily covered Surprise Lake. **Eaglesmere Trail** is found by keeping right just past the campground for another 0.5 mile. It runs off west and south to the Gore Range Trail by a 3 mile route meeting it 0.5 mile east of the Eaglesmere Lakes. Combining the three trails makes a 10 mile circle hike with a 2,300' elevation gain. A very heavily used 2 mile trail circles Cataract Lake from a parking lot 0.25 mile beyond the Surprise Lake Trailhead.

From the Eaglesmere Trail junction, the Gore Range Trail heads northwest and west 4.5 miles to a junction north of Mahan Lake with the jeep road from the Spring Creek Road.

The Upper Cataract and Mirror Trails leave the **Gore Range Trail** just west of Surprise Lake and climb southwest. Upper Cataract Lake is located in the cirque on the north side of Eagles Nest. Mirror Trail continues southwest along the north side of Eagles Nest and then descends into the upper Cataract Creek valley. The trail continues west, becoming more difficult to follow past Mirror Lake, climbs to Elliott Ridge, and intersects with the Elliott Ridge Trail.

Eagles Nest (13,400') is the northwest high point of a rough curving ridge directly east of Meridian Peak. Climbs of Eagles Nest and Mount Powell can be made by using Eaglesmere, Surprise, Gore Range and Upper Cataract Trails, or from the north via Elliott Ridge (see Spring Creek Road Access). Once in the upper Cataract Creek valley, follow the route descriptions given under the Spring Creek access. Other routes lead from Dora Mountain and Upper Cataract Lake, but the route-finding is difficult. Kenneth Segerstrom, attempting a first ascent of Eagles Nest via the northwest ridge from the lake in 1933, was disappointed when he and his partner found a gun shell in a crevice near the top, believing it to be evidence of a previous ascent. Ormes observed that this was not conclusive, "crows and ravens being what they are."

To climb Powell from Eagles Nest, return to the low point of the south ridge and either stay on the ridge or drop west and contour the roughest part of the ridge, until scree gullies lead upward. The opposite direction, Powell to Eagles Nest, is much harder and should be attempted only by experienced technical climbers.

Mount Powell (13,560') is the high point of the range. It was first climbed by John Wesley Powell (probably from the Cataract Creek Valley) in 1868, a month after his ascent of Longs Peak, and a year before he boated the Colorado River. The standard route is now from Piney River (see Vail Village Access).

Dora Mountain (12,292') is a flat-topped ridge end overlooking Black Lake. The normal route is from the Gore Range Trail just west of Surprise Lake, where you can bushwhack south through timber up the broad, gradual slope. Hike south on the plateau above the Otter Creek cirque to Dora Lake and then east to the summit.

EAST SIDE RANGE - Brush Creek Trail Access:

The next access point off Hwy-9 to the Gore Range Trail is across from the pioneer cemetery, a short distance north of the County Rd-30/Hwy-9 junction at the end of Green Mountain Reservoir. The **Brush Creek Trail** climbs southwest to meet the Gore Range Trail at Brush Creek. From here, it is 1 mile north to the North Lost Lake Trail or 1 mile south to the South Lost Lake Trail. These both circle to Lost Lake and also provide access to upper Black Creek and **Guyselman Mountain** (13,120'), named for Summit County pioneer William Guyselman.

From the end of the trail at Lost Lake, bushwhack south along the west fork of Brush Creek to gain the northeast cirque of Guyselman and climb a talus slide to the upper east ridge and the summit. **Little Powell-Peak 0**, (12,920') sometimes mistaken for the real Powell, is the northernmost mountain on the ridge directly south of Black Lake. Its easiest route is from Lost Lake via the northeast ridge. To proceed the short distance to the near neighbor **Peak N** (13,121'), descend south along the ridge from Peak O, bypassing a couple gendarmes, then up the north ridge of Peak N. Peak N can also be combined with Guyselman Mountain by scrambling north from the saddle between the two.

From the Brush Creek Trail junction with the Gore Range Trail to Surprise Lake it is 6.5 miles and you cross Black Creek, and there is no public access along Black Creek in either direction. For upper Black Creek, follow a very good trail (not shown on the Mount Powell Quad) that leaves the North Lost Lake Trail about a mile from its junction with the Gore Range Trail and follows the canyon sidewall along the south side of Black Creek. Bushwhack upstream along the south fork for any number of routes on the peaks at the head of the Black Creek valley. For a sample of this wild area, try these climbs.

From the marshy area just below the unnamed lake at the head of the valley, bushwack north to the middle one of a trio of small lakes. Easy slopes lead on up to a 12,300' pass and access to Bubble Lake and the drainage of the middle fork. From the pass, **Peak 12,845'** is a short and simple climb up the east ridge. For harder **Peak 12,865'**, scramble the southwest ridge from the pass, staying to the right of the summit cliffs until you can swing left.

The peaks at the head of the valley are well armed with steep walls. One route to the ridge crest goes from the unnamed lake at 11,540'. Head west from the lake for the prominent snow couloir leading northwest up **Peak H** (13,080'). From here you can easily gain **Peak 13,129'**, also called Black Benchmark, and continue north to **Peak G** (13,240'), bypassing obstacles on the left.

Bubble Lake (11,250'), situated on an alpine bench at the head of the middle fork of Black Creek affords an ideal campsite for exploring this remote corner of the range. While one can bushwack the long approach up Black Creek, most interested parties have taken to coming over "Kneeknocker Pass" from the west (see Vail Village Access). From the pass, descend the snowfields for about a mile then contour southeast and up onto the bench.

Another bench above Bubble Lake holds an unnamed lake where several routes to the crest begin, mostly up steep snow, so bring an ice axe and possibly crampons. For **Peak F** (13,230') or **Peak G** (13,240'), climb the large permanent snowfield due south from the lake to the col between the two. Third class scrambling leads right for Peak F or left for Peak G, passing a false summit on the way. A steep couloir provides an interesting climb of the north face of **Peak E** (13,200').

PARK RG

Go west from the unnamed lake, then turn left up the couloir, popping out on the northwest ridge and a short finish. **Peak D** (13,047') goes easily from the saddle directly west from the lake on snow and talus.

EAST SIDE RANGE - Rock Creek/Boulder Creek/Slate Creek Access:

It is in Rock Creek that the only extensive mining in the Gore Range occurred. The Boss, Josie and Thunderbolt Mines produced silver from 1880 to 1920. The trailhead is reached by driving 8 miles north of Silverthorne (I-70 exit 205) on Hwy-9 to the Rock Creek Road (Co Rd-1350) and turning west across from the Blue River Campground. It is 3 miles to the trailhead and then 0.3 mile on an old road to the Gore Range Trail junction and 1.2 miles farther to the Boss Mine dumps.

Keller Mountain (13,085') climbs best from the Boss Mine dumps via the east ridge with some rock scrambling across the top of the northeast cirque before gaining the summit.

Peak R   *David Anschicks*

Former access points off Hwy-9 at Brush Creek, Squaw Creek, Hay Camp Creek and Slate Creek are now closed by private property. Boulder Creek (Co Rd-1376), 8 miles south of the pioneer cemetery on Hwy-9, is also private but you may use the **Boulder Creek Trail** by parking outside a private property sign and hiking 1.5 miles to where the road ends and a trail begins. Access to Boulder Lake is recommended from Rock Creek. Follow directions for Rock Creek Trailhead (above), turn right at the Rock Creek-Gore Range Trail junction and go north 1.8 miles then west on the overused trail to Boulder Lake. The trail continues to Upper Boulder Lake but tends to be indistinct and requires bushwhacking. The Boulder Creek valley is surrounded by rough peaks including the northeast facing cirque of Keller Mountain and **Peak Z** (13,245'). To climb the latter, ascend from Upper Boulder Lake northwest for 1.5 miles to the saddle on the southwest ridge. Climb this ridge to intersect the southeast ridge and scramble this to the top.

For **Peak Y** (13,085') ascend from the lake as for Peak Z, but instead of going for the saddle, follow the drainage west, then climb northwest to meet the southwest ridge of the peak for an easy ascent. A close neighbor on the range crest, **Peak 12,710'** is approached the same way but one continues west to the saddle on the south ridge and a short finish.

Peak 13,090', also called Mount Solitude by it's solitary first ascender, is one of the few peaks on the southern rim of Boulder Creek basin that is not too guarded by headwalls for a simple ascent from this side of the range. Continue up Boulder Creek from the upper lake to the last small lake nestled beneath the headwall. Climb to the left of the prominent east ridge and gain the crest by climbing the broad gulley. Attain the summit by way of the south ridge.

Access to the **Slate Creek Trail** must be made from Brush Creek or Rock Creek. Either way, it is a long hike to Slate Lake and Upper Slate Lake and the summits surrounding the valley. Even so, this is one of the most rewarding places in the Gores and worth the effort with interesting climbing possibilites. From the junction of the Boulder Creek Trail and the Gore Range Trail, follow the latter 3 miles north to the Slate Creek Trail and follow it west past Slate Lake to camping at the east end of **Upper Slate Lake**.

One of only two thirteeners in the basin of Slate Creek and close above the lake, **Peak L** (13,213) is more frequently visited then most peaks in this area. Walk around the south shore of the lake to the far end, cross Slate Creek and head northwest up broken slopes to the southwest ridge. Scramble up the ridge and head right near the summit blocks to finish.

For summits further up valley, from the far end of the lake bushwack another mile to the large, unnamed lake at the head of the valley. For **Peak K** (12, 920'), go northwest from the far end of this lake to the southwest ridge and scramble

Peak L   *David Anschicks*

along the thin ridge. **Peak J** (12,942') on the ridge crest also goes from this same lake and is a steep and enjoyable scramble by the northeast ridge. Follow the same route as for Peak K but turn left at the ridge over a 12,685' sub-peak. Hop on the ridge, staying right of any obstacles on ledges as they present themselves.

Peak P (12,965') is a short scramble south from Peak J, combining well with it, bypassing any obstacles on the west. To descend after the traverse or to climb Peak P alone, go down Peak P's easy east ridge, then descend north down the permanent snowfield, back to the upper lake in the Slate Creek drainage.

The ridge dividing Slate Creek and it's south fork offer some of the more challenging scrambles in the area. Massive **Peak Q** (13,230') is the highest summit and readily recognizable from several points in the Gores. To climb it, ascend into the basin south of the upper lake in the Slate Creek drainage. Without getting on the east ridge, stay on it's right side, scrambling up through a steep bench system to gain the narrow, northeast ridge near the top. Close neighbor **Peak R** (12,995') offers a dramatic north ridge from the lake. Head directly for it but angle right into ramps and ribs before gaining the ridge proper a few hundred feet below the summit. **Peak S** (12,857') is climbed by the steep, snow couloir between it and Peak R. Head up from the marshy area just below the upper, unnamed lake, and finish on the short west ridge.

The trailless south fork of Slate Creek undoubtedly offers much solitude and numerous climbing possibilites but since most of the peaks contained there are better approached from Pitkin Creek or Boulder Creek, we have covered those possibilites elsewhere.

EAST SIDE RANGE - Mesa Cortina/Wildernest Access:

There is an access route up Willow Creek to the Gore Range Trail from the Willowbrook subdivision just north of Silverthorne, but private property has made the trailhead difficult to find, and there is no parking on the roads. It is better to use the **Mesa Cortina Trail** which begins in the Mesa Cortina development west of Silverthorne. Turn west on the Wildernest Road off Hwy-9 just north of I-70 exit 205. Cross the Blue River bridge, turn right on Adams Avenue, then immediately left on Buffalo Mountain Drive. Go 0.75 mile and turn right on Lakeview Drive; go right again in 0.5 mile to Aspen Drive, then left to the parking area and trailhead. At 2.5 miles you reach South Willow Creek and the junction of the Gore Range Trail. Follow the trail north another 4 miles to **Willow Lakes Trail**.

It is a stiff climb to the four Willow Lakes and the Zodiac Spires from the Gore Range Trail junction. One mile up the trail is the Salmon Lake cutoff, an unmarked right fork to the lake which lies out of sight of the trail. The trail ends in another 2.5 miles at the farthest west of the Willow Lakes in the cirque below the east side of the **Zodiac Spires**. Salmon Lake is a good starting point for the 13,357' peak that goes by both the names of "Mount Silverthorne" and **Willow Peak**, and its more spectacular eastern ridge point, the **East Thorn** (13,333'). The name Silverthorne honors an early Summit County judge, Marshall Silverthorn (who didn't bother with the "e").

For the higher peak, head into the basin west of Salmon Lake and climb it's headwall onto the upper plateau. Stroll up this to the top. East Thorn can also be tackled from the plateau by scrambling up the short west ridge. There is a false summit to go over and it's a bit narrow in places. By the way, that terrific east ridge, so prominent above Salmon Lake, offers a long extended technical climb, mostly fourth and low fifth class.

Red Peak (13,189') can be climbed via its north ridge from the westernmost Willow Lake or, more easily, from the south side off **Red Buffalo Pass**. Hike to the pass, either from the east on the Gore Range Trail or from the west on the **Gore Creek Trail**, and follow the ridge north and then east to the summit. Both approaches are about 6 miles one way and involve over 2,200' elevation gain.

The Wildernest housing development is reached by continuing west on the Wildernest Road past the Adams Avenue turnoff (see Mesa Cortina Trailhead above). Follow this road, which becomes Ryan Gulch Road, all the way up through the development to reach several short trails leaving from the top of the road loop. Buffalo Cabin Trail is a 1 mile trail leading to cabin remains at 10,320'. A good but steep trail continues up an old avalanche path (best not to do this in winter!) to the summit of **Buffalo Mountain** (12,777'). An immensely popular goal for locals and in full view from I-70, Buffalo is also reached from Mesa Cortina.

The **South Willow Creek Trail** (not shown on the Frisco and Dillon 1987 topographic maps) splits off from the Buffalo Cabin Trail and is a shortcut for those heading west on the Gore Range Trail along South Willow Creek. The most popular portion leads to South Willow Falls, but is hard to follow because of a maze of spur trails.

Lily Pad Trail starts from the Wildernest water tank and reaches Lily Pad Lake in 1.5 miles and a junction with the Meadow Creek Trail coming up from Frisco in another 0.5 mile.

Heading west on the Gore Range Trail from its junction with the Mesa Cortina Trail brings you in 6.2 miles to Red Buffalo Pass and the Gore Creek Trail coming over from the west side of the range; 1.5 miles farther is Eccles Pass and shortly beyond that, the junction of the Meadow Creek Trail. **Eccles Pass** (11,880') is interesting because it is a meeting point for five access trails (Gore Creek, Wheeler Lakes, North Tenmile Creek, Meadow Creek and South Willow Creek) that make up many combinations of long hikes and backpacks. Buffalo Mountain can be easily reached from here by climbing east and over a bump to the simple west ridge. This leads to the south summit, only a short scramble from the higher north summit. **Peak 12,902'** to the left of the pass is an even easier ascent. Contour around the south side of a minor ridge point to the northeast ridge.

SOUTH SIDE RANGE - I-70 Access:

The south section of the range is conveniently accessible from several exits on I-70 between Frisco and Vail Pass.

Meadow Creek is an initially steep, 4.5 mile climb going west from the access road on the north side of I-70, at exit 203 for Frisco/Hwy-9, up to the Gore Range Trail. Drive 0.6 mile northwest of the exit on a gravel road to the trailhead. This trail is often boggy into midsummer.

North Tenmile Trail begins near the Frisco water tower, 0.3 mile north of exit 201, and follows North Tenmile Creek west 3.5 miles to a junction with the Gore Range Trail, and continues another 1.5 miles farther into the upper valley. The first 2 miles is a heavily used jeep road and the first mile past the wilderness boundary is boggy, as is the section above the Gore Range Trail. To climb **Peak 12,736'**, continue trailless up to the head of the valley and climb the easy south ridge.

From Eccles Pass to **Uneva Pass** is 8.3 miles on the Gore Range Trail, and from Uneva Pass south to Wheeler Flats and Copper Mountain Resort is another 4.7 miles. This southernmost Gore Range trailhead is just north of I-70 at the top of the westbound exit ramp and overpass (exit 195) for Hwy-91. To park, continue across the overpass and turn left opposite the entrance to Copper Mountain. Follow the side road 0.4 mile to Wheeler Flats Trailhead; park then walk back on the road, following flimsy signs, and scamper across the ramps to get back to the trailhead proper. This same trailhead is access for a pleasant 2.2 mile hike to the lovely Wheeler Lakes.

Uneva Peak (12,522'), visible from I-70 at Vail Pass, can be climbed from Uneva Pass or more easily from the Vail Pass rest stop (exit 190), also the exit for Shrine Pass Road. From the rest stop, you can walk south on the Vail Pass-Tenmile Canyon Bikepath to the **Corral Creek Trail**, and then loop back northwards on an old logging road along the creek to timberline, and then to the summit. From the rest stop, a shortcut can be made by crossing to the east side of I-70 and hiking across the north side of a low hill to connect with the Corral Creek logging road.

WEST SIDE RANGE - Vail East Access:

The five trails starting from the Vail East access (I-70 exit 180) all begin within a 3 mile area, but fan out in an arc some 16 miles wide, making it possible to ascend one valley and descend another and still end up close to one's starting point.

The **Deluge Lake Trail** and **Gore Creek Trail** have a common trailhead reached from exit 180 on I-70. The trailhead is on the South Frontage Road 2.3 miles east of the exit. The Deluge Lake Trail takes a left fork at 0.25 mile and climbs northeast, steep all the way, out of the Gore Creek valley. At 2 miles, it crosses Deluge Creek and meets an old, unmaintained trail coming up Deluge Creek. The trail ends in 3.6 miles at Deluge Lake. **Grand Traverse Peak** (13,041') and **Mount Valhalla** (13,180') offer straightforward summit climbs from Deluge Lake. The former is a simple talus and grass pull northwest from the lake and the latter is a bit steeper climb northeast from the lake to finish on the northwest ridge. For **Peak 13,024'** go southeast from the lake up steep talus to the Valhalla-Peak 13,024 saddle, then climb the north ridge, scrambling left at the end.

Gore Range - Vail Accesses

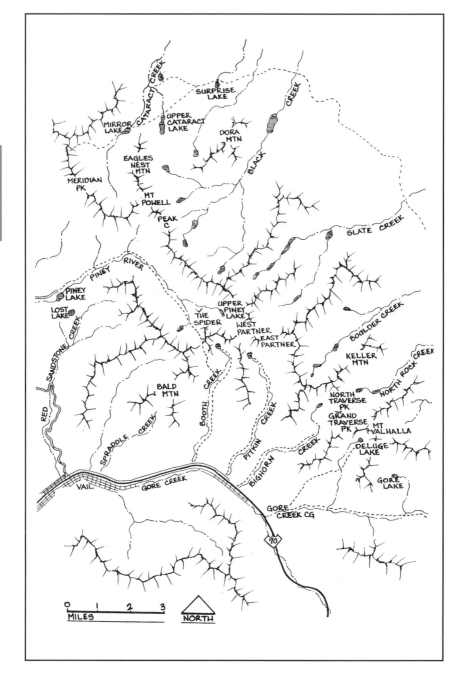

The Gore Creek Trail keeps to the north side of Gore Creek and meets the old Deluge Creek Trail junction in 1.5 miles. At 4 miles and the Recen gravesite, the left fork of the trail leads steeply to **Gore Lake**, while the main trail continues an additional 2.25 miles over Red Buffalo Pass to meet the Gore Range Trail near Eccles Pass. **Peak 12,904'** goes by following the drainage north before encountering Gore Lake, towards Snow Lake and leaving the creek before it turns west. Climb talus as the slope curves northwest to the top.

Bighorn Creek Trail is also reached from exit 180. Turn left off the South Frontage Road at Columbine Drive 0.7 mile east of the exit. Go under the interstate through a narrow underpass to a tiny parking area. The trail terminates in 3 miles at the Bighorn Cabin.

The north ridge of **North Traverse Peak** (13,079') can be climbed from the upper end of Bighorn Creek. Continue to the head of the valley, turn right and jump on the ridge. The high ridge across the head of the Bighorn valley is known as the "Grand Traverse". One of the fine ridge traverses in the Gore Range, it requires careful route finding. The "Grand Traverse" peaks and ridges have been photographed endlessly as a backdrop for the town of Vail.

Pitkin Creek Trail begins on the north side of I-70 just east of exit 180, behind some condominiums, and ends in 4 miles at Pitkin Lake. The first mile is steep. Pitkin Lake is west of **East Partner** (13,057'). The peak is climbed from the lake by its south or harder west ridge. **Peak 13,075'**, **Peak 13,090'** and **Peak 13,005'** are all climbed by leaving the trail at the second falls, about a mile before the lake, heading east and climbing the broad talus slopes to whichever summit.

The **Booth Creek Trail** starts from the Booth Falls Road, which runs off the North Frontage Road 1 mile west of exit 180. Also steep for the first mile, it is very heavily used as far as the falls. At 2.5 miles there is the junction with the Upper Piney River Trail and the trail ends 1.5 miles farther at Booth Lake. **West Partner** (13,041') is northeast of the lake and is climbed by its south or easier west ridge. For the latter, leave the trail 0.25 mile before the lake and head northeast for the saddle on the ridge. The two "pardners" were names suggested by the CMC because of their close proximity and height.

The Spider (12,692') is an outstanding peak as viewed up the Piney River but it is more often tackled from Booth Lake, where it is not even visible. From the lake, climb steeply northwest to the south ridge, passing an intermediate summit on the left.

PARK RG

WEST SIDE RANGE - Vail Village Access:

Spraddle Creek Trail begins as a jeep trail on the north side of I-70 just east of exit 176. It provides access to **Bald Mountain** (12,136') and outstanding views of the main chain of the range and Vail Ski Area. The trailhead will be relocated in the future as a result of a planned housing development.

Piney River Valley is the main approach point for the central section of this fine mountain range. From the main I-70 exit for Vail (exit 176), take the North Frontage Road west 1 mile to Red Sandstone Road (Co Rd-700) which, with FSR-701, leads in 11 miles to the Piney River Ranch and Piney Lake. The ranch is private property, but there is public parking near the lake. The trailhead is reached through the main ranch entrance.

The **Lost Lake Trail** has two trailheads off Red Sandstone Road. The east trailhead is found by taking the Lost Lake Road (FSR-786) at mile 3.1 on the Red Sandstone Road, and following it 2.7 miles, keeping left at all three road forks. The west trailhead is on the right side of Red Sandstone Road at mile 7.1. The heavily used trails both lead to Lost Lake and the distance between trailheads is 3.75 miles.

The **Upper Piney River Trail** begins at Piney Lake and follows the north side of Piney River. It is mainly used for climbs of Mount Powell, the **Cataract Points**, and lesser summits southeast along the range crest, but also gives access to Soda Lakes Trail and the Upper Piney River and Lake.

To climb **Mount Powell** (13,580'), high point of the range, hike 3 miles northeast up the trail and turn left on an unmarked trail at a flat area just before crossing an unnamed side stream, and before the Piney River turns southeast. Follow the small stream north, then northeast. It leads in a steep rough mile to a pleasant basin at 11,000', below Powell on the left and the dramatic Peak C on the right. Climb a prominent talus slide to the 12,260' saddle known as "Kneeknocker Pass" between the two mountains. Descend a short way on the east side of the saddle to the southeast side of Mount Powell, then climb to the plateau area and the summit on the east end. Note that there are variations on the route from the saddle to the summit.

The "west gully" route for Mount Powell is reached by following the directions for Eagles Nest (see below) as far as the 12,040' pass between the Cataract Points and Powell. Descend the pass a short distance and then angle right into the large gully and follow it to the summit plateau (see Spring Creek Road Access).

Eagles Nest (13,400') can be climbed from the 11,000' basin between Powell and Peak C. Go directly north over the obvious pass at 12,040' and drop into upper Cataract Creek valley. The route works up the west side to the low point of the south ridge. This is an extremely long climb and, if combined with Powell, should be attempted from north to south (see Cataract Creek Access).

Scrambling on Peak C   Chester Stone

Peak C (13,200') is the prominent pointed peak seen east from Piney Lake. From 3 miles east of Piney Lake, take the same trail as for Powell north and then northeast to the basin. Head for the eastermost couloir on the southwest ridge of Peak C in order to gain the southwest face of the peak. Climb the prominent couloir up this face, exiting left up a ramp before gaining the south ridge. The terrific profile of the north ridge offers a mid fifth class climb from "Kneeknocker Pass".

The Upper Piney River Trail continues along the east side of the river, bogging out in places and getting lost in others (keep on the east side of the river when in doubt) and reaches Upper Piney Lake in 7 miles from the trailhead. From a small lake before Upper Piney, a trail goes over 11,760' "West Booth Pass", and descends along a northwest fork of Booth Creek to join the Booth Creek Trail.

Peak D (13,047') is best approached by continuing up the Piney River Trail another 0.5 mile after the aforementioned turnoff for Mount Powell. From an open area, hike steeply into a small basin to the northeast containing Peak C and Peak D, as well as several small tarns. At the east end of the basin, climb a couloir to gain the easy south ridge. **Peak E** (13,200') is also accessed from the col at the top of this couloir. Scramble up the harder northwest ridge of this peak, passing over one false summit.

The Piney River Trial becomes rather faint long before you reach a drainage coming off the south slopes of **Peak F** (13,230') and **Peak G** (13,240'), at about two miles after the river turns to the southeast. Climb northeast up this drainage to the saddle between the two peaks and scramble left or right.

The Spider (12,692') is the rugged rock peak jutting up in the middle of the Piney valley. Named on an early CMC ascent for a denizen near the summit, it is climbed by going around the east side above Upper Piney Lake. From above the lake, climb wide ledges up to the south ridge and work back north to the summit.

The Soda Lakes Trail leaves the Upper Piney River Trail a short distance east of the Piney Lake Trailhead, and climbs northeast to a ridge and then north along the head of the East Meadow Creek valley to join the Elliott Ridge Trail about 1 mile north of Meridian Peak.

South Gore Group

Maps:

USGS: *Climax, Copper Mountain, Leadville North, Minturn, Pando, Red Cliff, Vail East, Vail Pass, Vail West*

Forest Service: *White River NF*

This area, normally included with the Gore Range, stretches from Vail south to Leadville, east of the Eagle River and US-24, and west of Tenmile Creek and Hwy-91. Black Gore and West Tenmile Creeks separate it from the Gore Range proper, and Tenmile Creek, from the Tenmile Range. The main appeal for mountaineers is for ski touring and for viewing other mountains. It has been necessary for the Forest Service to study how to limit conflicts developing from increasing wintertime use by cross-country skiers, hut-trippers, snowmobilers and commercial helicopter and snowcat outfitters for alpine skiers. Excellent maps of the area are available from the Tenth Mountain Trail Association in Aspen.

Vail Pass Access:

The Shrine Pass Road starts just south of the top of Vail Pass (exit 190) and runs northwest 2.5 miles to a crest at 11,060', then turns west-southwest down Turkey Creek to the town of Red Cliff and US-24. A turn in the canyon lets you see Mount Jackson and Mount of the Holy Cross. Snowmobilers and cross-country skiers vie for space on winter weekends when the Forest Service has instituted a fee for parking.

Eagle Park/Camp Hale Access:

The Eagle River East Fork Road (FSR-714) leads from Fremont Pass, the Continental Divide crossing of Hwy-91 at Climax, to the site of Camp Hale in Eagle Park and US-24. It is suitable for two-wheel drive vehicles with decent clearance. The road is public, although a portion of it is through Climax Mining property. You can park south of **Sheep Mountain** (12,376') and head up its southeast slope, or continue down FSR-714 to the east end of Eagle Park and catch the Colorado Trail north and east up Cataract Creek to **Kokomo Pass**, then south a mile to the summit, picking off **North Sheep Mountain** (12,400') on the way.

Ptarmigan Hill (12,143') is a good lookout point for little effort, accessible from US-24 at Camp Hale, or from the Vail Pass rest area on I-70 up Wilder Gulch to Ptarmigan Pass. From the north end of Camp Hale, drive the steep but good road (FSR-702) up Resolution Creek to 11,756' Ptarmigan Pass. Climb 0.5 mile and 400' west to the top. From Ptarmigan Pass, you can follow the ridge south around to **Sugarloaf Peak** (12,545'), **Elk Mountain** (12,693') and **Corbett Peak** (12,583'), ending up at Kokomo Pass.

For **Chicago Ridge** (12,542'), take the Eagle River East Fork Road at Fremont Pass, then turn left in 0.25 mile and proceed on the public road past the old Climax observatory, under the power lines and along the city of Pueblo's water ditch to a dead end. You can choose any number of routes to proceed up to Chicago Ridge and over to **Buckeye Mountain** (12,867'), which would have to be considered the very southern end of the Gore Range.

Copper Mountain/Hwy-91 Access:

Jacque Peak (13,208') is the highest peak in this section and is an easy climb and a good ski ascent. Access can be from the west end of Copper Mountain base area, via the Vail Pass-Tenmile Canyon Bikepath (also the route of the Colorado Trail here), 0.5 mile to Guller Creek. Follow the CT 6 miles southwest up Guller Creek, past Janet's Cabin to **Searle Pass** and up the windswept west ridge to the summit. You can also access the peak by driving 3.7 miles south of Copper Mountain on Hwy-91. Turn right on the old highway leading to the Climax water treatment plant and park near the Kokomo jeep road turnoff. Go up-road exiting northeast before Rose Gulch to gain the east-northeast ridge over point 12,631'and up-ridge to the summit. You can also continue to the public road end and follow Searle Gulch to Searle Pass, then east to the summit.

PARK RG

Tenth Mountain Huts and Trails System:

For winter ski tourers, the most dramatic change in recent years has been the expansion of the I0th Mountain Huts and Trails System. It started with two-huts near Aspen as a memorial to the 10th Mountain Division soldiers who trained at Camp Hale. The trails now stretch from Aspen across the Fryingpan River, along the northern Sawatch Range, to the Polar Star Inn on New York Mountain, west of Vail. Another string of huts starts with the Shrine Mountain Inn on Shrine Pass Road, loops south to Tennessee Pass, stays up high north of Turquoise Lake and connects to the original string at Hagerman Pass. A further extension looping north across I-70, up as far as Piney Lake and connecting back with the Shrine Mountain Inn is being considered. The huts are designed to be one day's ski tour apart for an intermediate cross-country skier.

Not to be outdone, Summit County has started a hut system, the first of which is Janet's Cabin in the Guller Creek drainage southwest of Copper Mountain. Five to seven huts are planned in the next few years and will eventually connect with the 10th Mountain system.

PARK RG

Tenmile Range

Jurisdiction:
White River NF, Dillon Ranger Districr

Map area reference:
Page 140 and 164

Maps:
USGS: *Breckenridge, Copper Mountain, Frisco, Vail Pass*
Forest Service: *White River NF*

This well-defined 12 mile range climbs south from Frisco on I-70, to the Continental Divide west of Hoosier Pass on Hwy-9, where it continues south as the Mosquito Range. Most of the peaks are visible from the Blue River valley and from the Boreas Pass Road, which goes southeast out of Breckenridge. Climbs to the peaks are usually approached from the east on Hwy-9, and to a lesser extent, from the west on Hwy-91.

Like the Gore and the Sawatch, the Tenmile Range has its flank trail, the Wheeler Trail. This trail crosses over the range diagonally from an obscure starting point at Hoosier Pass on Hwy-9 to Wheeler Flats Trailhead opposite Copper Mountain Resort on Hwy-91. The northwestern portion of this route has been adopted by the Colorado Trail, as has the Miners Creek Trail route on the east side of the range.

Monte Cristo Creek/Blue Lakes Access:

Quandary Peak (14,265') is the high point of the range. From 2 miles north of **Hoosier Pass** on Hwy-9 or 7.5 miles south of Breckenridge, turn west on Summit Co Rd-850 into the Monte Cristo Creek valley. Turn right at McCullough Gulch Road (Co Rd-851) for one mile to the white arrow on the left side of the road. Hike the jeep road to the intersection with the Wheeler Trail and follow for 0.25 mile on the Wheeler to the ridge. Turn left at the ridge to gain the broad east ridge and follow it 2 miles to the top. The crest is broad enough to be skied most of the way in spring.

A water board road climbs in Monte Cristo canyon to the dam incorporating Blue Lakes at 11,700'. Quandary Peak is a direct but extremely rough scramble on this side. **Fletcher Mountain** (13,951') is a 2 mile climb northwest up the ridge from the reservoir. **Wheeler Mountain** (13,690') is separated from Fletcher by a very slow serrated ridge with climbing problems along the way. We have not heard of a climb combining the two. The route to Wheeler goes from the reservoir straight west 2 miles to the ridge crest at 13,360' and south for the final pitch.

North Star Mountain (13,614') is very steep on this side. Save it for a road walk west from Hoosier Pass on Hwy-9, a route which climbs the south side to high mine buildings not far east of the summit.

Climbing Quandary Peak, east ridge   *Spencer Swanger*

McCullough Gulch Access:

McCullough Gulch has a walking road that starts 7 miles south of Breckenridge at 10,300' on Hwy-9 and climbs 2.5 miles to 11,250'. Another mile of old trail climbs 500' higher. The easy route in, however, is on a water board road. Start as for Monte Cristo Creek above on Rd-850 and in 500' take a right turn on Rd-851. You will go north around the Quandary east ridge and up to the 11,000' water diversion structure, where you are 2.5 miles east of the range crest.

Pacific Peak (13,950') is a steep short pull from either the south or the east ridge. Climb to the northwest corner of the widening valley and take your choice. Peak 13,841', unofficially **Atlantic Peak**, is 0.7 mile south of Pacific with a 600' dip.

Fletcher Mountain can also be climbed from this side, steeply, with a finish on its east ridge. The 5-point Rock Fountain makes an enjoyable obstacle route to Fletcher from its north saddle.

Pacific Peak can also be climbed from the west via Mayflower Gulch. Starting 5 miles north of Fremont Pass on Hwy-91, head southeast a mile up the old mine road and cross the creek east into Pacific Creek. Continue to the head of the drainage and head northeast towards the peak's west ridge for a finish.

Spruce Creek Road Access:

Spruce Creek has a road; sturdy vehicles can negotiate the 3.0 miles to the road end. Start 2.5 miles south of Breckenridge on Hwy-9, and turn on Summit Co Rd-800, Spruce Creek Road, opposite Goose Pasture Tarn. From the road end, a trail continues past Mayflower Lake and on up the bench to Mohawk Lake at around 12,000'.

Mount Helen (13,164') juts out east of the range crest between Spruce Creek and its north tributary, Crystal Creek. The peak is best climbed from the east ridge, about 2.5 miles up the Spruce Creek Road. You rise 2,000' in the mile.

Crystal Peak (13,852') is at the head of the valley on the right side. Hike past Mohawk Lakes, and the lakes beyond, choose a route for the saddle 0.2 mile east of the summit, and continue up the ridge. It is something under 4 miles from the road end.

Crystal Peak can also be climbed from upper Crystal Lake. The Crystal Creek jeep road (not recommended) forks right about 1.5 miles up the Spruce Creek Road. If you stay on the better Spruce Creek Road, continue to about mile 2.5 and follow a sharp right fork north for about 500' and look for the Wheeler Trail to leave the road at left. In something less than a mile, the Wheeler Trail connects with the 4WD road up Crystal Creek, which continues to lower Crystal Lake and then, more trail-like, to upper Crystal Lake. Crystal Peak and **Peak 10** (13,633') can both be climbed from their common saddle 0.3 mile northwest of the upper lake. **Father Dyer Peak** (13,615'), named for the 19th century "snowshoe itinerant" who is well know locally for his ministering to miners in the Fairplay and Breckenridge areas, is 0.6 mile east of Crystal on a rocky ridge.

Gold Hill Trailhead/Miners Creek Access:

The sequentially named summits on the north end of the range can be approached from the east on the **Miners Creek Trail**. Starting at the Gold Hill Trailhead on Hwy-9, 5 miles south of Frisco or 4 miles north of Breckenridge, hike the trail through a distressing area of logging activity, to a junction with the **Peaks Trail**, 3.2 miles from the trailhead. Follow the Peaks Trail 0.3 mile south, then head west on the Miners Creek Trail, also the route of the Colorado Trail. A closer alternate starting point for the same destination goes right on Summit Co Rd-1004 from 0.3 mile south of Frisco on Hwy-9. Following the Miners Creek jeep road takes you to Rainbow Lake, and 3 miles farther to an obscure trailhead at about 10,600' on the Miners Creek Trail at the end of the road. One requirement for this approach is a sturdy 4WD vehicle.

PARK RG

The Miners Creek Trail tops the range crest between **Peak 6** (12,573') and **Peak 5** (12,855'). Following the crest north takes you over **Peak 4** (12,866'), where your casual stroll ends. **Peak 3** (12,676'), **Tenmile Peak** (12,933') and **Peak 1** (12,805') are connected by a slow, rough ridge. These three can be approached from their east extending ridges (avoid the cliffy cirques) near timberline on the Miners Creek Trail.

Wheeler Flats Trailhead Access:

The northern summits of the range are also approached more directly from the west, on a shorter but steeper trail, starting at the Wheeler Flats Trailhead. Immediately after exiting I-70 (exit 195), turn onto the side road opposite the entrance to Copper Mountain Resort on Hwy-91 and travel 0.4 mile to the trailhead parking area at 9,680'. Follow the Tenmile Bike Path a few steps to a right turn (south) onto an overgrown side road, the route of both the Wheeler Trail and Colorado Trail. Continue 1 mile south, paralleling Tenmile Creek, then bear left on the Colorado-Wheeler Trail. Ascend steeply for 2 miles to a trail junction at 11,200'. Go left (north) on the Colorado-Miners Creek Trail to the Peak 5-6 ridge mentioned under Gold Hill Access. From the trail junction, take the right fork (southeast) on the Wheeler Trail 1.3 miles to the 12,408' saddle between **Peak 8** (12,987') and **Peak 9** (12,987'), from which a direct 0.8 mile climb north or south for either would begin. For **Peak 7** (12,665') head north 0.5 mile along the crest from Peak 8.

The approach to Fletcher Mountain   *Mike Endres*

Mosquito Range

Jurisdiction:
Pike NF, South Park Ranger District
San Isabel NF, Leadville Ranger District

Map area reference:
Page 140 and 164

Maps:
USGS: *Alma, Climax, Fairplay West, Jones Hill, Marmot Peak, Mount Sherman*
Forest Service: *Pike NF, San Isabel NF*

This linear range runs almost due south from Hwy-9 at Hoosier Pass to Trout Creek Pass on US-24. Along with the Tenmile Range to the north, the main ridge does not dip below timberline from Frisco to south of Weston Pass, a total of 33 miles. The range is separated by the upper Arkansas Valley on the west and the open expanse of South Park on the east, making it a highly visible and recognizable mountain chain from almost any point. High altitude mining has made for many old roads that make good walking and skiing routes. A good deal of the cap is of early Tertiary intrusive rock. The better accesses are on the east, off US-285 or Hwy-9.

Mosquito Range names are of Civil War political vintage, with a rebellious Democrat thrown in afterward. Legend says that a mosquito lighted on the blank space left for the yet to be decided name on a legal document, and thus gave the mine, mountain and the range its name. Fairplay, the long standing center for Colorado's placering operations, was named by protesting miners who were forced out of the earlier Tarryall camp.

Kite Lake/FSR-416 Access:

Mount Lincoln (14,286'), **Mount Democrat** (14,148') and **Mount Bross** (14,172') can be climbed in one day by a moderately strong party. At Alma, 6 miles northwest of Fairplay on Hwy-9, turn west in the middle of town on Alma Street (Park Co Rd-8 which becomes FSR-416) and travel northwest in Buckskin Gulch part or all of the 7 miles to **Kite Lake** at 12,000'. Camping is available in Buckskin Gulch before the last steep section of the road leading to Kite Lake. The Forest Service has initiated a parking fee for summertime users at Kite Lake. Climb 1 mile northwest to the summit of Democrat, then go east-northeast 2 miles along the ridge and over Cameron to the summit of Lincoln. Skirt back to Cameron and go 1 mile southeast to Bross, descend (a wild scree ride) to where you left your car.

PARK RG

Tenmile Range and Mosquito Range

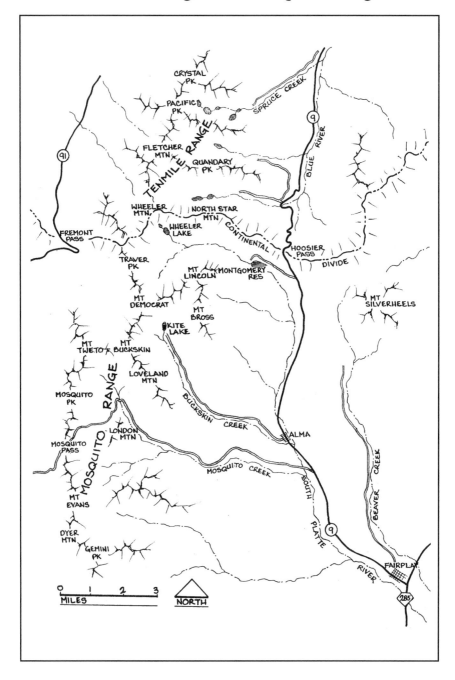

CRYSTAL PK
PACIFIC PK
SPRUCE CREEK
FLETCHER MTN
TENMILE RANGE
QUANDARY PK
WHEELER MTN
NORTH STAR MTN
WHEELER LAKE
CONTINENTAL
FREMONT PASS
HOOSIER PASS
DIVIDE
TRAVER PK
MT LINCOLN
MONTGOMERY RES
MT SILVERHEELS
MT DEMOCRAT
MT BROSS
KITE LAKE
MT TWETO
MT BUCKSKIN
LOVELAND MTN
MOSQUITO PK
BUCKSKIN CREEK
MOSQUITO RANGE
LONDON MTN
ALMA
MOSQUITO PASS
MOSQUITO CREEK
MT EVANS
SOUTH PLATTE
BEAVER CREEK
DYER MTN
GEMINI PK
RIVER
FAIRPLAY

91
9
9
285

0 1 2 3
MILES

NORTH

The Democrat-Cameron ridge drops to 13,400'; Cameron-Lincoln ridge remains above 14,000'; Bross ridge drops to 13,850'. There is something of a trail leading southeast to Bross, which continues in about the same direction into a steep descent couloir which takes you to the road just below Kite Lake. Ormes reported in an early edition of this guide that in 1921 Ellingwood descended this couloir using a pair of metal heels he had made. They were noisy for a few seconds but he was soon out of sight and sound below. Bross, in the right time of the right spring, offers a broad east front of smooth snow, a swisher's dream .

Mount Buckskin (13,865') is a quick climb up the north ridge from Buckskin Gulch. It starts well from Kite Lake or from further down the valley. The summit register is located to the west of the marked point of 13,865', although the point does not appear to be higher and the traverse is uncomplicated. The whole Buckskin southeast ridge, including the long lower ridge known as **Loveland Mountain** (13,692') is an interesting route, with mine roads and mines along the way.

In Buckskin Gulch one sees one or two arrastras, doughnut shaped pools formed in the rock of the streambed, where a stone dragged around a pole by a donkey provided a crude ore crushing process. It attests to the Spanish influence on early mining methods in Colorado.

Platte Gulch/Moutgomery Reservoir Access:

Democrat has a more interesting route if you follow the Platte Gulch-Montgomery Reservoir Road. Starting about 1 mile south of Hoosier Pass on Hwy-9, turn west onto Park Co Rd-4 and continue almost 2 miles to the head of the reservoir where the road deteriorates significantly. You can get pretty far up the gulch on the jeep road, then climb steeply to the Cameron-Democrat saddle and west along the east ridge to the summit.

Mount Lincoln is an abrupt climb from its northeast ridge, with slight problems near the bottom but good footing higher up.

Traver Peak (13,852'), **McNamee Peak** (13,800') and **Clinton Peak** (13,857') are clustered together along a mile of ridge at the west end of this valley, which is the headwater of the South Platte River. Start as for Democrat, but take the first right-hand road, which climbs west from 2 miles above the reservoir to Wheeler Lake at 12,183', where you can choose a route to the range crest. The three peaks named are west to southwest. Wheeler Mountain is a mile north-northwest, up past a higher lakelet, as easy a climb this side as from any other.

Near Mosquito Pass   *Neil Purrett*

Mosquito Pass Road/FSR-438 Access:

The **Mosquito Pass** Road (Park Co Rd-12, FSR-438) starts west off Hwy-9 from a mile south of Alma and climbs in 9 miles up the drainage of Mosquito Creek, past the ruins of the North London Mill and Mine, to the range crest and then descends 8 miles into Leadville. Topping out at 13,186', the road over Mosquito Pass is one of the highest in Colorado, but it is suitable only for sturdy 4WD vehicles.

Mount Evans (13,577'), at the head of South Mosquito Creek, is 2 miles south along the ridge crest from Mosquito Pass. **Dyer Mountain** (13,855') is another mile south on the same ridge, albeit with some rough spots and exposure. **Mosquito Peak** (13,782') is 2 miles north of the pass, and **Treasurevault Mountain** (13,701') is 0.5 mile north of Mosquito.

Mount Tweto (13,672'), previously **USLM Divide**, and recently named for the noted geologist Ogden Tweto, is a point on the range crest at the head of Mosquito Creek and a mile west of Mount Buckskin. **Mount Arkansas** (13,795') is reached from here via a nice 0.75 mile ridge scramble northwest from Tweto.

South Mosquito Creek, which branches off left at mile 5 from Hwy-9, opens into a broad ski touring area. **London Mountain** (13,194') splits the Mosquito Creeks. It is a short climb up ridge from the west end, where the Mosquito Pass Road and an old alternative route to the pass up the south branch meet.

Broadly sloped **Pennsylvania Mountain** (13,006') is an eastward extension off the main crest. Leave the South Mosquito Creek road near the London Butte Mine and saunter southwest to the Evans-Pennsylvania saddle to climb the mountain's west ridge.

Four Mile Creek Road/FSR-421 Access:

People go through private property to climb on this access. From Fairplay on US-285, travel south 1.2 miles and turn right (west) on Four Mile Creek Road (Park Co Rd-18). Stay straight at mile 1.2 towards the campgrounds and continue to the site of Leavick, about 10 miles in from the highway. A locked gate on the way to the Dauntless Mine prevents further travel by auto.

For **Mount Sherman** (14,036') head west-northwest from Leavick on the old road system to the high mines. Continue in the same direction to the saddle and southwest ridge of Sherman. **Gemini Peak** (13,951') is 0.5 mile north of Sherman with a meager 200' dip. **White Ridge** is a mile southeast of Sherman. **Mount Sheridan** (13,748') is straight west of the mine, a 0.5 mile climb of 550' from the same ridge saddle as for Sherman. Sheridan shows its stripe of snow to all of South Park. **Horseshoe Mountain** (13,898') displays its horseshoe cirque to the Fairplay area. To climb it, you leave the road above Leavick and go left up the benches to the ridge north of the precipitous cirque. **Peerless Mountain** (13,348') is just north of the saddle to Horseshoe.

Mount Democrat   *H. L. Standley*

Weston Pass Road/FSR-425 Access:

Weston Pass crosses the range on a general diagonal connecting US-285 south of Fairplay with US-24 south of Leadville. From US-285 10 miles south of Fairplay or 10.5 north of Antero Junction (US-285 and US-24 junction), travel west on FSR-429 7 miles and go left on FSR-425, 9 miles to Weston Pass.

Ptarmigan Peak (13,739') is a 2.5 mile climb up the steep hillside north of the pass by the west side and crest of the ridge. **Weston Peak** (13,572') is an easy 0.5 mile east from the ridge end south of Ptarmigan. **South Peak** (12,892') is a point 2 miles westsouthwest of the pass, a gentle walk with some mine relics to be seen en route.

Buffalo Peaks/FSR431 Access:

The **Buffalo Peaks'** west summit (13,326') and east summit (13,300'), the noticeable south point of the range, have been a good place to see elk and bighorn. Drive 8 miles north on US-285 from Antero Junction (US-285 and US-24 junction) and turn west onto FSR-431, Buffalo Peaks Road. Follow FSR-431 approximately 8 miles west to a saddle at 10,600', where the road begins a descent into the headwaters of Rough and Tumbling Creek. At the saddle, notice an old logging road, now closed to vehicles, which forks to the left (south) off FSR431. Hike up the road which switchbacks its way in about 2 miles to 11,600', bearing generally south. The road ends near timberline; continue south through the trees, noting the way for your return. Once in the open ascend approximately 1 mile south-southeast to the spacious 12,300' saddle northeast of the east summit, which you would approach from its smoother east face. Continue north-northwest 1 mile to the west summit with a 500' loss of altitude.

Leadville/US-24 Access:

The gulches east of Leadville, the Cloud City, offer close approaches for those who like to prowl the old mines or climb to the summits. Mount Evans is at the head of Evans Gulch, reached by driving east on East 7th Street in Leadville towards Mosquito Pass.

Iowa Gulch has a paved 4 mile road (Lake Co Rd-2) to the active Asarco mill. Begin in the south part of town on Toledo Street, 1 block east of Harrison Street. Rd-2 takes you southeast and east up historic California Gulch past old mine ruins, then over the hump to Iowa Gulch. Fork left onto a gravel mine road as the blacktop descends to the Asarco operation. Continue 2 miles east into the amphitheater circled by Dyer Mountain, Gemini Peak, Mount Sherman, Mount Sheridan and West Sheridan.

THE SAWATCH RANGE

On the ridge to Peak 13,282'   *David Anschicks*

Sawatch Range

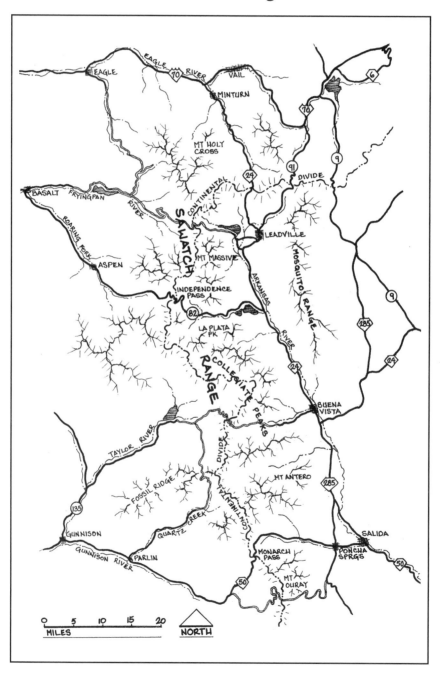

The Sawatch Range

The Sawatch is a long, complex range which stretches nearly a hundred miles, from the Eagle River on the north, south to Marshall Pass. The range is amorphous in the north section, near Vail, but from Mount Massive south it is a definite chain, referred to by Ferdinand V Hayden as one of the grandest of eruptive masses on the continent. Sawatch (or the traditional Ute spelling, Saguache) is a native American word for "water of the blue earth", supposedly in reference to the ancient lake which once covered the San Luis Valley.

The Sawatch Range accompanies the Continental Divide from Tennessee Pass south to Marshall Pass. It parts the waters into the Arkansas River on the east and into many tributaries of the Colorado River on the west (Eagle River, Fryingpan River, Roaring Fork, Taylor River, Gunnison River to name a few). Because of the singularity of the eastern watershed, the range possesses a dramatic line of summits viewed from the Arkansas valley, many of them exceeding 14,000'. In fact, no other mountain range in Colorado contains more fourteeners than the "skyscraping" Sawatch.

The Colorado Trail enters the Sawatch at Tennessee Pass and continues along the east slope of the range at elevations from 12,500' to 8,100'. The CT is not revered only as a tangible trail asset, but even more because of the way the job was accomplished. From the mid-1970's to 1990, volunteers headed to the hills to build this Denver to Durango trail, a success story that already lives as part of Colorado folklore.

At Marshall Pass, over 100 miles to the south, the Colorado Trail leaves the range behind and trends southwesterly in the Cochetopa Hills. Long portions of the CT in the Sawatch use the pre-existing Main Range Trail, which was initially built by the Civilian Conservation Corps (CCC) in the 1930's for fire protection. The Main Range-Colorado Trail has many popular trailheads within the range providing access to three wilderness areas (Holy Cross, Mount Massive and Collegiate Peaks) and destinations to numerous summits and isolated niches. An interconnecting system of less notable, but no less important, trails makes the Sawatch a favorite haunt for high altitude exploring.

Most of the high parts of the mountains from north of Harvard to south of Yale are gneiss and schist, wavy textured Precambrian rocks of the Idaho Springs Formation. From Mount Princeton through Shavano the rock is intrusive volcanic of Tertiary times. Although there are some rough places, the Sawatch Range does not generally have the grand cliffs one sees in the Front Range glaciated granite and in the Elk and San Juan areas. The Sawatch Range is treated here in four sections: Holy Cross, Leadville-Fryingpan, Collegiate Peaks and Southern Section.

SAWATCH

Mount of the Holy Cross
Inset: *Climbing the cross couloir*

Terry Root
Mike Endres

Holy Cross Section

Jurisdiction:
San Isabel NF, Leadville Ranger District
White River NF, Holy Cross Ranger District and Eagle Ranger District

Map area reference:
Page 170

Maps:
USGS: *Crooked Creek Pass, Fulford, Grouse Mountain, Homestake Reservoir, Leadville North, Meredith, Minturn, Mount of the Holy Cross, Mount Jackson, Nast, Pando, Red Cliff*
Forest Service: *San Isabel NF, White River NF*

This part of the range extends south from New York Mountain, Mount Jackson and Mount of the Holy Cross to Hagerman Pass. Red Table Mountain borders the west side, the Eagle River on the north and east, and the Fryingpan River and Hagerman Pass Road on the south. Access to this area's destinations begins south of I-70 in the vicinity of Eagle, or west of US-24 between Minturn and Leadville. Typically the terrain is cut by nearly parallel canyons, with many lakes, and presenting interesting, but generally not difficult, mountaineering opportunities. A large portion of this section is embraced by the Holy Cross Wilderness.

Halfmoon Campground Road/FSR-707 Access:

FSR-707, Tigiwon Road, starting 2 miles south of Minturn on US-24, travels southwest about 10 miles to Halfmoon Campground. At 1.5 miles up from US-24, you will pass Cross Creek Trailhead. Some backpackers enjoy the loop trip up Cross Creek to Fancy Pass, then back to FSR-707 at Halfmoon Campground via Holy Cross City and Fall Creek Trail; all within Holy Cross Wilderness and passing many potential climbs en route. If you want to do this, think ahead and spot a car at the campground to prevent an 8 mile trudge on the road back to your starting point.

Mount Jackson (13,670') is named for the famous photographer who took the first photograph of Mount of the Holy Cross. From the Cross Creek Trailhead at the second switchback on Tigiwon Road, pack 8.5 miles up Cross Creek. Then ascend west straight up the side valley to a high meadow above the waterfalls. Work up the short cliffs in the trees to above timberline. From here there is a fine snow climb up the southeast face couloir, or one can go to the end of the east ridge and make a long scramble west to the summit.

SAWATCH

Mount of the Holy Cross (14,005') became famous through the photograph by William H. Jackson of the Hayden Survey. The arm of the cross is about 700' across, and the steep, ice-filled couloir is about twice that in height. The photo generated sundry tales and legends, and the mountain became the goal of many religious treks.

The climb starts at Halfmoon Campground, with a 2 mile climb to **Half Moon Pass** at 11,600', then a drop of 900' in 2 miles to East Cross Creek. The trail then ascends the north ridge of the mountain on the west side, and along the top of the ridge to the summit. Since the 1930's, small parties of technical climbers have made the ascent up the cross couloir itself. This route is only for experienced, well equipped climbers.

On south from Holy Cross is **Peak 13,831'** along **Holy Cross Ridge**. It is only 0.5 mile to this point, but allow 1.5 hours for the additional round trip. For those doing the "thirteeners", this long, high ridge also has **Peak 13,768'**, another mile south.

Notch Mountain (13,237') is noteworthy for its view of Mount of the Holy Cross. It can be climbed via the **Fall Creek Trail**, starting at Halfmoon Campground, with a rise of 2,800' in 5 miles. It can also be climbed from Half Moon Pass.

The Fall Creek Trail connects Halfmoon Campground with Holy Cross City, about 10 miles. Lake Constantine is on the way, as is a side trail to the Tuhare Lakes, and 12,600' **Fall Creek Pass**. **Whitney Peak** (13,271') is an easy climb south-southeast from Fall Creek Pass. The climb can also be made from Whitney Lake; climb 1.5 miles up the east ridge.

Homestake Creek/FSR-703 Access:

FSR-703, the Homestake Reservoir Road, begins on US-24 about 8 miles south of Minturn and travels southwest to a dead end at the reservoir in 10 miles. Homestake Valley approaches have been partly spoiled by the siphoning of water from most of the alpine streams and the ugly pipes of the Homestake Water Diversion Project, but the timberline and areas above are gorgeous.

From Gold Park at 9,320', on Homestake Creek, the old jeep road for Holy Cross City leaves the valley. Don't take it! One mile beyond Gold Park Campground is a better road to the west which loops around to the Missouri Lakes trailhead. From there the road goes north and east about 2 miles with little elevation gain to a clearing. Now you rejoin the "old jeep road," and continue a rough trip up the French Creek drainage to the fork leading left (south) to Holy Cross City and right (north) to Fall Creek Pass. From Holy Cross City, the old mine road, now

Holy Cross Wilderness   *Chester Stone*

within Holy Cross Wilderness, passes Fancy Creek and a side trail to Mulhall Lakes in 1.5 miles. Still visible along the old Fancy Pass wagon road are traces of the steeply inclined boardwalk, where loads of ore from the nearby mill were transported. At the top of 12,400' **Fancy Pass**, you drop to Treasure Vault Lake and into the headwaters of Cross Creek.

A very popular backpack takes one from the Missouri Lakes Trailhead up to Missouri Lakes Basin, then over 11,986' **Missouri Pass**, past Treasure Vault Lake and over Fancy Pass. From here it goes down Fancy Creek to the trailhead, just 1 mile from the Missouri Lakes Trailhead parking. Of course, the reverse routing is also possible. There are short climbing possibilities from either pass. The end point for Holy Cross Ridge, **Peak 13,192'**, is a jaunt north from Fancy Pass, bypassing on the left (west) a few early obstacles. South from the same pass is **Peak 12,920'**. This time bypass the early obstacles on the right (also west) before gaining much easier slopes. The easternmost point is the higher, with an impressive cairn. From Missouri Pass head southwest and then south for **Peak 12,898'** in about a mile, with a 100' cliff band to scramble through at about 12,500'.

Savage Peak (13,139') is the prominent summit above the Missouri Lakes basin. It is easily climbed along the northeast ridge.

US-24/Tennessee Pass/Leadville Access:

The Colorado Trail enters the Sawatch at **Tennessee Pass** and parallels the Arkansas River Valley to US-50 west of Salida. Most trail approaches from this direction use, or at least cross, the CT.

From 1.5 miles southwest of Tennessee Pass on US-24, follow FSR-100 1 mile and fork right. Continue another mile on the Wurtz Ditch Road to a saddle where the ditch crosses the divide at 10,000'. A left fork continues up the ridge west-northwest for 2.5 miles to Slide Lake. **Homestake Peak** (13,209') is about 0.8 mile west-southwest of **Slide Lake**, 11,700'. For the climb, start just south of the lake and climb west to the saddle, then up the northeast ridge.

A jeep road starting out as the above mentioned FSR-100 southwest of Tennessee Pass, goes up West Tennessee Creek via Lily Lake 5.5 miles to the Homestake Mine at 11,727'. The West Tennessee Lakes are 0.5 mile north.

The Colorado Trail heads up Longs Gulch after crossing FSR-100, about 1.5 miles west of US-24. It heads 12 miles southwest through Holy Cross Wilderness by way of Porcupine Creek and Bear Lake to the Lake Fork.

The Colorado Trail at the Lake Fork is easily accessible by auto at the head of Turquoise Reservoir. From just south of Leadville at Malta on US-24, go west on Hwy-300 0.5 mile, then north to a skewed three way intersection. Turn left and ascend the blacktop to Sugarloaf Dam. Continue 7 miles to the head of the reservoir at a hairpin turn where a neglected side road, flooded by Mill Creek, opens into a small meadow. Better parking is available a mile down the road at either the Homestake or Boustead Tunnel outlets. An abandoned road continues up the Lake Fork 2.5 miles to **Timberline Lake**, a good sized body of water at 10,900'. 12,000' summits of the divide rise on 3 sides.

Galena Mountain (12,893') is best approached on the CT at the Lake Fork Trailhead mentioned above. Follow the trail north 1.5 miles to near timberline and before Galena Lakes, then head straight north up the broad south ridge to the summit.

Crooked Creek Pass/FSR-400 Access:

The Crooked Creek Pass Road (FSR-400) runs south from Eagle into the heart of the northern Sawatch. It eventually ties into FSR-105 at the head of Ruedi Reservoir about 20 miles east of Basalt on Hwy-82. FSR-105, as an almost jeep road, continues east over the Continental Divide at Hagerman Pass to tie into US-24 at Leadville, making an exciting high-country auto loop.

From Eagle on I-70 (exit 147), take the Crooked Creek Pass Road (FSR-400), marked Sylvan Lake, south 10 miles to the fork of East and West Brush Creeks. Take the West Brush Creek Road another 5 miles to Sylvan Lake, then another 5 miles to the pass, at 10,020'. About 5 miles down the southeast side (1 mile past the Crooked Creek Reservoir) turn east on a side road for **Woods Lake** and upper Lime Creek. Keep left (northeast) after a mile, then continue about 2 miles more to a parking area for Upper Lime Creek Trail. The trail leads about a mile to **Eagle Lake**, 2.5 miles on to Fairview Lake, and 3 miles more to Strawberry Lakes at the head of the valley.

The valley above Woods Lake is extremely rugged and rimmed with at least ten challenging peaks. A general rule for these peaks is that the interior valley approaches are quite difficult, and the ridges can involve very exposed climbing.

Fools Peak (12,947') starts from a trail at the north end of Woods Lake. Head north for the southwest side of this cone-shaped peak. This approach takes you to the saddle west of the summit. Go east a mile to the top.

Eagle Peak (13,043') goes from 0.6 mile above Eagle Lake. Work your way north through the glaciated cliffs to above timberline. Ascend the sloping south face which takes you to the east summit. To go to the lower west summit, cross the ridge west. The ridge between Fools and Eagle is very tricky.

Ribbed Peak (13,085') is the highest in this rough valley. It is a technical climb either along the ridge from Eagle Peak or the south face from Fairview Lake.

Avalanche Peak (12,803') is the other cone-shaped peak in the valley. Approach from as far west as possible, even from between Woods Lake and Eagle Lake. Go south from the valley to the west end and follow the long ridge system east-southeast to the final summit.

The remaining peaks in this valley either at its head or southeast section, including **Hammer Peak** (12,975'), all involve some technical climbing. Getting to the rim or ridges for final summit approaches usually involves going up the narrow snow couloirs that lie between the peaks.

East Brush Creek/FSR-415 Access:

The East Brush Creek Road (FSR-415) leaves the Crooked Creek Pass Road 10 miles out of Eagle, and leads 6 miles east and southeast to the Fulford Cave Campground. This is the trailhead to go up East Brush Creek 4.5 miles to Lake Charles, and on another 1.5 miles to **Mystic Island Lake** at 11,300' near the head of the valley.

SAWATCH

Gold Dust Peak (13,365') is climbed from about 4 miles up the trail from the Fulford Cave Campground. From the campground, take the East Brush Creek Trail. Follow the creek up to timberline, then head north for 0.5 mile and take the west ridge to the summit. There is an interesting technical route on the north face via a snow ramp to the west ridge.

Pika Peak (13,126') is the next summit south of Gold Dust. One can take the interesting ridge between the two. An easier approach is from just above Lake Charles 0.3 mile, working up the southwest side. The final route hits the broader west ridge, then east-northeast to the summit.

New York Mountain (12,550') can be climbed with a start at Yeoman Park, near the Fulford Cave Campground. A road (FSR-418) heads northeast to Fulford, 4 miles, then another 0.5 mile to a jeep road which climbs 2 miles to Polar Star Mine. A road fork just short of the mine turns right to a shoulder of the peak, 0.5 mile southeast.

Mountain goat   *CMC archives*

Leadville Fryingpan Section

Jurisdiction:
San Isabel NF, Leadville Ranger District
White River NF, Aspen and Sopris Ranger Districts

Map area reference:
Page 170

Maps:
USGS: *Granite, Independence Pass, Leadville South, Mount Champion, Mount Elbert, Thimble Rock*
Forest Service: *San Isabel NF, White River NF*

This group includes the Sawatch from Hagerman Pass to Twin Lakes Reservoir and Lake Creek. Most of the mountains are of schist and gneiss of the Idaho Springs formation. Mount Massive is granite, and the south part is intrusive volcanic rock.

Hagerman Pass Road/FSR-105 Access:

The Hagerman Pass Road (FSR-105) goes west from Leadville, following the abandoned grade of John J. Hagerman's Colorado Midland Railroad. The Midland was a short-lived but well-respected railroad, notable because it was built in standard guage, as opposed to the narrow gauge of other early Colorado railroads. Its twisting miles of track connected the silver mines at Aspen with the east slope via Leadville and the breathtaking 11,528' Hagerman Tunnel. Today, the Hagerman Road takes advantage of the old railroad grade on both sides of the Continental Divide, with the exception of a 6 mile section over the top suitable only for high-clearance vehicles. From Leadville, the road connects with Basalt on Hwy-82 via Ruedi Reservoir.

From just south of Leadville on US-24, go west on Hwy-300 0.5 mile, then north 1.8 miles to a skewed three-way intersection. Turn left and ascend the blacktop to the Tourquoise Reservoir Dam. Continue 3 miles west above the reservoir shoreline, and fork left off the reservoir road onto the Hagerman Pass Road. At mile 1 on the Hagerman Road, you will pass an obscure intersection with the Colorado Trail; at mile 4, just short of the more recent Busk Ivanhoe Tunnel outlet at 10,750', the **Highline Trail** winds south 3 miles up to **Native Lake** at 11,250'. Higher lakes in the Rock Creek drainage (Rainbow Lake, Three Lakes, Notch Lake and Pear Lake) can be reached by weaker trails to the glaciated cirques on the north shoulder of Mount Massive.

Railroad buffs enjoy the remains of the old routes on the Hagerman Pass Road. Most notable is a pleasant 3 mile hike to the **Hagerman Tunnel** starting 1 mile beyond the Busk Ivanhoe Tunnel outlet.

SAWATCH

West of the Continental Divide, FSR-505 leaves the Hagerman Pass Road at a sharp bend 3 miles up from Chapman Campground or 13 miles down from the top of the pass. FSR-505 goes southeast up the Fryingpan River to Marten Creek and a gauging station for the Fryingpan-Arkansas Water Diversion Project. A trail follows the river on the opposite side. Three miles above the Chapman Lake Resort, where Granite Creek comes in from the south, the trail follows the creek up to the **Granite Lakes**, at 11,400' and 11,600'. (The ridge above these lakes is a possible approach to Mount Massive).

From the end of FSR-505 at Marten Creek, the Fryingpan River Trail goes 10 miles; 5 miles to the Fryingpan Lakes, then on up to the divide. The ridge between this trail and the Marten Creek Trail includes some eight points over 13,000'.

Halfmoon Creek/FSR-110 Access:

Halfmoon Creek divides the state's two highest peaks, and provides access for scores of recreation enthusiasts. The drainage is easily accessible south-south-west of Leadville on US-24 at Malta, then west on Hwy-300 for 1 mile, and following the signs 6 miles south-southwest to Halfmoon Campground. Further up the valley lies Emerald Lake, Elbert Creek Campground, a popular Main Range-Colorado Trail trailhead and, eventually, the boundary of Mount Massive Wilderness.

Mount Massive (14,421') was named by the Hayden Survey, as Henry Gannett reports. Several attempts have been made to substitute such men's names as those of Gannett and Winston Churchill, but for the sake of superior descriptive designation, none has succeeded. It was long rated first in altitude in the state. The simplest route up the mountain begins at the Colorado Trail junction on Halfmoon Creek. To get there go west of Leadville 3 miles to Malta and take Hwy-300 west a mile to join Halfmoon Campground road. Go south and south-west (up Halfmoon Creek) about 6 miles, just past Elbert Creek Campground. Follow the signs. The trailhead gives access north to Massive and south to **Mount Elbert** (14,433').

The Massive route simply goes north 3 miles along the CT to a junction with the Mount Massive Trail, which you then follow west, then north to the summit, about 4 miles. Another, wilder route goes west from the same trailhead to, and along, North Halfmoon Creek. Hike until you are west of the south summit, then climb up the obvious gulch north-northeast to the saddle between the south and main summits. Go north from the saddle. This area has some fine glissading early in the summer.

Mount Massive   *H. L. Standley*

Mount Elbert is truly the top of Colorado, and gentle enough for winter ascents on skis. From the Colorado Trail trailhead (see above) go south up the ridge through the trees for 1 mile to a fork; take the right fork up a steep, eroded trail through the trees to gain the northeast ridge. Follow the ridge in undulating steps south to the summit.

Another route is to continue south on the Main Range-Colorado Trail 3.5 miles from the trailhead to the Mount Elbert Trail, then 2.5 miles up to the top. This Mount Elbert Trail actually starts at the hamlet of Twin Lakes, 6 miles west of US-24 on Hwy-82. The route heads north on the old Main Range Trail 3 miles, then west to the summit. There are many small lakes and potential campsites along the route below timberline.

Elbert can also be climbed from the west. From 2.5 miles west of Emerald Lake on the Halfmoon Campground road, a jeep road branches south along South Halfmoon Creek, and becomes a trail. Follow this 2 miles to 11,400' and select a couloir directly to the summit. From this trail, too, routes can be selected to **French Peak** (13,940'), **Casco Peak** (13,908') and **Bull Hill** (13,761'). This old south Half moon Creek road leads to the Iron Mike Mine at 12,600', and on to higher mining claims on the north ridge of Casco Peak. To get to French, descend this same ridge to the saddle, then climb north and east, passing over 13,876' "Frasco" along the way. **Peak 13,823'** is a bit isolated from the group. Follow the ridge crest southwest for two miles from Casco to gain it. Bull Hill is on the south rim of the basin. You'll have to leave the road at about treeline and head for the saddle below Bull's west ridge.

Mount Oklahoma (13,845') is climbed from the same western approach route to Mount Massive described above. In the North Halfmoon valley near North Halfmoon Lakes you will see Oklahoma's eastern ridge. Ascend this, staying south of the cliffs.

The Halfmoon Campground road continues west and then southwest along Halfmoon Creek to the Champion Mill at 11,600', and other old mining sites. By car, and then foot, this route leads to **Mount Champion** (13,646') and **Deer Mountain** (13,761'). For the former, hike up a jeep trail that parallels the old aerial tramway heading southwest from the mill. This leads to the grassy south ridge of Champion. Those continuing north can reach **Peak 13,736'** with a 500 foot dip between them. For Deer Mountain, go into the basin north of the mill and gain the south ridge, passing over an intermediate 13,445' point along the way. **Peak 13,535'** goes from a saddle just east of this ridge point by way of a west ridge.

Twin Lakes/Hwy-82 Access:

The ridge between Lake Creek and Clear Creek includes several interesting peaks in addition to the fourteener La Plata Peak. From a trailhead 2.0 miles west of Twin Lakes on Hwy-82, cross the footbridge and go right (west) on the trail about 200', then left on a side-trail which reverses direction to the east and meets the Colorado Trail in a mile at the lower end of **Willis Gulch**. Ascending south on the CT, you will come to a fork at 10,280'. The right fork continues southwest up Big Willis Gulch 3 miles to **Willis Lake**. About 0.5 mile before the lake, climb west into a small basin that gives access to the flat saddle south of **Rinker Peak** (13,783'). Finish the climb of Rinker by bounding up either of its two south ridges or the gully between. The **Twin Peaks** (13,333' and 13,276') are the two bumps 1 mile down-ridge and northeast from Rinker. This is easy walking, with the higher bump reached first. Don't try to descend east from either Twin into Willis Gulch, as cliff bands bar the way. Return back towards Rinker or bushwack down Twin Peaks very steep and direct northeast ridge.

The left fork up Little Willis Gulch continues south as the Colorado Trail for 2.2 miles, past a small unnamed lake at timberline, to 12,520' **Hope Pass** between **Quail Mountain** (13,461') and **Mount Hope** (13,933'). Quail Mountain is an easy 0.6 mile climb east from the pass. For Mount Hope, go directly up-ridge west from the pass, about 0.5 mile.

There are five summits over 13,500' between Mount Hope and La Plata Peak; these can be climbed from the Willis Lake area, or from the south, from Winfield on Clear Creek (Chaffee Co Rd-390). The Colorado Trail up Little Willis Gulch continues south over Hope Pass and down Sheep Gulch to Chaffee Co Rd-390.

La Plata Peak (14,336') was traditionally climbed from the Lake Creek side. Access problems have restricted north approaches, but a route starting near the base of La Plata Gulch at 10,100', 7 miles west of Twin Lakes on Hwy-82, offers a way to the north-northwest ridge, a 3 mile climb. A more interesting ascent is to take the rough **Ellingwood Ridge,** a jolly route, but longer and much more serious. Albert Ellingwood pioneered the route alone on this 1.5 mile long, northeast extension from La Plata Peak. Get an early start, as while the problems are not too severe, they are numerous with exposed moves. Most obstacles can be turned on the left (east) side.

From the road up the South Fork of Lake Creek there are routes west to the unbelievable color of **Ruby Red Mountain** (13,480') and to **Grizzly Peak** (13,988'). To get there, turn off Hwy-82 15.5 miles west from US-24. Grizzly, long listed as a fourteener, can be climbed by going up the road three miles and taking the McNasser Gulch trail and hopping on the east ridge. Also up McNasser Gulch are **Ouray Peak** (12,957') and **Star Mountain** (12,941'). Leave the trail about 1.5 miles up the gulch for a faint pack trail that leads north into Graham Gulch. These two are an easy stroll from the pass between the two gulches on grassy slopes.

CMC'ers on Mount Massive   *Dan O'Haire*

SAWATCH

Middle Mountain (13,100'), true to its name, splits the South Fork drainage. Jeep roads continue to the head of the South Fork, south of the peak and into Peekaboo Gulch to the north of it. The peak is easily climbed from either, by heading for the west ridge. Peekaboo Gulch is also the ticket to Ruby Red Mountain where mine trails lead up high on the colorfull flanks. **Garfield Peak** (13,780') lies on the ridge between Red and Grizzly and is a short scramble north from Red. Stay left of any obstacles.

The road, and then trail, to the head of the South Fork goes over Lake Pass, then south and down into Taylor River country. The two tiny lakes on the pass are a bit of a letdown considering the distance you have come but while you are there you might as well knock off the string of unnamed twelvers and thirteeners that make up the divide here. **Peak 13,322'** is a short walk east. **Peak 13,312'** is two miles to the west with a couple shorter summits to climb over on the way. Another mile north takes you to **Peak 13,447'** where you can descend easily back into the basin to pick up the South Fork road.

Independence Pass/Hwy-82 Access:

Hwy-82 over the Continental Divide at Independence Pass gives a hint of its harrowing origins as a mine trail in the previous century. The highway is a major mountain route, connecting US-24 south of Leadville to I-70 at Glenwood Springs, although the link is cut during winter when the highest portion of the road at Independence Pass is closed.

At the great hair-pin turn of Hwy-82, at the eastern base of the pass, a jeep road and then trail heads north following the North Fork of Lake Creek, splitting before crossing the Continental Divide in two passes and then descending along the Fryingpan River. Mount Champion's grassy south ridge can be reached by walking 0.25 mile up the road, then cross the river and go east up Lackawanna Gulch, taking the left fork in another 0.25 mile. Turn left and start trudging up the ridge at any place that looks good. From Champion, several other summits extend north along the ridge and are covered under the Halfmoon Creek access.

Lonely **Peak 13,202'** sits on the Continental Divide at the headwaters of the North Fork. Follow the trail north until it splits in about 3.5 miles and take the left pass at 12,700' in another 0.5 mile. Scramble west for 500' up the ridge. Following the right hand fork of the trail leads in 0.5 mile past a small lake to the other pass at 12,460'. Deer Mountain is close at hand to the east with a straight-forward scramble up its northwest ridge. To the west of the pass in 0.25 mile is the first of several points that reach around 13,200' in a very narrow and rugged ridge that extents north for several miles. We only have a report for one of them, **Peak 13,280'**, the first point north of the Continental Divide; a short and intense scramble from the 13,160' subpeak on the Divide.

Rugged **Williams Mountain** (13,382'), high point of a small western spur of the Sawatch, can be climbed from the Lost Man Campground, starting at 10,500', on the west side of Independence Pass. Take the **Lost Man Creek Trail** 5 miles to **South Fork Pass**, then head northwest into the basin beneath the south face. Go up the broad, hour-glass couloir just left of the center of the face to gain the south ridge and a short but intense scramble.

Geissler Mountain (13,360') is a grassy climb starting from the road 2 miles west of Independence Pass. Follow the trail north for 3 miles along the creek, past **Independence Lake**, to an unnamed pass (12,800'), then turn west to the true summit. Geissler's western summit, **Peak 13,301'**, is less than a mile to the west-southwest with another 12,800' unnamed pass between the two summits. Continuing north from both of these passes are trails leading into the Hunter Fryingpan Wilderness, joining up with the Lost Man Creek Trail just before South Fork Pass.

From the vicinity of the same trailhead for Geissler, bushwhack northeast up moderate slopes to reach the high point of the area around Independence Pass, **Twining Peak** (13,711'). It can also be reached directly from the pass by climbing north 2 miles, passing over **Peak 13,480'** along the way.

SAWATCH

Collegiate Peaks

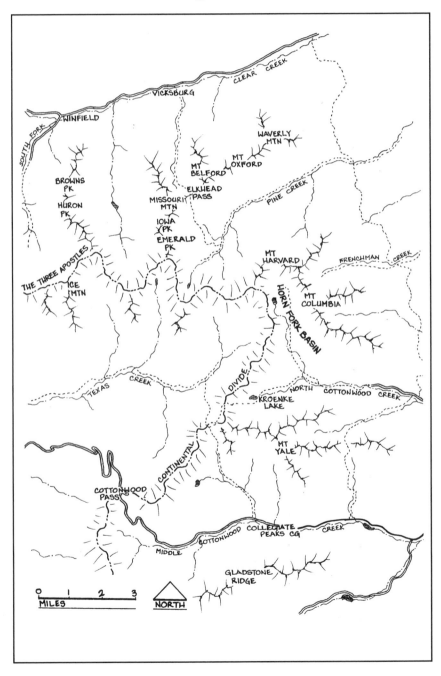

SAWATCH

Collegiate Peaks

Jurisdiction:

San Isabel NF, Salida and Leadville Ranger Districts
Gunnison NF, Gunnison Ranger District

Map area reference:

Page 170 and 186

Maps:

USGS: Harvard Lakes, Mount Antero, Mount Harvard, Mount Yale, Pieplant,
Winfield
Forest Service: San Isabel NF, Gunnison NF

Perhaps the most popular section of the Sawatch is the concentration of high summits known as the Collegiate Peaks. Peakbaggers know the area for its accessibility to no less than eight easily climbed fourteeners, almost all of which lie within the boundaries of the Collegiate Peaks Wilderness.

The name of the region was the result of an early survey led by Professor Josiah Dwight Whitney, head of the Hooper School of Mining and Geology at Harvard. The 1869 expedition was assembled to assess the height of the central Rockies, whose elevations had been rumored to be much higher than the Sierra Nevada, and to give Whitney's students some practical field work.

Clear Creek/Chaffee Co Rd-390 Access:

Chaffee Co Rd-390 heads west from US-24 at Clear Creek Reservoir, 14.5 miles north of Buena Vista. It gives access to the almost ghost towns of Winfield and Vicksburg, as well as many nooks and crannies within the **Collegiate Peaks Wilderness**.

For the shortest route to **Mount Hope** (13,933') and **Quail Mountain** (13,461'), go 9.5 miles west of US-24, about 1.5 miles west of Vicksburg. Here a short, narrow road leads north a short distance toward Sheep Gulch. From the end of the road, follow the Colorado Trail north up Sheep Gulch to Hope Pass. Hope is to the left and Quail is right. By this route, Quail Mountian is a 4.8 mile climb with a 3,600' gain, and Mount Hope is 5.0 miles with a 4,100' gain.

The preferred route now for **La Plata Peak** (14,336') is from the south. Travel west on Rd-390 12 miles, with a jog to the north out of Winfield, up the North Fork of Clear Creek. There are many campsites along the road. A mining road branches to the right. Take this to a gate, turn left just short of the gate and look for a trail. This trail leads up through timber to emerge into a small valley, just east of **Sayres Peak** (13,738'). There are signs of old mining activity here,

La Plata Peak *CMC archives*

including trails which can be taken north up the valley, then northwest steeply up to gain the ridge at about 13,200'. Follow the ridge to just west of point 13,581', then on north to the summit. It is 3 miles from the gate on the road to the top.

For Sayres, climb due west out of the small valley at about treeline and into the next basin. Go north through this basin to the 13,100' saddle, just east of the summit and finish on the ridge.

If one stays on the mining road mentioned above and continues up to old prospects at the head of Blackbear Gulch, several high unnamed thirteeners dominate the ridge. **Peak 13,686'** and **Peak 13,616'** are steep but easy slogs on the left and right sides of the basin, respectively. **Peak 13,531'** is another mile southeast and **Peak 13,642'** is a further mile northeast beyond that.

A mile beyond the Blackbear Creek turnoff, the road up the North Fork ends and an increasingly faint trail leads 3 more miles up the valley. At the head are several thirteeners with low saddle drops. The two most prominent are actually western spurs off the Continental Divide, not visible from below. For **Jenkins Mountain** (13,432') climb west from the basin past two small lakes to the Divide to gain Jenkins' east ridge. **Grizzly Peak** (13,281') goes from the same lakes by heading south up and along the crest to the north ridge.

The road south from Winfield, which follows the South Fork of Clear Creek, is passable by some vehicles for about 2 miles, past the Banker Mine and some ponds, to a road barrier near the wilderness boundary. This area is famous for late profusion of fringed gentians.

The trail for Silver Basin leaves the South Fork by crossing the creek at the Banker Mine and continuing another 2 miles to peter out on the south slopes of **Virginia Peak** (13,088') . To climb **Winfield Peak** (13,077') continue another mile north from Virginia or continue west following the ridges over several small unnamed thirteeners. Silver Basin seems to swarm with elk but seldom any people.

Granite Mountain (12,848') is an impressive little peak separating the South Fork from untrampled Silver Basin and gives an outstanding view of the Apostles. From the road barrier, take the trail south up onto Harrison Flat, veering north at treeline for Granite's easy south slopes.

At the head of the South Fork valley are the **Three Apostles**. Perhaps the most challenging climb in the Sawatch Range is **Ice Mountain** (13,951'). It is flanked by **Apostle North** (13,863') and the **Apostle West** (13,570'). From the road barrier, take a route up the creek through timber, then southeast up to the saddle between Ice Mountain and Apostle North. The latter is a moderate climb from here. Ice Mountain starts from down in the basin and climbs the steep shelves of the north-northwest ridge. It should only be attempted by technically experienced climbers, although one CMCer reports that his dog made it, as did Ormes on one notable occasion. As he describes it, "one continues S to and up the NWN ridge lifting Harry Standley's box of glass plates and a tripod, consisting of three joined oak trees from shelf to shelf of a slippery grass slope. Eventually, however, one stands up for the summit push." The west summit is done from the saddle between it and Ice Mountain. Scramble up Apostle West's southwest ridge. The ridge between all three is done commonly enough but involves real exposure and requires a rope.

Huron Peak (14,005') is climbed from the South Fork valley also. From the Banker Mine, ascend up the ridge southeast to **Browns Peak** (13,523'); then follow the ridge to the summit of Huron. There are other routes up Huron from the South Fork road, but they encounter scree and cliffy areas.

Browns Peak and Huron are also climbable from the east. From the ghost town of Rockdale, 2 miles west of Vicksburg, cross Clear Creek and take the Cloyses Lake Trail south up the Lake Fork. There is camping available in the vicinity of the lake, but there are problems with private property. From this valley, there are routes to the west up Browns Peak and Huron Peak, to the east to gain the northwest ridge of **Missouri Mountain** (14,067') and on south to **Iowa Peak** (13,831') and **Emerald Peak** (13,904'), and to some obscure thirteeners in the south end of the basin.

The **Missouri Gulch Trail** begins at a parking area near Vicksburg and leads south into the wilderness area to several fine climbs. Up the trail 1.5 miles, near treeline, there are campsites. From this vicinity there are several possible routes west to gain the long northwest ridge of Missouri Mountain. A couple early season snow gullys on the north face offer more direct routes. From timberline, a route southeast heads directly to **Mount Belford** (14,197'). From here a mile ridge connects east to **Mount Oxford** (14,153'). A longer, gentler route to Belford is to continue south on the trail to **Elkhead Pass** at 13,200'. From the pass head east then arc north to gain the rock outcropping of the summit. The trail continues over Elkhead Pass south into distinctive Missouri Basin, in the Pine Creek valley.

An alternate route for Mount Oxford is to take the Main Range-Colorado Trail from a trailhead on Rd-390 just west of the Clear Creek Reservoir, 3 miles from US-24. The trail crosses south through a ranch barnyard, then up through aspen. In a meadow at 9,640' and about 2 miles from the start, leave the trail and catch an old jeep road at right which leads to a pair of ponds and a filthy cabin not far below timberline. For the climb, head west along the north flank of **Waverly Mountain** (13,292'). With some luck you may catch the faint trail which leads to the summit of Oxford and perhaps see the large Waverly Mountain elk herd.

Pine Creek/Chaffee Co Rd-388 Access:

The Pine Creek valley offers many possibilities for hikes and climbs in the northern part of the Collegiate Peaks. The Pine Creek Trailhead is off US-24, 13 miles north of Buena Vista or 4.5 miles south of Granite, on Chaffee Co Rd-388. The road deteriorates after about 0.5 mile. Take the trail from there.

Winter climbing in the Sawatch   *David Anschicks*

The narrow trail follows Pine Creek. About 3 miles from the trailhead, at 10,400', the Main Range-Colorado Trail intersects at a bridge across the creek. **Mount Oxford** (14,153') can be climbed from here. Take the Main Range-Colorado Trail north 1 mile. In a meadow including the remains of an old cabin, take a route west-southwest over Waverly Mountain and on to the Oxford summit, 3 miles.

From the bridge over Pine Creek, there is access to Frenchman Creek. Take the Main Range-Colorado Trail south 4 miles, past Morrison Creek to Frenchman Creek, then 0.9 mile up the Harvard Trail to campsites in a meadowed area including ruins of several cabins. The Harvard Trail is also accessible from the south via the Colorado Trail crossing on North Cottonwood Creek and Chaffee Co Rd-365 as described below. For **Mount Harvard** (14,420') continue west on the Harvard Trail, then up the east ridge for 3 miles, keeping high on the south side. To climb **Mount Columbia** (14,073') there are several routes to the east ridge, to points 12,462' and 13,492', for an easy walk to the summit.

From the Main Range-Colorado Trail crossing at the bridge over Pine Creek, the Pine Creek Trail continues 7 miles southwest. Littlejohn's cabins are 2.2 miles upstream, built in 1881 and now registered as a National Historical Landmark. A trail south heads up very steeply to the South Pine Creek headwaters, about 1.5 miles, where there are some ponds and good campsites. Mount Harvard is on up the ridge 1.5 miles.

Up Pine Creek from the cabins 1.3 miles, is Bedrock Falls, and after another 1.3 miles there is a fork in the trail. The right hand fork leads to Missouri Basin. Near timberline, 0.5 mile from the fork, there is fine camping. Another 2 miles northwest up the basin is the Missouri Mountain-Iowa Peak saddle, and the summit of **Missouri Mountain** (14,067') to the north. An easy ridge walk south is **Iowa Peak** (13,831') and **Emerald Peak** (13,904'). Another climb is to continue north up the trail to Elkhead Pass at 13,200'. Mount Belford and Mount Oxford can be climbed from there.

The Pine Creek Trail goes on southwest past Twin Lakes at 12,190', and Silver King Lake at 12,634'. A discontinuous trail continues up past Silver King Mine and the lake over the Continental Divide ridge. Seldom visited **Peak 13,762'** is a gain of 600' by its northeast ridge from the saddle. The trail disappears on the south side, which can be negotiated with care down to the Magdalene Mine at 12,400'. Here a trail starts down Magdalene Gulch to Texas Creek, where there is a fine campsite.

An approach to Mounts Harvard and Columbia directly from the east is to take the Frenchman Creek Trail from US-24 at Riverside about 7 miles north of Buena Vista. This crosses private property near the highway so be certain to check for access. Mount Harvard is 7 miles from the trailhead.

North Cottonwood Creek/Chaffee Co Rd-365 Access:

Horn Fork Basin provides an approach from the south for Harvard and Columbia. From the traffic light in Buena Vista, the intersection of Main Street and US-24, go north 0.4 mile to Crossman Avenue (Chaffee Co Rd-350) and drive west 2 miles, then north and northwest on Chaffee Co Rd-361. A Forest Service sign there indicates a hard left turn onto North Cottonwood Creek Road (Chaffee Co Rd-365), which jogs south 0.2 mile, then west 5 miles to its end. There are several campsites along the last mile of road, from the beaver ponds onward.

From the end of the road, a trail goes 1.5 miles, first crossing a bridge to the south side, then recrossing shortly before a fork. The right fork turns north into Horn Fork Basin, with many campsites available to treeline. The route up **Mount Harvard** (14,420), some 4 miles from the fork to the summit, goes past Bear Lake, to gain the ridge near point 13,598' and to the top. The summit block requires some rock scrambling. To continue to Columbia, descend southeast off Harvard, avoiding a direct assault on Columbia's north ridge by dropping east into the shallow basin to the east of the ridge. Eventually work back up onto the ridge as you near the summit.

Mount Columbia (14,073') is accessible also from lower down. From the vicinity of the timberline campsites, 2 miles from the fork in the trail, traverse east to a steep ridge. A tedious, steady climb leads to point 13,544' and an easy ridge walk north to the summit.

From the trail fork, the Kroenke Lake trail goes left, 2.4 miles to the lake at 11,530' where there is camping. From **Kroenke Lake**, **Mount Yale** (14,196') is climbed by taking the trail west to about 12,000', then heading south to gain the long northwest ridge of Yale and on 2 miles to the top. **Birthday Peak** (12,730') is climbed by taking the trail to the Continental Divide at 12,520', then following the ridge north 1.5 miles to the summit.

Mounts Harvard and Yale were named by J. D. Whitney in 1869, when he brought Harvard's first Mining School graduates to Colorado. Henry Gannet, one of his students who became a noted geographer, later named Mount Princeton. Mount Columbia was named in 1916 by Roger Toll when he was placing Colorado Mountain Club registers on peaks in the area. Jerry Hart, CMC member and a Rhodes scholar, named Mount Oxford.

Middle Cottonwood Creek/Chaffee Co Rd-306 Access:

Mount Yale is normally climbed from the south. From Buena Vista take Main Street west, which becomes Chaffee Co Rd-306, following Middle Cottonwood Creek. The Collegiate Peaks Campground is 11 miles from town. The Forest Service has closed the traditional route directly north up Denny Gulch and recommends the route up Denny Creek.

The Denny Creek route starts 0.9 mile west of the campground. Take the Denny Creek Trail north, then north up Delaney Gulch, 1.6 miles from the road. Then head northeast 1.2 miles to gain the northwest ridge of Yale, and 0.5 mile southeast to the top.

The Main Range-Colorado Trail passes near Mount Yale, heading west-southwest from the North Cottonwood Creek Road (Chaffee Co Rd-365) up Silver Creek to an 11,880' saddle about 2 miles east of the summit. The saddle to summit ridge is a scramble at times. The trail descends 3.3 miles from the saddle to Avalanche Trailhead at 9,360', 9.5 miles west of Buena Vista on Chaffee Co Rd-306.

South Cottonwood Creek Road (Chaffee Co Rd-344) branches south from Middle Cottonwood Creek Road (Chaffee Co Rd-306) 7 miles west from Buena Vista. It proceeds 4 miles to Cottonwood Lake and another 7 miles to Mineral Basin. At the head of Mineral Basin is **Mount Kreutzer** (13,120'). Leave the road where it begins to turn south and climb west to the divide to get to Kreutzer's north ridge. Continuing south on the road another mile brings you up underneath **Emma Burr Mountain** (13,538'). Hike to the end of the valley to gain the easy east ridge. At Jonesy Gulch, 4 miles west of Cottonwood Lake, a route north up the gulch leads to **Gladstone Ridge**, 13,209'.

Gladstone can also be climbed from Middle Cottonwood Creek, from the Ptarmigan Trailhead, near Hangmans Cabin at 10,583'. Leave the trail after about a mile and head for point 11,925' and the north ridge. **Jones Mountain** (13,218') is one of the original sites where mountain goats were introduced in the 1940s and it still supports a healthy herd. To climb it, follow the Ptarmigan Trail south to a pass and stroll up the east ridge.

To reach **Turner Peak** (13,233'), take Chaffee Co Rd-306 to the top of the Divide at Cottonwood Pass, about 20 miles west of Buena Vista, and hike east 2 miles.

SAWATCH

Southern Section

Jurisdiction:

Gunnison NF, Gunnison Ranger District
San Isabel NF, Salida Ranger District

Map area reference:

Page 170

Maps:

USGS: *Crystal Creek, Cumberland Pass, Fairview Peak, Garfield, Maysville, Mount Antero, Mount Ouray, Pahlone Peak, St Elmo*
Forest Service: *San Isabel NF, Gunnison NF*

The boundaries of this section stretch from Chalk Creek south to Marshall Pass and west to Fossil Ridge in the Gunnison country. Much of the southern Sawatch honors the memory of the once mighty Ute Indian tribe, immortalized in the names of many summits from Antero to Ouray.

Chalk Creek/Chaffee Co Rd-162 Access:

Chalk Creek flows east from the vicinity of Tincup Pass at 12,154', to the Arkansas River, between Mounts Princeton and Antero. A detailed guide to the area by Helen Stiles was published by the CMC in the August 1969 issue of *Trail & Timberline.*

Chaffee Co Rd-162, the Chalk Creek Road, goes west from US-285 just south of Nathrop, 8 miles south of Buena Vista, and 16 miles north of US-50 at Poncha Springs. It climbs to St Elmo, mostly on the abandoned grade of the Denver South Park and Pacific Railroad, and then on a steepening route (FSR-267) to **Tincup Pass** on the Continental Divide. On the west side, the rough jeep road drops down to Mirror Lake, then a better road continues to Tincup and Taylor Park Reservoir. This, continuing via Taylor Pass, was part of the old stage route to Aspen.

From Tincup Pass, **Emma Burr Mountain** (13,544') is 2.5 miles east then north on the ridge. **Fitzpatrick Peak** (13,124') is 1.5 miles south of the pass.

Mount Arps (12,383') named in 1989 in honor of Louisa Ward Arps, a distinguished Colorado historian, author and librarian, and CMC member until her death in 1986, is approached via St Elmo. Continue on FSR-266 south from St Elmo 5 miles to the ghost town of Hancock. Hike from here west and northwest then west-southwest on a jeep trail toward **Williams Pass** to timberline. Turn left, southeast to ascend to the summit.

SAWATCH

The old Denver, South Park and Pacific Railroad grade heads westerly from Hancock to the ruins of the **Alpine Tunnel**. Built in 1882 under Altman Pass, it was the first tunnel through the Continental Divide, but was abandoned in 1910. **Mount Helmers** (12,858') west of Altman Pass and **Mount Poor** (12,442') southeast of the pass honor railroad historians Dow Helmers and Mac Poor.

Hancock Pass, 12,100', about 2 miles south-southwest of Hancock, serves as the starting point for climbs northwest 0.5 mile to **Mount Chapman** (12,755') and south 1 mile to **Van Wirt Mountain** (13,024'). The old road south-southeast from Hancock goes over 12,070' **Chalk Creek Pass**, then follows the Middle Fork of the South Arkansas River to Garfield on US-50. From the vicinity of Chalk Creek Pass there are short climbs of **Sewanee Peak** (13,132'), a cliffy peak to the northeast, **Monumental Peak** (13,369'), and **Van Wirt Mountain** (13,024') to the west. **Brittle Silver Mountain** (12,486') is 0.5 mile west beyond Van Wirt with a short drop between.

Mount Princeton (14,197'), the southernmost of the Collegiate peaks, is measured at one foot higher than Mount Yale, and thus is reported to be subject to removal of its top two feet of rock by certain ivy leaguers. The route from the east is made by turning north from Chaffee Co Rd-162 onto Rd-321 at Mount Princeton Hot Springs. Continue on Rd-322 in the vicinity of the Young Life Camp to FSR-322. Travel on FSR-322 to a TV relay station parking area at 10,800. Catch a trail on the north side of this area to the summit.

The first recorded climb of Mount Princeton was by William Libbey, Jr, on July 17, 1877. According to his diary, Libbey encountered no difficulty until he was within 1,500 feet of the top, "when his only way lay over a bed of debris. . .the size of the boulders being such that nothing but the hardest sort of crawling would answer."

The hot springs in the Chalk Creek gulch have been used since Indian times. Father Dyer, the Methodist minister known as the "Snowshoe Itinerant" in the 1860's, enjoyed the hot water after local climbs. Various hotels were built near the springs. The largest of these, a wonder of Victorian gingerbread, lasted until 1950, when it was torn down and the fine hardwood was shipped to Abilene, Texas. The present Mount Princeton Hot Springs resort provides a welcome soak for many weary mountaineers at the end of their climb.

The white "chalk cliffs" on the south side of Mount Princeton are of quartz monzonite, a rough, hard, crumbly rock.

Across the Chalk Creek valley from Mount Princeton is **Mount Antero** (14,269'), named for a Ute chief of the Uintah bend. This is truly a crystal hunter's mountain, with extensive deposits of aquamarine, clear and smoky quartz, and topaz crystals. Lieutenant Zebulon Pike and his men had Christmas dinner near the base of this mountain in 1806. To climb it, follow Rd-162 12.5

miles west from US-285 to Alpine. Baldwin Gulch Road heads southeast from here. The road deteriorates into a rough jeep road, but continues 5 miles to 14,200', 0.5 mile from the summit. One can take this road as far as the vehicle permits, and select a climbing route from there. Near the summit there is a bronze marker which designates this as a mineralogical site.

To the west of Antero is **Mount Mamma** (13,646') which is climbed by taking Deer Canyon south from Alpine, 3 miles. The highest point is actually the southernmost point on this elongated ridge. On the east side of Deer Canyon is **Boulder Mountain** (13,524') The Merrimac and Tilden mines were in this vicinity, noteworthy for their silver production. In Helen Stiles' *Chalk Creek Guide,* the scene as climbed from Baldwin Gulch is described, "A long mile of scree climbing on foot brings you to the top of Boulder Mountain. Here you realize the full extent of the great, precipitous gorge you've been climbing out of — the basin of Baldwin Lakes, backdropped by that unnamed "thirteen" to the south, and across to the north the white ridges of Princeton." To climb that "unnamed thirteen", **Peak 13,870'**, leave the Baldwin Gulch road near 13,000 feet and walk west across the flats to approach the east ridge.

Garfield/US50 Access:

A few of the peaks accessible from the upper Chalk Creek drainage can also be approached from Garfield, 12 miles west of Poncha Springs on US-50.

From the west end of Garfield, a jeep road climbs beside the Middle Fork 4.5 miles to its end on Mount Aetna's western flank. This was an old stage route to 12,100' **Chalk Creek Pass** at the northwest end of the valley. At mile 1.5, a good trail leads up to **Boss Lake**. **Bald Mountain** (12,856') is a mile west of the lake and only a bit more work. Another mile on west is **Hunt Lake** with **Banana Mountain** (12,339') directly south of the lake. At mile 2.1, **Mount Aetna** (13,745') may be climbed up the side of its spectacular southwest avalanche chute with an easy circle over to **Taylor Mountain** (13,651') and back to the Middle Fork Road. **Clover Mountain** (12,955'), **Vulcan Mountain** (12,973') and **Monumental Peak** (13,369') make a nice ridge walk from mile 3.0 to Chalk Creek Pass, providing evidence of extensive prospecting along this ridge in years past.

Browns Creek Trailhead Access:

Browns Creek Trail provides an approach to the seldom climbed mountains between Mount Antero and the Shavano-Tabeguache ridge. From 3.5 miles south of Nathrop on US-285, follow Chaffee Co Rd-270 west 1.5 miles. Then continue straight ahead on Chaffee Co Rd-272 for 2 miles and fork left with Rd-272. Continue south 1.6 miles to the trailhead.

The trail leads to a small lake at 11,300', 5 miles in. From this campsite, **Mount White** (13,667') is 0.3 mile beyond the lake, then north and up the right side of a gully 1.2 miles to the top. For **Peak 13,712'** head south, ford Browns Creek and climb another gulley to the saddle just southwest of the summit. **Jones Peak** (13,604') is 1 mile east along a modest ridge.

North Fork South Arkansas River Road/Chaffee Co Rd-240 Access:

The southernmost fourteeners of the Sawatch Range, **Mount Shavano** (14,229') and **Tabeguache Peak** (14,155'), normally climbed together, are separated by an easy mile with a 250' drop. Shavano was a medicine man and chief of the Ute Tabeguache band.

From Maysville, 6.4 miles west of Poncha Springs on US-50, take the North Fork Road (Chaffee Co Rd-240) 6.3 miles northwest to Shavano Campground, then another 1.7 miles to Jennings Creek where there is limited parking. Find a ragged trail north through the aspen, then go steeply up a burn area to the south-southwest ridge of Tabeguache, and on to the summit, 2 miles. Cross east and southeast to the Shavano summit. To return, drop south then west across the McCoy Creek drainage. Do not follow this creek down; the way becomes very difficult! Injuries and even a death has occured when climbers have been lured into descending McCoy Creek. Continue west over the Tabeguache south-south-west ridge and drop down to the Jennings Creek trail.

Another approach to Shavano, gaining popularity, is from the southeast. Take US-50 west 2 miles from Poncha Springs, turn north on Chaffee Co Rd-250 4 miles, then Rd-252 3 miles to Blank's Cabin site at 9,900'. Follow the Colorado Trail 0.25 mile north to the **Mount Shavano Trail**. The pleasant trail ascends through the alpine gully which holds the snowfield famous as the "Angel of Shavano" in early spring. The trail ends at the 13,400' saddle south and 800' below the summit. Look closely for the Mount Shavano mountain goat herd when using this approach.

The ghost town of Shavano at 10,130' is 8.5 miles from US-50 on the North Fork Road (Rd-240); it was active from 1880 to 1883. An old road, now usable as a trail, goes from Shavano up Cyclone Creek to **Calico Pass** at 12,050' and then down Grizzly Gulch to St Elmo on Chalk Creek.

Calico Mountain (12,949') can be climbed from the vicinity of the pass by heading east 0.5 mile, then south 1 mile. **Grizzly Mountain** (13,708') is also east but then north a mile. From the old site of Shavano, a trail goes north 3 miles up Cyclone Creek. From a small lake near where the trail ends, **Cyclone Mountain** (13,596') is a steep mile east, with **Carbonate Mountain** (13,663') a short walk from there to the southeast. These peaks can also be climbed from Jennings Creek.

SAWATCH

Hunky Dory Gulch, southwest of the town of Shavano, leads to **Mount Aetna** (13,745') with a climb of 2.5 miles and a gain of 3,000'. This approach also leads to **Taylor Mountain** (13,651') by taking a route south from the gulch to the Aetna-Taylor saddle and east to the summit. These two peaks can be climbed from the south, from the vicinity of Garfield on US-50 and up Columbus Gulch.

North Fork Reservoir Campground, 2 miles west-northwest of Shavano, is the starting point for climbs in the Billings Lake area. **Sewanee Peak** (13,132') is 1.4 miles west of the campground, and **Calico Mountain** (12,949') is less than a mile northeast. A road 1.5 miles north takes you to the base of **Pomeroy Mountain** (13,151').

Missouri Hill (12,707') and **Lost Mountain** (12,623') are just east of Taylor Mountain. They can be approached directly north from Garfield via the Taylor Gulch Road, or from the north on Rd-240, about 1.4 miles east of Shavano.

Whitepine/Tomichi Pass Access:

FSR-888, west of **Monarch Pass**, leaves US-50 a mile north of Sargents and continues 7 miles north to Snowblind Campground and White Pine. From White Pine north, FSR-888 parallels the ridge to the east by 1 to 1.5 miles. The ridge includes Bald Mountain, Clover Mountain, Vulcan Mountain and Monumental Peak. The road fades away as it nears Tomichi Pass, a mile west of Van Wirt

Mount Shavano and the angel

H. L. Standley

Mountain. Near its end the road gives access to **Granite Mountain** (12,598')
and **Stella Mountain** (12,597') to the west, and to **Paywell Mountain**
(12,630'), just northwest of the pass.

Pitkin/Cumberland Pass Access:

North of Quartz Creek on which nestles the town of Pitkin, an irregular spur
extends about 12 miles from the Continental Divide to **Fossil Ridge**. There are
access trails from the north and west, but the best routes are from the south. From
Parlin, 10 miles east of Gunnison on US-50, the Quartz Creek Road (starts as
Gunnison Co Rd-76) goes northeast 9 miles to Ohio City, 6 miles to Pitkin, then
10 miles north up North Quartz Creek to Cumberland Pass, and down to the
Taylor River via Tincup. From 12,000' **Cumberland Pass**, it is 2 miles east to
Fitzpatrick Peak (13,112'), and 3.5 miles west to **Fairview Peak** (13,214'). A
jeep road runs all the way from Pitkin to the summit of Fairview, passing the
Fairview Mine at 11,250'.

A road north from Ohio City runs to a campground on Gold Creek at 10,030'. A
trail leads north 3 miles past Lamphier Lake to **Gunsight Pass** at 12,167'. From
the pass it is 0.5 mile east-northeast to **Bronco Mountain** (12,834') and 1 mile
southwest to **Squaretop Mountain** (12,985'). From Squaretop, it is less than a
mile northwest to **Henry Mountain** (13,254') and 1 mile south to **Fossil
Mountain** (12,749').

Fossil Ridge gets its name from its Pennsylvanian, Mississippian and Devonian
rock. The ridge extends some 7 miles west-southwest from Fossil Mountain.
Access to the west area is via the Willow Creek jeep road, which runs north from
1 mile west of Ohio City. The east end is accessed via the Gold Creek
Campground as described above.

Just east of Pitkin on the Quartz Creek Road, a right fork leads up Middle Quartz
Creek following the old railroad grade to the west portal of the **Alpine Tunnel**.
This is a very spectacular shelf road. Peaks accessible from this side include Van
Wirt, Chapman and Mount Helmers.

US-50/South Access:

There are some southern access roads on US-50 just west of Poncha Springs.
Chaffee Co Rd-210, 2 miles west of Poncha Springs goes up Little Cochetopa Creek
4 miles, then becomes a trail. It climbs to cross the Continental Divide at 12,400'.

Green Creek, west of Poncha Springs via Chaffee Co Rd-220 and then Rd-221,
has a trail which goes southwest to the divide crest between **Pahlone Peak**
(12,667') and **Chipeta Mountain** (12,853'), 7 miles with a 3,500' climb.

SAWATCH

Fooses Creek Road (Chaffee Co Rd-225), 9 miles west of Poncha Springs on US-50, has a 3 mile road to a fork at 9,600'. The left fork is the route of the Colorado Trail up South Fooses Creek. It climbs 2,400' in 6 miles to the Continental Divide, passing the base of Pahlone Peak to the east on the way. The right fork, North Fooses Creek Road, goes some 5 miles to an old road, the route of the Continental Divide Trail, which it intersects on the divide a mile north of **Mount Peck** (12,208').

It is 10 miles on the Continental Divide Trail from Monarch Pass, on US-50, southeast to Marshall Pass. The midpoint is the south ridge of Pahlone Peak, whose summit is 2 miles north of the divide. This peak can also be climbed from the Colorado Trail on South Fooses Creek and from Green Creek Trail, starting about 10,400'.

Marshall Pass Access:

The road over Marshall Pass is the abandoned route of the Denver & Rio Grande Railroad. It can be accessed either from Sargents on US-50 west of Monarch Pass, or from 5 miles south of Poncha Springs on US-285, following Chaffee Co Rd-200 and then Rd-202 west. From either direction, it is approximately 13 miles to the top.

From the pass, **Mount Ouray** (13,971') is an obvious ridge walk north and east 3 miles. **Chipeta Mountain** (12,853') is 2 miles northwest from Ouray. Mount Ouray honors the well-respected chief who represented the Ute nation during the disastrous treaty proceedings in the 1870's. Chipeta was his wife.

The southernmost point of the Sawatch is marked by **Antora Peak** (13,269') which can provide a fine view of the Sangre de Cristo Range to the southeast. The origin of the name is uncertain, and it may or may not be a variation of Antero. The peak is 5 miles south and southeast of Marshall Pass. From the top of the pass, hike south on the Colorado Trail and Continental Divide Trail, which coincide here, for 3 miles to the head of Silver Creek, then crosscountry southeast to the summit.

THE ELK MOUNTAINS

The Maroon Bells   *Robert E. Thompson*

Elk Mountains

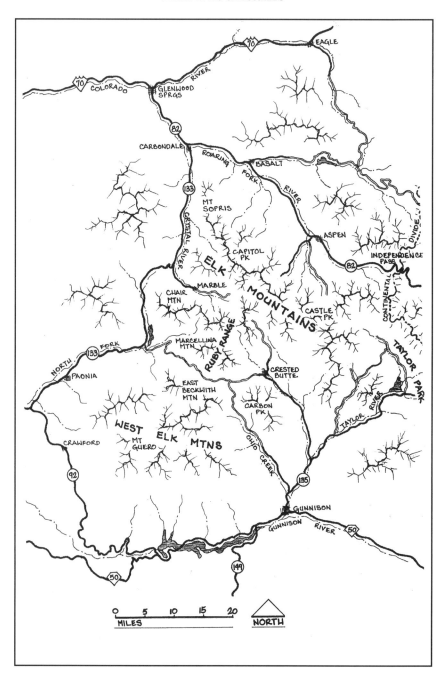

The Elk Mountains

The Elk Mountains stretch southeast from the Crystal River to the Sawatch Range and south to Crested Butte. This large region contains some of the most invigorating climbing possibilities outside the San Juans. While the Elk summits generally can be scaled without ropes, they are rough enough to offer route problems and give a lively mountaineering experience. For most parties the routes are slower than the distances indicate, so early starts are wise. As part of this section we include the related West Elks and the Ruby Range.

The major summits are of two geological types: first, the igneous rock, Tertiary intrusives of Snowmass, Sopris and Capitol, which are eaten away into thin, shattered ridges that swoop and rise gracefully from point to point; second, the stratified rock of Permian age which has been hoisted up with little folding, characteristic of Pyramid and the Maroon Bells. The combination of the light-colored intrusives and the purplish-red sedimentary formations, together with their unique shapes and forms, has resulted in a peculiar beauty distinct to this mountain region.

A relative dearth of mining activity in the Elk Mountain main peak area resulted in its isolation from the time of the Hayden and Wheeler Surveys in 1873 to 1907 when Percy Hagerman and Harold Clark began scoring summits, many of which the surveyors left for them as first ascents. Hagerman, son of Aspen mining magnate John J. Hagerman, and Aspen attorney Clark were, as Hagerman described later, "the first Colorado men to climb extensively just for the sake of climbing." Hagerman's delightful booklet, *Notes on Mountaineering in the Elk Mountains, 1908-1910*, is a rarity in Colorado's mountain literature.

The Elk Mountains provide many busy, if not overpopulated, pullouts, destinations and commanding viewpoints for the casual tourist. But thanks to the Maroon Bells Snowmass Wilderness, climbers can still experience large sections of the range as they appeared to the early mountaineers. For in Clark's own words, written in 1912 and still applicable today, "the true glory of (these) mountains will never be seen from the touring cars, to the walker and climber alone will it ever be revealed."

Central Section

Jurisdiction:
White River NF; Aspen Ranger District, Sopris Ranger District

Map area reference:
Page 202, 208 and 212

Maps:
USGS: *Capitol Peak, Hayden Peak, Highland Peak, Maroon Bells, New York Peak, Pearl Pass, Snowmass Mountain*
Forest Service: *White River NF*

The central Elks run from Lincoln Gulch and the tributary New York Creek west to the Capitol-Snowmass ridge. They include the range crest between the Roaring Fork and Gunnison drainages. These peaks are among the finest in the Rockies for a number of reasons. They have big streams and fine large lakes; they are rugged, steep and forbidding in appearance; some of them are richly colored; and finally, the upper stretches have not been scarred with mining claims which can be converted to private property, and so have achieved wilderness status.

The main peaks are clustered south of Aspen, at the head of Castle, Maroon and Snowmass Creeks. The road up Maroon Creek to Maroon Lake gives some of the state's most intimate closeups of mountain grandeur.

Lincoln Gulch Access:

The road up Lincoln Gulch (FSR-106) starts 8 miles east of Aspen on Hwy-82. **Difficult Peak** (12,934'), can be seen from the streets of Aspen. Drive 3.3 miles up the Lincoln Gulch road to a fork. The right fork goes up New York Creek a bit to a trailhead. A road, then trail, goes up to the aqueduct. Follow this to its end, past Brooklyn Gulch. A trail goes right and crosses New York Creek. At the highest west branch of the creek, you leave the trail and follow this branch to above timberline. Leave this valley, going northwest up the slope, and going right of the 12,700' point. Continue north on the ridge to the summit. **New York Peak** (12,811') is lower and less interesting.

Another 0.75 mile up the Lincoln Gulch road, Tabor Creek comes in from the south. A trail follows the creek 4 miles to a grassy pass into the Galena Creek drainage. Two miles in, turn right and follow the outlet creek coming out of **Tabor Lake**, benched at 12,300'. Impressive, knife edged **Peak 13,282'** can be climbed by skirting the lake on the north, then west to gain the short but steep, north ridge. From the pass, you can go west up a ridge to the crest, then scramble 300' northwest to grab **Peak 13,300'**.

Most cars can make it another six miles up the Lincoln Gulch road to where an old jeep road comes down on the right from **Anderson Lake**. Named for a miner in the first half of this century who defended his privacy at the point of a gun, this lake makes a good starting point for climbing several semi-rough peaks to the west and north. From the lake, head for the obvious short ridge to the west that leads up onto the crest at point 13,105'. Hike less than a mile south, then east to gain the high spot of the area, **Peak 13,631'**. Or go west, then north the same distance to reach **Peak 13,505'**.

North of Anderson Lake are several small but sharp summits, all with a bit of scrambling. Follow the trail northwest to Petroleum Lake, then due north to hop on **Larson Peak** (12,908') and its west ridge. The west summit of this twin is the higher.

Skirt around Larson Peak on the east to get into the Galena Creek drainage and hike up the steep grassy slopes to the saddle between **Truro Peak** (13,282') and its rugged satellite, usually called **West Truro** (13,120'). The main peak is a short but fun scramble east. The route to the smaller one starts out simple up a ramp but gets dicey. Drop off on the south to get past a tower, then scramble up a narrow gulley on the southeast face. West Truro alone goes much easier from the pass on its west ridge. Truro Peak is a showpiece from down on the road and has seen an epic rock climb on its north buttress.

The Lincoln Gulch road continues another mile from the Anderson Lake turnoff to end at the old ghost town of Ruby. Several cabins have been preserved in the area by locals with a sense of history. Its easy to hike further south in the basin and toil up **Peak 13,384'**, the easternmost limit of the Elk Range.

Castle Creek Access:

Aspen mining was largely silver mining. The area never died entirely but was a very quiet place until skiing and Walter Paepke brought it to life as a ski resort and culture center.

Two access roads run south into the mountains from 0.5 mile west of the bridge immediately west of Aspen on Hwy-82. The left one goes 12 miles up Castle Creek to the Ashcroft flats beyond Elk Mountain Lodge, where it splits. The left fork, for which you will need a 4WD vehicle, crosses the creek and climbs 6.5 miles from 9,400' to 11,928' **Taylor Pass**. There is a very steep and washed descent to little Taylor Lake. The top of the pass gives fine views all around, especially of the serrated Castle Peak ridge. You can drive east a mile to a 12,430' lookout summit and north from that road to points farther east. You can also follow a long jeep road over **McArthur Mountain** which continues down the ridge to **Richmond Hill** and the Castle Creek Road.

ELK MTNS

Follow the main road past the Ashcroft ghost town to a right fork at about 1.5 miles. This jeep road goes to 12,705' **Pearl Pass**. Follow the Hayden Peak and Pearl Pass Quads. At a junction on this road near the Taggert Hut the right fork goes to Montezuma Basin.

Castle Peak (14,265'), on the Hayden Peak Quad, is climbed from this basin. The standard route goes southwest up the valley, then west to the saddle between **Conundrum Peak** (14,022') and Castle. You will often find a gorgeous snow-field on your way. From the saddle, go southeast to the summit. A route preferred by the Aspenites begins at the basin, goes up the same valley a ways, then angles left up to the northeast ridge of Castle, which you then follow. Conundrum, not a true fourteener because of inadequate distance and saddle drop from Castle, is an easy detour from the latter.

Cathedral Peak (13,943') is reached from the trail to Cathedral Lake. The trail angles off right from the Castle Creek Road 0.5 mile south of the Ashcroft buildings and climbs in 3 miles to camp, northeast of the lake. To climb, proceed west from the lake and ascend an obvious, probably snowy couloir up to the south

ELK MTNS

Cathedral Peak   *David Anschicks*

ridge. This couloir is the one ending at the first saddle south of the summit. Follow the ridge north to the summit.

Hayden Peak (13,561') is reached from the **American Lake Trail**, beginning at a parking spot just west of Elk Mountain Ranch, 11 miles up Castle Creek Road. Note that the trail finally goes around to the south side of a ridge at a point about a mile below American Lake. You will soon leave the timber briefly and can see the valley where the lake rests. Steeply up to the right are some large rock cliffs and a gravelly gully east of them which you climb to the ridge top at about 11,600'. Now you will see Hayden Peak and the large bowl southeast of it. Hike a bit down, along the north slopes and then into the bowl to a point where the northeast ridge of the peak looks inviting. Once on it you will have an easy walk southwest to the summit.

Conundrum Creek Access:

The Conundrum Creek Trail leaves Castle Creek 5 miles from Hwy-82. It runs the length of the valley to climb out at **Conundrum Pass**, 12 miles south. Drive 1.25 miles to the trailhead; from there you enter the wilderness. From 12,900' Conundrum Pass you can go 0.5 mile northwest to **Triangle Pass**, 250' lower, and take one trail down into East Maroon Creek, or stay on the south side of the ridge another 1.5 miles to the 7 mile trail down Copper Creek to Gothic, or keep on west to **East Maroon Pass**. The East Maroon Creek Trail is a long one. In summer, the Maroon Lake Road may be closed during the day to cars, with travel only on the shuttle bus.

At 10,200', 1.5 miles in from the wilderness boundary, the **Electric Pass Trail** climbs off east from Conundrum Creek and zigzags to a crossing of Cataract Creek at 12,000' and on up the hill to 13,500' on the Hayden ridge. It descends to the Cathedral Lake Trail on the Castle Creek side. **Electric Pass Peak** is a short side trip. You climb on the main trail almost to its 13,635' summit. From Conundrum Creek to the pass logs out at 3.3 miles.

Hunter Peak (13,497') and **Keefe Peak** (13,516') are on the ridge between Conundrum and East Maroon Creeks and can be climbed from the Conundrum side, which is a little higher and closer.

Hunter Peak is climbed from the wilderness boundary in Conundrum Creek, 10,000'. Climb a steep 1.5 miles west and west-northwest toward the north-northeast ridge, to which you should find access at 12,600'. The top is an easier half mile from there to the left. Keefe Peak starts with a 2 mile walk up the trail inside the boundary. Leave the trail at 10,500' and climb west along the north edge of the trees. This graduates into a good ridge route leading directly to the east-southeast face and summit, 1.5 miles.

ELK MTNS

Hilliard Peak (13,409') is in the same club, easily climbed south 0.5 mile and southwest 0.3 mile more, from Keefe Peak. About a mile down-trail from the hot springs you would head west-southwest for the central rib of the broad valley facing you and climb, climb, climb. Ed Hilliard was an active CMC environmentalist who suffered a fatal mountain accident. **Peak 13,537'** is less than a mile southwest from Hilliard, with a 500' dip in between.

The rustic pools of Conundrum Hot Springs, some 6 miles up the valley, attract a lot of visitors. **Peak 13,803'**, one of the 100 highest peaks in the state, can be climbed by hiking south and east from the pools to trudge up the broad southwest face. In early summer, the broad couloir dropping west off the summit has been the scene of more than one wild ride that deposited glissaders neatly next to the pools. Bring your ice axe and bathing suit. **Peak 13,350'** is a short, steep scramble from the saddle between it and Peak 13,803'.

West Maroon Creek Access:

Maroon Creek Road starts 0.5 mile west of the bridge immediately west of Aspen on Hwy-82. Take the right fork which runs south and southwest 11 miles to **Maroon Lake**. In summer, the popularity of the lake area requires that day time visitors use the shuttle bus for the trip.

Maroon Bells Group

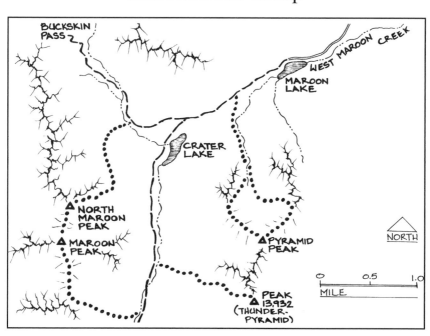

South Maroon, south ridge   *Roger Fuehrer*

The East Maroon Creek Trail starts officially from near the end of the road, part way up West Maroon Creek. This approach can be shortened if water is not too high, by a tricky crossing of West Maroon Creek near its junction with East Maroon Creek. From the Maroon Lake Trailhead it is about 12 miles to East Maroon Pass.

A trail from the Maroon Lake parking area at 9,600' runs southwest and south-southwest 8 miles up the creek to West Maroon Pass at 12,500', where it drops 3.5 miles to the road at Schofield Park, north of Gothic. Two miles southwest from Maroon Lake a trail runs off right, northwest, above the little Crater Lake and climbs 2.5 miles to 12,462' Buckskin Pass where it enters Snowmass Creek drainage and descends 4.5 miles to the large Snowmass Lake, 11,000'. Buckskin Trail is more open than some of the valley trails and looks out on fine mountain scenery. The pass was named for an overloaded buckskin pack animal who rolled down the slope, twice, in a vain effort to cross it during an outing in 1915, before there was a trail.

Pyramid Peak (14,018') is very rough and steep. You see it framed between the canyon walls from a mile below Aspen on Hwy-82. An ascent of Pyramid involves exposed, strenuous climbing on loose rock, not without route finding difficulties. Helmets are advised as may be a rope and ice axe. The climbs starts 1 mile southwest of Maroon Lake parking lot on the West Maroon Creek Trail (below Crater Lake) where cairns mark the trail over the moraine and up the

Pyramid Peak   *H. L. Standley*

obvious, partly grassy slope toward the amphitheatre at 11,250'. Once in this bowl there are two ascent routes. The first is safer and less technical. To begin, go steeply up to the saddle on the northeast ridge. Follow cairns up the ridge to the summit, staying generally on the southeast side of the ridge. The route is very loose and a small party is suggested, together with a rope. The other route is for very small, experienced parties. Go steeply southwest up to the low point on the northwest ridge. From there, follow cairns carefully up the ridge generally keeping to the western side. Find your way up a short loose couloir ending at a keyhole and climb south up exposed rock. The route continues up ledges on the west side to finish near the summit from a southwest rib after either a short chimney or ledge-and-mantel move to the summit ridge, take your pick. Descend by the northeast ridge. A Wheeler Survey man climbed to within 200' of this summit and turned back. Percy Hagerman is believed to have made the first ascent.

Thunder Pyramid (13,932'), a summit 0.7 mile south of Pyramid Peak, was climbed by a party which left the West Maroon Trail at about the 10,500' level, south of Crater Lake, and headed southeast into a basin directly west of the peak. They traversed from the basin north to get into a steep, rocky gully on the west face that leads up to the south ridge, and a short scramble of a couple hundred yards to finish. The first ascent crew named the peak for a counter attack from the sky.

Peak 13,722', 0.5 mile south, can be reached from the same basin by working east up the couloir that descends from the saddle between the two peaks. Conversely, it can be combined with Thunder Pyramid. Climb down the higher peak's south ridge until, at about the 13,800' level, a gully leads you down east to where you can traverse on steep slopes into the 13,400' saddle. The summit is a short jaunt south.

The mile-long ridge south from Peak 13,722' to **Peak 13,631'** is too rough and time consuming. It's better to hike further south to the head of the same basin and then cut left and up to the saddle, just northeast of the summit of Peak 13,631'. The final ridge is short but involves careful work past some steep steps. Len Shoemaker Ridge, commemorating a local, is the fine knife edge that extends northwest from the peak, bounding in this rugged basin.

North Maroon Peak (14,014') and **South Maroon Peak** (14,156') loom above Maroon Lake like peaks of the Canadian Rockies. These two and the peaks from Pyramid to Castle are the only high summits in Colorado of this conspicuously layered late Paleozoic sedimentary rock. They are named and photographed for the rich color and its contrast with the blue sky and with the aspens, whether green or gold. Though they go very well on the right route and under good conditions, the peaks have claimed the lives of experienced climbers.

To climb North Maroon, take the Buckskin Pass Trail from Maroon Lake, and climb on it to about a mile up from the trail junction near **Crater Lake**, where there is a large clearing, and obvious camping spots to the left. Cross the creek on a trail and pick up a cairned trail which leads up over the top of the large bench north of the peak. Once on top and in the open, notice particularly where to pick this up on your return. Traverse southeast over a boulderfield to a cairn on the northeast ridge of the peak. The route goes around to the left, and up, reaching a traverse to the left which soon arrives at a wide grassy gully. Cairns go up this gully. Exit at the top, up a short vertical climb. Go up and to the left to a cairn on the ridge. A short walk up this ridge leads to a leftward traverse into the second gully. Ascend this and exit from the top. Traverse right and a little upward, following cairns. A steep, short gully or chimney takes you toward the crest of the northeast ridge. The ridge goes up steeply. Bypass the difficulties to the left and proceed to the summit. As you ascend, look back frequently to see what the descent will look like. This mountain has claimed a number of lives, some of them from descent-route errors. A rope should be taken, particularly if the weather is wet, and for possible short rappels on the descent. The Dike Route, going up an obvious white dike in the northwest ridge from the east, offers a simpler route, but the trip up the dike is considerably more difficult. All routes are over very loose rock.

ELK MTNS

ELK MTNS

Central Elk Mountains

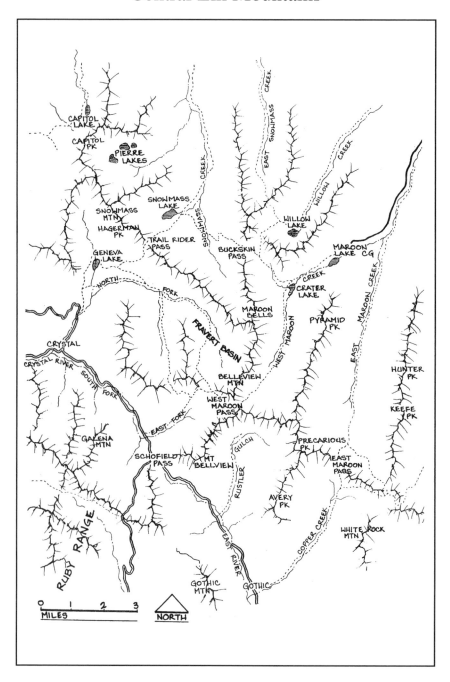

South Maroon Peak is climbed from a hike past Crater Lake on the West Maroon Pass Trail. About 1 mile beyond the lake, the trail crosses to the east side of the stream. Instead, stay on the west side and angle upward and a bit south until you finally reach the south ridge of the peak. As you ascend to the ridge, if in doubt go to the left, to avoid very steep, loose scrambling. Follow the cairned route on the main ridge north, just west of the ridge crest, to the summit. As you proceed, there are multiple cairned routes. Generally, the upper ones are actually simpler. This route also has much loose rock.

The ridge between the two Bells is practical, however it is painstaking. It requires time and some technical abilities. Rope should be taken, and the party should feel very comfortable on extremely loose rock and great exposure. If your destination is the North Peak summit, someone with complete knowledge of the descent should be along. For that reason, most climbers attempting the traverse, do it from north to south. As you leave the north peak, descend a gully, almost immediately, that takes you 150' down for a right (west) side traverse below the ridge. Staying on the crest would necessitate a rappel at a notch about 1/3 of the way along the ridge. Continue on this traverse below the ridge until past the lowest point on the ridge, then look for cairns to climb back up to the main pyramid of the south peak.

Sleeping Sexton (13,460') is the high point of the ridge between **Buckskin Pass** and the Maroon Bells. There is a probable route from where the pass trail crosses to the left side of Minnehaha Gulch Creek. The ridge leading west-southwest to a point north of the summit looks likely; it is a rock scramble from there to the top.

After all this scrambling on rotten rock, few peaks in the area are as easy to get up as **Peak 13,370'**, or "Buckskin Benchmark". To visit it from the top of Buckskin Pass, contour north to get left around a subpoint and into another saddle at 12,600'. Climb the simple south ridge from there.

Snowmass Creek Access:

The road up Snowmass Creek leaves Hwy-82 4 miles southeast of Basalt and runs 10 miles up the canyon to Snowmass Creek Campground and Snowmass Falls Ranch. There is a shortcut from Aspen via Snowmass Ski Area. It goes up to the top of the Brush Creek Road, and from there down to the Snowmass Creek Road.

The trail to **Snowmass Lake** climbs from 8,400' to 11,000' and goes 8 miles from the road end above the campground. At the lake, one branch turns back east to Snowmass Creek (the lake is on a side stream) and up to Buckskin Pass as noted above. The other climbs southwest 2.25 miles to 12,400' **Trail Rider Pass** and drops by Geneva Lake to Lead King Basin. Consult the Forest Service for information about high country pack trips on these wilderness trails.

ELK MTNS

The Maroon Peaks, together or separately, are less formidable if climbed from upper Snowmass Creek. You proceed as for Buckskin Pass, but at mile 1.5, where the trail starts to climb off left, you keep on up the valley to its end, 4 more miles, and pick your way up.

Snowmass Mountain (14,092') is named for the great sheet of snow that hangs between its two summits and is visible from numerous northern summits of the Sawatch Range. From the lake it is an inconspicuous hump to the right of Hagerman Peak, which rises handsomely above the water. From the outlet, take a fisherman's trail 0.5 mile along the south (left) side of the lake and climb west into the basin, keeping to the right (north) of Hagerman Peak. Then climb to the Hagerman-Snowmass ridge and follow it northwest to the summit.

Hagerman Peak (13,841'), the ridge-end a mile southeast of Snowmass Mountain and 0.8 mile north-northwest of Trail Rider Pass, is a photographer's dream as seen from the lake beneath. It has been climbed by routes of varying directness from Snowmass Lake, including everything from rope-work on the face to full flank attacks on both north and south sides. It combines as a ridge traverse with the **Snowmass Peak** (13,620') on the Snowmass Quad. The easiest route is probably on the south. You climb to Trail Rider Pass, contour right (westnorthwest) for a full 0.25 mile, and go to the right up a couloir to a saddle between the highest point and front point. Go through the saddle and choose your summit, high point or lake-overlook point.

Capitol Creek Access:

Capitol Peak (14,130') is the hardest of the Elks to reach and one of the most rewarding to climb. Like some others, it is named for a government building. Along with Snowmass, it is in a system of thin ridges that sweep from point to point in long, graceful parabolas. Under the north-south connecting ridge between the peaks, and draining east, is **Pierre Lakes Basin**, a bowlful of broken rock 2.5 miles wide. It is named for an Aspen youth who backpacked fingerling trout over the rocky benches into Pierre Lakes.

The standard route to the peak is also the most scenic. From old Snowmass, the post office, 4 miles southeast of Basalt on Hwy-82, drive south for 2 miles, then turn right to go another 8 miles to the end of the Capitol Creek Road. If you are lucky with road conditions, you will be at the Capitol Lake Trailhead, with its gorgeous views of the valley and Capitol Peak. You can go to your camp below **Capitol Lake** on this trail, initially dropping some 400 feet before climbing to the lake in a bit more than 6 miles. An alternate route and perhaps easier hike begins at the irrigation ditch at the west end of the parking area. Follow the trail southwest. It later leaves the ditch, and finally rejoins Capitol Creek and its trail on the east bank. A stream crossing is necessary either way. The Forest Service

Capitol Peak, the knife edge, 1999   *Linda Grey*

The knife edge, 1928   *CMC archives*

ELK MTNS

has set up designated campsites to protect the fragile environs of the lake. The Capitol Creek Trail then continues south from the lake to cross a 12,060' pass and drop into the Avalanche Creek drainage

To climb Capitol, begin just north of the lake and climb east to the Capitol-Daly ridge. A sketchy trail goes along the east side, dropping to snowfields. Proceed around and up to the west, reaching the point "**K2**", an unnamed 13,664' point on the way to the famous Knife Edge. Crossing K2 is easier if you drop a bit north as you go. After scooting along the Knife Edge ridge, you can continue up the ridge to the summit, or traverse generally leftward around the east side of the peak, with a northward finish. Although Capitol is not made of the red, flaky rocks composing its eastward neighbors, the route is nevertheless quite loose.

The northwest face of Capitol has yielded good rock climbs to roped parties, and so have the Cleaver Ridge and other parts of the Pierre Basin headwall. The long difficult Capitol- Snowmass ridge has been traversed.

Clark Peak (13,560') honors Harold Clark of Aspen who pioneered many first ascents in the range. To climb it, leave the snowfields below K2 and contour east in the basin. To get around a subpoint, look for a weakness in the short cliff band near the saddle just north of it. Contour around the northeast side of the subpoint and into another saddle to gain Clark's west ridge. A short, narrow scramble leads to the top.

Mount Daly (13,300') has a very direct snow route early in the season from a camp at Capitol Lake. A large southwest facing couloir tops out on the south ridge, barely a hundred yards from the summit. Later in the summer, it is insufferable scree. From the Capitol-Daly ridge, you can also, slowly and gingerly, pick your way up this same south ridge, generally passing obstacles on the right until easy slopes present themselves above 13,000'.

ELK MTNS

Crystal River Section

Jurisdiction:
White River NF, Sopris Ranger District

Map area reference:
Page 202

Maps:
USGS: *Chair Mountain, Marble, Mount Sopris, Oh-Be-Joyful, Redstone, Snowmass Mountain*
Forest Service: *White River NF*

The Crystal River comes into the Roaring Fork at Carbondale where Hwy-133 runs 17 miles south up the valley to Redstone. The road continues over McClure Pass and out to the Paonia country. At the foot of the pass, 4.5 miles south of Redstone, Gunnison Co Rd-3 goes southeast 6 miles to Marble. Here, at perhaps Colorado's most unique mining town, both a steam and an electric railroad brought out gleaming white stone from the cavernous quarries up Yule Creek, some of it for the Lincoln Memorial, some of it in every size from chips to great drum-shaped hunks that would fill a living room. After closing in 1949, the Yule Quarries are once again in production. The owners have provided public parking for 20 cars up a good road with a hiking trail to view the workings.

It was on this river, originally called Rock Creek, that "an evil mule called Gimlet" dumped a load of William Jackson's precious glass photographic plates, so that he had to go back over his weeks-long trail and do the work again. The Crystal River—it would be nice to know who had the felicitous idea to name it the Crystal, and when—is full of interest, starting with Carbondale at its mouth. There are fabulous cattle ranches around here, and this was where Eugene Grubb created the finest of potatoes. At Redstone, John C. Osgood, of the then Colorado Fuel and Iron Company, established a model village for the miners and coke workers about 1900, long before day laborers were recognized as human beings. Here, also, a posh hotel and stately mansion remind one of the world of wealth from steel and coal.

There is plenty for exploration: the beds of two abandoned railroads up the valley, a coal road west from Redstone, mines in the high country, and the town of Crystal, 5 miles east of Marble. Crystal is gaining popularity as an uncrowded backdoor access into the Maroon Bells Snowmass Wilderness. Marble is the terminus of car travel, but connects via Crystal with Gothic and Crested Butte by an infamous jeep road up steep hillsides and a stretch of all-rock canyon, known to locals as the Devil's Punch Bowl, over Schofield Pass. From Crystal, it is 4.5 miles to a good road starting at Emerald Lake, and 4.5 more to Gothic.

ELK MTNS

Hwy-133 Access:

Mount Sopris (12,953'), in the Maroon Bells Snowmass Wilderness, dominates the view coming up Hwy-82 from Glenwood Springs. From Carbondale, drive 1.5 miles southeast on Hwy-133 and take the Prince Creek Road to the left. It leaves Hwy-133 across the road from the fish hatchery. After 6 miles on Prince Creek, take the right branch, FSR-311, 2 more miles to Dinkle Lake Picnicground. Near Dinkle Lake, you will find the Thomas Lakes Trailhead. Follow the trail to **Thomas Lakes** and a possible camp. To the south is a ridge which is the route to the summits. Follow it south and then west. Sopris's two summits are of equal altitude. Captain Sopris was a Denver major who led a gold-hunting party of his fellow citizens into Roaring Fork country before it was settled.

Twelve miles south of Carbondale on Hwy-133, 5 miles north of Redstone, Avalanche Creek comes into Crystal River, flowing northwest off the slopes of Capitol Peak. A 2.5 mile road runs southeast up Avalanche Creek to Avalanche Campground at 7,300'. Avalanche Trail follows the creek. At mile 2.5, 8,200', a branch climbs out left up Hell Roaring Creek to a 12,050' pass and drops into Capitol Creek 2 miles above the guard station there. At mile 10 the main trail goes left to Capitol Lake by way of a zigzag through the timber and a 12,060' pass; a spur continues southeast 0.5 mile to **Avalanche Lake** under the precipitous west wall of Capitol Peak.

From the head of Avalanche Gulch there is a quite feasible shortcut pass to Siberia Lake in Lead King Basin. Take the left basin above 10,700' Avalanche Lake and climb to a lakelet at 12,100', then head to a 12,650' saddle 0.25 mile south. This report came to us from the Outward Bound folks whose camp is 2 miles east of Marble.

Gunnison Co Rd-3 Access:

Chair Mountain (12,721'), in the **Raggeds Wilderness**, is a showpiece from several points along the valley, a high-backed chair with high arms facing you. From Bogan Flats Campground, 2 miles in on Gunnison Co Rd-3 from Hwy-133, drive 1 mile farther southeast to the Prospect Ranch to leave the car, and inquire for Genter Mine, 0.25 mile west. A trail from the 7,800' mine climbs west and southwest through timber to 10,500' before fading out in the Chair Creek glacial wash. Keep track of where the trail ends for the return, since bushwhacking here is rough. Work up the valley close to Cleaver Ridge, which is on your left. After you pass the cleaver, the east arm of the chair, cross the saddle between it and the summit, and head straight south for 0.5 mile to a narrow east ridge. The final climb of 1,000' is on this ridge, on unstable rock. Chair Mountain lets you see the Elk Range from the west and look off southwest at the peaks toward Crawford.

ELK MTNS

Ragged Peak (12,641'), high point of the 6-mile curved ridge that forms an ending bulwark for the Elk Range, is at the end of the Rapid Creek Valley. For any but a very fast team, this should be a two-day excursion, with a camp at timberline on the route to Chair Mountain. The 2-mile ridge between the two peaks would be very slow going, even if they are climbed in one day. The better plan would be to retreat from Chair Mountain to the west side and continue nearly all the way to Ragged before climbing back up to the ridge.

Crystal Access:

A popular jeep road (FSR-314) runs east 5 miles from Marble to Crystal. It splits about 0.5 mile east of Crystal, straight ahead for **Schofield Pass** and Gothic, sharp left for **Lead King Basin**. The latter road, narrow and exposed in spots, climbs high above the North Fork of the Crystal River and reaches Lead King Basin in about 1.5 miles. From a trailhead at the first switchback going west out of the basin, a trail goes northeast into the Maroon Bells Snowmass Wilderness, then branches: left to **Geneva Lake** and **Trail Rider Pass**, right for the North Fork and **Frigid Air Pass**. The road continues, switchbacking up several more times then heading west across Silver Creek and returning down Lost Trail Creek as FSR-315 to Marble.

Snowmass Peak   *H. L. Standley*

ELK MTNS

Kicking steps   *Spencer Swanger*

Arkansas Mountain (11,853') in the Maroon Bells Snowmass Wilderness, is climbed from the above Silver Creek crossing, 10,700'. Head north up a trail paralleling Silver Creek to a flat pass at 11,300' in about a mile. From here, Arkansas is a short stroll southwest. Larger neighbor **Meadow Mountain** (12,840) can be gained by contouring northeast over to the south ridge and up.

Mineral Point (11,025') rising abruptly east of Crystal, gives fine views of the area. The trail to it starts from a little short of the bridge on the Lead King Basin Road, 1.5 miles from Crystal, and climbs east-southeast up a steep draw. Angle right to the ridge and down to the point.

Snowmass Mountain (14,092') is feasible from north of Geneva Lake to Little Gem or to Siberia Lake and climb east from there. Do not get on the ridge immediately, rather pick a route up any of several flutes that lead toward the ridge rather gradually. Expect unstable rock and some exposure. **Hagerman Peak** (13,841') may be climbed either across a difficult ridge southeast from Snowmass Mountain, or up easier slopes from the south.

John Beyer has written directions for several trail trips and climbs of the upper Crystal River. His article, "Hikes and Climbs from Crystal", which appeared with a map by Bob Hubbard in the October 1968 *Trail and Timberline*, is the source of the statements below.

A trail leads south 2 miles from Crystal, at 8,950', to 10,350' Bear Basin. Cross to it on the Outward Bound suspension bridge or on logs behind the southern-most house. Climb directly up the hill about 75 yards to find the trail. It follows a road upstream 0.25 mile then veers off to the right (south) paralleling but staying well to the west of the stream draining the basin. The trail climbs steeply through conifers and meadows, then disappears in a skunk cabbage patch just beyond a large outcrop of table rock. The stream separates into two branches. The right-hand branch leads toward a saddle between Treasure and Treasury Mountains, whereas the left branch leads to a saddle between Crystal Peak and Treasury Mountain.

Crystal Peak (12,632') is climbed from Bear Basin. Follow the left branch south near its right side but leave the stream and keep well to the west as a waterfall is approached about 0.5 mile upstream. Climb steeply and bushwhack through conifers and a few willow patches, until an old cabin is reached on the bench west of the waterfall. Follow the very gradual drainage system south heading directly for the saddle between Crystal and Treasury. Leave the stream well before reaching the saddle, but after passing a series of steep ledges, and climb east up to the ridge. Follow the ridge north to the summit, avoiding a rock outcrop by passing under and around it to the left (west).

Treasure Mountain (13,528') is climbed from the saddle heading the right hand stream branch, by way of a flat ridge to the right. Take an ice axe for a glissade return but avoid the north side cornices.

Treasury Mountain (13,462') has a route from 1 mile upstream on the right fork. Head east toward the prominent nose of Treasury's north spur. Contour around the nose then turn south and climb a steep pitch to the false summit 13,407' above the Treasury-Treasure saddle. Follow the ridge southeast to the main summit. Take your ice axe.

ELK MTNS

Crested Butte Section

Jurisdiction:
Gunnison NF, Gunnison Ranger District

Map area reference:
Page 202

Maps:
USGS: *Cement Mountain, Crested Butte, Gothic, Hayden Peak, Italian Creek, Marble, Mount Axtell, New York Peak, Oh-Be-Joyful, Pearl Pass, Pieplant, Snowmass Mountain*

Forest Service: *Gunnison NF*

This section centers around Crested Butte, the mountain and town, from Taylor Park west to the Ruby Range and north to the boundary of Maroon Bells Snowmass Wilderness in the main peak area. Crested Butte is connected to Marble at the head of the Crystal River by the 4WD Schofield Pass Road via Gothic and Crystal. Other access roads in this section include the Kebler Pass road (Gunnison Co Rd-12) west of Crested Butte connecting to Hwy-133 at Paonia Reservoir, and the Taylor Park Road (FSR-742) connecting Almont 15 miles south of Crested Butte on Hwy-135 to Cottonwood Pass on the Continental Divide.

Taylor Park Access:

Hwy-135 from Gunnison north to Crested Butte is 29 miles long. At Almont, mile 9, the Taylor River Road (FSR-742) turns off northeast and goes about 23 miles to the Taylor Park Reservoir. On the northeast side of the reservoir, FSR-742 joins the Cottonwood Pass Road (FSR-209) from Buena Vista and US-285/24 east of the divide.

Park Cone (12,100') is the symmetrical mountain south of the reservoir, well-timbered below a bare top. Hike southwest on the trail from Lakeview Campground, then bushwhack. Taylor River drains a lot of country, and is a most attractive fishing stream with numerous campgrounds.

Matchless Mountain (12,383') is 4 miles northwest of Park Cone on the opposite side of the valley. From about 1 mile north of the outlet on the west side of the reservoir, the Matchless Trail (#413) climbs 2 miles west to a timberline saddle, and then descends 3 miles in Dustin Gulch to join the Rocky Brook-Trail Creek Road (FSR-748) at 10,400'. From the saddle, you climb 0.3 mile southwest to the Matchless east ridge, then 0.5 mile up it to the top.

The Taylor River Road (FSR-742) swings north-northwest from the Cottonwood Pass Road junction east of the reservoir, and at mile 8 meets FSR-748 where you can turn southwest and go up Trail Creek through timbered country, over the low pass at 10,600', down Rocky Brook to the Spring Creek Road (FSR-744), then south to the Taylor River Road. You can reach the western end of the Matchless Trail by driving northeast up Spring Creek on FSR-744 then 3 miles northeast on FSR-748.

About 5 miles north of the reservoir on FSR-742, about 0.5 mile south of FSR-748, a road (FSR-742.8H) runs off to the north side for a mile and joins the Red Mountain Creek Trail. About 3.5 miles north and east from the start at 9,700' is the Pieplant Mine Trail (10,243'). The Red Mountain Creek Trail continues north up the creek and in about 2 miles enters the Collegiate Peaks Wilderness. The trail continues on up Red Mountain Creek and its right fork about 3.5 miles more to **Lake Pass** on the divide at 12,230'. It descends to the South Fork of Lake Creek. You can also hike east from the pass and drop into Sayres Gulch, a south fork of the South Fork.

Lake Pass has two flanking peaks very close to it. On the left (southwest) is **Peak 12,934'**, on the right (east) the abrupt summit of **Peak 13,322'**. Though steep, these peaks are of the plodding Sawatch type.

About 10 miles north of the reservoir on FSR-742, a jeep road (FSR-759) goes west up Italian Creek. Italian Mountain is about 8 miles west of the junction, and American Flag is about 2 miles southeast of Italian. At about mile 7 on FSR-759 you come to the Star Mine at 11,600', in a basin with lakelets.

Italian Mountain (13,378') goes nicely if you climb straight west from about 0.3 mile north of the Star Mine to gain the crest ridge from the north side of a sub-ridge jutting east. This puts you between summits 13,051' and 13,209', and you can walk and climb south up the dark rock of the main summit. From there the east ridge offers a good return to base.

American Flag Mountain (12,713') is an easy climb from the saddle a mile east-northeast of the Stewart Mine. Starting at 12,000', you go southeast up the gentle north ridge and summit plateau.

Brush Creek Access:

About 2 miles short of Crested Butte on Hwy-135, Gunnison Co Rd-738 goes off right on the south flank of Crested Butte. It is passable for cars for about 4.5 miles, where it branches. The left fork goes north-northwest along the East River on an inferior route to Gothic. It is locked off about 1.5 miles south of Gothic. The right fork is a jeep road that goes up Brush Creek a mile to another forking, left (FSR-738.2A) goes to West Brush Creek, right (FSR-738) goes to Middle and East Brush Creeks.

Teocalli Mountain (13,208') was so called by survey men for its resemblance to temple-like pyramids in Mexico. To climb it, take FSR-738.2A up West Brush Creek. It goes about 5 miles up creek where you are at 10,400' on the bare south side of Teocalli Mountain. A jeep trail takes off right (eastward) from near the end of the road, and gives you a half-mile of uphill trail work before you turn off and climb more directly toward the ridge east of the summit on the broad south slope.

There is a road branch at the junction of Middle and East Brush Creeks; the left, FSR-738, goes up the Middle Fork about 4 miles then climbs out to work its way east and north some 3 miles to **Pearl Pass**. For **Pearl Mountain** (13,362'), leave the road 0.5 mile before the pass and walk west across the basin to gain the south ridge. Lands west of Pearl Pass are in the Maroon Bells Snowmass Wilderness. This was once a wagon road, and the hardiest of jeepers go over it in either direction. But not fast. And not when the snow is deep. The right, FSR-738.2B, goes up East Brush Creek, over the pass northwest of **Crystal Peak** (12,777'), then along the Taylor River under **Star Peak** (13,521') and **Taylor Peak** (13,435') to 11,928' Taylor Pass. Lands east of **Taylor Pass** are in the Collegiate Peaks Wilderness. Except for some local fish, anything reached from Middle and East Brush Creeks is better reached from somewhere else.

Gothic Access:

Gothic is on up past the ski area (north) on Gunnison Co Rd-317, about 8 miles from the town of Crested Butte. It is a ghost town, revived as a place for alpine biological studies. Beyond Gothic the road deteriorates, though conventional automobiles can ascend without too much difficulty to the top of **Schofield Pass**. From the pass, the road continues northwest as a jeep connector to Crystal and Marble.

Crested Butte (12,162') is a good show from the south side. The rough cliffs are cut out of early Tertiary intrusive rock. To climb it, go up the ski area on the northwest side. The gondola top, 1,000' below the summit, gives a good view west, north, and east. If you want to see deeper into the Elks, you can climb on up to where the ridge ends at 11,800'. For the summit, you have to work around east to the southeast ridge.

Gothic Mountain (12,625') is the handsome and appropriately named peak directly west of the town. The ascent should start from a mile south of the townsite at 9,400'. Climb directly west 1,000' to timber, and then another 1,000' along the right edge of the timber to the top of the trees. A ridge, first broadish and then narrower, takes you up to easier grades near the top. Come back the same way.

A primitive road goes east up Copper Creek about 0.5 mile to Judd Falls and the Maroon Bells Snowmass Wilderness. Trail #739 continues up Copper Creek about 3.5 miles then forks west a mile to some lakelets and an old mine on the back side of Avery Peak. The right fork continues up Copper Creek about 0.5 mile and branches again. The left fork, #983, goes to **Copper Lake** at 11,321' and East Maroon Pass, and the right fork, #981, goes to **Copper Pass**.

White Rock Mountain (13,532') is a grandly rambling mass east of Copper Creek, and can best be climbed from about a mile south of the jog to the lakelets. Cut east-southeast from the trail on a very minor drainage line to the upper end of a strip of trees, then turn north-northeast to climb 600' higher in a direction a little left of the summit point. From there angle almost south to the west ridge for the last 1,000' of climbing.

Avery Peak (12,653') is named for a mine and mill operator in the heyday of Gothic. To climb it you go to the Virginia Mine in the basin south of the peak. The trail goes north from the east end of Gothic at 9,600' and branches off to the right from the packtrail 0.1 mile after the start. The mine is at 10,600' and you can climb in the basin the next mile to 11,800'. Then go west to the south ridge.

Avery Peak   *Andrew De Naray*

ELK MTNS

The problem is to decide what to call the summit. Tradition attaches the name to a 12,653' point visible from the East River above Gothic. It is on the west side of the little cirque. We vote for the point straight north of the cirque, but that only begins the problems. On to the north there are other tops and then the range crest. For that, however there is a new name.

Precarious Peak (13,360') is a very rough piece of ground between the head of Rustler Gulch and the wide upper basin of East Maroon Creek. From just south of **East Maroon Pass** you go northwest up a small basin and west past a lake, then northwest to a 12,650' saddle one mile west of the pass. Now you skirt left west-southwest and climb to a ridge at 13,200'. Climb to the point on the right and then work along west 0.3 mile to the summit, if you haven't already had enough of the precarious.

Three miles up the East River from Gothic, at 9,720', an old road (FSR-569) goes east, and north about a mile to the wilderness. A trail continues north and east up Rustler Gulch to a couple of old mines at 11,600'.

At the wilderness boundary, FSR-569 turns northwest off the Rustler Gulch Trail for about a mile to again meet the wilderness. A trail climbs north to the Silver Spruce Mine at 11,800'. This mine is just under and east of **Mount Bellview** (12,519').

From about 0.75 mile north of Schofield Pass, you find the trail that turns east up the East Fork of the South Fork of Crystal River, enters the wilderness, and goes over 12,500' **West Maroon Pass**, a favorite trail between the Crystal and Maroon drainages. There is a differently spelled **Belleview Mountain**, its summit at 13,233', a mile north along a sharpish ridge from the pass.

There are interesting trails on the north side of Schofield Pass. **Galena Mountain** (12,580') is approached from one mile north of Schofield Pass, where a trail runs off through woods 1.5 miles northwest and west into North Pole Basin. Leave the trail at the meadows to follow the stream one mile, then cut left across the basin to climb to the level south ridge of Galena.

From Schofield Pass, an old road (FSR-519) descends west into Elko Park, then south to the Paradise Mine and Paradise Basin at 11,200'. After a minuscule pass it joins FSR-734 and winds down to the Slate River and to the site of Pittsburg. From the last switchback before the pass, **Cinnamon Mountain** (12,293') is a short stroll to the northwest. **Mount Baldy** (12,805') can be reached by taking the fork to the mine, a mile before the pass, and heading up Baldy's steep west slopes to gain the south ridge.

From Gothic Campground, 3 miles north of Gothic, you can find a trail west to Elkton, a once lively mining area northwest of Gothic Mountain. The main approach to the camp was from the south on a road up Washington Gulch, now FSR-811. It can be driven a little way in a car, the whole 8 miles by jeeps. FSR-811 goes left from 2 miles north of Crested Butte town on the road to the ski area.

Ruby Range

Maps:

USGS: *Crested Butte, Marcellina Mountain, Mount Axtell, Oh-Be-Joyful*
Forest Service: *Gunnison NF*

This long southward extension of the Elk Range in the Raggeds Wilderness is worthy of its separate name but belongs within the Crested Butte sphere of interest. It has had a good share of mining activity high up as well as low. Access is generally from the roads to Pittsburg up the Slate River (FSR-734) and to Kebler Pass (Gunnison Co Rd-12).

Slate River Access:

The Slate River Road (Gunnison Co Rd-734) begins a mile north of Crested Butte. Just short of Pittsburg site, FSR-734.2A crosses the Slate and goes about 1.5 miles northwest up Poverty Gulch on a mild grade to 9,600', where FSR-522 tums off to meet a pack trail, #404, to **Daisy Pass** at 11,600'. The trail continues south to 11,000' in Democrat Basin, where there is a junction with trails from over the range to the west and down the valleys to the south.

Richmond Mountain (12,501') is about 0.75 mile northwest along a sharp ridge from Daisy Pass, with a false summit to climb en route. This peak is on the crest of the Ruby Range.

Schuylkill Mountain (12,146') is a mile southeast of the pass, with a similar wayside obstruction of 100' or so.

The Poverty Gulch road zigzags on up and across the creek and climbs up the left side to the Augusta Mine at 11,000'. At the point where it crosses the creek, you can leave the road and hike north 2.5 miles to reach **Purple Mountain**. (12,958'), not to be confused with Purple Peak further south in the range. Several old prospect holes dot the way up the broad south face. From the road's end at the Augusta Mine, the steep ridge to the south is **Cascade Mountain** (11,715'). Climb toward it for a pleasant little lake on a bench and finish by way of the west ridge.

Augusta Mountain (12,559') and **Mineral Point** (12,506') are about 0.75 mile northwest and 0.5 mile north from the mine. Climb up the creek to another bench lake and choose your route.

At mile 5 from Crested Butte on FSR-734, FSR-754 runs west up Oh-Be-Joyful Creek. After about 2 miles, it is for jeeps only. At mile 4 you are directly south of Schuylkill Mountain and 2,000' under it on a steep slope. Garfield and Peeler Peaks are to the south.

ELK MTNS

At mile 5 the road makes a short steep climb to the pack trail, #404, at 10,500'. A mile north is the trail junction in Democrat Basin. The climb from the Basin west to **Oh-Be-Joyful Pass** makes 800 feet in about a mile. Over the pass you drop into the timber of the Raggeds Wilderness on the west side of the range and hike south 9 or 10 miles to the Kebler Pass Road (Gunnison Co Rd-12), meeting it about 12 miles west of Crested Butte.

On Oh-Be-Joyful Pass, you are at the north end of a string of four named 12,000' summits, all on a 2-mile stretch of ridge. **Hancock Peak** (12,410), **Oh-Be-Joyful Peak** (12,400'), and **Afley Peak** (12,646') involve small altitude losses. South of Afley you drop 600' before climbing to **Purple Peak** (12,800').

Trail #404 south from the Oh-Be-Joyful Pass Trail junction turns east and crosses a pass at 11,900' into Peeler Basin, south tributary of Oh-Be-Joyful Creek. From this latter pass it is an easy stroll north to **Garfield Peak** (12,080'), which looked quite high on the valley side, and you can go on about 0.75 mile east to **Peeler Peak** (12,227') with little loss of altitude. Peeler Basin has several little lakes including two fair-sized ones in the timber. On the south side of the basin is Scarp Ridge, rough toward the basin, smooth along the top. It is a pleasant 4-mile ridge walk at altitudes of 12,000'-12,200', running southeast from the Joyful-Peeler Basin to 12,090' **Gunsight Pass**, a saddle west of Mount Emmons.

FSR-585/732 Access:

About a mile short of the turnoff at 8,950' to Oh-Be-Joyful Creek on FSR-734, a jeep road (FSR-585) cuts back along the old railroad grade to start climbing the steep ridges southeast of Oh-BeJoyful Creek. Note that this road has been locked off. It comes to a ragged 11,000' timberline in Redwell Basin in 5 miles, and in 2 more miles to 12,090' Gunsight Pass. In Redwell Basin it joins trail #404 to Peeler Basin and the upper end of the Oh-Be-Joyful valley.

Mount Emmons (12,392'), the summit overlooking Crested Butte from the northwest, is a half-mile walk east and northeast from Gunsight Pass. FSR-732, a jeep road, goes right from the Kebler Pass Road (Gunnison Co Rd-12) about 2 miles west of Crested Butte to join FSR-585. FSR-732 is also locked off. The road goes about a mile west up the hill to the Keystone Mine, then with one switchback, continues west parallel to Rd-12 about 2.5 miles to turn north up Elk Creek and to Gunsight Pass. These jeep roads are good hiking routes to Mount Emmons and Scarp Ridge.

ELK MTNS

Irwin/FSR-826 Access:

Kebler Pass at 9,980' is 7 miles west up Coal Creek from Crested Butte on Gunnison Co Rd-12. Just short of the pass, a secondary road, FSR-826, turns off north for the mining camps of Ruby and Irwin. Just beyond is **Lake Irwin**, prettily reflecting the images of Ruby Peak and its apparent twin Mount Owen (higher, but more distant) in the wilderness.

Ruby Peak (12,644') and **Mount Owen** (13,058'), high point of the range, are best climbed from Lake Irwin, and the campground there. A trail goes a mile northwest to mines at the base of Ruby and then turns north 2 more miles to a mine at 11,600' under the Mount Owen-Purple Peak saddle. From here, the ridges leading to Owen and Purple are steep and loose. Tackle the peaks from the easier ridge connecting to Ruby. You can take Ruby Peak by its southeast ridge and lose 800' of altitude in going on to Mount Owen. Or you can bypass Ruby. Take the first mile of trail from where it turns north, then climb left to 11,653' Green Lake on a bench between the two peaks, continue to the saddle west of the lake, then north on the narrow ridge crest to the summit. **Purple Peak** (12,800') can be combined well with Mount Owen, being only 0.5 mile around the ridge and rising only 200' from it.

ELK MTNS

West Elk Mountains

Jurisdiction:

Gunnison NF, Gunnison and Paonia Ranger Districts

Map area reference:

Page 202

Maps:

USGS: *Anthracite Range, Cathedral Peak, Crawford, Marcellina Mountain, Minnesota Pass, Mount Guero, Mt Axtell, Paonia, Paonia Reservoir, Squirrel Creek, West Beckwith Mountain, West Elk Peak*

Forest Service: *Gunnison NF*

This group includes Carbon Peak, the Anthracite Range and the West Elk Range. The main east side access road, Gunnison Co Rd-730, leaves Hwy-135 about 3 miles north of Gunnison and climbs along Ohio Creek 23 miles north-northwest to Ohio Pass at 10,074'. It joins Gunnison Co Rd-12, connecting Crested Butte west to Paonia Reservoir and Hwy-133, a mile farther north at 9,980' Kebler Pass. Carbon Peak, then the Anthracite Range, and then West Beckwith Peak come into view from down in the valley. There are glimpses of the ridge country of the West Elk Wilderness, bristling for a fight with rock climbers. As you climb up to Ohio Pass look at the water cascading off the Anthracite Range. The lesser-used western approaches are visually enticing too, from the Grand Valley communities of Crawford and Paonia on Hwy-133 and Hwy-92.

The extraordinary cliffs and pinnacles in the West Elks are in a formation called the West Elk Breccia, composed of volcanic agglomerate and breccia, probably Miocene in age.

Anthracite Range/Gunnison Co Rd-730 Access:

Carbon Peak (12,709') can be climbed from the switchback about 20 miles from Gunnison at 9,520'. Go east on a side road that turns into a trail and takes you up the north side of the mountain.

Ohio Peak (12,271') is the most tempting excursion on the Anthracite Range because of the cascades. Instead of going up to **Ohio Pass**, where you have an altitude advantage, leave your car at mile 19.5, 9,400', where the road jogs right and crosses a stream to go up the hillside. Climb up the little ridge left of the stream and enter the wilderness. Take a close look at the falls, then work farther left for the main east ridge. Where it steepens, climb northwest to the crest ridge for the major part of the work. The total distance to the peak is a couple of miles.

The **Anthracite Range** is a 4-mile long east-west curved mountain, with Ohio Peak being an east summit. The higher west summit, at 12,385', is about 1.5 more miles along the ridge, with a 300' obstacle summit and a dip to 11,800' after that on the way. Too much.

West Elk Wilderness/Gunnison Co Rd-730 Access:

The West Elk Mountains have a north-south backbone of 12,000' crest points. Deep-in parts are accessible only from trails through the wilderness.

The Castle Creek Road (FSR-728) that goes west from a little over a mile north of Baldwin is closed, but the **Pass Creek Trail** #439 goes west from a trailhead about 18 miles from Gunnison on Rd-730, and after about 1.5 miles joins a trail that goes south 2 miles to FSR-728. About 1.5 miles west and 0.3 mile south of the trail junction with FSR-728, the **Lowline Trail #438** goes east-southeast to the Mill Creek Road (FSR-727). FSR-727 is locked about a mile west of its junction with trail #438.

Trail #438/842 goes northwest over **Swampy Pass** and **Beckwith Pass** to the campground at Lost Lake Slough, 12 miles. A west branch, trail #441, goes over **Castle Pass** to the trail system west of the West Elks. Trail #450, the **Mill-Castle Trail**, goes south and southwest, climbs over 12,450' **Storm Pass**, and descends east along Mill Creek.

The Castles are a rough section of ridgetop between Castle and South Castle Creek, at about 12,000'. To visit the area, turn up the hill, right, from the Mill-Castle Trail, about where it finishes contouring in close to South Castle Creek. You can climb 700' on a ridge, and then work to the right to get close to the toothsome rocks. The summits are a matter for the technical climber.

West Elk Peak (13,035'), high point of the range, goes from the Mill-Castle Trail. Keep on it until you have climbed 2 or 3 double elbows toward Storm Pass, then head off a little over a mile west to the southeast ridge.

The Mill Creek Road (FSR-727, Gunnison Co Rd-727) goes west from mile 9 on Gunnison Co Rd-730. It joins the Lowline Trail #438 about 3 miles west of Rd-730. At 9,000', just short of the locked gate, it joins the Mill-Castle Trail #450. About 0.5 mile short of Storm Pass, a trail branches west and south a mile, and goes almost to the top of **North Baldy Mountain** (12,850'). **South Baldy Mountain** (12,380') is 3 miles of mostly grassy walking to the south, with a couple of bumps and dips along the way.

ELK MTNS

Kebler Pass/Gunnison Co Rd-12 Access:

The road over **Kebler Pass**, Gunnison Co Rd-12, connects Crested Butte with Hwy- 133 at Paonia Reservoir. About 7 miles west from Crested Butte, it intersects the Ohio Creek Road, Gunnison Co Rd-730, from Gunnison.

Marcellina Mountain (11,348') is north of the main West Elk group and rises 2,700' above the Kebler Pass road to the south. The mountain is a 2 mile long showpiece of Eocene roughness. It appears the rock was pushed up by a Tertiary intrusion and is still angry. To climb it, go west from Crested Butte on Gunnison Co Rd-12 about 16 miles to Trout Creek. Continue northwest about 1.5 miles to where Rd-12 makes a sharp left to descend into Grouse Spring Creek. Turn right on a jeep/pack trail and park. Enter the Raggeds Wilderness and follow the trail east and north along the Trout Creek-Ruby Anthracite Creek Valley. Where the trail crosses a small creek and starts its descent into Ruby Anthracite Creek, work west and northwest to the east ridge. Follow the ridge west a mile to the summit.

East Beckwith Mountain (12,432') is a ridge with 5 almost identical cirques cut into it from the north. The route to it starts about 9 miles west of Kebler Pass on Rd-l 2, where you go south on FSR-706 about 2.5 miles to **Lost Lake Slough** 9,623'. Cross to the east side of the outlet and follow the side of the lake and the creek south all the way up the big cirque; climb out on the cirque's far right corner and finish a little way along the southeast ridge. To do the whole ridge along to West Beckwith Mountain is perfectly possible but very long, and the traverse back to the lake would take you through very rough country. West Beckwith is one of several mountains in the area which seem to have started out as circular domes. Others are Carbon Mountain to the east, and Sand, Saddle, Landsend mountains, and Tater Heap.

Minnesota Creek Access:

The trail up Minnesota Creek East Fork starts from 14 miles east and south of Paonia at the end of FSR-710 at Beaver Reservoir. It crosses **Minnesota Pass** at 9,992' and **Curecanti Pass** at 10,450', and goes down Curecanti Creek to FSR-720, a total distance of 20 miles.

Mount Gunnison (12,719'), on Minnesota Pass and West Beckwith Quads, is a miniature version of Mount McKinley, given enough ice to fill the scooped-out valleys, which fall off from the massif in all directions from the summit region. It is a mountain not to get lost on. The approach is a long one. From Beaver Reservoir, go along the right shore and up East Fork to a trail junction at 8,500'. Find Hoodoo Creek, a little south of the junction, and climb along it east, southeast, east for about 3 miles. This may be the hardest part of the climb. Where the creek gradient becomes quite steep, at about 10,300', leave the valley and climb the slope to its right, a 1,700' rise in one mile. Work left near the top, and you will come out on the easy south-southwest ridge a mile from the summit.

The mountain was named for Captain John Gunnison, who was assigned in 1853 to explore the central of four possible railroad routes across the country. For the twenty wagons in his train, he built a road; over Sangre de Cristo Pass, over Cochetopa Pass, down the Gunnison, and out to Utah, where he was killed by Indians. Beckwith, who succeeded him in command, was honored in the naming of the peaks to the east.

West Access:

Mount Lamborn (11,395'), and **Landsend Peak** (10,806') are the conspicuous peaks near Paonia and Hotchkiss. From Paonia, go southwest on a road south of the North Fork of the Gunnison and parallel to the D&RG tracks. The road crosses the tracks about 1.5 miles from town, and a little later, after you have passed a gravel pit, turns off left and south. After going south 0.5 mile, go east a mile, then south 1.25 miles to a left turn on FSR-834 to Bell Creek Springs, which are

Finding the way   *Chester Stone*

ELK MTNS

3 more miles southeast. At the springs, take trail #894 east-southeast up Bell Creek about 3 miles to a saddle at about 9,650' on the Landsend-Lamborn ridge. Landsend is 2 miles southwest along a flat ridge. Lamborn is 1.5 miles north up-ridge, but if it looks too obstructed, keep on the trail. By way of left forks, it spirals northeast to northwest and in 3 miles puts you within 0.25 mile and 700' of Lamborn on its southeast side.

North and **South Saddle Peaks** (9,728' and 10,005') can be climbed from the south side. From Crawford, drive southeast on Hwy-92 to the Crawford State Recreation Area, then east about 6 miles to a pond at 8,214'. Climb 1.5 miles north-northwest to the south peak, then drop to a 9,340' saddle on the way to North Saddle. There is a lot of private property in this area, so this way may be closed. Another approach is from the north: from Crawford, drive east-north-east on FSR-712 about 7.5 miles to Cow Creek and park. Bushwhack southwest up-ridge to South Saddle Peak, then drop to the 9,340' saddle on the way to North Saddle.

There are other interesting peaks reached via FSR-712 east of Crawford. About 5 miles east of town, you pass just south of the local showpiece, **Needle Rock**. About 10 miles east of town, where the road turns south to Virginia Creek, at about 7,600', you can take a trail system (#860, #861, #862) southeast and east about 3.5 miles, then north about a mile, to **Tater Heap** (10,984'). For **Mount Guero** (12,052') don't turn north to Tater Heap. Continue east on the trail about a mile, then climb north-northeast about a mile to the summit.

To visit **Castle Rock**, the striking 11,205' south point of Mendicant Ridge, drive east and northeast from the Crawford State Recreation Area about 7.5 miles to the locked gate at the Forest boundary. Hike on east about 0.3 mile to a road junction, then turn south on FSR-814 and go about 2.5 miles to about 9,250'. Castle Rock is about a mile southeast.

ELK MTNS

THE SAN JUAN MOUNTAINS

Wham Ridge, Vestal Peak   *David Anschicks*

San Juan Mountains (Eastern)

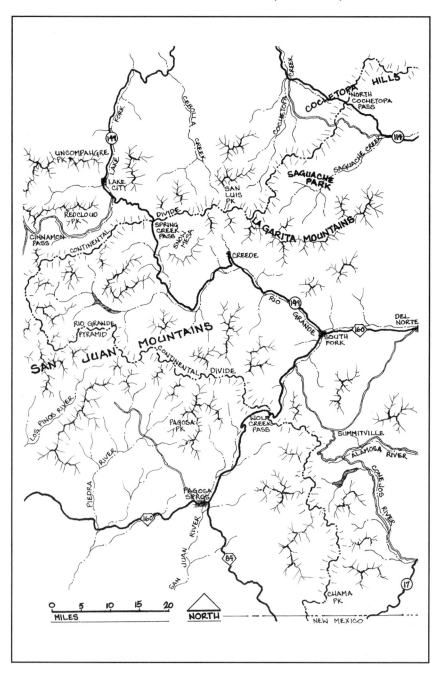

The San Juan Mountains

We tend to speak of the expansive jumble of summits and maze of watersheds in southwest Colorado as "the San Juan," not thinking of them so much as a range but as a large and varied mountain region. As part of this immense area west of the San Luis Valley and south of US-50, the outlying La Plata, Rico and San Miguels form ranges set off from the main group; and the La Garita Mountains and Cochetopa Hills are a muted collection of peaks connected to the mighty Sawatch.

Parts of the San Juan, particularly those around the present day towns of Creede, Lake City, Ouray, Telluride and Silverton, were prospected and mined from the 1860's on. Old homes, stores, churches and courthouses preserve the flavor of earlier times, and the abandoned mines with their dumps of colored rock, the mills, and the tramways are all a part of the scene for the visitor.

Fortunately, not all the San Juan produced pay metal enough to be built up with towns and roads. The Needle Mountains and Grenadiers are roadless, almost trailless, hard to reach, hard to get around in, and very wild and rough. All of us who have been there hope that man's propensity to develop things will not encroach on the wilderness areas that preserve large sections of the San Juan.

This uncompromising area of dazzling spires, jagged ridges, and glaciated valleys, has lured generations of mountaineers. The CMC began leading expeditions into the San Juan in the 1920's. A few years later, a small but enthusiastic group of climbers organized themselves into the San Juan Mountaineers (SJM) and began an ambitious goal of surveying the crags and needles for their like-minded peers. *The San Juan Mountaineer's Climber's Guide to Southwestern Colorado* by Dwight Lavender and Carleton Long, was never published, but remained in mimeograph form, mainly due to Lavender's untimely death in 1934. Only more recently was a comprehensive climber's guide published to the San Juan, (Bob Rosebrough's *The San Juan Mountains: A Climbing and Hiking Guide*) and all contemporary works refer to the SJM guide of nearly 60 years before. It remains a testament to the diligence and thoroughness of those fearless young climbers of another era, that we still refer to their work, especially since they didn't have modern transportation and equipment that we take for granted. For unnamed summits, we still refer to the SJM original terminology (example: T11, for Telluride #11; S5, for Sneffels #5; etc).

The Needles are granite. The Grenadiers and West Needles are quarzite. The great majority of the other peaks in the San Juans are volcanic in origin. This is important since it accounts for the looseness of the rock throughout the range.

Northeast Section

Jurisdiction:
Gunnison NF; Gunnison Ranger District
Rio Grande NF; Divide Ranger District-Creede, Saguache Ranger District

Map area reference:
Page 236

Maps:
USGS: *Baldy Cinco, Elk Park, Lake San Cristobal, Halfmoon Pass, San Luis Peak, Slumgullion Pass, Stewart Peak*
Forest Service: *Gunnison NF, Rio Grande NF*

This rarely visited section of the San Juan stretches southwest to northeast along the crest of the Continental Divide for nearly 80 miles; from Spring Creek Pass, the divide crossing of Hwy-149 between Lake City and Creede, to Windy Peak south of Marshall Pass. The main attractions are the contiguous routes of the Colorado and Continental Divide Trails, which follow on or slightly to one side of the crest, and an isolated fourteener, San Luis Peak. Included in this section are the almost unknown, but historically significant, La Garita Mountains and wilderness of the same name, and Cochetopa Hills, areas of intense solitude. Given their characteristic isolation, accesses can be long, and sometimes difficult.

Spring Creek Pass/Hwy-149 Access:

Hwy-149, the road between Creede and Lake City, is one of only two paved accesses to this section; both are Continental Divide crossings. At the crest of 10,898' **Spring Creek Pass**, the CT and CDT go east and west, giving easy access to the summits which top the lofty divide in both directions.

West of the pass, the trail route follows FSR-550, a jeep road, for 10 miles. The first 5 contour around the south side of **Jarosa Mesa** (12,054'), which has a smooth velvety look from willows you want to avoid. Follow FSR-550 to the west side of the mesa, then head north and east to the top. Or follow the old **La Garita Stock Driveway** due west from east of the mesa, staying in an ancient swath cut in the willows, to the top.

FSR-550 continues west and then southwest, to its end at the head of Big Buck Creek. From here, the trail continues southwest rounding several bumps on the divide, highest of which is **Coney** (13,334'), for which you would need to travel 16 miles from Spring Creek Pass. This is impressive country of rolling highlands. Coney is more often driven to by 4WD vehicle. Go 6.5 miles on the Wager Gulch Road up from the valley of the Lake Fork south-southwest of Lake City. You pass the ghost mining camp of Carson en route.

Solitude in the San Juans   *Rolf Asphaug*

A climb on the CT and CDT east of Spring Creek Pass takes you 1.8 miles to the western edge of impressive **Snow Mesa**, an almost unbelievable rolling alpine pasture encompassing some 5 square miles and elevated to 12,200'. Look for elk grazing in its broad recesses. North of Snow Mesa rises **Baldy Cinco** (13,383'), an easy climb 1.5 miles northeast from the west edge of the mesa. A further hike east on the trail route towards San Luis Pass skirts several unnamed high points exceeding 13,000'. Many are worthy of protracted side-trips, not mere bumps on the divide.

San Luis Pass/FSR-503 Access:

The area north of Creede is a world of seemingly endless mountaintops and ridges extending from the divide. It is accessible to sturdy and maneuverable autos. Go due north of Creede on FSR-503 6.5 miles to the Equity Mine. There is a pull-out here, but 4WD vehicles can continue 1.5 miles further north. Continue the last 1.5 miles north on foot to 11,960' **San Luis Pass** on the divide, the boundary between Gunnison NF and Rio Grande NF and the southern limit of the La Garita Wilderness.

A scenic alpine route, gaining popularity, to **San Luis Peak** (14,014') begins here. At the pass, follow the fairly legible footpath of the CT and CDT east, over a hump on the divide into Spring Creek valley, where there are some camping opportunities in a high spruce forest within the wilderness. Continue on the trail to the 12,600' saddle due south of the peak, a 3.8 mile walk from San Luis Pass. From here it is a 1.3 mile ridge-walk north to the summit. The more standard route to San Luis is described under Stewart Creek Trail Access.

Stewart Creek Trail Access:

San Luis Peak (14,014'), **Baldy Alto** (13,698') and **Stewart Peak** (13,983') extend in line on a north-south ridge, traditionally climbed from the east up Stewart Creek.

To find this remote point of departure deep within the forest, descend west 5.2 miles from **North Pass** (sometimes called North Cochetopa Pass), the Continental Divide crossing on Hwy-114 connecting Saguache and Gunnison, and turn left (south) on Gunnison Co Rd-l 7GG. Continue 5.2 miles and go right (west) on Rd-NN14. Go west 1.3 miles and turn left (south) on Rd-15GG. Continue following the main road, which is marked as "Stewart Creek", 20 miles to the parking area for **Stewart Creek Trail** at 10,500'.

Continue on foot 4.5 miles southwest to timberline, then west-southwest to the 13,200' saddle, from where it is a 0.75 mile ridge-walk south to San Luis. The thirteeners Stewart and Baldy are accessible north on the same ridge line. Stewart is at the head of Nutras Creek, the next drainage north of Stewart Creek. From here you would need to contour to return to the parking area. A one point Stewart was considered a fourteener but subsequent measurements have reduced it to merely a "centennial".

Organ Mountain (13,799') is the high point of a ridge extending east from San Luis Peak. It gets its name from a cluster of thin pinnacles guarding the summit but like most others in the area, the climb is long and gentle. Continue another mile on the road past the Stewart Creek trailhead to where the **Skyline Trail** heads south along the west side of Cochetopa Creek. Follow the trail 5.5 miles, as it winds around the massive east ridge of Organ. Climb it by leaving the trail for the drainage that descends off the grassy, southeast flank.

La Garita Mountains

Maps:

USGS: *Bowers Mountain, Creede, Halfmoon Pass, Lookout Mountain, Mesa Mountain, Pool Table Mountain, Wagon Wheel Gap*
Forest Service: *Rio Grande NF*

The La Garita Mountains are a spur off the divide north of Creede and continue 20 miles east to the western edge of the San Luis Valley. The east section is largely in timber, while the west end rises higher, and is more distinctly a ridge, flattened at its crest, giving the main range area a unique alpine mesa appearance. Accesses are straightforward, from the north, south, east and west. The western section is within the boundary of the La Garita Wilderness, and the showcase of the range is a square mile of weird spires and crevices comprising the Wheeler Geologic Area.

La Garita Access:

The town of La Garita, 6 miles west of US-285 on Saguache Co Rd-G in the San Luis Valley, has a road running 10.5 miles northwest up Carnero Creek to a junction. The left road (FSR-675), in South Carnero Creek, runs from this junction 11 miles northwest to Moon Pass at 10,600'. About 2 miles short of the pass, FSR-676 to Miners Creek runs off left (west) along the creek. At mile 3 is the crossing of South Carnero Creek at 10,800' and the start of the La Garita Stock Driveway.

Bowers Peak (12,449') is at the head of South Carnero Creek, and a mile north of the stock driveway. From where the road crosses the creek, hike southwest on the trail up-creek for 2.5 miles, then cut right for a 0.5 mile climb north.

Hwy-149 Access:

The high section of the La Garitas stair-steps south to the Rio Grande, making the drive from South Fork to Creede on Hwy-149 a most scenic approach.

One of the southernmost high points, **Pool Table Mountain** (12,218'), is approached 0.5 mile west of South Fork on Hwy-l 49. After crossing the Rio Grande, turn right onto an unmarked road. Travel 1.2 miles and turn onto the Alder Creek Road (FSR-610). Continue north to Pool Table Park at 11,000'. The mountaintop is 1.5 miles further north.

La Garita Peak (13,710') is the southeast corner piece of a 4 mile northwest-southeast ridge of middling high thirteeners, 7 miles northeast of Creede. Start on the Wason-Wheeler Trail from Creede's lower east side at 8,800' (100 yards south of the Baptist Church), and climb via Inspiration Point 6 miles to the 11,700' flats northeast of **Mammoth Mountain** (11,658'). Loaf 3 more miles in Wason Park to an intersection. From there the route proceeds directly northeast to the peak, 1,700' higher and 1.5 miles distant. **Peak 13,895'** is to the northwest in 3 miles following this high, handsome ridge.

Pool Table Road (FSR-600), starting 13 miles northwest of South Fork on Hwy-149, runs east-northeast 9 miles to the Hanson Mill, then continues 15 more miles as a notorious jeep road to **Wheeler Geologic Area**. To hike the same, park at mile 9 near the Hanson Mill camping site and follow old FSR-790, now trail #790, about 8 miles to the Wheeler Area. There is also a walking route via the wilderness area (see Saguache Park Access).

Saguache Park Access:

FSR-787, Saguache Park Road, is the backdoor approach to the La Garitas and the wilderness area. To begin the long road in, descend west 5.2 miles from **North Pass** (sometimes called North Cochetopa Pass), the Continental Divide crossing on Hwy-114 connecting Saguache and Gunnison, and turn left (south) on Gunnison Co Rd-17GG. Continue 5.2 miles and go left (east) on Rd-NN14, the Cochetopa Pass Road. Drive 1.1 miles east and go right (south) on Rd-17FF, Saguache Park Road. It is 8 miles south to the divide, where you cross into the Rio Grande NF, Saguache County, and where expansive **Saguache Park** opens up, displaying a panorama of the La Garita main range, west to San Luis Peak. From the divide, it is 4 miles further to Stone Cellar Campground, 10 miles to the South Fork Saguache Creek Trailhead, and 12 miles to the road end at the Sky City Mine.

From the South Fork Saguache Trailhead, you enter the wilderness almost immediately, and go to 12,480' **Halfmoon Pass**. You can get there by continuing southwest up the South Fork, or by taking a side trail to the right at mile 0.5 from the trailhead. This route goes almost due west up an unnamed side drainage. The two trails meet at the head of Twin Peaks Creek, a mile northeast of, and 800' below, the pass. At Halfmoon Pass, you stand on one of the main crossings in the La Garitas. Although La Garita Peak might be too long and tedious a trudge from here, **Palmer Mesa** (12,231') is a 3 mile hike southeast along the flattened crest of the range via the old La Garita Stock Driveway. And **Wheeler Geologic Area** is a pleasant 1.2 miles walk south.

The sometimes obscure trail system continues from upper Twin Peaks Creek northwest to **Machin Lake**, north of the main range crest, with spurs continuing northeast down Halfmoon and Middle Creeks to Saguache Park, or north into the Cochetopa Lake Fork. This is lonely country, bring your map and compass.

SAN JUAN

Cochetopa Hills

Maps:

USGS: *Chester, Cochetopa Park, North Pass, Sargents Mesa, West Baldy*
Forest Service: *Gunnison NF, Rio Grande NF*

The Cochetopa Hills carry the Continental Divide southwest 50 miles from the three county corner 3 miles south of Marshall Pass, to the junction with the La Garita Mountains, 7 miles northeast of Creede. Unlike other ranges in the state which host the Continental Divide, the Cochetopa Hills are a rambling string of summits which rarely top out above timberline. Marshall Pass, once an exciting ride over the divide on rails, and now a tedious trip by auto, is a landmark on the CT and CDT. South of the pass, the contiguous trails follow the rolling forested divide to Hwy-114 at North Pass, with only brief detours into Tank Seven and Razor Creeks. On the way, the trails either skirt or mount the major summits of the range. This trip is a 2 day backpack at minimum, plus a long car shuttle. The individual points can be visited by car, with lengthy strolls in one direction or the other on the divide.

Marshall Pass Access:

Marshall Pass Road, the abandoned meandering grade of the D&RGRR, is a more historic road over the divide than its paralleling US-50 Monarch Pass route, for those who enjoy such drawn-out diversions. It connects US-50 at Sargents with US-285 5 miles south of Poncha Springs.

From the road cut at the top of the pass, the CT and CDT continue south and west as one well-marked route 5 miles to **Windy Peak** (11,885'). The first section of the trail takes you to the head of Silver Creek, the last mile on an old road. Then continue west 1.5 miles to the south face of the peak, the trail climbs to within 200 vertical feet of the summit.

Hwy-114 Access:

Few Colorado passes over the divide have such a lengthy and impressive history as North Cochetopa Pass on Hwy-114, and its twin 4 miles south, **Cochetopa Pass**, on FSR- 750. This unusual low swath on the divide, linking the Sawatch and San Juan, was used for centuries by Indians and buffalo shuttling between the continental watersheds. When the white man appeared, the trails were already well-established. Today's roads, following those ancestral trails, still carry the Ute word for "pass of the buffalo."

SAN JUAN

A series of isolated summits north of Hwy-114 is reached by lengthy hikes on logging roads, from either of two directions. **Long Branch Baldy** (11,974') and **Middle Baldy** (11,680') are on the route of the CT and CDT. The first approach begins 1 mile west of North Pass on Hwy-114. Head up Lujan Creek Road (Rd-31CC) 2 miles to a cattle guard, which marks the top of the divide. Continue on the left fork 0.1 mile and watch for the CT to bear left from the road. Follow the trail northwest on the undulating divide 9 miles to Middle Baldy, then 2 miles east to Long Branch Baldy. **West Baldy** (11,449') is a 1.5 mile bushwhack west from upper Razor Park on your way.

For a longer drive, but a shorter walk to the same summits, turn on Rd-EE38 from Hwy-114, 10.5 miles west of Saguache. Continue 6 miles to Rd-32JJ (FSR-855) and go right. Travel 10 miles and go left at the fork marked Cameron Park. In 0.4 mile the improved road ends but 4WD vehicles can go another 0.7 mile to the broad open summit of **Sargents Mesa** (11,719') where you will intersect the CT and CDT. From here it is 7 miles west and northwest on the divide to Long Branch Baldy

Big Blue Wilderness   *Spencer Swanger*

Lake City and Vicinity

Jurisdiction:

Gunnison NF, Gunnison Ranger District
Rio Grande NF, Divide Ranger District-Creede
Uncompahgre NF, Ouray Ranger District
BLM, Montrose District, Gunnison Resource Area

Map area reference:

Page 236 and 249

Maps:

USGS: *Finger Mesa, Handies Peak, Lake City, Lake San Cristobal, Pole Creek Mountain, Redcloud Peak, Uncompahgre Peak, Wetterhorn Peak*
Forest Service: *Gunnison NF, Rio Grande NF, Uncompahgre NF*

The mountains covered here are those around the two streams flowing from the west into Lake City: the Lake Fork, named for Lake San Cristobal, and Henson Creek. The green, rolling basins and gentle walk-up summits were probably all visited early on by miners, surveyors, and the like; except for rugged Wetterhorn, which was not climbed until 1906. Practically the whole area has been identified as one huge, ancient caldera, where the volcanic rocks achieve high coloration in areas like Redcloud Peak. Lake San Cristobal itself was formed by a giant landslide, which continues to creep imperceptibly down the slopes south of town.

Access is on roads driveable for long distances up both main valleys. The roads continue as jeep routes west into the Ouray-Silverton country. The one up Henson Creek is the more scenic, climbing to 12,950' Engineer Pass, with a steep side road to Uncompahgre Peak and a 360 degree view of the San Juans. The other road, climbing 26 miles to near the end of the Lake Fork, crosses at Cinnamon Pass, way down at 12,600' where you can't see much. Both go down the Animas to Silverton. A rougher, more northerly branch goes down Mineral Creek to US-550 and Ouray.

Henson Creek Access:

The road up Henson Creek begins in Lake City and continues west 19 miles to **Engineer Pass**. Beyond Rose Cabin, the road is suitable only for 4WD vehicles.

Uncompahgre Peak (14,309') has a slanted anvil profile well known to the San Juan's high country visitors. The trail up the broad south ridge is the standard route. Drive 5.5 miles west up Henson Creek from Lake City. Starting at 9,310', hike or jeep north up Nellie Creek, going left at the junction 4 miles to the Big Blue Wilderness boundary. The trail continues about 4 miles west, and then north

Uncompahgre Peak   David Anschicks

to the summit. If coming from Wetterhorn, examine the west face for a prominent gully near the middle. Steep and with rock problems, it at least avoids an end run around the south ridge, and joins the trail near the summit. Once on the top, those who aren't faint-hearted should peer carefully down the dramatic north face.

North and east of Uncompahgre are several peaks, many unnamed, spread over a rolling tundra landscape. **Silver Mountain** (13,714') and **Peak 13,681'** are a couple of the more prominent, and can be reached from the same trail up Nellie Creek as for Uncompahgre. Less than a mile past the wilderness boundary, a trail to the right goes north over a 12,400' pass into the Big Blue Creek drainage. At 11,400' a trail heads northwest toward Silver's easy south ridge. To gain it, leave the trail at about 12,200' and hike directly west to a low point on the ridge and turn north. Peak 13,681' is another mile north from there across the tundra. If you head east from the above mentioned pass, you can go either over or around several bumps and in 3 or 4 miles reach **Crystal Peak** (12,933'). To descend, hike west to pick up an old trail that comes up the east fork of Nellie Creek.

A not very imposing **Matterhorn Peak** (13,590') is sometimes climbed en route between the area's two notable fourteeners. Travel through the grassy basin and up the south ridge, finishing with broken, yet easy, third class. **Broken Hill** (13,256') can likewise be reached as a side excursion between the fourteeners by hiking up its grassy, rolling north ridge.

For **Wetterhorn Peak** (14,015'), hike west 3 miles or so across the basin from Uncompahgre. For an alternate route for both peaks or Wetterhorn alone, drive 9.5 miles west from Lake City to Capitol City (not much there) and take the right fork for 2 miles to Matterhorn Creek at 10,350'. Four-wheelers can go up the road a mile or so to the wilderness boundary, otherwise walk north 3 miles up into the basin, and then cut across a mile to the southeast ridge of the peak. Follow this on the east side until you pass through the prominent notch, and finish on the southwest face. This last 400' is exciting: on small ledges sprinkled with sand, and occasionally ice. Parties should have a rope along just in case. Long approaches up the trails of the Cimarron River from the north have also been used for access. There is a six pitch technical route on the fine north face.

Wildhorse Peak (13,266') is an abrupt, conspicuous peak seen from Montrose or US-550. From a little off Engineer Pass on the Lake City side, it is a 3 mile walk, mostly by trail, north over American Flats. Hike up the grassy slope from the southwest. If this isn't enough, there are half a dozen unnamed "twelvers" and "thirteeners" on the long rolling ridge heading northeast to Wetterhorn. Approach these from American Flats, or drive up the North Fork of Henson Creek to the road end, about 11 miles from Lake City. Several stock trails access this country from there.

The designated point **Dolly Varden Mountain** (12,932') isn't exactly attached to the high point of the ridge. It can be reached from American Flats by a 2 mile trek southeast across the tundra from near American Lake. The higher point is a half mile east with an easy 300' drop on the way.

Lake Fork Access:

This popular access forks right off Hwy-149 about 2 miles south of Lake City. The first several miles to the head of Lake San Cristobal are paved, after which the road experiences stages of deterioration. A 4WD vehicle is required to reach the crest of **Cinnamon Pass.**

The ridge between Henson Creek and the Lake Fork has several high points that are easy enough to climb if you have the ambition. Mostly this country can be described as hillside walking. **Red Mountain** (12,826') has a trail part way up it from the north end of Lake San Cristobal. A stroll of 2 miles to the south-southwest will take you up its near neighbor, **Grassy Mountain** (12,821').

Wetterhorn Peak   *Mike Endres*

The obscure **Peak 13,832'** and its unnamed neighbors have only recently gained attention because of their inclusion on lists of the highest 100 and 200 peaks in the state. To climb the peak, drive 15 miles up the Lake Fork from Lake City, and take the right-hand road toward Cinnamon Pass. Continue for 4.2 miles to Silver Creek at 10,400'. Take the trail up Silver Creek about 5 miles to a pass, turn left and hike northeast and then southeast, following the crest over a false summit. **Peak 13,811'** is usually climbed with its near companion Peak 13,832', by hiking 1.5 miles east from the latter along the crest of the ridge. The false summit along the way can be easily skirted on the south.

For **Redcloud Peak** (14,034'), begin at the trailhead for Silver Creek as described above for Peak 13,832', but head southwest from the pass for the final 0.5 mile pull. It is also possible to climb the mostly grassy northwest side of the peak from lower down the creek. The peak gets its name from the lovely rouge of its rocks, a rhyolite that is visible on several surrounding peaks.

Sunshine Peak (14,001) is a close companion of Redcloud and is usually climbed with it by hiking 2 miles south from the Redcloud summit, taking a 700' drop along the way.

Sunshine and Redcloud Peaks

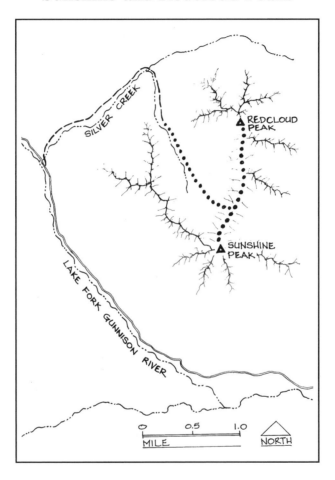

Ormes was fond of calling **Peak 13,688'** "Three Faces Mountain", apparently as seen from Alpine Gulch to the east. Though easy to climb from this side, a more common approach is by Cooper Creek to the west. Drive up the Lake Fork as described above but continue another 1.5 miles beyond Silver Creek to the parking area at Rock Creek. An old road begins here and travels east and then north about three miles to a trail junction. Take the right-hand trail as it doglegs east into the basin. It is more pleasant to climb the talus to the 13,400' point a half mile north of the summit, than to climb it directly. **Peak 13,691'** is climbed by hiking 1.5 miles northeast from Peak 13,688'. To descend, go west a mile along the ridge to pick up the trail that drops into Cooper Creek.

For **Peak 13,566'**, hike up the Cooper Creek Trail noted above, but contour west at the trail junction for Cooper Lake and then hop on the northeast ridge. **Peak 13,312'** is a mile further southwest, losing 700' along the way. More obscure thirteeners exist west along this ridge toward Cinnamon Pass. One could continue hiking southwest from here and tackle the entire 6 miles or so of ridge and descend Cleveland Gulch to the road for a long 15 mile loop. Whew!

Grizzly Gulch, known for its summer display of alpine flowers, is the preferred trailhead for a small group of peaks dominated by the fourteener Handies. For **Peak 13,795'**, head south, across from the Silver Creek trailhead on the Lake Fork Road, where a bridge allows hikers to cross the river. Follow the trail 2.5 miles southwest up Grizzly Gulch to the lake at 12,323', then ascend south into the small basin directly beneath the peak. Climb steeply up grass and talus to the saddle 0.25 mile west of the summit, then stroll to the top. Further east, around a curving cirque, is **Peak 13,454'**. There is a 400' walk up from the low point between the two.

Handies Peak (14,048') is climbed from Grizzly Gulch, as above, to about 11,900', then turn west and ascend mostly grassy slopes a mile to the Handies-Whitecross saddle. The north ridge provides easy slopes to the summit. Some parties drive another 5 miles along the Lake Fork Road from Silver Creek and hike another 2 or so miles to **Sloan Lake** in American Basin. A scenic place with steep headwalls, it is an steep pull up Handies' southwest face.

Whitecross Mountain (13,542') goes up Grizzly Gulch to the Handies-Whitecross saddle as above. Head right for the Whitecross south ridge, 500' of grass and talus.

Wager Gulch/Cataract Gulch Access:

The Continental Divide takes a big sweep to the west, just south of the Lake Fork Road. Previous editions of the guide referred to this 50 mile horseshoe curve between **Spring Creek Pass** at the northeast end and **Weminuche Pass** at the southeast end as the "Bend." Several of these summits have access from Lake City.

Bent Peak (13,393') and **Carson Peak** (13,657') can be reached from Wager Gulch. Drive 8.5 miles up the Lake Fork Road from its junction with Hwy-149, about 2 miles south of Lake City. The Wager Gulch jeep road takes you south 5 miles, passing the ghost town of Carson en route, to a saddle at 12,360' on the divide. The road continues as a rough jeep road over a 13,000' ridge and then south and east to Heart and Pearl Lakes. From the saddle on the divide, Bent Peak is a mile west-northwest, Carson another mile.

A camp at **Cataract Lake** gives access to some of the more interesting peaks in the area. To get there, follow the Lake Fork Road to Cottonwood Creek, the tributary of the Lake Fork which comes in at Sherman, mile 16 from Lake City. The jeep road west from Sherman can be followed for 4.5 miles up Cottonwood Creek to the mouth of Cuba Gulch, 10,800'. It continues as a trail 5 miles southwest to the crest trail on the divide.

At mile 1 west of Sherman, wade to the south side of Cottonwood Creek, and follow the trail up Cataract Gulch 5 miles to Cataract Lake at 12,082'. On the way you will pass some beautiful waterfalls and have access to some fine 13,000' summits 2 miles to the west. Notable among these is **Half Peak** (13,841'). To climb it, head for the saddle on the northeast ridge, a fun scramble starting on talus and finishing with steep third class. To visit **Peak 13,674'** to the north, return to the same saddle and climb north up the ridge to about 13,300'. Drop into the basin to the northeast about 400' so as to pass the pinnacles on the ridge just south of the summit. Climb northwest and finish on the north ridge. From here, take a gander at Half's rugged north face, one of the few serious technical climbs in the area.

South of a camp at Cataract Lake is a huge, isolated mass called **Pole Creek Mountain** (13,716'). Climb to the 12,400' pass southeast of the lake and walk southwest along the ridge tops. There is an optional side climb of **Peak 13,660'** along the way. The true summit for this second peak is a rotten block involving some exposed scrambling. Bypass a few obstacles on their west side, just before the summit of Pole Creek.

From the same pass on the divide, the trail comes into the La Garita Stock Driveway, now the route of the CT and CDT. East along the driveway there are trail connections down East and West Lost Trail Creeks to Lost Trail Campground at the head of Rio Grande Reservoir. There are trails up the west and north forks of Pole Creek leading to Continental Divide passes. These go down Minnie and Maggie Gulches to the Animas Forks Road (San Juan Co Rd-2) out of Silverton.

Head east on the driveway to reach more unnamed thirteeners. **Peaks 13,450'** and **13,580'** are easy ascents north and south respectively from where the trail crosses a 12,900' pass. A bit more than 0.25 mile north of the former is **Peak 13,524'**. It would probably go by either its short west or east ridges, after dropping to the 13,080' saddle from Peak 13,450'.

Peak 13,581', the end point on the ridge southeast of the 12,900' pass, is a difficult scramble once beyond the 13,568' sub-peak. Drop down a couple hundred feet and pass the pinnacles in the low point on their north sides and regain the crest.

SAN JUAN

Southeast Section

Jurisdiction:

Rio Grande NF; Divide Ranger District-Creede, Conejos Peak Ranger District, Divide Ranger District-Del Norte
San Juan NF; Pagosa Ranger District

Map area reference:

Page 236

Maps:

USGS: (*as detailed in each access*)
Forest Service: *Rio Grande NF, San Juan NF*

This section covers an immense area including the Continental Divide from Hunchback Pass at the head of Vallecito Creek, southeast to the border of New Mexico, encompassing some 140 lineal miles along the crest. The area from Hunchback Pass to Wolf Creek Pass on US-160, is within the Weminuche Wilderness. South of Wolf Creek Pass is the large and rarely visited South San Juan Wilderness. Within the boundaries of the two wilderness areas, it is the dramatic lay of the land that attracts introspective CDT backpackers and day hikers from the remote trailheads. Rio Grande Pyramid is the most prominent peak in this section.

Rio Grande/Hwy-149 Access:

Maps:

USGS: *Finger Mesa, Palomino Mountain, Pole Creek Mountain, Rio Grande Pyramid, South River Peak, Spar City, Storm King Peak, Weminuche Pass, Workman Creek*

The more conspicuous summits of the section are perhaps best approached at the head of the Rio Grande, west of Creede on Hwy-149. The drive into the site of Beartown, your closest approach to **Hunchback Pass**, will require a 4WD vehicle.

From Creede, drive west on Hwy-149 21 miles. Go left, continuing west, on FSR-520 marked as "Rio Grande Reservoir." The graded road goes in 19 miles, just beyond the head of the reservoir, and continues 5 more miles as a 4WD road to a fork. The right fork begins a long pull to Stony Pass on the divide, the historic route to Silverton. The left fork goes 4 miles southwest to the Beartown site and one more mile to a deadend at **Kite Lake**, just below the divide. The trail to Hunch back Pass starts south of the road about half way between Beartown and the lake. This is also the east approach to the Grenadiers.

From 0.25 mile west of the old Beartown site, just after the crossing of Bear Creek, the trail to **Starvation Pass** (also called Ute Pass in earlier editions) goes southeast 2 miles to the 12,702' saddle between the two southwestern-most summits of **Ute Ridge**, a curious offshoot from the divide. Its 6.5 miles have a profile of ten summits, the first five above 13,000'.

Pole Creek Mountain (13,716') takes up most of the USGS map named for it. Start one mile beyond the Rio Grande Reservoir at the trailhead for Lost Trail Creek. Hike north 2 miles, and go west up West Lost Trail Creek trail 4.5 miles to timberline. Head southwest, maneuvering through willows in a shallow cirque on trail remnants created by grazing sheep, around point 13,066'. Follow the main ridge south to the summit.

Rio Grande Pyramid (13,821') has its shortest approach from Thirty Mile Campground, just short of the reservoir on FSR-520. Take the trail west 1.5 miles along the south side of the reservoir, then southwest up Weminuche Creek 4 miles to 10,630' **Weminuche Pass**. Follow the trail west 4 miles and up to the summit by its long east ridge.

South River Peak (13,149') and **Piedra Peak** (12,328') are approached from either the north or the south. The north access starts 6 miles southwest of Creede on Hwy-149, using the Middle Creek Road. The jeep road up Red Mountain Creek may be closed by private property, if so, use the Ivy Creek Trail approach. For both, take Middle Fork Road (FSR-523) 4 miles and fork left on FSR-528. Travel 2.6 miles and then take FSR-526 3 miles to Ivy Creek Campground. The jeep road up Red Mountain Creek starts here with a ford of the creek. If there are no private property disputes, you can continue within 2 to 3 miles of the wilderness boundary. Piedra Peak is directly south. Keep left up the drainage to 11,500' Piedra Pass where you climb west 1.5 miles to Piedra Peak or east 1.5 miles to South River Peak. The trail approach starts at Ivy Creek Campground and Trailhead. It is 9 miles to **Goose Lake** just below South River Peak, and another mile further to the divide.

The south approach to the peaks goes up the West Fork San Juan River. Start at West Fork Campground, 9 miles west of **Wolf Creek Pass** on US-160. Head northwest 10 miles up the creek to a trail junction near the divide between the two peaks.

Piedra Road Access:
Maps:
USGS: *Bear Mountain, Cimarrona Peak, Granite Lake, Granite Peak, Oakbrush Ridge, Pagosa Peak, Palomino Mountain*

Piedra Road (FSR-631) turns off US-160 2 miles west of Pagosa Springs. It has forks and spurs that run into Williams Creek, Weminuche Creek and the Middle Fork, to name a few.

SAN JUAN

Pagosa Peak (12,640') is a conspicuous peak straight north of Pagosa Springs. To get near it, turn right off the Piedra Road 12.7 miles from US-160 onto FSR-633. Three miles farther, a more conspicuous road (FSR-634) heads off right (east) toward the timbered massif of **Black Mountain** (10,909'). Where this road turns abruptly south on a switchback at mile 2.5, there is a little used road running toward Black Mountain. Some cars drive this road toward and around right of Black Mountain for about 4 miles, where it comes to Little Pagosa Creek. Walk up the road until it takes a right fork, then climb through a certain amount of downed timber to the saddle south of Pagosa. Go up the steep but clean south ridge to the summit.

At 17.5 miles from US-160, the Middle Fork Road (FSR-636) goes right 5 miles to near the wilderness boundary. **Piedra Peak** (12,328'), on the divide, has a 10 mile trail from the end of the road. The first part is a steep climb out of the canyon, the rest winds northeast passing **Sugarloaf Mountain** (12,593') and **Palomino Mountain** (12,230') en route.

At mile 21.5 from US-160, go right on FSR-640 4 miles to the head of Williams Creek Reservoir and Cimarrona Campground. Long trails take you up Williams Creek, Indian Creek and Cimarrona Creek to the divide. There they meet the Squaw Creek and West Trout Creek Trails from the Rio Grande side. The most interesting of these is the Cimarrona Creek trail. **Cimarrona Peak** (12,536'), a handsomely jutting point 0.5 mile southeast of the divide, is approached from this trail by a short climb up ridge from the north.

Bighorn Sheep   *CMC archives*

Hossick (12,967') is only a designated triangulation point, but it is a fine peak for a look at the area. To reach it, turn left at the head of the Williams Creek Reservoir onto FSR- 644, and travel 3 miles to the trailhead at Poison Park. In about 2 miles, the trail splits, straight ahead for **Granite Lake**, right for Hossick. Go northeast to Hossick Lake, then make a steep hill climb to the peak. This trail meets with the one which almost ascends neighboring Cimarrona Peak, making for a circle trip back down to the reservoir.

Graham Peak (12,531') is conspicuous for its notch and for its isolation as seen from the Piedra Road. Take the left fork into Weminuche Creek at mile 21.5 from US-160, and go 20 miles west into the timbered country until you reach the Pine Piedra trail. The trail takes you northwest then north to the mountain top. **Granite Peak** (12,147') is 2 miles southwest along the easy ridge from Graham.

Summitville/Platoro Access:
Maps:
USGS: *Elwood Pass, Greenie Mountain, Jasper, Platoro, Summitville, Summit Peak*

There is a delightful plateau of grassland, timber, and moderate but varied summits centered around Summitville and Platoro. The area is generally east of the Continental Divide, between US-160 and the Conejos River. The main roads in are: 1, up FSR-250 along the Conejos River to Platoro, starting about 22 miles west of Antonito on Hwy-17; 2, up FSR-250 along the Alamosa River, starting about 20 miles south of Monte Vista on Hwy-15 (the first two routes connect above Platoro); 3, up FSR-380 along Park Creek to Summitville, starting about 6 miles south of South Fork on US-160; 4, up FSR-14 then FSR-330 along Pines Creek to Summitville going southwest from Del Norte (the last two routes connect near Summitville). These four routes are linked together, from Summitville to Platoro, by a 10 mile long extension of FSR-380 over **Elwood Pass**.

Summit Peak (13,300') and **Montezuma Peak** (13,150') on the Continental Divide are off the Elwood Pass Road. From either Summitville or Platoro, drive to Lakes Annella and De Nolda, 4 miles south of Elwood Pass on FSR-380, and go west on FSR-243 up Treasure Creek. The road ends in about 3 miles at 10,880' near the boundary of the South San Juan Wilderness. From the road end, follow an indistinct steep route up the north (right) side of the creek, where the cascades provide an attractive distraction, until you can safely cross to the south side of the creek. Then cut south a mile to get past the east ridge of Summit Peak, and come up to the summit on the southeast face. For Montezuma, which is 1.5 miles north of Summit Peak, drop to the Continental Divide Trail and pick a route for the final 500' climb. Return east and south to Treasure Creek.

SAN JUAN

Lookout Mountain (12,448') is tempting for the flat rhombus which is its summit, and for its high coloring. From 1 mile east of Lakes Annella and De Nolda, near where FSR-380 crosses Iron Creek at 10,520', follow a jeep trail about 0.75 mile, and climb to the right on one of the ridges 1 mile to the summit. **Cropsy Mountain** (12,578') is 1.5 miles north over a ridge that drops off sharply at both ends to a low point of 11,800'.

Conejos Peak (13,172') is just inside the South San Juan Wilderness boundary. Drive west up FSR-105, Saddle Creek Road, from 6 miles southeast of Platoro on the Conejos River Road. Travel 7.5 miles to the Tobacco Lake Trailhead, the last 0.5 mile on FSR-105.3A is rough. The trail goes 2 miles to the 12,280' lake, then rambles southwest a mile further to the summit.

Bennett Peak (13,203') is the eastern-most high point of the region. From Monte Vista on US-160, drive 2 miles south on Hwy-15, then west on the Rock Creek Road (FSR-265). Continue beyond Comstock Campground to the end of the road and take the trail to the head of South Fork Rock Creek and the saddle south of the peak. Take the trail 1.5 miles north to the summit.

Navajo River/Rio Chama Access:
Maps:
USGS: *Chama Peak, Chrome, Harris Lake*

This group consists of some striking 12,000' summits east and west of the Navajo River, north of the New Mexico line. Access is via the south, on US-84 and Hwy-17 which connect Pagosa Springs and Antonito via Chama, New Mexico.

US-84 crosses the Navajo River at Chrome, about 25 miles south of Pagosa Springs. The Navajo River Road (Archuleta Co Rd-382) runs east from Chrome, then angles northeast. At mile 7.7, FSR-731 climbs 7.5 miles to the southwest side of Navajo Peak, passing Price Lakes en route. From the road end, a trail takes you northwest 3 miles to the Little Navajo River, and 6 more northwest to **V Mountain** (10,744'). (V Mountain has a closer approach using FSR-663 up from US-84, starting 3 miles north of Chrome.)

Navajo Peak (11,323') dominates this part of the valley with its belligerent rock face. To climb it, go north-northwest on the trail toward Little Navajo River, to where you are a mile west-northwest of the peak. Cut east 0.5 mile where the likeliest ridge for the climb starts. The ridge runs east-southeast, rising 1,200' to a saddle a short distance north of the peak.

At mile 5 northeast of Chama on Hwy-17, the Rio Chama Road (FSR-121) runs north 6 miles into the Rio Grande NF. After entering the national forest at a cattle guard, go left on FSR-121.3B descending slightly to the informal camping area and the trailhead for Archuleta Creek at about 8,800'. **Chama Peak** (12,019') is 4 miles west from the road on the Rio Chama. To climb it, cross the river and go northwest 2.5 miles on the trail up Archuleta Creek. When the trail turns north up a side creek, leave it and take the stream fork which goes west-southwest. After about 2 miles of climbing, work off to the right of the peak to finish on the northeast ridge.

Banded Peak (12,778') is very handsome from the north side. Earlier editions suggested a climb from the flats around **Chama Lake**, which is at the head of the Rio Chama West Fork. That access is no longer available because of private property. Joe Kramarsic, in the May 1987 *T&T*, describes a route from the southeast using the national forest. Proceed up Archuleta Creek to below the cliffs at the head of the valley, where you can climb a gulley to get on the flats from which the peak rises. Banded Peak and a lot of the top country northeast of it belong to the Potosi volcanic sequence, which has layering and a tendency to flat-topping.

San Juan Mountains (Western)

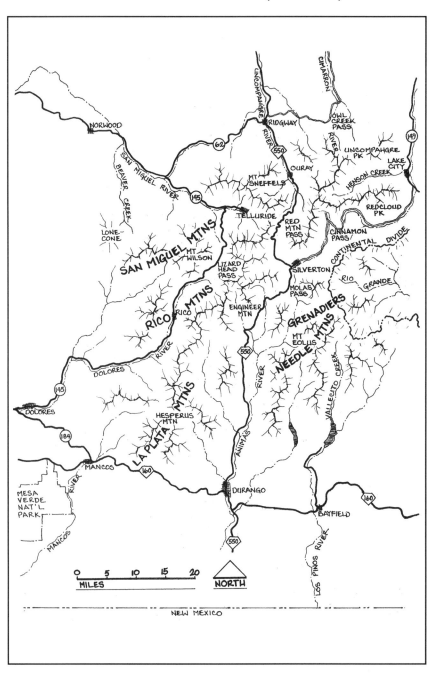

Cimarron River Group

Jurisdiction:
Uncompahgre NF, Ouray Ranger District

Map area reference:
Page 258

Maps:
USGS: *Courthouse Mountain, Sheep Mountain, Uncompahgre Peak, Wetterhorn Peak*

Forest Service: *Uncompahgre NF*

This group centers around the Cimarron River, mainly the West Cimarron. Many of the weirdly-shaped peaks were first climbed on CMC outings in the 1920's and 1930's; several have a pitch or two where rope is needed. The higher peaks are capped with tawny and gray rock, and the ridges along the canyons below them are so lined with little salmon-colored buttresses and pinnacles as to suggest a whole lifetime of rock climbing possibilities. Except for the valley floors, all of the surrounding peaks are in the Big Blue Wilderness, and typical restrictions apply beyond major trailheads.

From near Ridgway on US-550 you have glimpses of the fine Courthouse-Chimney Rock ridge. While the valley of the West Fork is exclusively used for most of the major peaks, the Middle Fork is often overlooked. But Precipice, Fortress and Redcliff all appear to have been named from the Middle Fork for their striking east faces; and further up valley, Heisshorn, El Punto and the Wetterhorn's fine north face are seldom seen or visited.

Cimarron River/Silver Jack Reservoir/Owl Creek Pass Access:

Camping and approach are best on the West Cimarron River. Leave US-50 2.5 miles southeast of Cimarron, and drive south 18 miles, 1 mile past Silver Jack Reservoir and the Jackson Ranger Station. Continue, keeping right twice, circling west to the West Fork of the Cimarron, and go south up that fork. Camping is available at facilities north of the reservoir, or about a mile south of the junction with the Owl Creek Road. To reach the other two branches of the Cimarron from the road, fork just south of the reservoir, turn right then left for the middle fork; go straight through for the east fork.

If approaching from the west, leave US-550 12 miles south of Colona, 2 miles north of Ridgway, and drive 16 miles east; go over **Owl Creek Pass** and a little way south to meet the Cimarron West Fork Road.

SAN JUAN

Chimney Rock (11,781') was first climbed in 1934 by Melvin Griffiths and Robert Ormes. The route is up the obvious south side chimney, with a large chock rock high up. Hike up a logging road from about a mile south of the Owl Creek-West Fork Road junction, and work your way through the lower cliff band to the small amphitheater beneath the chimney. Four short pitches of 5.5 bring one to the top of the chimney. Bob Rosebrough notes that from the top of the chimney, you traverse to the right along highly exposed rocks, and climb another roped pitch before topping out. Take along large pieces and several slings for the numerous small chock stones along the way. The first ascent climbers recorded a curious boo-boo. When they found the second man had climbed up the opposite side of the chock rock from the leader, they concurred in his retreating and doing it over, instead of sitting on top to untie and retie. Must have been exciting.

Courthouse Mountain (12,152') has some wicked overhangs on three sides, but it is no problem to climb from the Cimarron side. From 1.5 mile south of the road junction for Owl Creek Pass, a well marked trail climbs over the ridge south of the peak. However, leave the trail early and head directly up the steep east ridge, passing easily through several cliff bands. Courthouse is a popular climb as a strong hiker can often make the summit in an hour.

Courthouse Mountain   *Andrew De Naray*

Coxcomb (13,656') is at the head of the West Fork valley on the east; a strangely imposing peak, well-fortified against walking routes. To reach it, drive up the West Fork as far as you can. Cars with high clearance often make it all the way to the wilderness, but it does involve a stream fording. Hike up to the 12,500' pass west of the peak, and traverse around on generally sliding talus to the southwest end of the summit block. A wide chimney presents itself. It starts with a difficult 10' climb into the chimney, then after some scrambling comes a 50' section where protection has been used. Scramble to the ridge crest and follow it east to an abrupt notch. Most parties rappel it and leave their rope hanging to facilitate a belayed return. Scramble a short way to the summit. Another route that has gained a lot of popularity in the last few years, because of its short approach and generally interesting mixed climbing, is on the north face. At about 11,400', leave the West Fork Trail and hike up the small drainage coming off the north face. Alternating bands of snow, and a couple pitches of 5.2 rock, lead up just east of the summit, for a short scramble to the top.

Redcliff (13,642') starts from the West Fork Trailhead as for Coxcomb. Leave the trail at about 11,400', and head up to the Redcliff-Coxcomb saddle. The south ridge of Redcliff is an easy half mile with a 400' rise. For **Peak 13,241'** (**Fortress Peak**), leave the West Fork Trail about a mile from the trailhead and climb around the right-hand side of the prominent buttress to the ridge above.

Coxcomb   *Elvis Guin*

SAN JUAN

On **Precipice** (13,144'), several reports stress the importance of noting your point of ascent for return use, in case of doubtful weather. All leave the West Fork Trailhead and bushwhack generally east and a bit north to gain the south ridge. There are several alternatives when picking a best line of sight to get through the lower cliff bands. Eventually grassy slopes lead up the easy summit ridge.

For **Dunsinane Mountain** (12,742'), start about a mile south of the Owl Creek turnoff on the West Fork Cimarron Road. A old logging road takes off east across the creek but fades away in less than a mile. Bushwack to the Dunsinane-Turret Ridge saddle and head up the north ridge. At the first cliff band, scramble to an outsloping ledge and find a slight break about 40' to the west of the ridge. The route is steep, loose and exposed here and may require a rope belay. Traverse south on scree below the upper cliffs to reach a straightforward scramble leading to the summit.

Peak 12,260' is the high point of an impossible looking group of spires called **Turret Ridge**, just north of the above mentioned saddle. The first ascent was in 1979 by a group from the Iowa Mountaineers. It rivals Lizard Head as the state's hardest summit to reach. Scramble up the prominent west facing gulley beneath the highest spire. Three pitches lead up the obvious chimney system. The second and crux pitch is described as poorly protected 5.8.

Peak 13,411' (Heisshorn), which is 1.3 miles north of Wetterhorn, is described as looking like an upthrust tooth. A car can be driven all the way to the Middle Fork trailhead, from which a trail leads south high into the basin, before turning east to cross over into the East Fork by way of a 12,595' pass just north of Heisshorn. It was first climbed in the 1920's from a flat stretch on the north ridge at 13,250', by a route that works south, around from the pass, to the east face on the 12,800' level. One can then reach the platform by climbing a loose gully on that face or taking the more solid arete on its right side. The final bit of ridge from the platform to the top is an exposed knife edge.

At the head of the Middle Fork basin are two more seldom visited thirteeners that give outstanding views of nearby Coxcomb and Wetterhorn. Leave the Middle Fork trail just as it turns east at about 11,600' and bee-line due south to reach the saddle between **Peak 13,206'** and **Peak 13,377'**. Head right for the former, a very short walk-up. Or turn left for the taller one, passing one obstacle on the right. Don't attempt the ridge between Peak 13,377' and Heisshorn to the north because of several severe notches.

Peak 13,280' (El Punto) is 1.8 miles north of Matterhorn Peak. It has an aiguille summit like a small replica of the Lizard Head. Dwight Lavender and F. Greenfield first climbed it in 1929, hiking north from the above mentioned 12,595' pass and approaching by a couloir on the southwest side. The final pitch was made by a little 15 foot ledge on that side. Numerous small holds facilitate climbing the small cliff bands.

Pinnacle Ridge is the six mile long ridge running north from El Punto, ending in the small forest of pinnacles that you see along the Middle Fork Road. Despite the name, the cluster of 12,000' and 13,000' points along the way aren't too difficult to reach. Hike south along the Middle Fork Trail, then a mile southeast on occasional game trails, into Porphyry Basin. Gain the ridge and choose your destination, bypassing the occasional obstacle on the west side.

Sheep Mountain (13,168') gives a fine look at the rough and steep north faces of Uncompahgre, Wetterhorn and company. Unfortunately, to reach it is a marathon. From US-50, 3 miles southeast of Cimarron, turn south on Little Cimarron Road for about 15 miles to reach the **Little Cimarron Trail** (#229). Where the trail turns briefly west and crosses the 11,000' contour, turn due west to follow a drainage to treeline and then hike up Sheep's broad southeast ridge to the summit. It's a long ways in here and you might want to make it a weekend by bagging both **Silver Mountain** (13,714') and **Peak 13,681'**. They can be reached by continuing south along the Little Cimarron Trail, which eventually crosses Silver's east shoulder on the way to hooking up with other trails around Uncompahgre Peak.

SAN JUAN

SAN JUAN

Potosi Peak from the hole in the "teakettle"   *John Devitt*

Ouray and Vicinity

Jurisdiction:
Uncompahgre NF, Ouray Ranger District

Map area reference:
Page 258, 268 and 274

Maps:
USGS: *Handies Peak, Ironton, Mount Sneffels, Ouray, Sams, Telluride, Wetterhorn Peak*
Forest Service: *Uncompahgre NF*

The area covered in this group lies west of Poughkeepsie Gulch, north of Red Mountain Pass on US-550, and north and east of the Uncompahgre River-San Miguel River divide. Included in the group is Mount Sneffels, the only fourteener in the vicinity, and the landmark from which the surrounding wilderness gets its name. The connecting summits in spectacular Yankee Boy Basin are sometimes given the collective name Sneffels Range, and are known for their magnificent alpine beauty, climbing challenges, and steep faces of loose rock for which you might keep a rope and hard hat handy. The San Juan Mountaineers explored the area thoroughly, and left their designations on many of the peaks.

From the north, Mount Sneffels is both symmetrical and rough, and gives the most exciting prospects. Together with its associated summits, it is visible as a rugged stretch of mountains as one travels south on US-550 from Montrose.

US-550 Ouray South Access:

US-550, the Million Dollar Highway, is the main route from the Grand Valley communities south through the heart of the San Juan country to Durango. South of Ouray the route begins a twisting 13 mile ascent to **Red Mountain Pass**.

Hayden Mountain (13,206') is the bulky unexciting ridge west of Ironton Park, 6 miles south of Ouray on US-550. It is composed of at least 5 summit masses, the southernmost of which is the highest. From a mile northwest of the last switchback as US-550 descends north from Red Mountain Pass, an old and sometimes obscure trail, whose beginning is difficult to find, climbs northwest to 12,567' **Richmond Pass**, and then down the west side to Imogene Creek. The official summit of Hayden is 0.5 mile north of the pass. **T8** (13,315') and **T7** (13,359') are a greater distance up-ridge to the southwest of Richmond Pass.

The colorful Red Mountains 1, 2 and 3, get lots of attention from motorists descending Red Mountain Pass to the north. Those wanting a closer look should travel northeast 1.6 miles from the last switchback as US-550 descends north from the pass, and turn right (southeast) as marked for Corkscrew Gulch, and Brown Mountain. Go 0.2 mile and fork right, which takes you 2 miles into Corkscrew Gulch, between **Red Mountain #1** (12,592) and **Red Mountain #2** (12,219'). **Red Mountain #3** (12,890') is 0.8 mile south of #2, on a connecting ridge. The jeep road continues south, ascending out of Corkscrew, connecting eventually with Cement Creek at Gladstone.

For a less motorized route to Red Mountain #1, via **Gray Copper Gulch**, go left at the fork above marked Brown Mountain and ford the stream. Continue 0.2 mile where an old miners road intersects at right. Hike up the abandoned road, which for the first 0.8 mile is wide and obvious. Thereafter the route deteriorates significantly, and crosses to the west side of the drainage. Ascend on bits and pieces of trail to the right of meager but precipitous Gray Copper Falls. Continue 1 mile to the head of the valley, then follow the east ridge to the summit.

Brown Mountain is the long ridge east of Ironton Park, tapering bumpily from 13,330' at the south end to 12,801' **Abrams Mountain** at the north. Abrams is of interest because of the framing it gets as you look up the valley from Ouray. To climb Abrams, take directions above for the Red Mountains, and take the left fork, 0.2 mile in from the highway, marked Brown Mountain. This road is an old mine access road which continues about 2.5 miles from the highway to the 11,600' level near timberline. From there, one can easily pick a route to the extended north-south ridge of the mountain. The southern high point of the mountain is directly accessible following directions to Red Mountain #1 above, via Gray Copper Gulch to the head of the valley, then ascending the southwest ridge to the 13,339' summit.

Bear Creek Trail, a dramatic old mine trail, and a designated national recreation trail, is a very exciting and scenic trip. The trail starts at 8,400' on the south side of the tunnel 2 miles south of Ouray on US-550. Beyond the Yellow Jacket Mine, you get up to **American Flats**, where **Wildhorse Peak** (13,266') rises to the north from the alpine meadows, and where you have an intersection with the upper end of the **Horsethief Trail**. The lower trail head for the Horsethief Trail is found by driving 1.5 miles north of Ouray on US-550 to the Dexter Creek turnoff (Ouray Co Rd-14). It is 2.5 miles to the Dexter Creek Trailhead (go right at mile 1), where you can park and walk, if you wish, up the continuing rough road. Take the middle of 3 forks at mile 2.7 and follow another mile to the Horsethief Trailhead. Ascend via the sculptured mountainsides east of Ouray finally attaining the ridges above the Amphitheater, and beyond to American Flats and Bear Creek Trail as noted above.

Whitehouse Mountain (13,492'), the large northeast corner of the Sneffels Range west of Ouray, is most noticeable from US-550 just south of Ridgway. Its large flat summit is protected with battlements of dramatic chalk-white cliffs and spires. Isolated by the area's craggy canyons, the mountain is difficult to approach. Perhaps the most direct route starts on Oak Street in Ouray, west of the Uncompahgre River, and then goes uphill on the only intersecting side road. The beginning of the **Oak Creek Trail** is 0.5 mile beyond at 8,000'. Follow first on the south side then on the north side of Oak Creek Canyon. The SJM suggested a difficult bushwhack route up the canyon to the basin east of the mountain, then on to the summit by way of the southeast ridge. From the opposite direction, the mountain is 0.5 mile east of Mount Ridgway with a sub-summit on the way (see Blaine Basin Access).

A less demanding destination is **Twin Peaks** (10,798'), which is the easternmost point of the descending ridge from Whitehouse. To climb the peaks, start as for Whitehouse via Oak Creek Trail, then veer onto Twin Peaks Trail for a walk to the top.

Yankee Boy Basin Access:

Noted for its ascending wildflower terraces draped against sculpted mountainsides, and decaying mine structures, **Yankee Boy Basin** and its intersecting drainages hold a certain magical charm, unique to the San Juan. But it is a shame that this ideal setting is marred by long lines of vehicles headed up the canyon to enjoy, if not at the same time to depreciate, this special location. Fortunately, Mount Sneffels Wilderness is closed to motor vehicles. The popular approach to the area begins on Ouray Co Rd-361 barely 0.2 mile south of Ouray on US-550, and travels southwest up the canyon on a narrow, steep and winding mountain road. Beyond the townsite of Sneffels, you will need a 4WD vehicle to take you into upper Yankee Boy and Governor Basins, or for the exciting ride over **Imogene Pass** and down into Telluride.

At 6 miles up from US-550, near the townsite of Sneffels, a left fork begins the jeep road over Imogene Pass, bypassing the Camp Bird operations lower in the valley. Continuing 0.5 mile beyond Sneffels townsite (6.9 miles from US-550), the main road forks and begins jeep routes in two directions. The left fork takes you to Governor Basin and the right fork into Yankee Boy Basin.

It is possible, but difficult, to drive into upper Yankee Boy within a mile of **Blue Lakes Pass**. West of the pass, the Blue Lakes Trail zigzags down inside Mount Sneffels Wilderness to **Blue Lakes**, and the East Fork of Dallas Creek.

Mount Sneffels (14,150') has a Nordic name meaning snowfield, which Jules Verne used in his Journey to the Centre of The Earth. It was given to the peak by Endlich and a companion member of the Hayden Survey, at the time of the 1874 first ascent. The usual route goes from upper Yankee Boy: leave the **Blue Lakes Trail** and work to the right under cliffs until you reach the saddle east of the summit.

SAN JUAN

Sneffels Group

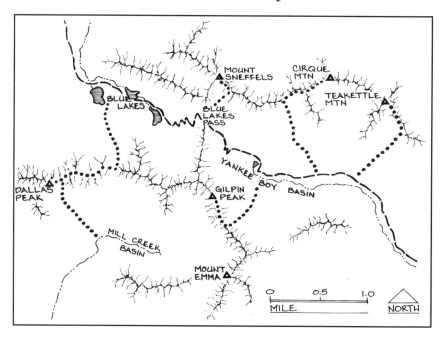

A steep and narrow couloir climbs to the left up the mountain's southeast face. Keep left again in a smaller couloir to the top. The couloir is not a rock climb, yet steep enough to create a rolling rock hazard.

The mountain is rated a good climb, not without a problem or two and some exposure, from the top of **Blue Lakes Pass** via the southwest ridge. Using this route, you will pass the pinnacles known as **The Monolith** (13,480') and **Blue Needle** (13,480'), and 0.5 mile to the west on an extended ridge, **Wolf Tooth** (12,720') — all well respected by the SJM.

Gilpin Peak (13,694'), directly south of Mount Sneffels and Blue Lakes Pass, can be climbed from Yankee Boy Basin. Start at the 11,800' level, at a switch-back on the road where a trail continues ahead. Angle southwest from the trail, aiming for the main ridge descending south from the summit. Climb a steep and rotten 200' cliff pitch to the main ridge, perhaps with protection, then walk the ridge north to the top. The SJM were intrigued with a route descending from the summit northwest and north to Blue Lakes Pass. This route passes an irresistible collection of irregular chopped high points 0.2 mile to the west of Gilpin called the **Block Tops** (13,543') by the early climbers. This alternative route can be used as a descent from Gilpin, however, be careful in spotting the right couloir for your return, to avoid the cliffs just north of the summit.

Dyke Col is a 13,040' pass between Kismet and Cirque Mountain. Though steep on the north side, it is a route between Yankee Boy Basin and **Blaine Basin**. It is named for the prominent rhyolite dyke on the Blaine Basin side.

Kismet (13,694') is the cluster of points directly north of Wrights Lake and 0.5 mile east-southeast of Sneffels on the range crest. From the top of Dyke Col, climb west over or around a couple of false summits to the base of the main needle. The SJM also suggested a route straight north from **Wrights Lake**, directly to the southeast side of the summit. There is the likelihood of rope protection being needed on top.

Cirque Mountain (13,686') is 1.2 miles east of Mount Sneffels on the continuing range crest. It has a gentle west ridge, but a rougher summit. The prominent cliffs when viewed from the north in Blaine Basin, give obvious significance to the mountain's name. It is best approached from Dyke Col and the ridge.

Teakettle Mountain (13,819') continues the range summits east of Sneffels. The standard approach begins at the last timber patch near 11,400' about 1 mile up the Yankee Boy Basin jeep road from the turnoff to Governor Basin. Start north toward the jutting southwest ridge of the peak, then as you climb, veer right into the cirque just south of the summit. The standard approach climbs up the loose rock slope which rises east from the cirque, and leads to the southeast ridge between the summit and the little protruding knob named **S1** (13,568'). It is sometimes referred to comically as the **Coffeepot** by today's mountaineers. Towards the top of the loose rock slope, veer left below "The Window" into a grungy dirt-rock couloir, and ascend to the southeast ridge. Follow the ridge northwest along the base of its spires to another couloir, which can be full of snow well into July. This puts you on the upper ridge, where it is a walk northwest to the eastern base of the summit block, which is ascended through a chimney, usually with protection.

Potosi Peak (13,786') is the southeast termination of the Sneffels Range crest, and worthy of being part of it. To include Potosi with Teakettle, return to the Coffeepot as noted above, and descend southeast to the 13,000' saddle between Coffeepot and Potosi. Potosi has a formidable looking summit block from this side, but is more easily climbed from the east, where there is a break in the cliffs. For this, ascend from the saddle to below the summit block, and traverse to the east side of the mountain, where the route to the top occurs. Note your route for a return. The route home is tricky because the ash-grey cliff and spire-band that make the photographer's plates so striking, stand as an awaiting danger. Retrace your steps to the Potosi-Coffeepot saddle, and descend until you can veer right onto upper grass slopes. Stay high, and traverse until the grassy bottom of the cirque south of Teakettle comes into view, where you began your climb earlier. Descend, staying right, retracing your earlier steps to the road.

SAN JUAN

Teakettle Mountain, with Dallas Peak in the hole   *CMC archives*
Inset: *Climbing the crack on Teakettle*   *Neil Purrett*

Aptly named **Stony Mountain** (12,693') is the little peak that splits Governor Basin off from Yankee Boy basin. It is a short, fun scramble up its west ridge.

Governor Basin Access:

Governor Basin is a side drainage to Yankee Boy Basin. Follow directions as for Yankee Boy to the fork just beyond Sneffels townsite, then go left about 2 miles to Governor Basin, under **Saint Sophia Ridge**. Although the approach to Saint Sophia is more gentle on the Governor Basin side than the imposing buttress displayed from upper Comet Creek above Telluride, Mel Griffiths of the SJM found the ridge full of unstable rock, and the pinnacles themselves too rotten to be tempting. **Mount Emma** (13,581') forms the north end of Saint Sophia. It is climbed to the northwest from upper Governor Basin or southwest from the jeep road in Yankee Boy Basin.

An intermittent old miners trail begins off the road in Governor Basin near the 12,000' level, and ascends difficultly, and steeply at times, south 1 mile to a notched pass at 13,050', on the rough ridge between the Uncompahgre and San Miguel drainages. The trail divides 0.3 mile south of the pass. The almost unrecognizable left fork continues south into **Marshall Basin** to the Imogene Pass Road; the right fork rises slightly to pass over the south ridge of Mendota Peak and down Comet Creek. Both routes end in Telluride.

Mendota Peak (13,275') forms the south termination of Saint Sophia Ridge, and is approached from the above mentioned notched pass. Drop down 150' on the Telluride side of the pass and traverse west until you can climb back up to the ridge.

East Dallas Creek/Blue Lakes Access:

The northwest section of the Sneffels Range is approached via **Blue Lakes** and Blaine Basin from East Dallas Creek Road. It is possible to gain access to Blue Lakes by the jeep road to upper Yankee Boy Basin then by foot over **Blue Lakes Pass**. However, the walk up East Dallas Creek to Blue Lakes, being within Mount Sneffels Wilderness, provides a quiet transition from the trailhead to a world of spectacular cirques and summits at the lakes; a personally rewarding experience in stark contrast to that in busy, noisy Yankee Boy Basin.

To reach Blue Lakes and Blaine Basin Trailhead, travel west of Ridgway 4.8 miles on Hwy-62 to Dallas Creek Road. The first seven miles is a county road, through private property until you reach the forest boundary. Go left at 0.4 mile and then right at 2.1 miles from the highway turnoff. After entering the national forest, continue 1.5 miles through the camping area in the meadow to the trailhead parking at 9,320'.

The trail to Blue Lakes begins to the right a few steps beyond the locked gate at the trailhead, and ascends 3 miles to the lower lake at 11,000'. The upper lakes are about a mile further up the basin at 11,480' and 11,720', and Blue Lakes Pass is 1.5 miles beyond the upper lake at 12,960'. The same peaks that are accessible from upper Yankee Boy Basin are feasible via Blue Lakes, i.e.. Sneffels, Gilpin, etc, although Sneffels, from this approach, is a much more formidable looking mountain.

The SJM did a fair amount of exploring in these northern cirques, and on the rugged twisting divide between the Uncompahgre and San Miguel Rivers, reconnoitering beyond the few summits in the area that are so well-known to today's mountaineers.

Accessible from the upper cirque 1.2 miles west of lower Blue Lake, **S3** (13,410') and **S5** (13,360') rise on the divide crest. The summit of **S4** (13,242') is perched on a ridge extending 0.5 mile east from S5, and is also most accessible from the basin west of the lower lake. The SJM designated S4 as **Wolcott Mountain**. However, the updated USGS map shows that peak as the 13,041' high point of an isolated ridge 1 mile northwest of S4. Today's Wolcott and the massive frontal cliffs of S4 are spectacularly viewed from a clearing about 2 miles up the Blue Lakes Trail from the parking area.

S6 (13,441') is a peak of several craggy summits offering "good bits of climbing" on the main divide crest 0.2 mile northwest of S5, and connecting 0.5 mile north with present-day Wolcott. **TO** (13,735') is 1 mile southwest of S3 on the divide bend, and likewise accessible from the lower lake with a longer walk up the cirque.

Much has been written lately on **Dallas Peak** (13,809') as one of Colorado's most challenging Centennial Peaks. The standard route is up the mountain's east face, and the standard approach is from the Telluride side in the San Miguel drainage, thereby avoiding the cliffs south of Blue Lakes. However, early in the summer the mountain is often climbed from Blue Lakes on snow all the way to the low point of the east ridge. From there follow the ridge, swinging south around any obstacles, and finish by the standard route as treated under Telluride and Vicinity.

Blaine Basin Access:

The **Blaine Basin** approach provides more challenging routes up peaks that are generally most accessible from the south in Yankee Boy Basin. However, the seldom

Mount Sneffels   *David Anschicks*

experienced grandeur of the area is easily accessible to the casual dayhiker as well as the technical climber. Take directions as above to the East Dallas Creek-Blue Lakes Trailhead. From the trailhead, continue south beyond the locked gate on the old road and past the trail to the Blue Lakes. In a few steps, the road crosses the creek and ascends to the north-northeast. Follow approximately 1 mile, bearing left when in doubt, to Wilson Creek, and intersect another road marked as Dallas Trail. Continue southeast another 0.7 mile paralleling Wilson Creek and go left at a fork, marked with an ancient sign as Blaine Basin, which ascends on an unmaintained trail to the lower basin 0.5 mile beyond at 11,000'. From here continue south into the main basin or contour to the left around a prominent ridge jutting north from Cirque Mountain into East Blaine Basin.

The north face of Sneffels is a technical climb, accessible from 2 couloirs, which diverge right and left from roughly the same point at the 13,000' level, in the southwest quadrant of the main basin, below the towering summit. Both steep routes are mostly on snow, which becomes hard-packed ice as the summer progresses.

Blaine Peak (12,920') is 0.7 mile north of Sneffels' summit. The SJM climbed it by the southwest ridge, which the climbers reached by heading southwest up the main basin under Sneffels.

Some of the aiguilles pointed out from the Blaine Basin approach, but not necessarily climbed, by the SJM are as follows: **Purgatory Point** (13,640'), 0.2 mile north-northwest of Sneffels, is part of the mountain's impressive northern massif; **The Hand**, **Penguin** and **Thumb** form a 3 part summit hovering around 13,000' on the ridge 0.5 mile northwest of Sneffels.

From East Blaine Basin, attempts can be made up the eastern end of the cirque on **Mount Ridgway** (13,468'), known as **S2** to the SJM, or to the top of the ridge extending 0.7 mile northwest of Ridgway called **Reconnoiter Peak** (12,960') by the climbers.

SAN JUAN

San Juan Mountains
(Ouray to Silverton)

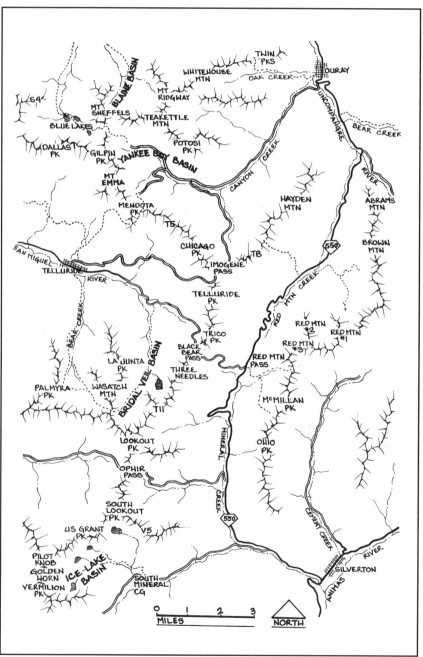

SAN JUAN

Telluride and Vicinity

Jurisdiction:
Uncompahgre NF, Norwood Ranger District

Map area reference:
Page 258 and 274

Maps:
USGS: *Gray Head, Mount Sneffels, Ophir, Sams, Telluride*
Forest Service: *Uncompahgre NF*

This section is centered around the picturesque little community of Telluride. The town is ringed with elevated alpine valleys, soaring spires and sculptured mountainsides in the headwaters of the San Miguel River. Evidence of the area's once heavy reliance on mining is everywhere. Plan a visit to the Telluride Museum to make your wanderings among the ruins in the high country more meaningful. The limits of this section follow the contorted Uncompahgre-San Miguel River divide, from which many of the summits rise, south to an arbitrary line drawn east and west from the town of Ophir.

As you drive south from Placerville on Hwy-145, the road splits 3 miles west of Telluride. The main route goes right (south); a highway spur continues a few miles east into town. There are many trails and jeep roads off this spur, most of which began as mine accesses in the previous century, and most of which still give convenient approaches to the peaks today.

Imogene Pass Road Access:

One of the most popular jeep routes over the divide begins on the north side of town on a city street, ascends to 13,114' **Imogene Pass**, and continues down into lower Yankee Boy Basin as a route to Ouray.

About 0.2 mile up from Telluride, a side road with a locked gate ascends at left. A trailhead sign identifies this as access to the **Jud Wiebe Trail**, although old timers know it more historically as the Liberty Bell Road. It switchbacks steeply above Comet Creek to the Liberty Bell Mine. About a mile up from the Imogene Road, the Jud Wiebe Trail bears to the left as an eventual extension to the Deep Creek Trail further west. Continue to ascend on the Liberty Bell Road and fork to the right in about 0.5 mile. The mine ruins are visible below as the road skirts the upper basin near timberline.

Towering to the north are **Greenback Mountain** (12,997') and **Mount Emma** (13,581'), both climbable from the grassy saddle connecting them, albeit with some judicious route finding. Leave the road a short distance beyond as it orients southeast under the scathing cliffs of **Saint Sophia Ridge**, and when you can pick out a very obscure trail which ascends east to a shallow dip on Mendota Peak's south ridge. The unmaintained trail drops briefly into the extreme upper portion of **Marshall Basin**, where a maze of old mine roads all descend ultimately to the Imogene Road. The trail ascends northwest obscurely, then disappears into the scree just below a pass connecting with the Governor Basin side, only to rise to a surprisingly inviting portal on the divide crest. From this seldom visited pass, **T5** (13,436') is a short 0.5 mile climb east.

Those who choose to follow the main jeep road the full 7 miles from Telluride to Imogene Pass, will encounter various motorized sightseers going to, or coming from Ouray via Yankee Boy Basin. However, once on the pass, one can travel peaceably on the crest of the divide 0.7 mile north-northwest to **Chicago Peak** (13,385') or 0.5 mile south to **Telluride Peak** (13,509').

Bear Creek Access:

South of Telluride, the two main valleys worth exploring are Bridal Veil Basin and Bear Creek. Both connect conveniently by trail at their upper ends and make for a long but worthwhile excursion.

Begin south of town on a city side street which crosses the San Miguel River and continues as the Bear Creek Road. Follow the road south up the valley 2 miles to the beginning of the **Wasatch Trail**. The trail switchbacks steeply to a dramatic gorge crossing, and passes the ruins of the Nellie Mine. A short distance beyond, at 10,880', take a right for the Wasatch Trail to lower **Lena Basin**, or a left fork for the **East Fork Trail**; both trails reconverge 1.5 miles further on. Continue 0.7 mile on the Wasatch Trail to a mid-level basin at 11,600' where the trail forks again. The left fork is a continuation of the Wasatch and the right fork ascends to the lower north ridge of **Gold Hill**, the highest point of the ski area and where you can watch hang gliders launch during their annual celebration in early September.

For Lena Basin, leave the trail here and ascend south and southwest. **Silver Mountain** (13,470') is an extended east-west ridge with its main summit at the head of the basin. **Palmyra Peak** (13,319') is a north extension of Silver Mountain, accessible from Lena Basin by its northeast ridge. **San Joaquin Ridge** is likewise a north extension of Silver further east, and reached by a steep climb out of the basin's east fork.

The Wasatch Trail rejoins the East Fork Trail at 12,000'. The main summit of **Wasatch Mountain** (13,555') is a steep but straightforward climb 0.75 mile to the east from this point. The converged trail ascends steadily 1.5 miles southeast to a 13,080' pass south of Wasatch Mountain, separating Bear Creek and Bridal Veil Basin.

SAN JUAN

Bridal Veil Basin Access:

Bridal Veil Basin is accessible 1.5 miles east of Telluride on a county road which skirts the Idarado Mill, then switchbacks opposite Bridal Veil Falls. Parking is scarce beyond the falls view point, and private property in the vicinity of the old cliff-hanging power house forbids vehicle access, and strictly constrains foot traffic to the road.

For **La Junta Peak** (13,472'), take a very obscure trail 0.3 mile beyond the power house, and cross to the west side of the stream. Ascend steeply southwest into lower Jackass Basin, mount the northeast ridge and continue to the summit.

The old mine road ascends 3 miles to the head of the basin, where it meets the Wasatch Trail from Bear Creek. **T12** (13,614'), at the southernmost tip of Bridal Veil Basin, is 0.2 mile north of Lookout Peak. **T11** (13,510') is 0.5 mile east of the Lewis Mine, but perhaps easier to reach from the old mine trail over the pass 0.5 mile south of the summit.

Mill Creek Basin Access:

Dallas Peak (13,809') is perhaps Colorado's most notorious Centennial Peak. In the mid-1970's, Spence Swanger climbed the mountain, and assumed his was the first ascent because of the unmolested condition of the summit, and the lack of information on the mountain. (Long and McBride climbed it in 1934 on a CMC outing.) Two excellent detailed accounts on routes exist in the *T&T*. One by Art Porter in the July-August 1980 issue, and the other by Bob and Kent Beverly in the October 1984 issue.

The first suggests starting at the Jud Wiebe trailhead north of Telluride on the Imogene Road, continuing to the Liberty Bell Mine, then north into and out of Pack Basin, then to upper **Mill Creek Basin**. The second approach is more direct, starting 1 mile west of Telluride on the highway, at a nondescript side road just opposite the gas station-convenience store. Head north on the mountain road approximately 2 miles, where you will pick up the **Deep Creek Trail** and follow it to a divide between Mill Creek and Elder Creek. From here a newly constructed trail leads northeast into lower Mill Creek Basin. At this point, the two descriptions approximate each other: go up the steep gullies and chimneys on the southeast face. At the east corner of the summit block, swing well around the north face on the obvious ledge system. Finish the last 100 feet up the prominent fourth class chimney that leads directly to the top. Rotten and exposed, most parties appreciate a rope here. This climb should only be attempted by experienced mountaineers with much contemplation and the proper equipment.

SAN JUAN

Dallas Peak, east ridge   *Terry Root*

Last Dollar Road Access:

The western portion of this group is most accessible from the Last Dollar Road, connecting Hwy-145 3 miles west of Telluride to Hwy-62 1.5 miles west of **Dallas Divide**. From about 3 miles west of Telluride, turn north off Hwy-145, and follow the recently paved and realigned road towards the airport. Turn right onto a dirt road after 1.7 miles and follow 2 more miles to the crossing of Sheep Creek. From here the road deteriorates and continues 6 miles to **Last Dollar Pass**, then 10 additional miles to Hwy-62.

A sign at Sheep Creek identifies a trail on an old roadway as the **Deep Creek Trail**. Actually, it is a connector trail that rises in 0.5 mile to an abandoned earthen flume, and the route, east and west, of the Deep Creek Trail. Bearing to the right here will take you east, traversing the lower slopes of **Iron Mountain** (12,747') and **Campbell Peak** (13,213') from which a steep but uniform ascent could begin. In approximately 6 miles, the trail connects to the Mill Creek Trail, and eventually to Telluride on the Jud Wiebe Trail extension.

Following the Deep Creek Trail to the left at the flume above Sheep Creek, will lead you quickly down on a new trail to a crossing of the East Fork Deep Creek, then up a bit to the old Iron Mountain Road. Here the Deep Creek Trail descends at left, eventually making its way north into the main fork.

For **Mears Peak** (13,496'), ascend the old Iron Mountain Road northeast to the head of the East Fork Deep Creek, deep within **Mount Sneffels Wilderness**, then make your way north to the prominent summit. **Ruffner Mountain** (12,304') is on an extended ridge separating the East and Main Forks of Deep Creek. The main summit of Ruffner on the divide was known as **S7** (13,200') to the SJM.

S8 (13,252') and **S9** (13,134') can be climbed by following the Deep Creek Trail north into the main fork drainage. Shortly after you enter Mount Sneffels Wilderness, leave the trail as it begins a more westerly orientation towards **Whipple Mountain Pass** and bushwhack up the drainage to the mountaintops.

The trailhead for **Alder Creek Trail** is hidden in the trees at the summit of 10,663' Last Dollar Pass, 10 miles up from Hwy-145. **Hayden Peak** (12,987') and **North Pole Peak** (12,203') can be reached on this trail, which descends slightly from the pass, then traverses the peaks on their rugged west side. From the trail, climb steeply east and northeast to the ridge between the two mountains; route finding through the cliffs and gullies suggests a longer than would be usual ascent.

Silverton and Vicinity

Jurisdiction :
San Juan NF, Columbine District-West

Map area reference:
Page 258 and 274

Maps:
USGS: *Engineer Mountain, Handies Peak, Howardsville, Ironton, Ophir, Silverton, Telluride*
Forest Service: *San Juan NF*

This group centers around Silverton, perhaps best known by tourists as the charming Victorian era destination of one of the nation's few remaining narrow gauge railroads. Lesser known is the area's past and continuing reliance on mining, particularly north of town and east of US-550. The resulting network of roads, both active and abandoned, is an off-road vehicle area, where hikers might feel alienated by their overwhelming presence.

The boundaries of the section range from the north on US-550 to Red Mountain Pass, west to the top of the Animas-Dolores River divide, east to the Continental Divide and south to the Needle and West Needle Mountains. The peaks themselves range from steep and seldomly rugged, to challenging slopes where ropes are called for. The rock is volcanic flows and tuffs, dramatically eroded in such places as Ice Lake Basin. A visit to the Silverton Museum beforehand will help you decipher the tangled historic remains in the cirques and valleys above the town.

US-550/Red Mountain Pass Access:

It is approximately 10 miles north on US-550 from Silverton to **Red Mountain Pass**. Just before you top the pass, there are inconspicuous gravel turnoffs in both directions from the highway. A turn to the left (west) will take you in 3 miles to **Black Bear Pass**, and then down into **Ingram Basin** and Telluride. Only experienced 4WD vehicle drivers should attempt the hair-raising descent at Ingram Falls. A turn to the right (east) from US-550 opposite the Black Bear Road will take you into **US Basin**.

The double summit of **T10** (13,477') is 0.5 mile southwest of Black Bear Pass, and **Trico Peak** (13,321') is 0.5 mile in the opposite direction. Those who want to visit the **Three Needles** (13,481'), which received high praise from the SJM for its beauty and climbing possibilities, should exit the Black Bear Road to the left, approximately 1 mile up from US-550. This jeep road climbs south and west into **Porphyry Basin** with the Needles at its head.

For **McMillan Peak** (12,804') and **Ohio Peak** (12,673'), follow the US Basin Road approximately 2 miles south-southeast of US-550, with a sharp right at mile 0.7. Both peaks are climbed north and south from this gentle basin. An alternate route up **Red Mountain #3** and McMillan starts on the US Basin Road at US-550 as above, but keeps straight at mile 0.7 to Carbon Lake. Head to the pass between the two peaks, from where you climb north or south.

Ophir Pass Access:

Ophir Pass, normally one of the easiest jeep roads to maneuver, starts approximately 5 miles northwest of Silverton on US-550 and continues 4 miles to its summit at 11,789'. A descent on the west side takes you in 5.5 miles to Hwy-145.

Lookout Peak (13,661'), 1 mile north of Ophir Pass, is approached on the road 0.2 mile east from the pass. From the road, head north to the rocky 12,500' basin south-southeast of the summit. This basin is circled by impressive red-orange cliffs and spires to the north and northeast. Climb the steep scree slope to the north-northwest, which leads to a small and narrow red couloir. This puts you on the south ridge, which you follow to the base of the main summit mass. The final push to the top deserves careful route finding over steep ledges.

South Mineral Creek Access:

The road up South Mineral Creek (San Juan Co Rd-7) begins 2 miles west of Silverton on US-550. The graded dirt road continues 4.5 miles west to South Mineral Campground. At the height of summer, campers are strung out along the length of this attractive valley. Fortunately, the hordes rarely venture too far beyond their wheels, leaving the dramatic, unseen cirques far beyond the highest treetops, a more pleasant destination for those willing to invest the time and energy. The road continues beyond the campground, albeit rough and narrow, 2 more miles to dead end after the creek crossing just beyond the abandoned site of the Bandora Mine.

Just opposite the campground is a trailhead parking area for those who wish to visit **Ice Lake Basin**. The trail begins a few hundred feet up the road. The lower basin, reached after a 2 mile climb, is a protected place to camp. Another mile by trail and 750' takes you into the upper basin. About halfway up, fork right to 12,257' **Ice Lake** or left to 12,585' **Fuller Lake**. Upon arrival in the basin, an impressive line of peaks to the west awaits you. For an interesting account of first ascents on six of these summits during a CMC outing, consult the October 1932 *T&T*.

SAN JUAN

Fuller Peak (13,761') is the southernmost summit, and an easy climb up its west ridge. From Fuller Lake, ascend the snow of the north face to the Fuller-Vermilion saddle. **Vermilion Peak** (13,894'), the highest of the group, is best ascended up its southeast ridge from this saddle. If planning a 3 summit day, finishing up on **Golden Horn** (13,769'), avoid the north slopes of Vermilion and backtrack to the saddle. Proceed to the Vermilion-Golden Horn saddle, then up Golden Horn's southwest ridge.

Pilot Knob (13,738'), a most impressive collection of volcanic bulkheads, can be climbed by tricky couloirs and chimneys on the west or east sides to an exposed summit. Best to have a rope along. If approaching from the east, climb either of two yellow couloirs on the east face that gain the ridge between the central summit and the northern summit. A difficult and exposed scramble along this ridge leads to the higher northern one. **Yellow Mountain** (13,177') is a long series of summits extending northwest from Pilot Knob.

US Grant Peak (13,767') is best approached from Ice Lake. Pick up an unmaintained trail east-northeast of the lake, and follow 0.5 mile across an old mine dump, then north to **Island Lake**. From there, ascend west-northwest to the saddle between Grant and **V4** (13,520'), as designated by the SJM. Continue up the southwest ridge where you will encounter a difficult cliff, then along a ledge to the south face.

South Lookout Peak (13,360') is approached by jeep road to **Clear Lake**, beginning approximately 1 mile short of South Mineral Campground. This well-buttressed peak is difficult to ascend, especially the needle on the northern end of the massif that the SJM called **North Summit** (13,357'). Because of a new mining venture, the road up Clear Creek is now closed at treeline. As you hike up the road, give a wide berth to the mine operation on the right, where you are not welcome. From Clear Lake, it is an easy ascent on grass to the southern summit of South Lookout. To gain the true summit further north, traverse down a bit and well around to the east face of the central summit block on loose junk. Scramble up an east facing couloir a few feet to where a ledge leads diagonally 30 feet over to the right hand rib of the couloir. Scramble this to the top. This loose but moderate route is difficult to find, so take a rope, as all other possibilities, including the obvious crack on the south face, are fifth class.

For **Rolling Mountain** (13,693') follow South Mineral Creek Road 2 miles beyond the campground to the site of the abandoned Bandora Mine. Descend slightly on the left fork to a creek crossing and a barricade to vehicles. The old mine road continues south as the **Rico-Silverton Trail**. Ascend the trail 1 mile to timberline, and continue into the marshy meadow called South Park. To your right (west) is a prominent cliffy drainage just below the summit. For a somewhat easier, though longer route, continue 0.5 mile south up the trail to the next drainage. Turn west and follow the drainage to the ridge extending south from the summit. From here it is 0.2 mile and 500' to the top.

Twin Sisters (13,432'), on the opposite side of the valley, is guarded with cliffs here and there and booby trapped with frustrating pockets of scree. It is perhaps more easily climbed by way of its southwest ridge above the Colorado Trail.

Those continuing on the Rico-Silverton Trail to 12,480' Rolling Mountain Pass should keep an eye peeled for a new section of maintained trail. It will bear right off an older, abandoned section of trail, south of South Park. Just below the pass, the Rico-Silverton joins up with the Colorado Trail. Following the CT to the left (southeast) will take you into a pleasant rolling highland punctuated with ponds, the largest of which is trail-side at 12,160', unofficially called **Engine Lake**. From here, a lazy stroll 0.7 mile south will put you on top of **Jura Knob** (12,614').

The route to **San Miguel Peak** (13,752') starts near the Bandora Mine on the closed-to-vehicles right fork of the road. Ascend west 2.5 miles on the old mine road to 12,445' **Hope Pass**, then descend to **Hope Lake**, where you might have difficulty setting up camp on its steep grassy shoreline. Climb west from the lake to the summit. San Miguel via Hope Lake is more directly approached from the west. Start at Trout Lake on Hwy-145, south of the Ophir turn off. Skirt east of the lake on FSR-626, then ascend FSR-627 2 miles to Hope Lake Trailhead. From here it is 2.5 miles to the lake.

Coal Bank Pass Access:

Engineer Mountain (12,968') is the prominent colonnaded cone observed by northbound drivers on US-550 beyond Purgatory. We never go by without thinking we would like to climb it and look around. The most direct ascent starts at **Coal Bank Pass** on US-550, opposite the parking area and goes up **Pass Creek Trail**. Go 1.5 miles on the trail, until the mountain's northeast ridge comes into view. Ascend the summit on the steep exposed ridge.

Little Molas Lake Access:

The objective from this vantage point is **Sultan Mountain** (13,368'), a large massif southwest of Silverton, with many possible destinations. Drive south from Silverton on US-550 approximately 6 miles to the **Little Molas Lake** turnoff (not Molas Lake). Drive west 1 mile to the lake and park. Climb north into and up a werl-defined narrowing basin between two rocky points. These were called **West Turkshead Peak** (12,849') and **Turkshead Peak** (12,734') by the SJM. Once above the basin, follow the undulating scenery northeast to **Grand Turk** (13,160') and finally to the summit of Sultan.

SAN JUAN

Molas Lake   *Chester Stone*

Howardsville/San Juan Co Rd-2 Access:

At the northeast end of Silverton, take a right turn onto Hwy-110 and follow it a couple of miles east-northeast up the valley. Where the blacktop ends, the road changes its designation to San Juan Co Rd-2 and continues as a well graded gravel road 2 miles to Howardsville. Beyond Howardsville, this road continues with variable quality 3.5 miles to the razed site of Eureka, and then 4 additional miles to the ghost town of Animas Forks. Beyond Animas Forks, only 4WD vehicles are recommended. The vicinity around Animas Forks is a center about which jeepers and dirt bikers explore old mine trails east over **Cinnamon Pass**, north over **Engineer Pass**, and west, from Picayne Gulch to Corkscrew Gulch. Those on foot may find the activity miserable, but likely will find a peaceful mountaintop above it all.

At a couple miles up Hwy-110 from town is the entrance to Boulder Gulch, just behind the settling ponds before the Mayflower Mill. An old trail goes north up the gulch for five miles before crossing over a ridge and down to Gladstone. To climb **Peak 13,325'**, leave the trail just past a small lakelet at 12,000 and climb the steep but broad southeast face. **Storm Peak** (13,487'), a large, rough peak with pronounced ridges radiating from it, is close to the west but unreachable from Peak 13,325' because of a severe saddle between them. Instead, leave the trail further down the gulch, where the valley forks, following a faint mining trail northwest into the basin beneath the south face of Storm. From two lakelets at 12,800', climb due north to a platform at about 13,100' and on the east ridge. The resulting scramble to the summit is left up broken and exposed rock.

A large collection of 13,000' peaks cluster about **Silver Lake**, high in **Arrastra Basin**, southeast of Silverton. An arrastra was a crude, early ore crushing device, and this area is littered with remnants of mining days. Some claims are still active, and it is important to observe all gates and private property signs. Silver Lake is reached by driving 2.25 miles northeast from Silverton to the Mayflower Mill, where you turn south, and perhaps try for the mine, 3 miles of not-too-steep road up the gulch. It's at 11,200', and another 1.5 miles takes you to the lake, 1,000' higher. Old trails fan out through the basin to nearly all the summits of the surrounding peaks, including the high point, **Kendall Peak** (13,451') on your right. The ridge west and north of the peak is called **Kendall Mountain** (13,338'). From Silverton you can reach it by an old road, visible across the Animas River, that winds around the southwest flank almost to the summit.

Tower Mountain (13,552'), where you are more likely to be accompanied by a herd of domestic sheep rather that vehicles, starts on the county road about 0.5 mile southwest of Howardsville. The trail on the left side of Hematite Gulch is not obvious for the first 0.5 mile, but continues through an infinite number of switchbacks to **Hematite Lake**, where the peak is a grassy walk up to the north-northwest. Including **Macomber Peak** (13,222') involves heading south from the lake and ascending the mountain's east ridge, then going north to Tower.

Dome Mountain (13,370') is a rocky scramble on the ridge 1.5 miles east of Tower. It's much better climbed independently, starting about a mile northeast of Howardsville, then by way of an old miners' road to the base of **Cataract Gulch**. Bushwhack up the appropriately named gulch, bypassing the falls on the left, to the lower lake and onto the southeast ridge to the summit, using a couloir on the south face as a finish.

The name **Middle Mountain** (12,984') is attached to the endpoint of a two-mile-long ridge that extends west from the Continental Divide. There are half a dozen points on it. **Maggie** and **Minnie Gulches**, both with old mining roads that originate down by the Animas River, flank the ridge, and provide easy access. To climb the named point, drive about 6 miles out of Silverton and turn off into Maggie Gulch. The road ends in a steep mile, where a trail continues up to the divide. Leave the trail in less than a mile, and head straight up the south face. To reach the higher east end of the ridge, continue up until near the divide and then hike north over easy slopes and pick your point.

From the leveled townsite of Eureka, a good road sidehills west into Eureka Gulch, offering an approach to several easy thirteeners. Most cars can make it to about 11,600', below the workings of the old Sunnyside Mine. For a grand tour, follow the road, then trail, northwest another 1.5 miles, past Lake Emma to the 12,800' **Sunnyside Saddle** where **Hurricane Peak** (13,447') and **Hanson Peak** (13,454') are short climbs northwest and northeast respectively, on grassy slopes. Return to the saddle and march up the north ridge of **Bonita Peak**

SAN JUAN

(13,286') in about a mile. Then continue south another mile, losing 500' along the way, in order to reach the 13,310' point called **Emery Peak**. This isn't really the high point though and you may want to continue southwest along a narrowing ridge to visit **Peak 13,330'**. Drop east into McCarty Basin and pick up an vague mining trail that turns north and back to the Eureka Gulch road.

One route reported for **Crown Mountain** (13,569') goes straight up the hanging valley east from Eureka. A few scraps of trail did little to ease the difficulties of cliffs and waterfalls, but once past 11,800' no significant problems were encountered. The party descended by picking their way north a mile to Niagara, then descended Burns Gulch; they recommend this as the wisest route.

A high country tour of three Centennial Peaks starts 2.5 miles above abandoned Eureka. Take a jeep road 2 miles southeast up **Burns Gulch**. Continue southeast on foot to a saddle between **Jones Mountain** (13,860') and **Niagara Peak** (13,807'). Climb the ridge west to Niagara or northeast to Jones. For unofficially designated **American Peak** (13,806'), descend to the saddle northeast of Jones, and follow a cairn route east just below the tops of the 13,744' ridge to the summit of American. To loop back, try heading back to the saddle and then dropping to the lakelets in Burns Gulch, then continue west-southwest to the road. Or you can climb west over sub-peak 13,444' and go down **Grouse Gulch** nearly back to your starting point. This peak has also been climbed from American Basin to the north.

Stony Pass/Cunningham Gulch Access:

Galena Mountain (13,278') is perhaps best known for its cliff-hanging Old Hundred Mine. At Howardsville, 4 miles northeast of Silverton, turn right, and drive up Cunningham Gulch 2 miles. Then fork left at the jeep road to **Stony Pass** on the Continental Divide. Take this road for 0.5 mile to where it forks again, and hike up the switchbacks to the old mine in Sterling Gulch. Grassy slopes lead northeast to the summit ridge.

The road to 12,588' Stony Pass also provides access to the "Bend" area of the Continental Divide, as referred to in earlier editions. From the top of the pass one can hike northeast 0.5 mile to **Canby Mountain** (13,478') or southwest 0.5 mile and then northwest another 0.5 mile to **Green Mountain** (13,049'). For **Sheep Mountain** (13,292') or **Greenhalgh Mountain** (13,220') descend 1 mile east down from the pass, and go up Sheep's easy west slopes. In fact, from the pass one can hike for miles over this gentle, rolling landscape. About 70 years ago, Ormes and a friend started confidently up Stony Pass in a Model T. As he relates it, "It was on the map. A few rods above the Animas it began to be rough, and we found a man to talk to. 'Well,' he said, 'the first car into Silverton came over this road. But it was in some wagons.'"

Engineer Pass/Cinnamon Pass Access:

From Animas Forks, 12 miles northeast of Silverton the road branches: north to **Engineer Pass** on the Animas-Gunnison Lake Fork divide, east for a short climb to **Cinnamon Pass** on the same crest. Both branches are suitable for 4WD vehicles only, and continue into the Lake City country.

Park your vehicle right in Animas Forks to climb **Houghton Mountain** (13,052). It is the gentle ridge, curving northwest from the last mine dump above town. To visit **Tuttle Mountain** (13,203') walk 2 miles west from Houghton, losing 400' along the way.

Engineer Mountain (13,218'), one of several such named peaks in Colorado, can be driven to the top by 4WD vehicle. Otherwise, drive as far as Animas Forks and hitch a ride the 3 or so miles north to Engineer Pass. Hike 0.5 mile south and 500' to the summit.

Handies Peak   *John Devitt*

SAN JUAN

Seigal Mountain (13,274') can be climbed on your way to Engineer Pass, from about 2 miles north of Animas Forks, where you are due west of the peak at 12,020'. An old mining trail heads southeast across the slope and climbs to **Denver Pass** at 12,880', 0.25 mile down ridge from the summit.

Wood Mountain (13,660') is climbed from Cinnamon Pass east of Animas Forks. The summit is 1.5 miles north of the pass over generally easy slopes. **Peak 13,722'** can be combined with Wood by proceeding west along the ridge one mile to the 13,708' sub-peak. Stroll the half mile "catwalk" south and finish on short, steep talus. The steep east ridge can also be ascended easily from the bowl just northwest of Cinnamon Pass.

Peak 13,688', also usually combined with Wood, is one of the more interesting peaks in the area, and involves some careful route finding. Climb west from Wood, past the beginning of the spired south ridge of 13,688'. Descend about 250' into **Hurricane Basin** from the 13,300' saddle just past this ridge, and traverse underneath the spires of the ridge towards the low point. The best gully to take appears to be the second one past the last major pinnacle. Ascend this on third or fourth class rock to gain the south ridge, and an easy third class scramble to the top. Ice has been reported up to July in the shady recesses of the traverse, so take an axe.

Cinnamon Mountain (13,328') and its higher neighbor, **Peak 13,535'** a mile southeast, are easy hikes from Cinnamon Pass. To loop Animas Forks, travel south off Peak 13,535' to the trail in **Grouse Gulch**, and follow it west 2 miles to the road.

SAN JUAN

Needle Mountains

Jurisdiction:
San Juan NF, Columbine-West and Columbine-East Ranger Districts

Map area reference:
Page 258, 290 and 302

Maps:
USGS: *Columbine Pass, Mountain View Crest, Snowdon Peak, Storm King Peak, Vallecito Reservoir*
Forest Service: *San Juan NF*

The Needle Mountains are a vast climber's paradise. The fact that they are wild and rugged, with few roads and trails, has tended to make them a preserve for mountaineering. Only the Chicago Basin area saw any of the mining activity that swarmed over the rest of the San Juan in the last century. As a result, the Needles have remained as wilderness until this day. Except for ascents in Chicago Basin, and of Pigeon Peak, many of the first ascents of major peaks were not accomplished until CMC and SJM expeditions of the 1920's and 1930's. Each decade since has seen new routes and climbs established, especially technical ones. There still are new routes to be explored on remote pinnacles and cold, dark north and east faces. In fact, there is a lifetime of climbing possibilities here.

The Needles proper, as part of the large Weminuche Wilderness, lie between the Animas River to the west and Vallecito Creek to the east. In a general sense, the term Needle Mountains also encompasses the West Needle Mountains, west of the Animas River, and the Mount Oso Group, to the east of Vallecito Creek.

It can be hard to get into the Needles, and even harder to get around in them once you are there. Very few maintained trails exist, but there are high cols that link the various climbing basins, making possible extended trips and loops. By avoiding popular Chicago Basin, you can pass several days in this wilderness without seeing another party. An ice axe and possibly crampons are required early in the season, and a rope is recommended, even for many of the standard climbs.

Access to the Needles comes by way of its major drainages, the Animas and Vallecito. The most common, and unique, approach uses the historic narrow gauge railroad, the Durango & Silverton, which runs several trains daily during the summer via spectacular Animas River Canyon. The train carries backpackers and climbers each morning, and makes stops at Needleton and Elk Creek. The Needleton stop is for approaches to the west side of the range, including popular Chicago Basin (Needle Creek), Ruby Basin, and Noname Creek. There is a Forest Service bridge there for crossing the Animas. Needleton can also be reached from US-550 at Purgatory Campground, about halfway between Silverton and Durango, where a 10 mile trail takes you down to and across the Animas, then east-northeast to the Needleton whistle stop.

Needle Creek Access:

One hundred years ago, there was a small mining boom at the headwaters of Needle Creek in **Chicago Basin**. A railstop named Needleton sprang up along the Animas River to service the mines, and for a few years the place prospered. Little remains of the short boom, but the Durango & Silverton still stops at Needleton, and the trail to Chicago Basin seems as busy as ever in summer, as hundreds of climbers and backpackers are attracted to this basin capped with fourteeners.

Leave the train at Needleton at 8,212', cross the footbridge to the east side of the Animas, and follow the trail a mile south, where it turns east along the banks of Needle Creek. Continue 5 more miles into lower Chicago Basin. About 1.5 miles after the trail reaches Needle Creek, a hard to find trail climbs south to the four jewel-like lakes beneath **Mountain View Crest**. From any of the lakes, it is easy to gain the crest and stroll along this tilted plateau to **Overlook Point** (12,998') or **Mount Kennedy** (13,125'), three miles east. Though of little mountaineering interest, they provide fantastic views back into the heart of the Needles.

Chicago Basin Group

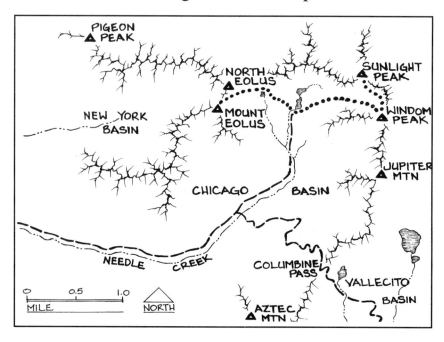

There are good, though crowded, camp sites at 11,000' in Chicago Basin. The trail splits here, with one branch heading east and over **Columbine Pass** into the Vallecito Creek area via Johnson Creek. The other climbs north an additional 1,500' into Twin Lakes basin. Here you are right underneath 3 fourteeners and a high col that leads north into Noname Creek basin.

Mount Eolus (14,083') is normally climbed from Twin Lakes basin by heading for the low point of the Eolus-North Eolus saddle, a mile west of the lakes. From here, either scramble the ridge, difficult and exposed, or traverse south, and out onto the east face where a cairn marked route winds to the top. The south ridge has also been ascended directly from Needle Creek. It is reported as third and fourth class. A few parties travel over to **North Eolus**, although it is not recognized as a separate fourteener. It is a short scramble from the low point between Eolus and North Eolus.

For **Glacier Point** (13,704'), head up its easy southeast ridge from the lakes. **Twin Thumbs** (13,420') and **Peak Eleven** (13,540') are both climbed from the col between them, due north from the lakes. The North Thumb is the harder, a rope may be needed for a short ways. Peak Eleven goes by contouring around Point 13,460' on the north.

Mel Griffiths and Bob Ormes made the first traverse of pinnacled **Needle Ridge** (13,480') in the 1930's, going from east to west. Ormes remembers it as "airy, with firm rock and no problems but the rappels."

Sunlight Peak (14,059') is usually combined with Windom, the latter recommended first. If coming from Windom, stay high in the basin at about 13,500'. But in any case, scramble up the south face. On top is a jumble of huge boulders, with the highest involving an exposed move. Some may require a short rope at this point, although it is recorded that a few individuals have stood on their heads on the narrow apex. A short distance east along the ridge is Point 13,995', sometimes called **Sunlight Spire**. This blocky pinnacle is climbed only by a difficult aid route in a jam crack on the northwest side.

For **Windom Peak** (14,082'), head east 0.5 mile from Twin Lakes, and then cut up to Windom's west ridge for a scrambling finish. **Peak 13,472'** (Peak Eighteen), is at the west end of this scrambling ridge.

Though the ridge between Windom and **Jupiter Mountain** (13,830') to the south has been climbed, it is a slow and tedious bit of work. It is better to drop into the upper basin just west of the ridge, and cross to the west ridge just below the summit. Jupiter can also be climbed from the 11,000' camp on Needle Creek, via its steep, grassy southwest face. Gain the west ridge at about 13,400' and scramble to the top. It has also been climbed by its long south ridge from Columbine Pass. This pass also is the way to approach **Aztec Mountain** (13,310'). Go 15 miles south, then boulder hop along the mountain's tedious east ridge.

SAN JUAN

Windom Peak   *H. L. Standley*

Noname Creek Access:

Noname Creek is the preferred approach for the rugged peaks centered around Jagged Mountain. It also offers high cols into the Grenadiers to the north, and Chicago Basin to the south. From the Durango & Silverton whistle stop at Needleton, cross over to the east side of the Animas River and hike north to "Watertank Hill," where you will be forced up through the cliffs. Once over this ridge, it is an easy mile or so to Noname Creek, where a good trail leads four miles east to the basin. There is good camping at 10,800', near the fork of the two branches of the creek, and high up the basin as well. The small lakelet on the northwest side of Jagged is a popular and lovely spot.

You can pass into the **Balsam Lake** region and the Grenadiers by continuing up the left fork of the creek, and over the easy 12,900' saddle just west of Peak Six. To reach Chicago Basin, take the right fork heading due south to the high col called **Twin Thumbs Pass**, between Glacier Point and Twin Thumbs. Ice axe and crampons may be required early in the season on this cold north side.

The **Heisspitz** (13,262') and **Peak Four** (13,410') can both be climbed from a camp at 10,800'. For Peak Four, head up the prominent gully running north from the camp, staying slightly to the right. The Heisspitz is best climbed by another prominent gully about 0.25 mile down the valley. This will get you to the ridge; another 0.25 mile of third and fourth class scrambling to the northwest is required to get you to the top.

Peak Five (13,283') and **Peak Six** (13,705') both go from the 12,900' pass between them. Six is an easy walkup to the east, while Five is described as a good scramble by its northeast ridge. Five has also been climbed from the lakes which flank it on the east and west.

It has been said that well named **Jagged Mountain** (13,824') is "one of the more difficult and certainly one of the most rewarding climbs in the Needles." The route finding will test your skills and the moves are hard enough and exposed enough that carrying a rope may be prudent. From the lakelet east of Peak Five, climb east 0.25 mile to the 13,000' saddle north of the peak. The summit is the first aiguille to the right of a prominent snow couloir on the north face. Traverse from the col to just short of the couloir, where a series of sandy ledges lead a couple hundred feet up to an impasse under which you traverse west into the next gully. This leads to a ridge just west of the summit. Here you swing onto the south face and contour to cracks which lead to the summit. Avoid starting in a good-looking gully to the left of that specified. It leads to a lower summit separated from the true one by a gap. Avoid also the snow couloir, it leads to the ridge, but not to the summit—"Finding the route on Jagged is a delight."

The sharp aiguilles that make up the western end of the Jagged Mountain ridge are interesting technical climbs. Bob Rosebrough says **Gray Needle** (13,430') is best approached from the north. **Noname Needle** (13,620'), just east of Gray, goes from the saddle between them and Peak Ten, and has a 5.6 pitch.

Leviathan Peak (13,528') is climbed by its southwest ridge. The approach is via the same col as Jagged. From here you traverse northeast 0.25 mile to the col which starts the ridge. It is not too hard to descend the southeast ridge to 11,250', and go up **Vallecito Mountain** (13,428') 0.5 mile east. There is a bit of third class climbing on both these peaks.

Knife Point (13,265') and **Peak Ten** (13,400') are climbed from the col between them. Approach them by the east branch of Noname Creek, swinging southeast toward a prominent gully that leads toward the col. To ascend the lowest cliffs, get into the bottom of the main gully. Eventually work up to the second couloir to the south (right) and follow it onto the upper grassy slopes. From the col, it is an easy walk up Knife Point. The south ridge of Peak Ten involves some tedious scrambling. As an alternative, it is possible to descend 200' from the col down the Sunlight Creek side, and traverse over to finish on the southeast face, where one source says "you feel like a mouse trapped in a maze" of gullies and boulders.

Needle Ridge, **Sunlight** and **Windom** are occasionally climbed from this side by heading east 0.5 mile from the 10,800' camp and then south two miles to the col between Needle Ridge and Sunlight. Then descend south into Chicago Basin to finish on the standard routes.

SAN JUAN

Chicago Basin can also be reached with about the same effort by way of **Twin Thumbs Pass** at 13,050'. You climb directly up the south fork two miles from camp. A camp just below the pass at the lake at 11,754' provides a decent base for the peaks in this basin. For **Peak Eleven** (13,540') and **Twin Thumbs** (13,420'), climb southeast into the cirque between the two. A direct ascent of the snow north of the Thumbs leads to chimneys and slabs, and eventually to the high col between the peaks. A rope may be needed to finish the North Thumb. **Glacier Point** (13,704') can be climbed from Twin Thumbs Pass by swinging out onto the southeast ridge for an easy finish.

To climb **Peak 13,120'** (Peak Twelve), climb due east from a camp at the lake to the 12,700' pass south of the great wall of Monitor Peak. Peak Twelve goes easily up the ridge left of the pass. This pass offers a good route into Ruby Basin for climbs on Pigeon and Turret.

Monitor Peak (13,695') boasts an intimidating 1,200' high east face that has seen some of the longest rock climbs in the San Juans. Since the first ascent in 1947 by Joe Stettner and others, four routes have been established on this face,

Jagged Mountain   *David Anschicks*

all rated about 5.8 or 5.9, with most having a bit of aid. Sunrise on this face from a camp on the south fork of Noname Creek is a spectacular sight. But to climb Monitor by its more pedestrian route, as well as its neighbors, a camp in the Ruby Basin is preferred.

Ruby Creek Access:

The route up Ruby Creek has caused more than a few epic bushwhacking tales from those who never found the rough, obscure trail. It starts above a meadow about 0.25 mile north of Pigeon Creek on the east side of the Animas River. Several strategies have been suggested for finding the illusive start. Suffice it to say the trail contours from above the meadows, crosses the next unnamed creek north at about 9500' and crests the ridge between the unnamed creek and Ruby Creek at about 10,300', then contours east to reach the Ruby Creek at about 10,400'. It is better not to camp at Ruby Lake, as it provides poor access to the main peaks. Another mile of willow-bashing upstream leads to good camping at 11,600'. If this sounds like a lot of hard work, it is; but **Ruby Basin** is dramatic, uncrowded, and offers some of the finer climbs in the Needles. Bring a rope, even for most of the standard routes. There are unclimbed technical routes on the north faces of the Turret Needles and the spectacular east face of Pigeon, both looming over the lovely campsite at 11,600'.

The Index (13,400') is the point 0.5 mile northwest of Animas Mountain. Leave camp at 11,600' and hike north up steep, grassy slopes, staying west of the cliffs and gaining the northwest ridge at about 13,100'. Traverse to the base of the first summit block, climb up through a gully to reach the second block, climb up that and rappel to the col between it and the third and true summit. Climb up and south to reach the southeast face. Most climbers rate it at about 5.7 in difficulty.

The small basin 0.25 mile northeast of camp is used for the standard routes on **Animas Mountain** (13,786'), **Peak Thirteen** (13,705') and **Monitor Peak** (13,695'), which combine well for one long day. For the first, head for the 13,500' saddle just east of the summit area, then move out to finish on the southeast face. For Peak Thirteen, work up until below the cliffs on the south face, contour around them to the east face, and scramble up the ledges. Monitor goes by way of its loose north ridge, third class up from the Peak Thirteen-Monitor saddle. Both Animas Mountain and Peak Thirteen have technical routes reported from their steep Noname Creek sides, involving steep snow climbing and finishing on exposed ledges.

New York Basin provides the practical way up **Little Finger** (13,200'), **Peak Sixteen** (13,500') and **Peak Fifteen** (13,700'), but getting there is a job in itself. Parties starting from the 11,600' camp head for the saddle between Pigeon and

Turret. Go southwest about 0.25 mile, drop into New York Basin, and contour on the 12,000' line for 0.5 mile to the south side of the peaks. Head for the saddle just east of Little Finger, and traverse west out onto the south face. Climb the west chimney about 100' and then switch over to the right one to finish on the summit ridge. Climb west to the top of the spire. It is rated at about 5.7. For the other two peaks, climb the south facing couloir to the saddle between them, often snow filled early in the season. From this airy spot, turn right to climb Peak Sixteen by moving east and then north up the summit block. Take a moment to study the route on Fifteen. Several variations exist up its east ridge; all offer tricky footing and a rope may be a welcome addition.

The finest peak in Ruby Basin is undoubtedly **Pigeon Peak** (13,972'), a striking sight from many viewpoints in the San Juan. Pigeon has a rich climbing history, starting with the 1908 first ascent by Cooper and Hubbard, and continuing to this day with assaults on the great east face. The standard route involves getting into the basin high on the northwest side. From the 11,600' camp, hike up over the Pigeon-Turret saddle, drop southwest to the 12,700' saddle, descend northwest to 12,200', and contour into the basin. Head for the northwest ridge and move west at the finish. There is a much more direct route that lies west of the first large gray rock ridge that runs from the north face of Pigeon. It climbs grassy ledges and continues up the northwest ridge. Under ideal conditions and excellent route finding it is not too difficult, but it is easy to get into technical trouble here, and a rope and protection ought to be along for those anxious moments. The common descent off Pigeon, particularly if the next objective is Turret, is the southeast chimney. To find it from the top, use a couloir which descends south from west of the summit and splits about 400' down, then rap the chimney to the saddle. Two double rope rappels are required. The first from a chockstone 30' below the start, the second 120' long, from hardware, 80' lower. This grungy chimney would not be a good ascent route.

It is perhaps with relief that one now approaches **Turret Peak** (13,835'), the only true walkup in the basin. Hike up the talus covered northwest face from the Pigeon-Turret saddle.

Vallecito Creek Access:

For the seldom used approach from the east up Vallecito Creek, drive to Vallecito Campground, north of **Vallecito Reservoir**, 22 miles north of Bayfield on US-160. A trail runs 19 miles north up Vallecito Creek to **Hunchback Pass** on the Continental Divide, and then down to meet the jeep road up Bear Creek. Vallecito Creek is high well into the summer, and difficult to cross. The bridge at Johnson Creek is the only one to the west side of the drainage.

Vallecito Basin, at the head of Johnson Creek, can be reached by packing 9 miles up the Vallecito Creek Trail to where the bridge will get you west across the stream. Take the trail up Johnson Creek about 5 miles where there is good camping at about 11,200'. After another mile, the trail goes over 12,700' **Columbine Pass** and west into **Chicago Basin**.

Hope Mountain (13,012'), which splits the upper basin, is a mile east of Columbine Pass, and can be approached on an old road that crosses north of it going east to **Hazel Lake**. Here you are looking at the rough cliffs of the south face of Jupiter Peak, and the southwest face of **Grizzly Peak** (13,700'), both within a mile. Climb Grizzly by way of the obvious ramp system that starts under the Jupiter-Grizzly saddle and heads for the broad gully that splits the southwest face, climbing to the 13,500' saddle just west of the summit. Finish on the north face. The ridge from Grizzly to **McCauley Peak** (13,554') is reported bumpy but offers no real difficulties. Descend McCauley's broad west face.

Echo Mountain (13,309'), the end point of the ridge, is well guarded by cliffs. One party seems to have ascended the steep southwest slopes to the ridge west of the summit, worked its way around some pinnacles and scrambled up the northwest face of the summit block. It is 4,000' down to the Vallecito from here; try the acoustics.

About a mile up **Johnson Creek Trail** from Vallecito Creek, seldom visited Grizzly Gulch comes in from the northwest. One well-known climber has been said to conjure up horror stories, "the bushwhack from hell", to inquiring parties about the difficulties of traveling up Grizzly Gulch in an attempt to discourage anyone from going there. But in truth, it is a surprisingly easy 1.5 mile bushwhack up the gulch, on good game trails, on either side of the creek. Once at treeline, you pass through a dramatic notch cut by the stream and into the open. Now you can understand that climber's fierce possessiveness, surrounded as you are by great cliffs, cascading waterfalls and emerald basins. Familiar peaks from Chicago Basin, like Windom and Jupiter, are quite a bit more rugged on this side, and reflect from azure lakes.

Thunder Mountain (13,108') has a 0.5 mile long, sheer cliff face that stops any attempts from the basin. Better to climb this one by its southeast ridge, starting down where Grizzly Creek enters Johnson Creek. The only walk-up in the Grizzly Gulch basin, **Greylock Mountain** (13,575'), can be climbed from the lake at 12,235' by ascending grassy slopes to the saddle 0.25 mile east of the summit, or by its equally easy west ridge. A high col above the 13,100' lake sitting under Windom, provides access into the Sunlight Creek drainage.

Florida Mountain (13,076') can be climbed most of the way by an old road that traverses south out of Vallecito Basin to 12,840' **Trimble Pass**. **Bullion Mountain** (13,182'), 0.5 mile west of the pass, and **Mount Valois** (13,185'), an equal distance southeast, are easy walk-ups. These summits are part of the south-ernmost extension of the Needles, culminating in **Endlich Mesa**, several miles south. To visit some of the other thirteeners, follow the trail south from Trimble Pass, three miles to the Florida River, where there is camping. Bushwhack north-east up the middle fork of the river to the 11,960' pass and contour east into the small basin beneath the north face of **Emerson Mountain** (13,085'). Emerson can be ascended by the saddle just east of the top. **Sheep Mountain** (13,070') is 0.5 mile south from this saddle over easy terrain. For **Amherst Mountain** (13,165') hike up its southwest face from the same basin, then continue to **Organ Mountain** (13,032') 0.25 mile further with a 600' drop between.

The **Sunlight Creek Trail** leaves Vallecito Creek 12 miles north of the trailhead at the Vallecito Campground, and climbs 4.5 miles from 9,700' to 12,033' Sunlight Lake, close under Sunlight Peak. You will have to wade Vallecito Creek to get to the trail on the south side of Sunlight Creek. There is good camping en route, and two passages into the Noname Creek drainage, the 13,000' pass just north of Jagged, and the 12,850' pass just north of Knife Point. The latter is steep, long and grassy on the Vallecito side, but somewhat frightening when you look down into Noname Creek. This drainage is seldom visited and you are like-ly to have a lot of solitude here, but the climbing possibilities are endless. See the Noname Creek access for the standard routes on Knife Point, Peak Ten, Jagged and many others.

The Guardian, endpoint of the Grenadiers, looms over the Vallecito some 13 miles north of the trailhead, where Leviathan Creek comes in from the west. Wade the Vallecito and follow the trail on the north bank of Leviathan Creek for about 2 miles, where there is good camping near treeline. One mile northwest is an easy pass with a small pond in it that gives passage into the Balsam Lake area, and the surrounding Grenadiers. **Peak Seven** (13,682'), the northernmost peak of the Needles proper, is climbed from this pass by angling over to its easy north ridge. A couple of 13,000' cols are convenient for getting into the Sunlight and Noname drainages. About 0.25 mile southwest of **Leviathan Lake** is the first, the other is only a few 100 yards southwest of the first, and north of Jagged Peak.

Mount Oso Group

Jurisdiction:
San Juan NF, Columbine Ranger District-East

Maps:
USGS: *Columbine Pass, Emerald Lake, Rio Grande Pyramid, Storm King Peak*
Forest Service: *San Juan NF*

This group is bordered on the north by the Continental Divide, by the deep gorge of the Vallecito to the west, and the Los Pines River on the east. Geologically the peaks have a lot in common with their neighbors across the Vallecito, sharing the same granites and quartzites as the Needles but without the latter's height and ruggedness. The area was first visited by surveyors in the 1870's, and the high point was climbed by the Hayden team.

Mount Oso, the high point, lords over a collection of mostly unnamed twelvers and thirteeners that in the past have attracted few climbers. But the large number of fine lakes, and an excellent trail system, make this part of the Weminuche Wilderness very popular with backpackers and fishermen. With only a few exceptions, these remote peaks require two days of packing to reach.

Vallecito Creek Access:

Directions for both the north approach from Kite Lake and Beartown, and the south approach from Vallecito Campground, have been given elsewhere. The **Kite Lake** approach is the shorter for those equipped with a 4WD vehicle. From the lake, hike south over 12,493' **Hunchback Pass**, then 4 miles down Vallecito Creek where the good Rock Creek Trail climbs southeast from 10,100' to **Rock Lake** at 11,841' in another 4 miles. Those without a 4WD vehicle must march up Vallecito Creek from the south some 13 miles to reach the Rock Creek Trail.

From Hunchback Pass, one can climb **Mount Nebo** (13,205') which affords a marvelous view into the Needles. It can be reached on a 3 mile walk southeast along the divide, with one 400' summit to climb or bypass. Or from down on the Vallecito, the best route starts up a steep watercourse 1 mile north of Rock Creek. After you reach timberline, head a mile northeast for a drink in the 12,500' lake, and take the peak by the southeast ridge.

A decent alternative exists for those only wishing to visit the higher core peaks of the group. Go up the Vallecito from the south, and turn off after about 8 miles, a little short of Johnson Creek, to bushwhack northeast up Irving Creek. This is reported to be steep and tough the first mile or so, but soon one reaches camping at **Irving Lake** at 11,662'. **Mount Oso** (13,684') is at the head of the basin, a mile further, by way of either its southwest or southeast ridges. A mile south is

Peak 13,417' which combines well with Oso. Expect a touch of fourth class near the summit on its north ridge. **Irving Peak** (13,218') can be climbed from the lake by going for the saddle between Irving and Point 13,006' and walk up the north ridge to finish.

It is also possible to do Irving directly from the Vallecito, a little north of Johnson Creek. Go east up the obvious avalanche gully and toil up the talus to the saddle.

Emerald Lake Access:

Emerald Lake might seem an interesting goal in itself, and quite as practical a way to approach Mount Oso and the host of lesser summits neighboring it. From the road junction north of **Vallecito Reservoir**, turn right and drive 6 miles to the trailhead at the Pine River Campg round. Hike 5 miles along the Los Pines River to a trail junction, where you go north another 5 miles to Emerald Lake. From here you can continue along the east shore of this huge, natural lake, and hike another 4 miles to **Moon Lake** at 11,620'. The trail climbs north from here over a 12,400' pass to reach **Rock Lake** and a branch swings east past Flint Lakes. Any of these high alpine lakes provides an excellent base for exploring the unnamed summits around them. We don't have reports on all of them but try these for a sample.

Peak 13,220' and **Peak 12,961'** are both easy ascents from tiny **Half Moon Lake** under the pass between Moon and Rock Lakes. Head east 0.25 mile to the saddle between the peaks and take your pick. Peak 13,220' reportedly also has an enjoyable scramble on its rugged east ridge. **Peak 12,965'**, just south of the upper of the **Flint Lakes**, is said to be an easy ascent from the lakelets on its east side, and **Peak 12,882'** likewise is a short climb from the same vicinity.

Buffalo Peak (12,728') is only a 1,000' stroll up its south ridge from the west shore of Rock Lake, and **Peters Peak** (13,122') is a rougher scramble from the saddle between them.

Finally, **Mount Oso** can also be easily reached from this side. Work up into the basin beneath its southeast face and follow grassy ledges to gain the southeast ridge for a boulder hop to the summit.

West Needle Mountains

Jurisdiction:
San Juan NF, Columbine Ranger District-West

Maps:
USGS: *Snowdon Peak*
Forest Service: *San Juan NF*

The West Needle Mountains are a small, but fairly rough north-south collection of peaks south of Molas Pass. They are separated from the main mountain chain by the plunging Animas River on the east, the meandering Lime Creek on the west. The main summits are casually viewed to the east as one drives north on US-550 to Molas Pass.

Andrews Lake Access:

The usual starting point into the West Needles is **Andrews Lake**, a 0.5 mile south of **Molas Pass** on US-550.

Snowdon Peak (13,077') as viewed by motorists atop Molas Pass, displays a most fearsome armor of vertical rock slabs, which seem to glisten like scales with a reptilian sheen. Fortunately, the route to the summit is not nearly as daunting. Begin at Andrews Lake, and ascend the trail on a series of switchbacks about a mile to an open area with some scattered ponds. Leave the trail and head east to a saddle just north of the summit. Go south along the ridge, which progressively tightens into an exposed sawtooth. The final pitch is a short chimney, which opens onto a broad summit. An alternative route contours left for a less challenging route up the east face.

For **North Twilight Peak** (13,075'), continue on the trail from Andrews Lake, south to **Crater Lake**. Ascend the summit by way of its east ridge. **Twilight Peak** (13,158') and **South Twilight Peak** (13,080') are scrambles, 0.5 mile and 1 mile respectively, south from North Twilight.

SAN JUAN

Grenadier Range and Needle Mountains

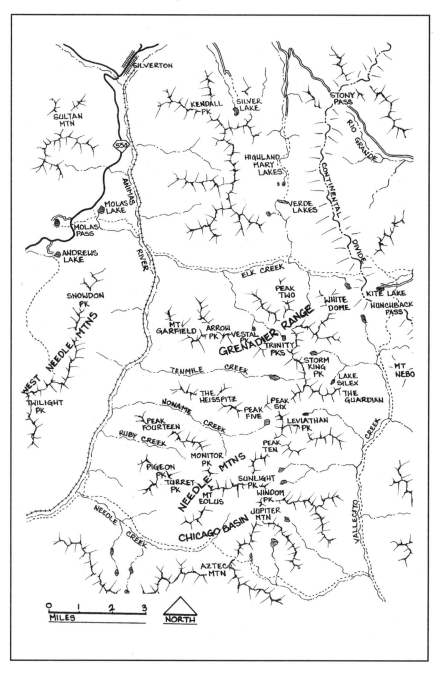

Grenadier Range

Jurisdiction :
San Juan NF, Columbine Ranger District-West

Map area reference:
Page 258 and 302

Maps:
USGS: *Snowdon Peak, Storm King Peak*
Forest Service: *San Juan NF*

The Grenadiers offer some of the finest mountaineering in the entire state. Soaring faces of hard quartzite, remote alpine campsites and pristine wilderness, have gladdened the hearts of Colorado climbers since the days of pitons and hob-nailed boots. And evocative names like Arrow, Storm King, and The Guardian, add to the lure for modern day climbers. The high quality of the rock has earned a reputation for fine rock climbs; everything from the "classic" Wham Ridge fourth class romp, to a demanding 18-pitch climb of Silex's east face. If you travel to this country, bring a rope and friends you trust.

As a small but impressive sub-set of the San Juans north of the Needle Mountains, the Grenadiers are a continuous ridge of quartzite, slate and conglomerate running roughly west-northwest from The Guardian. They include a two-pronged northern spur at the head of Elk Creek, and are within the boundaries of the Weminuche Wilderness. Like the Needles, the Grenadiers are conspicuously absent of past mining operations, and hence the numerous paths and roads those activities created. The result is an isolated wilderness, devoid of maintained trails, appropriate for these rugged peaks and valleys. The north faces of the peaks in this range are particularly beautiful. The most popular climbs are from a camp around Vestal Lake. The south side approaches from Balsam Lake are less remarkable, generally long pulls up talus and scree.

US-550/Molas Trail/Elk Park Access:

The most popular approach, especially for the more heavily visited western half, is by way of Elk Creek to Vestal Creek. For those wanting to preface their adventure on a relic of the past, arrange a lift on the D&SRR, which connects Durango and Silverton by narrow gauge rails, and disembark at **Elk Park**. The more conventional passage begins at the popular trailhead 1 mile north of **Molas Pass** on US-550. The **Molas Trail** descends to the Animas River just north of Elk Park on the railroad. Then follow the Colorado Trail about 3 miles up Elk Creek to some beaver ponds at an old cabin site. Leave the CT and skirt the ponds on the east and south, and drop suddenly down to Elk Creek. Cross the creek and search for a vague trail that climbs south up through the trees to join the large drainage of Vestal Creek, coming off the north slope of the Grenadiers. Continue up the left (east) side of this drainage. You will find good camping where the basin orients southeast and levels out a bit at 11,400'. Some parties head due south up to the bench holding **Vestal Lake**, directly beneath the spectacular Wham Ridge, an idyllic spot as fragile as it is beautiful. From this area, all climbs west of East Trinity are accessible, as well as Peaks Two and Three.

A backpack over the saddle between Vestal and West Trinity leads down to Balsam Lake, and access to the south side of the range. One can also continue up Vestal Creek to the saddle that leads down to Trinity Lake, for climbs on the north side of Storm King, and for standard approaches to Silex and The Guardian.

Mount Garfield (13,074'), is often combined with Graystone Peak and Point Pun. Hike into the Arrow-Electric Peak drainage, traverse around Graystone on angled slabs to Garfield Lake, and climb steeply up to the Garfield-Point Pun saddle. Easy third class leads along the ridge to the summit.

Point Pun (13,160') has two summit blocks, the eastern point is higher. Take the same approach as for Garfield, but before reaching the lake, head straight up the north face on steep, third class rock. A bit wet and loose in spots, it's an exciting scramble. The lower western summit is best reached by fourth classing its west ridge.

Approach **Graystone Peak** (13,489') from the Arrow-Graystone saddle, and hike up the northeast ridge. As fourth class difficulties present themselves near the eastern false summit, move out onto the east face to finish. Its easy to continue on to Point Pun and Garfield, then circle back through the Graystone-Electric Peak saddle.

Most parties on their way to **Electric Peak** (13,292') head up the drainage between Electric and Arrow and make for the south ridge. From here it's a scramble up steep and, at times, loose rock to the surprisingly bland summit area. More than one party has reported that Electric Peak lives up to its name during a storm.

The most popular route up **Arrow Peak** (13,803') takes off from the Vestal Lake camp and ascends ledges towards the north ridge of Arrow. From here two routes present themselves. The easiest is up the main gully that comes northeast off the peak. Steep and slabby, and often filled with snow early in the season, it joins the north ridge about 150 feet below the summit. Third class scrambling from here gains the top. The alternate route gains the north ridge at about 12,600' and follows it direct to the summit, with a fun and exposed knife edge just before joining the gully route.

Vestal Peak   *Linda Grey*

There are also several technical routes for those so inclined. The original south face, or "water gully", route pioneered in 1932 by Long and Nelson of the SJM features low fifth class climbing. Other good climbs include: the southeast ridge (reported to be 5.6), the east face (eight pitches of lower fifth), and extended multi-pitch climbs up to 5.7 on the northwest face and the north ridge.

Vestal Peak (13,864') and **Wham Ridge**, an imposing sight from a camp at Vestal Lake, have become a Colorado classic, since their first exciting ascent in 1941 by CMC members. It's easy to see why. On smooth slabs of quartzite, the rock is a joy to climb. Several lines exist up what is really a triangular face rather than a ridge, with the easiest being no harder than fourth class. But it is possible to get into trouble, especially if the weather threatens, so bring a rope. The easiest lines appear to be either a bit left or right of center, with the rock more broken near the summit. Most parties descend off the south face down the prominent gully, loose and grungy in spots, until they can traverse around to the Arrow-Vestal saddle and hike north and then east to camp.

The **Trinity Peaks** (13,765', 13,805' and 13,745'), usually climbed together, offer one of the finest scrambling traverses in the San Juans, challenging your route finding abilities. For a good circle trip from Vestal Lake, boulder hop up to the Vestal-West Trinity saddle, then scramble up the broken southwest ridge to the West Trinity summit. Descend directly to the West Trinity-Middle Trinity saddle, and begin a rising traverse on the south side of the 13,700' false summit,

SAN JUAN

staying as high as possible. A few cairns mark the way up to some ledges. This portion is fourth class but the easiest route can be hard to spot, so a rope may be useful. Once past the false summit, it's an easy 300' scramble to the top of Middle Trinity. Descend east down a gully to the saddle and scramble up the broad, third class gully on East Trinity's west face. Good scrambling leads down the northeast ridge, where at about 13,000', one can hike back west through the basin to Vestal Lake, passing the intimidating north faces of these peaks.

To gain **Peak Three** (13,478') from a camp in the Vestal Creek drainage, climb steeply out of the drainage to the flats above 12,800'. Walk up the west ridge. A moderate climbing route also is possible by way of the Vestal Creek-Trinity Creek saddle and the south ridge. Walk up **Peak Two** (13,475') from the flats by ascending its south ridge.

Beartown/Hunchback Pass/Kite Lake Access:

The peaks on the eastern end of the range are more commonly climbed from Beartown, a once bustling 1890's mining community. It has few remains, and is a historical site on the Colorado Trail. From Hwy-149, 20 miles west of Creede, follow the signs to Rio Grande Reservoir. Travel on a graded dirt road to the reservoir, then a mile beyond, where the road continues as suitable for 4WD vehicles only. Follow the jeep road approximately 6 miles and fork left into Bear Creek, where it is 4 miles to the site of Beartown. Go another mile to **Kite Lake** just below the crest of the Continental Divide. This point is also accessible from Silverton and Cunningham Gulch over the divide at **Stony Pass**.

If headed for the peaks centered around Balsam or Silex Lakes, take the trail from near Kite Lake over **Hunchback Pass**, and drop down into upper Vallecito Creek. A sketchy trail goes up Storm Gulch to camping at **Trinity Lake**, and another trail goes up Leviathan Creek. A 12,800' pass above the rock strewn basin containing Lake Silex gives access west to camping at **Balsam Lake**.

Although more popular with backpackers than climbers, the trail up Vallecito Creek from **Vallecito Reservoir** offers a scenic, albeit long approach to the southeast end of the range. Allow a couple of days walking if you go in this way.

The route to **Storm King Peak** (13,752) starts at a camp near Balsam Lake or **Silex Lake**. Hike up the talus to the pass between these two drainages and scramble the loose rock up the south ridge. Afine 15 pitch, 5.7 route, has been described for the magnificent north face.

The standard climb up **Mount Silex** (13,628') is up talus slopes on the south side, for which you need to reach the 12,800' pass on its southwest ridge. Drop a few hundred feet off the pass before traversing out onto the south face. Better yet, bring a rope and try the steep, fourth class, southwest ridge itself. Stay to the right of major obstacles. **The Guardian** (13,617') is often combined with Mount Silex by descending several hundred feet down the latter's south face before starting a tedious traverse on sloping ledges strewn with loose rock. Finish by ascending a gully to the northwest ridge and an easy finish.

Several parties reported **Peak Nine** (13,402') is one of the more difficult ascents in the area. One report says head for the saddle between Peak Eight and Peak Nine from the north. Early in the year, this route can be a good snow climb. Beyond here the difficulties start in the form of a short rock wall, needing a rope and protection. This party skirted the wall by descending about 200 feet on the south side, then climbed back to the ridge. The ridge features up to fifth class climbing on rotten, unstable rock. Traverse slightly below the summit on the south side for a finish on the southeast ridge. Another report on a route up the southeast ridge from the Leviathan drainage sounds equally hard. For **Peak Eight** (13,228'), start the same as for Peak Nine, except at the saddle head right. The route on the east ridge is straightforward enough, but quite exposed, with treacherously loose rock. The west ridge has also been climbed on a fifth class route.

White Dome (13,627') along with its close neighbors of Peaks One, Two and Three, doesn't quite fit the rugged profile of a Grenadier. From the trail above Kite Lake, leave the Continental Divide and head south on the 12,800' contour to the east ridge. **Peak One** (13,589') is combined with White Dome by descending the latter's moderate southwest ridge to the saddle and up Peak One's easy northeast ridge.

San Miguel Mountains

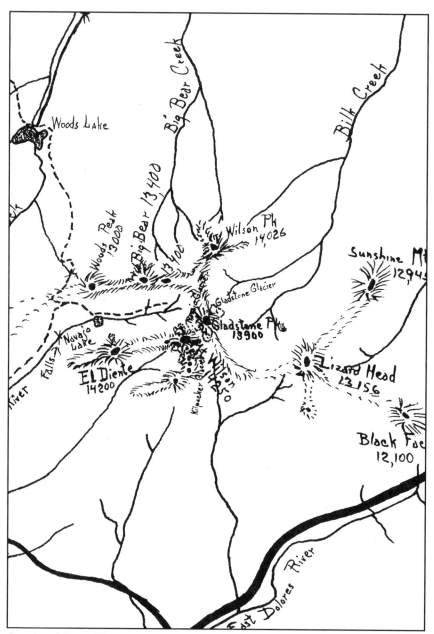

Reprinted from "The San Juan Mountaineer's Climber's Guide to Southwestern Colorado"
Dwight Lavender

San Miguel Mountains

Jurisdiction:
San Juan NF, Mancos/Dolores Ranger District
Uncompahgre NF, Norwood Ranger District

Map area reference:
Page 258, 308 and 311

Maps :
USGS: *Beaver Park, Dolores Peak, Groundhog Mountain, Lone Cone, Mount Wilson*
Forest Service: *Uncompahgre NF, San Juan NF*

This compact mountain range, known for its climbing challenges, is a westward extension of the San Juan uplift in the latitude of Telluride and Ophir. The San Miguels are bounded by the Lake Fork on the east, the Dolores River on the southeast, the San Miguel River on the north and the rolling plateau country on the west. A sizable part of the area, centered around Navajo Lake, is within Lizard Head Wilderness. Many of the trailhead and access points radiate towards the main climbing center in Navajo Basin, providing a rich variety of approaches and routes to the many mountaintops.

FSR-611/Beaver Park/Dunton Access:

FSR-611 begins at the boundary of Uncompahgre NF south of Norwood and Hwy- 145 and continues south over the San Miguel-Dolores River divide into the San Juan NF near Dunton on the West Dolores River Road. It then connects via FSR-535 to Hwy-145 just south of **Lizard Head Pass**. Along the way, this backcountry tour of nearly 40 miles gives access to several of the more notable but seldom climbed peaks of the western San Miguels. Whether you choose to begin from the Norwood or Lizard Head directions is a matter of choice, and convenience, but the description is laid out beginning from Norwood.

Lone Cone (12,613') sweeps upward to a sharp summit from the rolling plain of high mesas surrounding it. Considering its solitary location, it has a reputation for attracting fierce electric storms. From 1.5 miles east of Norwood on Hwy-145, drive south 11 miles on Lone Cone Road. Turn east following the signs to **Beaver Park** and enter Uncompahgre NF in 5.5 miles. At 2.8 miles inside the forest boundary, leave the Beaver Park Road and continue right on West Beaver Road (FSR-612). Go right again in 1.7 miles and travel 2.6 miles where the Goat Creek Trail descends on the right. Ascend on foot due west 1 mile to the peak's northeast ridge. Continue on that ridge, with a cliffy band and rock slabs on your way to the summit. Or cross the **Devils Chair** to the west near timberline, for an easier finish on the northwest ridge.

For **Dunn Mountain** (12,595'), drive as for Lone Cone above, but stay left on the Beaver Park Road at mile 2.8. At Beaver Park, continue right on FSR-611. In 3 miles, at the road fork, Dunn Peak's accessible south face is a 2 mile hike to the southeast. FSR-611 continues 4 miles southwest to its high point on the San Miguel-Dolores River divide. **Groundhog Mountain** (12,165') is a short climb northwest.

Middle Peak (13,261') and **Dolores Peak** (13,290'), connected with a long rambling ridge, are accessible from the south, up Fish Creek drainage, on FSR-611. From the Beaver Park access, continue south into San Juan NF over the San Miguel-Dolores River divide as described above. Descend for 2.5 miles and fork left. From this intersection, follow FSR-611 6 miles as it descends and then levels out to a crossing at Fish Creek. The peaks are climbed as seen, up the steepening drainage within 2 miles of the short side road.

FSR-611 descends from Fish Creek 4.5 miles to the West Dolores Road (FSR-535) north of Dunton. It is 10 miles on FSR-535 to a point on Hwy-145 6 miles south of Lizard Head Pass.

Middle and Dolores Peaks are also accessible, although not as directly, from **Woods Lake** at the end of the Fall Creek Road, which begins 3 miles southeast of Placerville on Hwy-145. Both the **Lone Cone Trail** and the **Woods Lake Trail** begin at Woods Lake. The former trail will put you at the bottom of Middle's formidable looking north ridge, and the latter will take you south to the 11,560' San Miguel-Dolores divide for a considerable ridge walk west to Dolores Peak, or a short steep ascent a mile east to **Woods Peak** (13,123').

Some peakbaggers use this Woods Lake Trail as a less congested point of departure to Navajo Basin.

Navajo Basin Trailhead Access:

Mount Wilson (14,246'), **Wilson Peak** (14,017') and **El Diente Peak** (14,159') are traditionally climbed as a unit from **Navajo Basin**, although Wilson Peak alone is closer by way of Silver Pick Basin or Bilk Creek Basin. These challenging mountains are usually avoided by peakbaggers, until they have gained their climbing legs and earned some mountaineering experience. Ice axes and crampons may be called for on the north face of the mountains well into July.

The bizarre naming of the two Wilsons is no coincidence, and honors Allen D. Wilson of the Hayden Survey who climbed the summits while triangulating the area in 1874. Why his name deserved two fourteeners is a matter of conjecture.

Navajo Basin is a popular destination because it is ringed with the three well known fourteeners, and rigid wilderness regulations apply. Start on FSR-535 6

Wilson Group

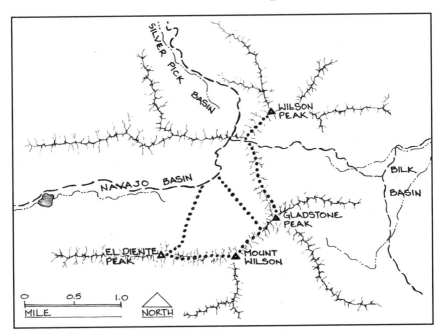

miles south of **Lizard Head Pass** on Hwy-145, a large sign here identifies this junction as Dunton. Follow the dirt road west 7 miles. Be on the lookout for a side road which forks sharply to the right as FSR-535 descends into the narrow gorge of West Dolores River. This short side road leads to Navajo Lake Trailhead. The trail north almost immediately enters Lizard Head Wilderness, and continues 4 miles to **Navajo Lake**.

Wilson Peak is located on a ridge extension in the extreme northeast quadrant of the basin and is most commonly climbed by its southwest ridge (see Silver Pick Basin Access). For **Mount Wilson**, hike to the head of the basin and bear southeast to the peak up the steepening face, aiming for the northeast ridge. The last bit up this ridge is a hand over hand scramble to the summit pinnacle.

If the weather is good, and time is in your favor, you might be tempted to try the difficult Wilson-El Diente ridge, otherwise, leave it for another day. Generally, obstacles are taken on the left (south), most notably, at the "Pipe Organs", where if you persist in staying too high, you'll be forced to rappel. **El Diente** is climbed alone about half way up the basin from the lake, then south to the low spot just east of the summit. Well into summer, this steep north slope may require an ice axe, and even crampons.

SAN JUAN

Another approach to Navajo Basin is on the **Kilpacker Trail**. This approach is popular because it starts higher than the Navajo Lake Trailhead parking area, thus avoiding about 800' of elevation gain. The Kilpacker Trail ties into the Navajo Lake Trail about 10,160' at a very obscure intersection identified only by a small sign. Access the Kilpacker Trail by traveling west on FSR-535 about 5.5 miles. Before FSR-535 begins a descent into the West Dolores River, look for a short side road at right to a small grouping of trees. Park here and walk a few hundred feet west to a barricade on the road and the beginning of the trail.

The Kilpacker Trail to Kilpacker Creek is gaining popularity as an alternate approach, from the south, to El Diente. For this, follow the trail about 3 miles to the crossing of Kilpacker Creek, 10,200'. After crossing to the north side of the creek, leave the trail and ascend a grassy slope northeast rising well above the creek, which shortly comes back into view as a dramatic waterfall at the upper end of the valley. Proceed up the valley northeast and east, staying to the left (north) of the waterfall, to about the 12,800' level. Then pick your way steeply north to the low spot just east of the summit.

Silver Pick Basin Access:

For **Wilson Peak** alone, or perhaps a different approach to **Mount Wilson** and **El Diente**, drive 6.5 miles southeast from Placerville on Hwy-145 and turn right (south) on Silver Pick Road (FSR-622). Go left at mile 3.2 and take the middle fork at mile 4, then continue on FSR-622 to the parking area. The road may be closed off well before the parking area. On foot, follow the old mine trail to the Silver Pick Mill and continue into the basin west of Wilson. Ascend south to the 13,000' Rock of Ages saddle west of the summit. Make your way to the east side of the peak's southwest ridge, where a rough route ascends to and along the ridge northeast to the summit. Careful route finding is necessary as you approach the top. Attempts on Mount Wilson and El Diente can be made across Navajo Basin to the south from the Rock of Ages saddle.

Bilk Creek Basin Access:

This access is rarely used when compared with Silver Pick and Navajo Basins, but gives a convenient approach to Wilson Peak. The disadvantage is that, like Silver Pick Basin, it requires an ascent of a high ridge to access Navajo Basin and the other fourteeners. Upper Bilk Creek is worth exploring for its aesthetic qualities alone, if not for its other notable climbing possibilities, Gladstone Peak and the immortal Lizard Head.

Scrambling on Wilson-El Diente Ridge   *Glenn Ruckhaus*

El Diente   *Robert E. Thompson*

Start on Hwy-145 6 miles west of Telluride, and turn south on South Fork Road. Drive 2.2 miles to the site of Ilium, and turn right on FSR-623, which ascends in 0.2 mile to the former railroad grade. Travel south on this ledge road nearly 3 miles, then ascend steeply 0.5 mile and go left at a fork. A 4WD vehicle can proceed for the next 1.2 miles to a meadow with a few abandoned structures. Park here and continue on foot 2 miles to the ruins of the Morningstar Mine, where you will intersect the **Bilk Creek Trail**, just outside the wilderness boundary.

A climb up **Sunshine Mountain** (12,930') begins 0.2 mile before the road intersects the trail at the mine. Climb along the north side of a steep drainage to the falls. Then angle left to the main north-northwest ridge, and follow the narrowing terrain to the summit.

From Morningstar Mine, the trail leads into **Bilk Creek Basin**, and after nearly 2 miles of ever-expanding views, to a junction with an old mine road. The left fork takes you in a long mile to a saddle between Cross Mountain and Lizard Head. The right fork will take you into the upper basin and eventually to the north-south ridge separating you from Navajo Basin. Wilson Peak can be climbed from the upper basin using the standard southwest ridge approach described under Silver Pick Basin.

Gladstone Peak (13,913') can be cautiously climbed by way of its steep northwest ridge from either upper Bilk or Navajo Basins. Another possibility is from lower Bilk Basin where you would ascend the mountain's east face, carefully picking your route to the top. The north face of the mountain from upper Bilk makes a rigorous ice or snow climb on the Gladstone "glacier", calling for appropriate equipment.

Lizard Head Trailhead/Cross Mountain Trailhead Access:

These two trailheads are described together because they end up at the same location, the base of the infamous Lizard Head. **Lizard Head Trail** starts at the top of **Lizard Head Pass** on Hwy-145, whereas **Cross Mountain Trail** starts on an obscure side road 2 miles southwest of the pass. Either trail could be used as an alternate starting point into Bilk Creek Basin. On the way, Lizard Head Trail takes a dramatic route over an elongated ridge called **Black Face** (12,147'). About 2 miles beyond, you will reach the 11,979' pass into Bilk Creek Basin. Head east up to the southwest corner of the monument where the technical climb to Lizard Head begins.

Wilson Peak   *Stephen Weaver*

SAN JUAN

Lizard Head   *CMC archives*

Lizard Head Peak (13,113') is a volcanic neck. It is one of the most difficult of Colorado's summits to reach. However, based on the reports of recent climbing parties, about 50 or more a year, the number of ascents has removed a lot of the lose stuff, and now the rock is fairly sound, especially the upper two pitches. The standard route, pioneered by Albert Ellingwood and Barton Hoag in 1920, begins in a shallow chute on the west face near the southwest corner. The first pitch is the most rotten. Two more pitches takes one to the top, with the last pitch being 5.8 in difficulty.

Another route is on the south side, rated about the same as the older one, sharing the third pitch. It has an airy traverse on its second pitch. Our advice however remains as in the earlier editions; when you reach the base, take picture and go home.

Rico Mountains

Jurisdiction:
San Juan NF, Mancos/Dolores Ranger District

Map area reference:
Page 258

Maps:
USGS: *Hermosa Peak, Rico*
Forest Service: *San Juan NF*

This small, often ignored range of mountains is a sub-group of the immense San Juans, located west of the Animas-Dolores River divide in the vicinity of Rico. Although most of the summits barely rise beyond 12,000', they are nevertheless notable due to their prominent location at the edge of the Colorado Plateau country and their accessibility.

CalicoTrailhead Access:

The closest approach to the west section of the range starts from Hwy-145 6 miles south of **Lizard Head Pass**. Turn right on FSR-535 marked as Dunton. Ascend through several switchbacks 4.5 miles to The Meadows. Turn left on FSR-471 and continue 1 mile to Calico Trailhead, or continue 5 more miles to the road end for an even closer approach to the summits on **Fall Creek Trail**.

The **Calico Trail** extends southwest ascending towards **Elliot Mountain** (12,340'), **Sockrider Peak** (12,308'), **Johnny Bull** (12,012'), **Calico Peak** (12,026'), **Eagle Peak** (12,113'), **Expectation Mountain** (12,071') and **Anchor** (12,327), all of which are climbed in sequence from the trail.

From the southern end of the group, the trail descends to an alternate trailhead point at Priest Gulch, 13 miles south of Rico on Hwy-145.

FSR-550 Scotch Creek/Hotel Draw Access:

FSR-550 accesses the southeast section of the range. This jeep road begins 3 miles south of Rico on Hwy-145, and rises in 5 steep and rocky miles to the Dolores-Animas River divide. On the divide, FSR-550 also happens to be the route of the Colorado Trail. Travel north 1.5 miles on the rambling divide to where the Colorado Trail leaves the road at left and continues beyond a locked gate as FSR-550A. FSR-550 descends to Hotel Draw in the Hermosa Creek drainage, eventually to tie into FSR-578 for an alternate access from US-550 at Purgatory Ski Area (see FSR-578/Bolam Pass Access below).

At its departure from FSR-550, follow the Colorado Trail north 4 miles to 12,000' **Blackhawk Pass**. **Blackhawk Mountain** (12,681') is a short 0.5 mile west. A trio of peaks radiate from the summit of Blackhawk, **Harts Peak** (12,540') to the north, **Dolores Mountain** (12,112') to the west and **Whitecap Mountain** (12,376') to the south. Following the CT northeast from the pass will bring you in 7 miles to FSR-578 just south of Bolam Pass.

FSR-578/Bolam Pass Access:

FSR-578 connects Hwy-145 6 miles south of Lizard Head Pass with US-550 at Purgatory. On the way, you will top out at 11,400' **Bolam Pass**. It is a generally well-graded road but calls for 4WD vehicles at the Hermosa Creek ford, 10 miles from Purgatory, and on the rough ascent to the pass.

From 0.4 mile north of the entrance to Purgatory Ski Area on US-550, ascend FSR-578, following the signs to Hermosa Park and Sig Creek Campground. Just north of the ford at Hermosa Creek, FSR-550 forks left to Hotel Draw and Scotch Creek. Stay north on FSR-578 several rough miles to the crossing of the Colorado Trail at a small pond. Top out at Bolam Pass 1 mile further on. Follow FSR-578 1 mile as it descends slightly to the west and its intersection with FSR-149 at left. FSR-578 continues to drop northwest into Barlow Creek and joins Hwy-145 after 7 bouncy miles.

Flattop Mountain (12,098') is a 2 mile stroll northwest from the FSR-149/578 intersection up the broad forested ridge. For **Hermosa Peak** (12,579') follow FSR-149 west- southwest 1.8 miles and park at 11,500'. Climb southeast to a 12,000' saddle then ascend the summit ridge northeast.

La Plata Mountains

Jurisdiction:
San Juan NF, Columbine West and Mancos/Dolores Ranger Districts

Map area reference:
Page 258

Maps:
USGS: *Hesperus, La Plata*
Forest Service: *San Juan NF*

The La Plata Mountains are an extreme southwest spur of the San Juans, separated from the range by the Animas River on the east, bounded on the north by the Rico Mountains, and on the west by the Dolores River. The La Platas are a compact mountain group of 12,000' and low 13,000' peaks, centered around the old La Plata mining district. The mountains are known for their climbing challenges where steady nerves and ropes are often called for.

FSR-571 La Plata Canyon Access:

This popular access, which receives weekend assaults from the citizens of Durango, Farmington and Cortez, ascends the main drainage of the La Plata River and bisects the range into relatively straightforward east and west sections. From Durango, drive west on US-160 to 0.5 mile beyond Hesperus and turn right (north) on FSR-571 (La Plata Co Rd-124), marked as La Plata Canyon. The road continues north 13 miles to the head of the range near 11,760' **Kennebec Pass**. Many of the side drainages, from which the climbs begin, and the last 2 miles of the road before the pass, are restricted to 4WD vehicles. Some of these side drainages are closed to the public due to mining operations.

A trio of walk-ups in the southwest quadrant of the range starts 6.5 miles north of US-160 just beyond Kroeger Campground, and opposite a private picnic ground. Ascend west through several switchbacks on the north side of Root Creek to a prominent gully just short of the Lucky Discovery Mine. Follow the drainage west to a saddle between **Parrott Peak** (11,857') and **Madden Peak** (11,972'). The former commemorates Tibercio Parrott, an absentee prospector from California, whose Colorado representative was Captain Moss. **Star Peak** (11,761') is 0.5 mile north of Madden on the same connecting ridge.

Gibbs Peak(12,286') is best reached from the Bedrock Creek Road (FSR-344) starting 7.5 miles from US-160. Stay on the main fork as it bends into the upper drainage of Madden Creek. Just before the road tops out near timberline at a mine digging, bear left (west) and ascend the peak's east ridge. If you choose the right spot to exit the road, you will pick up an old mine trail that leads to the base of the final summit scramble.

SAN JUAN

The most challenging summits of the range, for which you might carry a rope in reserve, form a tight group of 13,000' summits within a 1 mile radius of Mount Moss. The southern approach begins just beyond La Plata townsite and ascends the 4WD road on the north side of Boren Creek. At timberline, you will look due north, straining your neck in a vain effort to check out the unseen summit of Babcock Peak. Although Babcock can be climbed from the Boren Creek approach via the east ridge, or straight north up to its west group of peaks, it is more traditionally scaled by way of Tomahawk Basin as described below.

Spiller Peak (13,123') can be climbed from the Boren Creek Road at the upper mine workings by a scramble up its south ridge. Lesser **Burwell Peak** (12,664') is a climb to the south on the same ridge, with a detour around a large notch north of the summit. Both of these peaks are accessible on the same ridge from the west in Rush Basin by following the Echo Basin Road turnoff on US-160 2 miles east of Mancos, and then continuing by 4WD vehicle to the Doyle Mine at timberline.

Babcock Peak, east ridge   *Terry Root*

Two miles beyond the turnoff to Boren Creek north of La Plata townsite on FSR-571, a tight turn to the left will take you northwest well above timberline into Tomahawk Basin. Multi-summit **Babcock Peak** (13,149') forms the southwest fringe of the basin. When inspected from a distance, it appears that a needle in its western group of pinnacles is perhaps slightly higher than the official eastern end. The east summit is best approached from the east ridge. The west group of pinnacles goes best up the couloir in the extreme southwest corner of the basin. The western summits of Babcock are connected to Spiller by an east-west ridge known affectionately, and accurately, as **The Knife**.

Mount Moss (13,192') forms the northwest head of the basin. Head up the talus slope for the left side and ascend the south ridge.

Lavender Peak (13,160'), whose summit is reached in an unnerving scramble, is barely 0.2 mile northwest of Moss. It was named for Dwight Lavender, one of the SJM who explored and triangulated in the area and wrote the original San Juan Guide in 1932. The mountain should be considered as also honoring his surviving brother, David Lavender, an early SJM explorer, and author of many western historical narratives. Originally christened as **L1** in the early 1930's by young Dwight, the mountain no doubt inspired the eager climber to describe the north ridge as "virtually festooned with needles and daggers". Because of these obstacles, recommended ascents on both Hesperus and Centennial begin from the west as mentioned under Sharkstooth Access rather than continuing from the Lavender-Moss approach.

The high points at the northeast section of the range begin at the upper end of the valley. For **Lewis Mountain** (12,655'), drive 12 miles up the valley from US-160, and go right at the fork into Columbus Basin. Park at the gate, but proceed on foot to the head of the basin at 11,700'. Aim for a low saddle 0.2 mile northwest of the summit. Another good approach to Lewis is via a 4WD road up Lewis Creek to Eagle Pass. For this route, go one mile north of Boren Creek to a right turn down to a bridge over the La Plata River. The road may be blocked off a mile before the pass, but this can be hiked easily. At the pass turn left and climb another mile to the summit.

The last 2 miles on FSR-571 goes on north at the above fork marked Kennebec Pass, and officially ends at the trailhead parking area for the Highline and Colorado Trails. **Cumberland Mountain** (12,388') is 0.7 mile to the southeast on an obvious grassy ridge. **Snowstorm Peak** (12,511') is 1 mile south, across upper Cumberland Basin, and is best approached through the noticeable notch on the Bessie G Mine Road, then up the grassy east face.

SAN JUAN

Sharkstooth Trailhead FSR-350/FSR-561 Access:

A group of the most notable peaks in the La Platas are easily accessible by way of the remote and obscure Sharkstooth Trail. From Durango, travel west on US-160 to Mancos, and go north 0.5 mile on Hwy-184, to a county road at right marked Jackson Reservoir and/or Transfer Campground. Follow the road, which becomes FSR-561, beyond the reservoir and campground to Aspen Guard Station and after another 0.5 mile, bear right on FSR-350, Spruce Mill Road. Continue 8 miles to a small parking area at Sharkstooth Trailhead. From this point, the **Sharkstooth Trail** ascends 2 miles to **Sharkstooth Pass**, then drops into upper Bear Creek, eventually to tie into the northeast section of the range at **Kennebec Pass** and FSR-571. The new **West Mancos Trail** descends from the trailhead to the Owens Basin Trail, and west 3 miles down West Mancos Canyon to Transfer Campground.

The highest point in the range is **Hesperus Mountain** (13,232'), a natural zig-gurat best viewed from the plateau country to the west. From the trailhead, descend slightly on the West Mancos Trail to the south side of the drainage below the awesome north precipice of the mountain. Leave the trail and traverse west at approximately 10,600', being careful to avoid the impressive cliffs and rock avalanches below them. Intersect the mountain's northwest ridge and follow it over several ledges to the summit.

Centennial Peak (13,062'), Banded Mountain until changed in 1976 to honor the Centennial State, is a walk-up the mountain's north ridge from Sharkstooth Pass. **Sharkstooth Peak** (12,462') is a close, although steep climb, over sliding rocks north of the pass.

NORTHWESTERN PLATEAU

Colorado National Monument   *CMC archives*

Northwestern Plateau

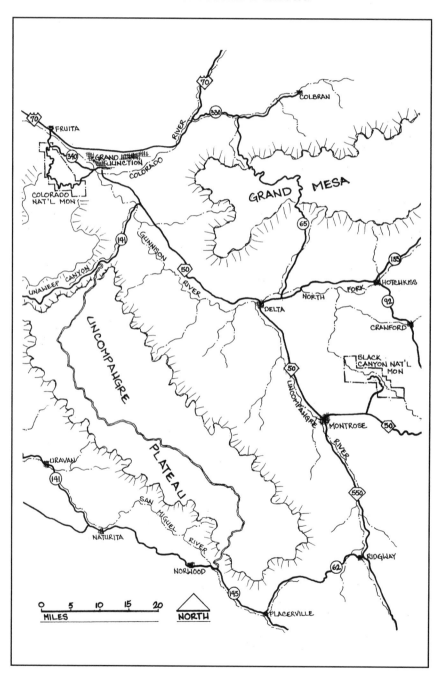

Northwestern Plateau

Colorado is known for its mountains. They draw the people, summer and winter. These popular mountainous regions occupy roughly the middle one third of the state. East of the mountains lies an expanse of fertile plains, referred to by disillusioned early day pioneers as the Great American Desert; and west of the main mountain chain is a vast area of plateaus, under the general designation of Colorado Plateau, whose escarpments have been sculpted by such legendary watercourses as the Colorado, Gunnison and the Yampa.

This section is an addition to earlier editions, inspired by the fact that Colorado has much more to offer than its mountainous areas. Included are plunging gorges, sandstone canyons and table-topped plateaus largely overlooked by non-local recreationalists, but as worthy of exploration as are the most dramatic mountain valleys and summits. It may be that only after some substantial persuasion, or insight, are the few moved to consider the "other" Colorado, and are then able to appreciate the state for its remarkable diversity.

You can expand your exploratory adventure beyond what is described here, by studying maps and visiting the local land management office. Most of the public land in northwestern Colorado, the true plateau country, outside of the Flattops, Grand Mesa and Uncompahgre Plateau, is under the jurisdiction of the BLM. Not to be by-passed are the three national monuments on the plateau, under the jurisdiction of the National Park Service.

The Mesas

The most notable landforms in the Grand Valley are the large mesas that define its borders, and stand as mighty sentinels of the plateau country. Grand Mesa, stretching west from the Elk Mountains, towers over Grand Junction and the confluence of the Colorado and Gunnison Rivers. The Uncompahgre Plateau forms the western edge of the valley, an isolated flat-topped range between the Uncompahgre River on the east and the Dolores River on the west.

Uncompahgre Plateau

Jurisdiction:
Uncompahgre NF; Norwood Ranger District
Map area reference:
Page 324
Maps:
USGS: *Antone Spring, Casto Reservoir, Keith Creek, Snipe Mountain, Starvation Point, Uncompahgre Butte, Ute, Windy Point*
Forest Service: *Uncompahgre NF*

Uncompahgre, say Borneman and Lampert in their 1978 work *A Climbing Guide to Colorado's Fourteeners*, is a Ute word that means hot water spring. Perhaps best thought of as a sawed-off mountain range, the Uncompahgre Plateau stretches some 60 miles, from Placerville on Hwy-145, northwest to the Colorado National Monument, west of Grand Junction on I-70. Innumerable canyons slice through the edges of the plateau, which is flat and even enough to sustain a linear road (FSR-402) for almost its entire length.

There are minor humps along the crest, none of which would be of particular interest to the mountaineer. However, it is for the side canyons that one would visit the Uncompahgre Plateau. The history of this unusual range can be told by the many Indian trails up the canyons and over the range, many of which still exist today as recreation trails and stock drives; and by the presence of the open range and cow camps that developed when the land was finally wrested from the Utes, their last concession of a once huge domain in western Colorado.

PLATEAU

Divide Road/FSR-402 Access:

One can access the Divide Road from several approaches; the Delta-Nucla Road (FSR-503), or via Montrose on FSR-9 (old Hwy-90). But the classic auto tour of Uncompahgre Plateau is the full length of the range from Sanborn Park Road off of Hwy-145 4 miles east of Norwood, to the road end at **Unaweep Canyon** on Hwy-141 10 miles southwest of Whitewater on US-50. Unaweep Canyon is notable as the ancestral course of the Gunnison and Colorado Rivers where water flows in two directions; from East Creek to the Gunnison, and West Creek to the Dolores.

Columbine Pass is the intersection of the Divide Road (FSR-402) and the Delta-Nucla Road (FSR-503) and the approximate halfway point on the Divide Road. Approximately 11 miles northwest of the pass on FSR-402, a rough side road, FSR-600, goes southeast 2.5 miles to **Spruce Mountain** (9,731'). At about mile 18 from the **Columbine Pass**, FSR-402 passes Monument Hill (9,519'), and at about mile 23, it skirts **Uncompahgre Butte** (9,679'). All of these points are molehills on the featureless crest of the plateau.

Some of the nicest excursions on the Uncompahgre Plateau are on its extreme northwestern section. To get there, follow the Divide Road about 41 miles north of Columbine Pass or 10 miles southwest of Hwy-141 in Unaweep Canyon; here the Big Creek Road (FSR-403) goes west from the Divide Road. Follow FSR-403 6 miles to a trailhead area. The **Unaweep Trail** is the focal point, but other trails radiate from the area; the Gill Creek Trail to the north and west, the Basin, Cabin and Snowshoe Trails to the south and west, all of which can be used as access to the Unaweep. The lengthy Unaweep Trail winds around the rim of the plateau, offering optional returns to the trailhead when combined with the Basin or Cabin Trails. The maze of trails and roads here are mostly unmarked, making possible temporary disorientations within the unrelenting forest, even with the aid of map and compass. When you come for a visit, plan to stay awhile for extended explorations.

The Uranium Road (FSR-404) goes west from the Divide Road about 6 miles southwest of the Big Creek Road, and provides an alternate approach to the trail system above via the Ute Creek Trail and Rim Trail Road (FSR-416). The Uranium Road leads southwest, eventually to BLM land which was the site of much uranium mining in the 1940's and 1950's.

PLATEAU

Grand Mesa

Jurisdiction:
Grand Mesa NF; Collbran Ranger District, Grand Junction Ranger District

Map area reference:
Page 324

Maps:
USGS: *Grand Mesa, Hells Kitchen, Leon Peak, Skyway*
Forest Service: *Grand Mesa NF*

Grand Mesa lies between the Colorado and the North Fork Gunnison Rivers. Its west end juts prominently above Grand Junction and Delta; the east tapers to lower mesa country west of the Elk Range. The chief charm is the lake-strewn west part, reached by Hwy-65, which crosses from the Colorado River on I-70 between DeBeque and Palisade, south to Cedaredge. It was traversed by Dominquez and Escalante in the year of American Independence, before he crossed the Colorado River north of DeBeque.

Hwy-65 Access:

Leon Peak (11,236') is a little oval mesa that gradually rises 200' from a larger triangular mesa, which is 200' above the surroundings. The approach road, FSR-121, runs east from the settlement of Grand Mesa, 8 miles to a pair of Twin Lakes a mile south of the peak.

The **Crag Crest Trail** starts at the north end of **Island Lake** on Hwy-65, 0.5 mile northwest of the visitor information center. It climbs to, and follows, the **Grand Mesa Crest**. It drops and terminates at Crag Crest Campground on FSR-121.This is a distance of 7 miles. Travel is by foot or horse only. The trail over-looks the mesa's nearby lakes and much of western Colorado.

The **Land O'Lakes Trail** starts from the parking lot on the south side of Hwy-65 about 1 mile west of Grand Mesa Lodge. It is a loop trail to basalt rock over-looks which provide a panoramic view of the mesa's lakes. Four interpretive signs assist the traveler. The trail is asphalt paved and limited to foot traffic only. Round trip is roughly 0.75 mile.

The **4 X 4 Trail**, road width and about 4 miles long, runs from Island Lake Campground southwest to and through a cluster of reservoirs, 3 miles. The **Cottonwood Trail**, starting with the Crag Crest Trail from Island Lake, climbs north-northeast over the crest and on to Cottonwood Lake and points north. West of **Cottonwood Lake** it meets the **High Trail**, which goes west 5 miles to a gooseneck in Hwy-65, passing lakes on the way.

The National Monuments

The plateau country of northwestern Colorado is the home of three national monuments: Black Canyon of the Gunnison, Dinosaur and Colorado. All three contribute to the integral uniqueness of this stark landscape, and are at least partially surrounded by BLM land offering an expansion of explorations, particularly in the case of Dinosaur and Colorado National Monuments.

Black Canyon of the Gunnison National Monument

Jurisdiction:
National Park Service

Map area reference:
Page 324

Maps:
USGS: *Grizzly Ridge, Red Rock Canyon*
Forest Service: *Gunnison NF*

The Gunnison River was known to the Ute Indians as Tomichi. Roughly translated, it means "land of high cliffs and plenty water", an obvious referral to the Black Canyon of the Gunnison. There are deeper canyons than the Black Canyon; certainly there are more impressive gorges of immense magnitude. But for a narrow cleft of sheer depth in relation to width, the Black Canyon of the Gunnison is hard to equal.

Black Canyon gets its name from the fact that it is almost perpetually shrouded in shadows. However, the stark walls of dark metamorphic schists and gneisses are sometimes beautifully banded, as in the famous and often photographed Painted Wall. The essential lack of sedimentary formations on top of the Precambrian rocks that form the canyon walls, a puzzling unconformity, lend the gorge an extra brutal uniqueness.

Black Canyon National Monument is located at the southeast edge of the Grand Valley. There are accesses to both the south and north rims: just east of Montrose on US-50 for the more popular south rim; and south of Crawford on Hwy-92 for the north rim. Both accesses provide short, scenic rim drives of the spectacular plunging depths, with pull-outs, view point trails, and nature walks. The adventurous might want to challenge themselves with a descent into the chasm. For this, you would need to register with the park rangers, who can advise you of the dangers and precautions necessary for this wilderness adventure. Several routes

PLATEAU

are available for a descent to the river on both the north and south rims. Remember that once down, you must climb back out.

In 1999, legislation was passed by Congress that will have a profound effect on this unique area. Greatly expanding the boundaries of the present monument, this bill will create **Black Canyon of the Gunnison National Park**, the third jewel of the National Park system in Colorado.

Dinosaur National Monument

Jurisdiction:
National Park Service

Maps:
USGS: *Dinosaur National Monument (1:62,500)*

Dinosaur is somewhat of a misnomer for this large park located in extreme northwestern Colorado and northeastern Utah. The actual dig area at the westernmost point of the monument, from which it draws the name, was proclaimed an 80 acre preserve in 1915 by President Woodrow Wilson. In 1938, President Franklin Roosevelt expanded the monument to 326 square miles, encompassing an impressive canyon region centered around the confluence of the Green and Yampa Rivers. The canyon walls here, in contrast to Black Canyon, are more colorful and stair-stepped, characteristic of their sedimentary origins.

The best way to see Dinosaur is by float trip, and most do. But those on foot can still get a good sense of the place from the overlooks and river access points. If you plan on doing much exploring, a 4WD vehicle would be helpful. The main monument entrance, and the dinosaur quarry visitor center, are accessed from the south off of US-40. The famous **Canyon of Lodore** on the Green River is approached on Hwy-318, west of Maybell.

A good introduction to the monument, beyond the dinosaur dig center, is **Harpers Corner Overlook**, due north from the monument headquarters. Here, from a lofty perch, you can observe **Whirlpool Canyon**, **Steamboat Rock** and **Echo Park** at the confluence of the two rivers. In the 1950's, a heated controversy raged when a dam was proposed for this junction. Obviously, the monument was preserved, and an alternate site for the dam was chosen further up the Green, at Flaming Gorge in Wyoming. Other excursions are the **Island Park Overlook** and **Ruple Point Trail**, **Pats Hole** in Echo Park, and its extension, the Yampa Bench Road. A more isolated canyon, but proportionally rewarding, is **Jones Hole Canyon Trail** at the end of a long unpaved road north and east from Jensen, Utah.

PLATEAU

Colorado National Monument

Jurisdiction:
National Park Service

Map area reference:
Page 324

Maps:
USGS: Battleship Rock, Colorado National Monument, Mack

To its infrequent, but awestruck, visitors, Colorado National Monument ranks second only to Rocky Mountain National Park as one of the state's outstanding crown jewels, bedecked with canyons of pink sandstone, rim rock arches, and towering monoliths. One of the first zealots of these stark canyons on the extreme northern reaches of the Uncompahgre Plateau, was John Otto. We owe him gratitude for the creation of Colorado National Monument and its system of trails. As a young pioneer to Colorado, Otto was a benign but enthusiastic eccentric, who generally accomplished his goals, but not without certain unintended insults to the sensitivities of Victorian society of the period. Perhaps his greatest accomplishment was to have the area preserved for all time. Currently there is talk of expanding the Monument to Park status.

Unlike Black Canyon and Dinosaur, there are no major watercourses through Colorado National Monument, hardly even a rivulet. That such a dramatic canyon could be sculpted from the multi-colored sandstones is a testament to the erosive forces of wind, weather, and the freeze-thaw cycle.

The monument is easily accessible west of Grand Junction, or south of Fruita on Hwy-340. You can explore the canyons and monoliths from easy overlook trails, such as the **John Otto Trail** to the Pipe Organs. For longer excursions, consider the scenic **Monument Canyon Trail** or the **Liberty Cap** and **Corkscrew Trails**.

Rattlesnake Canyon Access:

Of all the nooks and crannies in Colorado, **Rattlesnake Canyon** could be one of the most unique and dramatic. Now on BLM land just west of the Monument, it would be included as part of an expanded park. Stop for directions and information at the Colorado National Monument visitor's center before proceeding. The usual route goes from the Monument's Rim Rock Drive to the unpaved Black Ridge Road, which is notoriously gummy during inclement weather. Proceed about 8 miles northwest to Rattlesnake Canyon. If you should traverse the rim for views below, be on the lookout for thin rock which conceals domes and arches underneath. The most often used descent route into the canyon is from the head of the canyon to the south, near the **Old Ute Indian Trail**, now a jeep road.

PLATEAU

When explored from a bench at about the 5,600' level, the canyon reveals near-ly a dozen arches on its sidewalls. Exit the bench for a rise to the rim about 2 miles north of your entry, on the east side of the canyon, using a descending northwest ridge. Good route finding abilities are important here, where a mis-placed step could result in a fall of several hundred feet; perhaps you should even keep a rope handy for potentially unnerving ascents and descents.

Dinosaur National Monument   *CMC archives*

The Flattop Plateau

Jurisdiction:
Routt NF, Yampa Ranger District
White River NF, Blanco Ranger District

Map area reference:
Page 334

Maps:
USGS: *Big Marvine Peak, Deep Lake, Devils Causeway, Dome Peak, Dunckley Pass, Lost Park, Orno Peak, Pagoda Peak, Sugarloaf Mountain, Sweetwater Lake, Trappers Lake*
Forest Service: *Routt NF, White River NF*

The Flattops Wilderness is a land of lakes and forests at altitudes generally 9,000' to 11,000', between Steamboat Springs and Glenwood Springs. It is all andesite and basalt from late Tertiary and perhaps Quaternary flows, which remain as plateaus with abrupt drop-offs at the edges. Crumbly and rotten rock is common in these formations.

The first of the state's national forests was established on the White River Plateau in 1891, with the idea that its many resources might be saved from depletion. Ironically, its forests have suffered a tremendous devastation by beetles, and off trail travel below timberline can be difficult because of the downed trees.

Trails and their branches run all over the Flattop Plateau, and beautiful tours past the lakes and cliffs can be put together with forest service maps and advice. The main northeast-southwest trail connects Stillwater Reservoir to South Fork Campground via Trappers Lake. The routes below are for those who want to try their ingenuity, or even their ropes, on those little mesas on the mesa or the peak tops, while their relatives whip the lakes.

Stillwater Reservoir Access:

Access from the east is by Hwy-131, running south from near Steamboat Springs on US-40 to Wolcott on I-70. **Stillwater Reservoir** is reached by 15 mile FSR-900 (starts as Routt Co Rd-7 in Yampa) southwest from the south side of Yampa on Hwy-131.

A main cross trail starts along the north side of Stillwater Reservoir and continues southwesterly 30 miles or more to South Fork Campground, 10 miles south-southeast up the White River South Fork from Buford on Hwy-132. From the reservoir, about 9,500', it climbs over a plateau pass at 11,300' and at mile 7 reaches **Trappers Lake**. At miles 14-16 it passes the **Twin Lakes**, and connects with trails up the Marvine Creeks.

PLATEAU

Flattop Plateau

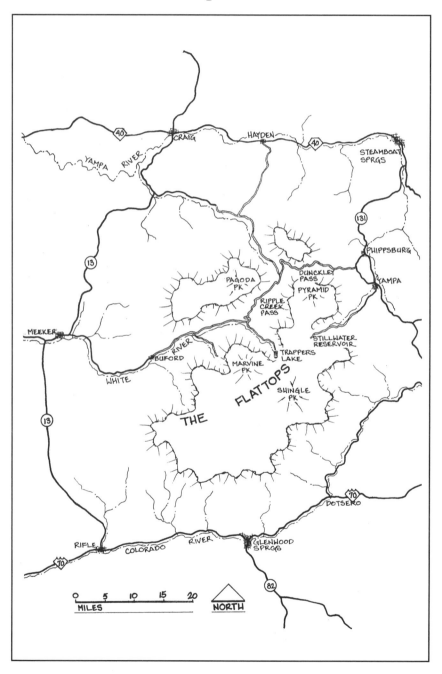

A trail runs from Stillwater Reservoir 7 miles south to **Stump Park** and a 4WD road that runs down the plateau west of Derby Creek to Burns, just up from Dotsero.

Flattop Mountain (12,354') and **Dome Mountain** (12,207') are a conspicuous sector of the plateau's east rampart. To climb the former, take the above trail 2.5 miles south to the smooth side of the west ridge, which is an easy 2.5 miles long. For Dome Mountain, you drop east off Flattop and follow the ridge around southeast and south 2.5 miles. On the return you follow the same ridge but contour around the south buttress of Flattop. For Dome Mountain and Dome Peak by themselves, take the road northwest from Burns, keeping right at mile 1.5 and left at mile 7. From mile 10.5 a jeep road heads toward the peak. You can either climb the last mile head on, or zig left and zag right for easier grades. A 250' dip separates the Peak and Dome.

Derby Peak (12,186') fronts the North Derby Creek Trail with angry cliffs. To climb it, take the trail running west-southwest along the north side of Stillwater Reservoir for about 3.5 miles. When you are part way up the mesa from **Mosquito Lake**, cut off left and head southeast overland for the flat summit, some 3.5 miles.

Ripple Creek Pass/FSR-16 Access:

A main crossroad, pretty well north in the area of prime interest, connects Phippsburg and Yampa on Hwy-131 west to Buford and Meeker via **Ripple Creek Pass** and **Dunckley Pass** (FSR-16).

Pagoda Peak (11,120') is a little sharpie with a good look around. From Ripple Creek Pass, cut straight west 1 mile to the trail for Pagoda Lake and follow it 2.5 miles. The summit is 0.7 mile north.

Pyramid Peak (11,532') is reached from the road to Sheriff's Reservoir (FSR-959), starting about 12 miles west of Phippsburg on FSR-16. Take a trail 2.5 miles southwest and south from the reservoir. Take off west-southwest 0.5 mile for the low point of the saddle and climb the east-southeast ridge.

The above trail continues south 3 more miles, to meet with one coming south up the east fork of the Williams Fork from Pyramid Guard Station, then continues south 2 miles to another junction. The right branch heads west for several small lakes. The left branch heads south and southeast past Causeway Lake to Stillwater Reservoir, 5 more miles.

PLATEAU

Manine Creek Access:

Hwy-132 running east out of Meeker has a turnoff 9 miles east of Buford for Marvine Creek. The Marvine Creek Road runs 4 miles southeast to Marvine Campground at 8,200', where the creek forks. Each branch has a trail to the main cross trail between Stillwater Reservoir and White River's South Fork. The right one takes you by a 12 mile route past Marvine Lakes. The left or east one climbs 6 more miles to the plateau between the Marvine Peaks, Little on the left and Big on the right.

The highest of the **Little Marvine Peaks** (11,947) is about 2 miles north up-ridge from where the above trail finishes its climb to the plateau. **Big Marvine Peak** (11,879') is about 1.5 miles west-southwest over high country from the same trail point. It is fairly well bulwarked with those big steps you see on the peaks, but nevertheless has a trail route through to the top.

Trappers Lake Access:

Trappers Lake, in the heart of the Flattops, is the traditional jumping off point. It lies at the end of FSR-205, some 26 miles east of Buford.

For **Trappers Peak** (12,002') take the 5 mile signed trail to Wall Lake from the parking area at the end of Trappers Lake Road. From the west side of **Wall Lake**, it is possible to make a direct route to the summit.

Shingle Peak (11,995') is about 6 miles southeast up Fraser Creek from Trappers Lake (west side). From the trail junction on the plateau, take the left branch 0.5 mile, then a right branch going south for 2.5 miles. Cut across toward the left side of the peak so you can climb it from the south side, another 2.5 miles.

For **Sheep Mountain** (12,241') you take the same approach as for Shingle, but go only 1 mile after you turn south from the second trail junction. Take the east branch, descending toward **Island Lake** for 1 mile. The second of the two right forks takes you southeast along the east side of Upper Island Lake and zigzags up to the west ridge of Sheep, which you follow northeast and southeast to the summit, totaling another 2 miles or so.

APPENDICES
INDEX

Climber on Otis Peak   *David Anschicks*

Colorado Mountain Bibliography

NOTE: This bibliography is only a partial listing of the guidebooks and histories to Colorado's mountains. Because most of the guides are updated with new printings or editions every few years, the publication dates given are those of the first edition unless otherwise noted.

GENERAL COLORADO

Boddie, Caryn and Peter. *Hiking Colorado.* Falcon Press, Helena, Montana, 1997.
A guide to 100 hikes throughout Colorado.

Borneman, Walter R., and Lyndon J. Lampert. *A Climbing Guide to Colorado's Fourteeners.* Pruett Publishing Company, Boulder, Colorado, 1978, 1989, 1998.
A guide to the 54 Colorado summits above 14,000 feet.

Bueler, William M. *Roof of the Rockies: A History of Colorado Mountaineering.* Cordillera Press, Evergreen, Colorado, 1986 second edition.
Coming Fall 2000: New, third edition of this definitive history of Colorado mountaineering from Colorado Mountain Club Press, Golden, Colorado.

Chronic, Halka. *Roadside Geology of Colorado.* Mountain Press, Missoula, Montana. 1980.
Best overall introduction to Colorado's geology.

Crouter, George. *Colorado's Highest.* Sundance, Denver, Colorado,1977.
Aerial, color photographs of Colorado's fourteeners.

Dawson, Louis W. *Dawson's Guide to the Colorado Fourteeners Vol. 1 & 2.* Blue Clover Press, 1999.
Winter and summer routes to the fourteeners, divided into two volumes (north and south).

Edrinn, Roger. *Colorado Fourteeners Grand Slam.* Above the Timber, Fort Collins, Colorado, 1991.
Color photography, text and maps to Colorado's fourteeners.

Garratt, Mike, and Bob Martin. *Colorado's High Thirteeners: A Climbing and Hiking Guide.* Johnson Books, Boulder, Colorado, 1984, 1989, 1992 third edition.
A guide to 169 summits above 13,000 feet, including the Centennial peaks below 14,000 feet.

Hart, John L. Jerome. *Fourteen Thousand Feet: A History of the Naming and Early Ascents of the High Colorado Peaks*. Colorado Mountain Club, Denver, Colorado, 1972.
The 1931 history of Colorado's 14,000-foot peaks; still available in a 1972 reprint.

Kramarsic, Joe. *Bibliography of Colorado Mountain Ascents, 1863-1976*. Self-published, 1979.
The most-thorough listing of Colorado mountaineering literature and references.

Jacobs, Randy. *The Colorado Trail*. Westcliffe Publishers, Englewood, Colorado, 1988, 1994.
The complete guide to the Colorado Trail from Denver to Durango.

Jones, Tom Lorang. *Colorado's Continental Divide Trail*. Westcliffe Publishers, Englewood, Colorado.
Comprehensive guide to the Colorado portion of the trail.

Martin, Bob. *Hiking the Highest Passes*. Pruett Publishing Company, Boulder, Colorado, 1984.
A guide to hiking 50 popular passes in the state.

Martin, Bob. *Hiking Trails of Central Colorado*. Pruett Publishing Company, Boulder, Colorado, 1983.
A guide to hikes in the Sawatch, Elk, and Mosquito ranges.

Roach, Gerry. *Colorado's Fourteeners*. Fulcrum Publishing, Golden, Colorado, 1999 second edition.
Another guide to Colorado's highest peaks.

Savage, Ania. *Colorado Mountain Club Pocket Guide to the Colorado Fourteeners*. Johnson Books, Boulder, Colorado, 1997.
Brief guide to the standard routes on the fourteeners.

Wolf, James R. *Guide to the Continental Divide Trail*. Volumes 4 and 5. Continental Divide Trail Society, Bethesda, Maryland, 1982.
A guide to the divide trail from Canada to Mexico.

FRONT RANGE and NORTHERN RANGES

Arps, Louisa, and Elinor Kingery. *High Country Names*. Rocky Mountain Nature Association, Estes Park, Colorado, 1978.
Place name history of Rocky Mountain National Park and vicinity.

Chapin, Frederick H. *Mountaineering in Colorado: The Peaks about Estes Park*. University of Nebraska, Lincoln, Nebraska, 1987.
Reprint with a foreword and notes of 1889 original printing by Appalachian Mountain Club.

Kramarsic, Joe. *Mountaineering in the Gore Range: A Record of Exploration*, Climbs, Routes, and Names. Self-published, 1989.
Major compilation of Gore Range routes and history.

Murray, John A. *The Indian Peaks Wilderness Area: A Hiking and Field Guide*. Pruett Publishing Company, Boulder, Colorado, 1983.
Natural history guide to Indian Peak hikes.

Roach, Gerry. *Colorado's Indian Peaks: Classic Hikes and Climbs*. Fulcrum, Golden, Colorado, 1989, 1998.
Climbing guide to Indian Peaks summits.

Roach, Gerry. *Rocky Mountain National Park: Classic Hikes and Climbs*. Fulcrum, Golden, Colorado, 1988.
Climbing guide to summits in Rocky Mountain National Park.

Rossiter, Richard. *Climber's Guide to Rocky Mountain National Park*. Chockstone Press, Evergreen, Colorado, 1991.
Guide to technical climbs in Rocky Mountain National Park.

SAN JUANS

Gebhardt, Dennis. *A Backpacking Guide to the Weminuche Wilderness in the San Juan Mountains of Colorado*. Basin Reproduction and Printing Company, Durango, Colorado, 1976.
Backpacking guide to Weminuche Wilderness with pocket maps.

Murray, John A. *South San Juan Wilderness Area*. Pruett Publishing Company, Boulder, Colorado, 1990.
Natural history and hiking guide to South San Juan Wilderness Area.

Pixler, Paul. *Hiking Trails of Southwestern Colorado*. Pruett Publishing Company, Boulder, Colorado, 1981.
Day hikes in the San Juan Mountains.

Rhoda, Franklin. *Summits to Reach: Report on the Topography of the San Juan Country*. Edited by Mike Foster. Pruett Publishing Company, Boulder, Colorado, 1984.
Rhoda's report from the Hayden Survey in the San Juans.

Rosebrough, *Robert F. Climbing Colorado's San Juan Mountains*. Falcon Press, Helena, Montana, 1999.
Complete guide to history, trails and summits of the range.

Land Management Agencies

BUREAU OF LAND MANAGEMENT

BLM-Colorado State Office
2850 Youngsfield Street
Lakewood, CO 80215
303-239-3600

Northwest Center
Grand Junction Field Office
2815 H Road
Grand Junction, CO 81506
970-244-3000

Uncompahgre Field Office
2505 S. Townsend Avenue
Montrose, CO 81401
970-240-5300

Southwest Center
2465 S. Townsend Avenue
Montrose, CO 81401
970-240-5300

San Juan Field Office
15 Burnett Court
Durango, CO 81301
970-247-4874

Front Range Center
Royal Gorge Field Office
3170 East Main Street
Canon City, CO 81212
719-269-8500

Saguache Field Office
46525 Highway 114, PO Box 67
Saguache, CO 81149

La Jara Field Office
15571 County Rd T5
La Jara, CO 81140
719-274-8971

Glenwood Field Office
50629 Hwys 6 & 24
PO Box 1009
Glenwood Springs, CO 81602
970-947-2800

Little Snake Field Office
455 Emerson St.
Craig, CO 81625
970-826-5000

Kremmling Field Office
1116 Park Avenue, PO Box 68
Kremmling, CO 80459
970-724-3437

White River Field Office
73544 Highway 64
Meeker, CO 81641
970-878-3601

Gunnison Field Office
216 N. Colorado
Gunnison, CO 81230
970-641-0471

COUNTY PARKS

Jefferson County Open Space
700 Jefferson County Parkway
Golden, CO 80401
303-271-5925

COLORADO STATE PARKS

Colorado State Parks and Recreation
1313 Sherman
Denver, CO 80203
303-866-3437

NATIONAL FOREST SERVICE

USDA Forest Service
Rocky Mountain Regional Office
740 Simms, PO Box 25127
Lakewood, CO 80225
303-275-5350

Arapaho & Roosevelt
National Forests

Boulder Ranger District
2995 Baseline Rd., Room 110
Boulder, CO 80303
303-444-6600

Canyon Lakes Ranger District
1311 S. College Ave.
Ft. Collins, CO 80526
970-498-2770

Estes Park Office
161 Second St.
Estes Park, CO 80517
970-586-3440

Clear Creek Ranger District
101 Chicago Creek, Box 3307
Idaho Springs, CO 80452
303-567-2901

Sulphur Ranger District
9 Ten Mile Drive
Granby, CO 80446
970-887-4100

Grand Mesa, Uncompahgre &
Gunnison National Forests

Collbran Ranger District
218 E. High St., Box 330
Collbran, CO 81624
970-487-3534

Grand Junction Ranger District
2777 Crossroads Blvd.
Grand Junction, CO 81506
970-242-8211

Norwood Ranger District
1760 E. Grand, Box 388
Norwood, CO 81401
970-327-4261

Ouray Ranger District
2505 S. Townsend
Montrose, CO 81401
970-240-5300

Paonia Ranger District
N. Rio Grande Ave., Box 1030
Paonia, CO 81428
970-527-4131

Gunnison Ranger District
216 N. Colorado
Gunnison, CO 81230
970-641-0471

Medicine Bow & Routt
National Forests

Hahns Peak/Bears Ears Ranger District
925 Weiss Drive
Steamboat Springs, CO 80487
970-879-1870

Parks Ranger District
210 S. Sixth, Box 1210
Kremmling, CO 80459
970-724-9004

Yampa Ranger District
300 Roselawn Ave., Box 7
Yampa, CO 80483
970-638-4516

Pike & San Isabel National Forests

Leadville Ranger District
2015 N. Poplar
Leadville, CO 80461
719-486-0749

Pikes Peak Ranger District
601 S. Weber St.
Colorado Springs, CO 80903
719-636-1602

Salida Ranger District
325 W. Rainbow Blvd.
Salida, CO 81201
719-539-3591

San Carlos Ranger District
3170 E. Main St.
Canon City, CO 81212
719-269-8500

South Park Ranger District
320 Hwy. 285, Box 219
Fairplay, CO 80440
719-836-2031

South Platte Ranger District
19316 Goddard Ranch Ct.
Morrison, CO 80465
303-275-5610

**San Juan & Rio Grande
National Forests**

Columbine Ranger District - East
367 S. Pearl St., Box 439
Bayfield, CO 81122
970-884-2512

Columbine Ranger District - West
110 W. 11th St.
Durango, CO 81301
970-385-1283

Conejos Peak Ranger District
15571 County Rd. T-5, Box 420
La Jara, CO 81140
719-274-8971

Divide Ranger District - Creede
3rd & Creede Ave., Box 270
Creede, CO 81130
719-658-2556

Divide Ranger District - Del Norte
13308 W. Highway 160, Box 40
Del Norte, CO 81132
719-657-3321

Mancos/Dolores Ranger District
100 N. Sixth, Box 210
Dolores, CO 81323
970-882-7296

Pagosa Ranger District
180 Second St., Box 310
Pagosa Springs, CO 81147
970-264-2268

Saguache Ranger District
46525 State Hwy. 114, Box 67
Saguache, CO 81149
719-655-2547

White River National Forest

Aspen Ranger District
806 W. Hallam
Aspen, CO 81611
970-925-3445

Blanco Ranger District
317 E. Market St.
Meeker, CO 81641
970-878-4039

Dillon Ranger District
680 Blue River Parkway, Box 620
Silverthorne, CO 80498
970-468-5400

Eagle Ranger District
125 W. 5th St., Box 720
Eagle, CO 81631
970-328-6388

Holy Cross Ranger District
24747 US Hwy. 24, Box 190
Minturn, CO 81645
970-827-5715

Rifle Ranger District
0094 County Road 244
Rifle, CO 81650
970-625-2371

Sopris Ranger District
620 Main St., Box 309
Carbondale, CO 81623
970-963-2266

Listing the Peaks

Tackling "lists" of mountains in Colorado has been a popular goal for climbers ever since Carl Blaurock and Bill Ervin systematically climbed all the fourteeners in the 1920's. Over time, attempts to develop a complete and final list of the peaks were hampered by remeasurements that altered published values for elevations. Indeed, Blaurock and Ervins' original list had 46 summits but subsequent surveys discovered several "new" fourteeners, while down-grading others out of the exclusive club. Today's climber faces 54 summits, a figure widely accepted and popularized in most guidebooks and the publications of the Colorado Mountain Club and the Colorado Fourteeners Initiative. The CMC reports that by the year 2000, nearly 1000 climbers will have registered with the club as having completed all the fourteeners on this list.

Curiosity of what lay beyond the fourteeners induced Bill Graves in 1968 to publish in *Trail and Timberline* a list of the 100 highest peaks in Colorado, where-in a "300-foot rule" was first proposed to establish what constituted a separate summit. This rule states that a summit must rise at least 300 feet above all saddles connecting it to any higher summits, in order to be considered as a separate peak. This rule was generally accepted and the original list revised by others, resulting in present-day lists of the "Centennials" and "Bicentennials" in various publications.

The separate evolution and establishment of a list of the highest 100, and that of the fourteeners, gave rise to a curious situation for the climber interested in both of these goals. The current fourteener list omits several summits that fail the 300-foot rule: Conundrum Peak (14,060'), Mount Cameron (14,238'), North Eolus (14,039'), "North Massive" (14,340') and "South Elbert" (14,134') are the most prominent. Yet North Maroon Peak and El Diente also fail but are typically included in the list, as climbers traditionally have thought of them as separate summits. Challenger Point, which probably barely meets the 300-foot rule, has not caught the attention of most climbers doing fourteeners and is normally omitted. But strict adherence to the 300-foot rule for inclusion on the list of the highest 100 has meant that North Maroon Peak and El Diente drop out and Challenger comes aboard. Thus there are 53 fourteeners on this list.

If these criterion and attendant lists bring out the emotions in climbers, its nothing new. People have been arguing about them since Blaurock and Ervin. Personal whims of guide book authors, remeasurements, and redefinitions of what constitutes a peak, highlight how arbitrary lists can be. The only certain thing is that lists change and these will too. But certainly someone who completes any of these lists will travel widely through all the ranges and gain a deep appreciation of everything our Colorado mountains have to offer.

The 200 Highest

✔	14er	200	Peak & Elevation	Page
❑	1	1	Mount Elbert (14,433') 180
❑	2	2	Mount Massive (14,421') 180
❑	3	3	Mount Harvard (14,420') 192
❑	4	4	Blanca Peak (14,345') 121
❑	5	5	La Plata Peak (14,336') 183
❑	6	6	Uncompahgre Peak (14,309') 245
❑	7	7	Crestone Peak (14,294') 107
❑	8	8	Mount Lincoln (14,286') 163
❑	9	9	Grays Peak (14,270') 72
❑	10	10	Mount Antero (14,269') 195
❑	11	11	Torreys Peak (14,267') 72
❑	12	12	Castle Peak (14,265') 206
❑	13	13	Quandary Peak (14,265') 159
❑	14	14	Mount Evans (14,264') 74
❑	15	15	Longs Peak (14,255') 44
❑	16	16	Mount Wilson (14,246') 310
❑	17	17	Mount Shavano (14,229') 197
❑	18	18	Mount Princeton (14,197') 195
❑	19	19	Mount Belford (14,197') 190
❑	20	20	Crestone Needle (14,197') 107
❑	21	21	Mount Yale (14,196') 193
❑	22	22	Mount Bross (14,172') 163
❑	23	23	Kit Carson Mountain (14,165') 107
❑	24	---	El Diente (14,159') 310
❑	25	24	Maroon Peak (14,156') 211
❑	26	25	Tabeguache Peak (14,155') 197
❑	27	26	Mount Oxford (14,153') 190
❑	28	27	Mount Sneffels (14,150') 267
❑	29	28	Mount Democrat (14,148') 163
❑	30	29	Capitol Peak (14,130') 214
❑	31	30	Pikes Peak (14,109') 90
❑	32	31	Snowmass Mountain (14,092') 214
❑	33	32	Mount Eolus (14,083') 291
❑	34	33	Windom Peak (14,082') 291
❑	---	34	Challenger Point (14,081') 114
❑	35	35	Mount Columbia (14,073') 192
❑	36	36	Missouri Mountain (14,067') 189
❑	37	37	Humboltd Peak (14,064') 107
❑	38	38	Mount Bierstadt (14,060') 73
❑	39	39	Sunlight Peak (14,059') 291
❑	40	40	Handies Peak (14,048') 250
❑	41	41	Culebra Peak (14,047') 127

✔ 14er	200	Peak & Elevation	Page
❏	86	Hagerman Peak (13,841')	.214
❏	87	Half Peak (13,841')	.251
❏	88	Atlantic Peak (13,841')	.160
❏	89	Turret Peak (13,835')	.296
❏	90	Peak 13,832'	.248
❏	91	Holy Cross Ridge (13,831')	.174
❏	92	Jupiter Mountain (13,830')	.291
❏	93	Peak 13,828'	.118
❏	94	Jagged Mountain (13,824')	.293
❏	95	Peak 13,823'	.181
❏	96	Mount Silverheels (13,822')	.80
❏	97	Rio Grande Pyramid (13,821')	.253
❏	98	Teakettle Mountain (13,819')	.269
❏	99	Peak 13,811'	.248
❏	100	Dallas Peak (13,809')	.277
❏	101	Niagara Peak (13,807')	.286
❏	102	American Peak (13,806')	.286
❏	103	Trinity Peak (13,805')	.305
❏	104	Arrow Peak (13,803')	.304
❏	105	Peak 13,803'	.208
❏	106	Organ Mountain (13,799')	.240
❏	107	Peak 13,799'	.107
❏	108	Mount Arkansas (13,795')	.166
❏	109	Peak 13,795'	.250
❏	110	Rito Alto Peak (13,794')	.103
❏	111	Square Top Mountain (13,794')	.73
❏	112	Animas Mountain (13,786')	.295
❏	113	Potosi Peak (13,786')	.269
❏	114	Rinker Peak (13,783')	.182
❏	115	Mosquito Peak (13,782')	.166
❏	116	Garfield Peak (13,780')	.184
❏	117	Golden Horn (13,769')	.282
❏	118	Peak 13,768'	.174
❏	119	U S Grant Peak (13,767')	.282
❏	120	West Trinity Peak (13,765')	.305
❏	121	Peak 13,762'	.191
❏	122	Bull Hill (13,761')	.181
❏	123	Deer Mountain (13,761')	.182
❏	124	San Miguel Peak (13,752')	.283
❏	125	Storm King Peak (13,752')	.306
❏	126	Mount Sheridan (13,748')	.167
❏	127	Mount Aetna (13,745')	.196
❏	128	East Trinity Peak (13,745')	.305
❏	129	Argentine Peak (13,738')	.73
❏	130	Grizzly Peak (13,738')	---

✔ 14er	200	Peak & Elevation	Page
❏	131	Pilot Knob (13,738') 282
❏	132	Sayres Peak (13,738') 187
❏	133	Peak 13,736' 182
❏	134	T0 (13,735') 272
❏	135	Vermejo Peak (13,723') 129
❏	136	Peak 13,722' 288
❏	137	Peak 13,722' 211
❏	138	Pole Creek Mountain (13,716') 251
❏	139	Silver Mountain (13,714') 346
❏	140	Peak 13,712' 197
❏	141	Twining Peak (13,711') 185
❏	142	Grizzly Mountain (13,708') 197
❏	143	Colony Baldy (13,705') 106
❏	144	Peak Six (13,705') 293
❏	145	Grizzly Peak (13,700') 297
❏	146	Peak Fifteen (13,700') 295
❏	147	Baldy Alto (13,698') 240
❏	148	Monitor Peak (13,695') 295
❏	149	Gilpin Peak (13,694') 268
❏	150	Rolling Mountain (13,693') 282
❏	151	Peak 13,691' 249
❏	152	Wheeler Mountain (13,690') 159
❏	153	Peak 13,688' 249
❏	154	Peak 13,688' 288
❏	155	Cirque Mountain (13,686') 269
❏	156	Bald Mountain (13,684') 80
❏	157	Mount Oso (13,684') 299
❏	158	Peak Seven (13,682') 298
❏	159	Peak 13,681' 246
❏	160	Purgatoire Peak (13,676') 129
❏	161	Peak 13,674' 251
❏	162	Mount Tweto (13,672') 166
❏	163	Mount Jackson (13,670') 173
❏	164	Mount White (13,667') 197
❏	165	Carbonate Mountain (13,663') 197
❏	166	Lookout Peak (13,661') 281
❏	167	Peak 13,660' 251
❏	168	Peak 13,660' 122
❏	169	Wood Mountain (13,660') 288
❏	170	Carson Peak (13,657') 250
❏	171	Coxcomb Peak (13,656') 261
❏	172	Taylor Mountain (13,651') 196
❏	173	Mount Champion (13,646') 182
❏	174	Mount Mamma (13,646') 196
❏	175	Redcliff (13,642') 261

✔ 14er	200	Peak & Elevation	Page
❑	176	Bard Peak (13,641')	.68
❑	177	Electric Pass Peak (13,635')	.207
❑	178	Peak 10 (13,633')	.161
❑	179	Peak 13,631'	.211
❑	180	Peak 13,631'	.205
❑	181	Mount Silex (13,628')	.306
❑	182	White Dome (13,627')	.307
❑	183	Peak 13,626'	.---
❑	184	West Spanish Peak (13,626')	.126
❑	185	The Guardian (13,617')	.307
❑	186	Peak 13,616'	.188
❑	187	North Star Mountain (13,614')	.159
❑	188	Pico Asilado (13,611')	.115
❑	189	Tijeras Peak (13,604')	.110
❑	190	Gray Wolf Mountain (13,602')	.73
❑	191	Electric Peak (13,598')	.103
❑	192	Cyclone Mountain (13,596')	.197
❑	193	Matterhorn Peak (13,590')	.247
❑	194	Peak One (13,589')	.307
❑	195	Cottonwood Peak (13,588')	.102
❑	196	Mount Emma (13,581')	.270
❑	197	Peak 13,581'	.251
❑	198	Clark Peak (13,580')	.216
❑	199	Mount Powell (13,580')	.154
❑	200	Twin Peaks (13,580')	.122
❑		Peak 13,580'	.114
❑		Peak 13,580'	.251

NOTE: Elevations are as per the latest editions of the USGS 7.5 minute topographic map series (1:24,000), with a few corrections obtained by correspndence with other USGS sources. Peaks that do not have a published value are interpolated to be 20 feet (one half of a contour) above the last contour shown on the maps. Obviously, as fixed elevations are established for these points over time, peaks will shift up or down in their rankings.

For over twenty years the CMC has collected and printed an annual list of those climbers who have finished the fourteeners, the centennials, and the bicentennials in the pages of the club journal, *Trail and Timberline* (January/February issue). To report the completion of one of these goals, send climber's name, first peak and last peak ascended, and approximate dates to:

Trail and Timberline
c/o The Colorado Mountain Club
710 10th St. #200
Golden, CO 80401

Index

C

T